Reminiscences Of A Newburyport Nonagenarian

Emery, Sarah Smith, 1787-1879.

REMINISCENCES

OF A

NONAGENARIAN.

EDITED AND ILLUSTRATED

BY SARAH ANNA EMERY.

AUTHOR OF "THREE GENERATIONS."

NEWBURYPORT:
WILLIAM H. HUSE & CO., PRINTERS, 42 STATE STREET.
1879.

PREFACE.

THIS volume, as its title implies, has been chiefly derived from the recollections of my mother; but recitals by my father, grandparents and other deceased relatives and friends have aided the work, and I have obtained many anecdotes and facts from several aged persons still living. My thanks are due to others less advanced in life, especially to J. H. HAMLIN, esq., of Portland, Maine, for details respecting the Poyen family, and for the description of their ancestral home in Gaudaloupe; to Miss REBECCA INGERSOLL DAVIS of East Haverhill, for others relating to the Countess De Vipart; to Mr. LYMAN COLE of Newburyport, for his family history; to GEORGE EDWIN EMERY of Lynn, Mass., for facts respecting our ancestors, and their home in England, and for the history of the name of Emery; also to THOMAS C. AMORY, esq., of Boston, for Amory records; to JAMES CHUTE PEABODY, esq., for valuable information. I am indebted to the "Genealogy of the LITTLE Family," compiled by GEORGE T. LITTLE; to that of HALE by ROBERT S. HALE, LL.D.; to EDMUND SMITH, esq., for the "Heraldry of SMITH, London, JOHN RUSSELL SMITH, 36 Soho square, 1870;" to BENJAMIN HALE, esq., and other persons and families who have kindly loaned genealogies and ancient documents. I have received assistance from the Histories of Newbury and Newburyport by JOSHUA COFFIN, esq., and Mrs. E. VALE SMITH; and JOHNSTON'S History of the Campaign on Long Island in 1776; from the Record of Schools, by Mr. O. B. MERRILL, published by the "Antiquarian and Historical Society" of Old Newbury; GAGE'S History of Rowley and Genealogical Register, 1869. In the family records I have aimed at an arrangement that will enable the descendants of the present generation to trace their lineage, and I have endeavored to note those born within the limits of Newbury and Newburyport, who have been college graduates, or have otherwise become distinguished.

My desire has been to give a graphic history of "Ye Olden Time"; to faithfully portray the domestic, religious, political, literary and social life of a past age, with a description of "Ould Newberry," and of the business and aspect of Newburyport prior to the great fire of 1811. The ancient town has been rich in matters of world-wide interest and historic value.

About 1650, at the Dummer, now Glen Mills, was set up the first cloth mill in America. In the Byfield parish was the first woolen and cotton factory in Massachusetts, and there the first broadcloth manufactured in the country was made. There, Perkins the inventor of the plate for engraving bank notes, set up the first nail factory. In the same parish, in 1680, at the head of tide-water on the river Parker, the first vessel was built in New England. Later, the first academy was founded by Gov. Dummer, and still later, the first incorporated rifle company was formed. In the West Precinct, now West Newbury, the first horn combs and buttons were manufactured by Mr. Enoch Noyes. In Newburyport Master Pike published the first Arithmetic, and the stalwart ship carpenter, Eleazer Johnson, burned the first tea in ante-revolutionary times, previous to its destruction in Boston. His son Nicholas, commanding a Newburyport ship, the "Count de Grass,e" was the first to display the Stars and Stripes on the river Thames. Newburyport has also the honor of having founded the first Sunday and female high schools in Massachusetts. That the book may satisfy the expectations of relatives and friends, and prove a source of instruction and interest to the public generally, is the sincere wish of

SARAH ANNA EMERY.

Newburyport, 1879.

SMITH PLACE.

REMINISCENCES OF A NONAGENARIAN.

CHAPTER I.

Ninety years is a long period to review. The world of to-day is an entirely different thing from that of my earliest recollection. How vividly I recall the old homestead — the large brown house, built in 1707, with its wide, sloping back roof, and many sized and shaped windows; the long barn and other farm buildings in the rear; the well, with its graceful sweep in front, and the usually huge wood pile at the back. Before the house stretched a large garden, well stocked with pear, peach and cherry trees. Currant and gooseberry bushes grew luxuriantly beneath the sheltering board fence, that separated the enclosure from the broad fields and orchards around. There was a clump of quince bushes in one corner, and in another two Plum Island plum bushes, that had grown from stones taken from fruit brought from the island. There was also a great variety of medicinal and sweet herbs, and from early spring till late in autumn the borders on either side of the gravel walk were gay with flowers. These flowers were one of the greatest delights of my childhood. How distinctly I remember every shrub and bush, and the pleasure I received in dispensing my treasures amongst my less favored neighbors, who often came to beg a rose, a bunch of pinks, or some spearmint or lavender "to take to meetin' to keep 'em awake Sabba' day."

Crossing the broad, unhewn doorstone and opening the wide front door, you saw a narrow entry with a flight of winding stairs at the back. As you stepped across the threshold your feet fell upon a trap door in the floor. Through this cavity passed all the farm produce that was annually stored in the cellar. Carts filled with potatoes, turnips, etc., were backed up to the door and their contents chuted into the subterranean regions below, while from the iron stanchion in the unplastered ceiling overhead was lowered, by rope and pulleys, barrel after barrel of apples and cider. The house was constructed in the style common to the period, two spacious rooms on either side of the front entry, with wide fireplaces, and low ceilings crossed in the centre by a broad beam. The two front windows in both rooms were long and narrow;

the one in the end was square. Opening from these apartments were the summer kitchen, bed-rooms and the dairy. The fireplaces, both below and in the chambers, showed an attempt at architectural ornament, in the high mantel pieces. Those in the two front rooms were both furnished with a large oven in a corner to the right, and a smaller one in that opposite. These were closed by brightly-painted red oven lids; and in the right-hand corner stood a long, low form, for the accommodation of the smaller members of the household. There were long dressers, also, showing some effort at elegance in the carving of the shelves, which were loaded with pewter ware, as bright as silver, and a corner cupboard, in the country phraseology termed a "beaufat," which displayed rare treasures of China, glass and silver.

My father and mother, recently married, occupied one half of the house; my widowed grandmother, with another son and daughter, resided in the other half. Young people, their fortune still to be made, my parents' rooms were plainly furnished, with common tables and flag-bottomed chairs. A high case of drawers was the chief ornament to the best bedroom, the others boasting of only a chest of drawers. These were about the height of a bureau, with a chest atop and one or two drawers beneath. The square, high-post bedsteads were tastily hung with muslin and chintz curtains, and covered with the prettiest of coverlids, woven in love-knots and other dainty patterns, or with quilts stiff with the most elaborate quilting. Grandmother's rooms were much more elegant. While my mother, the oldest of nine children, was provided with a common fitting out, my grandmother, the heiress to quite a fortune, had received an outfit that, at the time of her marriage, had been the chief topic for tea-table talk throughout the country-side. The bridal trousseau and the best furniture had been imported from England expressly for her, by indulgent and somewhat aristocratic parents. The green damask dress, and brown camblet circular cloak and riding hood, with the high-heeled brocade slippers, were, at the time of which I am speaking, still as fresh as new, and a peep at them was a rare treat which was sometimes vouchsafed when I was especially good. Grandmother's front room had bow-backed chairs with flag seats, and tables supported by curiously-carved and twisted legs, a candle stand that screwed up and down like a piano stool, a handsome mirror, and the buffet was resplendent in its appointments. Her best bed was hung with green moreen curtains, edged by heavy gimp trimming; the case of drawers was decorated with fluted drawers in the upper tier, and surmounted by ornaments of carving. There was a handsome dressing table, a fine specimen of the sculptured frames of the period, with several drawers and compartments. Over this hung a glass, the plate surrounded by an ornamental wreath, and a frame of colored glass, set in mahogany moulding. The back chamber — the large one under the long, sloping back roof — was set apart for manufacturing purposes. Here the chief part of the clothing and other household goods for the family were spun and woven. The apartment was conveniently fitted up with looms, woolen, linen and spooling wheels, swifts, reels, cards and warping bars. Here, also, stood the great grain chest, well stored with wheat, rye, oats and barley. Our farm was well adapted to the growth of wheat. My father raised enough to supply his family, and had a surplus for the market. The large garret, besides being the receptacle for all the odds and ends of housekeeping, was annually filled with Indian corn, a corn barn being a later addition to the premises.

CHAPTER II.

My parents had married young. Their chief capital for commencing life was youth, health and mutual love. My grandfather's decease dated a few years prior to his son's marriage, and the large farm, with the exception of the widow's dower, had been divided between the five sons. At this time my father had purchased one of these shares, and he was making strenuous exertions to secure the rest of the paternal acres. Industry and economy were the watchwords of the household: still, there was no overtasking nor stint.

In those summer days, when my recollection first opens, mother and Aunt Sarah rose in the early dawn, and, taking the well-scoured wooden pails from the bench by the back door, repaired to the cow yard behind the barn. We owned six cows; my grandmother four. Having milked the ten cows, the milk was strained, the fires built, and breakfast prepared. Many families had milk for this meal, but we always had coffee or chocolate, with meat and potatoes. During breakfast the milk for the cheese was warming over the fire, in the large brass kettle. The milk being from the ten cows, my mother made cheese four days, Aunt Sarah having the milk the remainder of the week. In this way good-sized cheeses were obtained. The curd having been broken into the basket, the dishes were washed, and, unless there was washing or other extra work, the house was righted. By the time this was done the curd was ready for the press. Next came preparations for dinner, which was on the table punctually at twelve o'clock. In the hot weather we usually had boiled salted meat and vegetables, and, if it was baking day, a custard or pudding. If there was linen whitening on the grass, as was usual at this season, that must be sprinkled. After dinner the cheeses were turned and rubbed; then mother put me on a clean frock, and dressed herself for the afternoon. Our gowns and aprons, unless upon some special occasion, when calico was worn, were usually of blue checked home-made gingham, starched and ironed to a nice gloss.

In the sultry August afternoons mother and Aunt Sarah usually took their sewing to the cool back room, whose shaded door and windows overlooked the freshly-mown field, dotted by apple trees. Beyond the mossy stone wall stood the homestead of Uncle Samuel Thurlow (at that time this name was pronounced Thurrell), our next neighbor. Other buildings came to view, interspersed with hill and meadow, forest and orcharding. The line of brown houses — very few were at that time painted — marked the position of the main road. Across rose the square meeting-house, crowning the high, precipitous hill upon which it was perched. Farther on, the spires of the distant seaport town glittered in the afternoon light, which fell in brilliant beams upon the sands of the beaches and Plum Island, and whitened the sails of vessels far away upon the blue sea, whose line blended, almost imperceptibly, with the tints of the sky in the eastern horizon.

My grandmother, after her afternoon nap, usually joined her daughters, with a pretence at knitting, but she was not an industrious old lady. There was no necessity for work; and if idle hours are a sin, I fear the good woman had much to answer for. Leaning back in her easy-chair, she beguiled the time with watching the splendid prospect, with its ever-varying lights and shades, or joined in the harmless gossip of some neighboring woman, who had run in with her sewing, for an hour's chat.

At five o'clock the men came from the field, and tea was served. The tea things washed, the vegetables were gathered for the morrow, the linen taken in, and other chores done. At sunset the cows came from the pasture. Milking finished and the milk strained, the day's labor was ended. The last load pitched on the hay mow, and the last hay cock turned up, my father and the hired man joined us in the cool back room, where bowls of bread and milk were ready for those who wished the refreshment. At nine o'clock the house was still, the tired hands gladly resting from the day's toil. Except during the busiest of the hay season, my father went regularly once a week to the neighboring seaport town, taking thither a load of farm produce. For years he supplied several families and stores with butter, cheese, eggs, fruit and vegetables. These market days were joyful epochs for me, as at his return I never failed to receive some little gift, usually sent by some of our "Port" relatives and friends.

Butter making commenced in September; only "two meal cheese" were made, that is, one milking of new milk and one of skimmed to the cheese, the cream of one milking going to the butter. The weaving of woolen cloth was begun, in order that it should be returned from the mill where it was fulled, colored and pressed in time to be made up before Thanksgiving. This mill was in Byfield, at the Falls, on the site of the present mill, and was owned and run by Mr. Benjamin Pearson. The winter's stocking yarn was also carded and spun, and the lengthening evenings began to be enlivened by the busy click of knitting needles. As Thanksgiving approached, the hurry both in doors and out increased.

With awe I would tiptoe to the edge of the open trap door which I had been strictly enjoined not to approach, to peep at the things which had been carried into the cellar; then I would patiently toil after perspiring Uncle Burrill, my favorite amongst the hired men, as he wearily bore basket after basket full of the long, golden ears of Indian corn into the large garret, which to my childish vision appeared so very vast and mysterious.

While of an evening the males of the family were busy husking on the barn floor, by the light of the hunter's moon, the females were equally engaged around the sparkling fire, which the chilly evenings rendered grateful, peeling apples, pears and quinces, for cider apple-sauce and preserves.

After the cloth had been brought from the mill, tailor Thurrell from the

Falls village appeared, goose in hand, remaining several days, to fashion my father's and uncle's coats and breeches. Mother, a manteau-maker before her marriage, had her hands more than full, as she was not only called upon to make the gowns for our family, but to fit the dresses for her own mother and sisters and others in the vicinity. As the cold increased the cheese were carried to the cellar, and the cheese room was scoured. The week before Thanksgiving the ox which had been stalled for the occasion, was killed. Part of the beef was salted, the remainder put in a cool place, and as soon as the weather was sufficiently cold it was frozen, in order to preserve it fresh through the winter. The house was banked up; everything without and within made tight and trim, to defy as much as possible the approach of old Boreas.

Thanksgiving brought a social season. There was much visiting and distribution of good cheer for a week or two after that holiday. Towards Christmas the fat hogs were killed, the pork salted, the hams hung in the wide chimney to cure, and the sausages made. The women began to comb flax and spin linen thread; the men went daily to cut and haul the year's firewood. We were too good Puritans to make much account of Christmas, though sometimes the young people at the main road got up a ball on Christmas eve, but at New Year, there was a general interchange of good wishes, with gifts and festivity.

As soon as the spring weather would permit weaving without a fire, the looms in the back chamber were set in motion, weaving the next season's linen. Next came candle-dipping, the making of soap, and house cleaning. The calves had been sold, churning commenced, and butter was made until the warmer weather brought the summer routine.

CHAPTER III.

Thanksgiving day I accompanied my parents to my Grandfather Little's. A visit to my mother's maiden home was at all times one of my highest pleasures. My grandmother, a daughter of the first pastor of the upper parish, the Rev. William Johnson, was one of those rare women whom every one, old and young, rich and poor, loved and revered. A minister's daughter, and highly educated for those days, the wisdom of my grandfather's choice as regarded his worldly success, had been a subject of doubt throughout the family. His thrifty sisters all declared that "Brother Jose could never get ahead with a wife so genteel as to wash her hearth every day, have a border of posies afore her front door to tend, besides ruffles on her leetle gal's sleeves to iron." Notwithstanding these dire prognostications, Brother Jose had reared a large family in comfort and some elegance. The house was similar to ours, the parlor furnished in much the same style as my Grandmother Smith's, with the addition of a pretty carpet of home construction in the centre of the floor. The arm chairs were also decorated with wrought cushion covers, and a pair of worked holders hung on either side of the fireplace, these ornaments being the handiwork of deft Mollie Johnson before her marriage. At this time only two daughters had left the paternal roof tree. Three sons and four daughters, with two or three apprentices, (my grandfather carried on shoe business in addito his farming), made a large, but pleasant and orderly household.

Father and mother, grandsir, grandma'am and Uncle Bill went to meeting. Aunt Betsy and Aunt Judy remained at home, ostensibly to get the dinner, but they were so busy preparing for a party to which they had been invited for the evening that most of the cooking fell upon the younger, but more quiet and staid, Aunt Sukey. Rollicking Aunt Hannah, a girl of eight or nine, ran hither and thither, poking fun and helping everybody. Seizing the broom, she drew the freshly-strewn sand on the kitchen floor into a remarkable combination of zig-zags. Next she fell to basting the turkey, roasting on a spit, which rested on brackets on the tall iron andirons, flourishing the long-handled butter ladle in such a manner as to call forth the animadversions of Aunt Sukey, who declared that she would have the drippings, which fell into a pan beneath, "all over her clean hearth."

Uncle Ben, a lad of twelve, brought wood and did other chores, meanwhile playing so many practical jokes on his gay elder sisters that they laughingly threatened to turn him out of the house. Roly-Poly Uncle Joe, only three years my senior, sat beside me on the form in the corner, where, with great glee, we watched the proceedings of our elders. The merry forenoon glided away. The hands of the tall clock in the corner of the room pointed to twelve. Aunt Hannah set the table with the best napery and ware, the pickles and apple-sauce were brought, the cider drawn, and the chafing dish filled, ready to put on the table to keep the gravy hot. How long those expectant moments seemed! Uncle Joe and I ensconced ourselves at the window, while Aunt Hannah zealously basted the turkey, with the wish that Parson Toppan would end that "everlasting sarmon." At length the sleighs appeared. There had been a fall of snow — the first of the season — the night before, and it was pretty good sleighing. The party entered, accompanied by Aunt Nannie, the second daughter, and her husband, Mr. John Peabody. This young man was descended from Lieut. Francis Peabody, born at St. Albans, Hartfordshire, England, in 1614. He came to New England in the ship Planter, Nicholas Frarcie, master, in 1635. Mr. Peabody first resided at Ipswich. In 1638 he went to Hampton, N. H., with the Rev. Stephen Bachilar and twelve others. He was made a freeman in 1642,.and in 1649 was chosen, by the town of Hampton, one of the three men "to ende small causes", and was confirmed in that office by the justices of that court. "Being minded to live nearer Boston," he sold his estate in Hampton and purchased a farm in Topsfield, and became a large landholder in Topsfield, Boxford and Rowley. He set up the first mill in Topsfield, on a stream that flows past the spot where he lived. Lieut. Peabody was a man of great capacity and influence. His wife was a daughter of Reginald Foster, whose family is honorably mentioned in "Marmion" and "The Lay of the Last Minstrel". He died February 19, 1697 or 1698. His widow died April 9, 1705. Children: John, Joseph, William, Isaac;

Sarah m. How of Ipswich; Hepsibah m. Rea of Salem Village; Lydia m. Jacob Perley; Mary m. John Death of Framingham; Ruth died before her father; Damaris died Dec. 19, 1660; Samuel died Sept. 13, 1677; Jacob d. in 1664; Hannah d. before her father; Nathaniel d. in 1715 without children. Of this large family three sons settled in Boxford, and two remained in Topsfield. The Peabodys have been a patriotic and brave race. Two officers and two privates served in the French war. Lieut. Jacob Peabody fell on the plains of Abraham in 1759. Six officers, one chaplain, a surgeon, and assistant surgeon, a 1st officer in marine service, and five privates rendered military service during the Revolution. Capt. Richard Peabody commanded a company in the Continental army, and sent his sons to war as fast as he was able. Nathaniel Peabody of Atkinson, N. H., commanded a regiment in the war of the Revolution, and subsequently represented his state in the Continental Congress. Amongst the clergy the Peabodys count many eminent men. The Rev. Oliver Peabody, who died in Natick; the twin brothers, William Oliver Bourne and Oliver William Bourne; Rev. David Peabody, professoa in the college at Hanover; Rev. Andrew P. Peabody D. D., professor of Harvard University, and Rev. Ephraim Peabody of Boston. Professor Silliman of Yale College, descended from a Peabody. In medicine, law and the various walks of life, the family reputation has been ably sustained. Capt. John, the oldest son of Lieut. Francis Peabody, lived in Boxford, was made a freeman in 1674, representative from 1689 to 1691. He married first, Hannah Andrews; second, Sarah Mosely. He died in 1720 aged 78. Children: John; Thomas; Mary married Richard Hazen; Lydia m. Jacob Perley; David born July 12, 1672; Elizabeth m. David Andrew; Nathan; Hannah m. Jos. Buckman; Ruth m. John Wood of Boxford; Moses. Ensign David Peabody m. Sarah Pope of Dartmouth. He lived in Boxford, died April 1, 1726 aged 48. His widow d. Sept. 29, 1756, aged 72. Children: Thomas; Hannah m. Jona. Fuller of Sutton; Sarah m. Daniel Wood; Mercy, d. Sept. 26, 1793; John; Deborah, d. Aug. 21, 1736; Rebecca, m. Richard Dexter; Susanna, d. Oct. 1794; David, born Oct. 4, 1724; Mary, d. in 1736; David Peabody m. Mary Gaines of Ipswich, and settled on a farm in Andover. Having become a zealous member of the Baptist communion, he moved to Haverhill, where a church of that denomination had been established. A short time after his removal he died, on Aug. 16, 1774, aged 50. His widow died in Newburyport, at the residence of her son-in-law, Mr. Leonard Smith, April, 1806, aged 77. Children: Lucy m. Peter Middleton, lived in Haverhill and Bradford; David d. in the West Indies; Sarah m. Leonard Smith; Mary m. William Farmer of Bradford; Judith m. William Butler, lived in Newburyport; Thomas m. Judith daughter of Jeremiah and Judith (Spofford) Dodge. These were the parents of David, George, the well-known banker; and Jeremiah Dodge Peabody of Ohio. Deborah m. James Becket, resided in Salem; Abigail in 1765, m. Edmund Greenleaf of Newburyport; John born Feb 22, 1768; Josiah Gaines m. Edna Greenough, resided in Porstmouth. Mrs. David Peabody at her husband's death, was left with this large family of young children. John was apprenticed to learn the trade of a shoe-maker to Mr. Josiah Bartlett of Newbury. Upon coming of age he established himself at the main road. In addition to the shoe trade, he set up a general furnishing store. March 30, 1791, he married Anna, second daughter of Joseph and Mary (Johnson) Little, of Newbury. The young couple set up housekeeping in a house contiguous to the shop, which stood next below the residence of Dea. John Osgood. The Peabodys date back to Boadie, a gallant British chieftain, who, in the year A. D. 61, came to the rescue of his noble and chivalrous Queen and kinswoman, Boadicea, when "bleeding from the Roman rods." From the disastrous battle in which she lost her crown and life, he fled to the Cambrian mountains, in Wales. There his posterity lived and became a terror to the Lowlands. From their frequent raids into the Roman territory, he was designated Pea Bodie (Mountain Man; Pea signifying mountain, and Bodie man). Some members of the family retained the British name, Peabody; others anglicysed it into Hillman, some as the German Bergmann, while others divided it into its constituents, thus originating the names of Hill and Mann. There was a Peabody among the Knights of the Round Table, the name being registered with due heraldric honors, by command of King Arthur.

Boadie, with his own hand, killed Galbuta, a distinguished Roman general, and, following the custom of assuming the arms of the vanquished if he were a person of note, Boadie copied the two suns proper from the armor of Galbuta and adopted them as his own arms.

PARTY PER FESS NEBULE, GULES, AZURE, TWO SUNS PROPER, WITH A GARB, CREST AND EAGLE.

Dinner was immediately set upon the table. Grace having been said, due justice was given to the turkey and plum pudding. Aunt Sukey received many encomiums upon her cooking, part of which Aunt Hannah declared she should appropriate. "Sukey never would have basted that turkey as I did, for fear of injuring her fine complexion." Then the wild little minx, as her sisters termed her, fell to clearing the table, having first stirred the kettle of boiling dish-water with the knives and forks, "in order that it should not boil away the beaux." The girls washed the dinner things; the others repaired to the "fore room", where Uncle Ben had a bright fire blazing across the shiny black fire-dogs, with nigger faces, which my roguish young uncle wished me to admire. Aunt Hannah called me to go with her up stairs, to see the girls dress.

When Nannie was married, their father had given his two next oldest daughters silk dresses. This had called forth severe animadversion from his sisters. "To think of Brother

Jose's extravagance; and he had bought all of them, but Hanner, gold necklaces, ear-drops and a finger ring! Well, they allers said he never could be forehanded when he married Mollie Johnson, she was so high bred and had so much 'Port' company." These and similar speeches, which, somehow, always got reported to the subject of them, caused my grandfather's family much diversion. Miss Betty Bradstreet, a wealthy cousin of my grandmother, a maiden lady, and a resident of the "Port", had upon a recent visit brought my two aunts each a brooch to match their ear-drops, and the girls made themselves very merry over what their father's sisters would say to this addition to their finery, each devoutly hoping that they would never know but their brother had purchased them. The brown silks were vastly becoming. They were made with full skirts, tight waists, low square necks, with tight sleeves reaching just below the elbow, finished by a ruffle, with an under one of lace. The neck was covered by a square white muslin handkerchief, doubled and tucked under the dress, immensely puffed out in front, long black net mitts covered the hands and arms, and when the jewelry was added, to my childish eyes my two girlish aunts presented the very acme of splendor.

My mother and aunts were very handsome women. Never did six sisters more closely resemble each other. I have often heard it remarked, that in after years, when dressed alike in mourning, at a funeral, it was difficult to distinguish one from another. I would that their portraits were extant; they would form a rare galaxy of beauty. Of medium hight, trim figures, small hands and feet, black hair and eyes (with the exception of Nannie's, whose were deep blue), fair skin, cherry lips, white teeth, a brilliant color, the eyes sparkling, with much expression in conversation, a lively mien, tempered by much grace and sensibility, great courtesy and kindness of heart—little wonder that the six Little girls should become the reigning toasts of the period. Their toilets completed, my aunts joined the rest in the parlor. Nuts were cracked, apples roasted, a mug of flip was made, songs sung and stories told. At dusk father went home to do his chores; soon after, Amos Chase and Stephen Bartlett came to take their affianced to the party. These young gentlemen were arrayed in blue coats, with brass buttons, buff vests, satin breeches, silk stockings, silver knee and shoe buckles, their hair frizzled, powdered and cued.

The evening's entertainment was at Deacon Tenney's. Mrs. Tenney, my father's eldest sister, like my grandmother Little, had a house full of girls. The deacon, though honoring his office, was the prince of hospitality, and an invitation to his house gave occasion for much satisfaction. After the young people had gone, Mr, and Mrs. Peabody and Uncle Bill having accompanied them, grandsir, grandma'm and my mother drew round the fire for a quiet chat. We children went into the kitchen to play blind man's buff, aunt Sukey, much to our delight, condescending to join in the sport. At seven o'clock, my father having returned, supper was served. Soon after, as my eyelids, notwithstanding strenuous exertions to the contrary, would shut, mother declared it was time for home.

The next day we dined and spent the evening in my grandmother Smith's room. Uncle and aunt Thurrell came to tea, and other neighboring relatives dropped in for the evening. Saturday afternoon mother had company, but as Saturday night was considered holy time, they left at an early hour. The next week was one continued festival. Visiting was general throughout the parish. Each one's skill in cooking was discussed, and the merits of different persons' mince pies and plum cake pronounced. Nor was the visiting confined to the females, the gentlemen often came alone. Two of four neighbors for years made it a practice to come together to take tea with us the week following Thanksgiving. Never shall I forget the gusto with which they demolished the huge piles of dipped toast, or the way they smacked their lips over the pies and cake, all the while declaring "that for cooking, little Prudy Smith bore the palm."

CHAPTER IV.

The Puritan Sabbath commenced at sunset Saturday night—a literal interpretation of the scripture text "And the evening and the morning were the first day." Supper eaten, silence and rest settled over the household. To most this was a grateful period of repose, in which, in the long evenings, they were only to happy too fold their hands and doze away the hours till the early bedtime, eight o'clock being the usual hour for retiring on that night. Others were glad of this leisure for reading, but many could not have been induced to peruse anything save the Bible, psalm book, a sermon or some religious treatise. My father and mother were less strict. Father usually passed the time in conning the columns of the "Independent Chronicle and Universal Advertiser," a weekly sheet of small size, printed by "Nathaniel Willis, Boston, opposite the New Court House," which was taken conjointly with Uncle Amos Dole. In 1793 "The Impartial Herald," (Newburyport Herald) was established in Newburyport.

Deacon Tenney had a thriving tobacconist business, and he went to Boston two or three times a month, with snuff and cigars; upon his return he usually brought some reading matter. This was a rare treat, especially to my mother. Saturday evening was an oasis in her life of toil; the one space of soul refreshment eagerly anticipated through the week, but I fear her studies would not always have been pronounced canonical. Great-grandfather Johnson's youngest daughter married Master Simon Chase, a school teacher of much renown, and a man devoted to literature. Besides many books of his own, to which he was constantly adding, he had, through his wife, come into posession of most of her father's library. This couple resided in the former parsonage, everything still remaining as it had been in the minister's lifetime. Mother, being a frequent visitor at her aunt Hannah's, was usually supplied with a book from their shelves, and father sometimes brought her one of the love-laden romances of the period, loaned to her by some of her "Port" friends.

Sunday, if in health, everybody was expected to attend public worship. In warm weather, grandmother and Aunt Sarah drove together in the square topped chaise. Uncle Enoch usually walked; my father rode on his handsome horse, my mother riding on the pillion behind him. At a very early age, as I was a quiet little girl, much to my joy I was permitted to go to meeting, and usually rode between my grandmother and aunt in the chaise, but sometimes was perched on mother's lap, a ride I vastly enjoyed, especially if father put his horse to a gallop.

Never shall I forget my first advent at meeting. Great had been the preparation for this public appearance, for mother had a good share of wholesome sort of pride, and, as was natural for a youthful matron, wished her little daughter to look as pretty as possible. Grandmother Little owned a famously embroidered, linen cambric christening frock, and this garment having done service at all the baptisms, was now remodelled for my Sunday dress. Mother constructed a tasty green silk bonnet, and Grandfather Little presented a pair of red shoes, of his own make.

The meeting house, a square, weather embrowned structure, without steeple or bell, crowned a high hill, up which a stony road wound in steep ascent. A horse block for the convenience of the pillion riders stood by the front steps, and a long row of low sheds, shelter for the horses, extended to the left. The interior was a handsome specimen of the ecclesiastical architecture of the period. The wide front door led through a broad aisle to a high pulpit furnished with green cushions. A sounding board depended from the ceiling above, and the communion table stood in front. A sounding board usually was about eight feet in diameter, and shaped like an inverted wine-glass flattened toward the brim; it hung some six feet above the pulpit cushion. Generally this adjunct to the sacred desk displayed gracefulness of design and beauty of decoration. A circular moulding enclosed the suspending rod where it entered the ceiling. This appendage was to aid the speaker by equally diffusing the sound of the voice in every part of the building.

The broad aisle was intersected by a narrower one, into which side entrances opened. Another aisle ran around the edifice, separating the wall pews from those in the body of the house. These pews were enclosed by handsomely turned balusters. Front of the pulpit were rows of seats, for the accommodation of those wishing to be near the preacher, or elderly persons who were not pew holders. The benches to the right were for females, those to the left for males. The singers occupied the front gallery, to which a flight of stairs led each side of the front door. The side galleries were furnished with one long pew, extending the length of the wall; the space in front was filled with benches. The wall pew to the right was set apart for the young women; girls occupied the centre tier of benches, while the front was filled by middle-aged women. The opposite gallery was similarly occupied by young men in the wall pew, boys and men on the benches. The large, square pews, in addition to the seats, were furnished with one or two high-backed chairs, which stood in the centre. These were commonly of rich wood, handsomely carved, with flag seats. These chairs were the posts of honor, and were usually occupied by elderly ladies. Besides the chairs, there was generally one or more high stools, for the accommodation of the more infantile portion of the congregation. Ours was a wall pew, the second to the right from the front door. My grandmother led me in and placed me on a stool beside her chair. Mother, somewhat flustered, but looking proud and pleased, seated herself behind me, and Aunt Sarah fidgeted around, placing the highest footstool beneath my feet. How vast and splendid everything seemed! At length I began to take in details and recognize my relatives and acquaintances. There were Grandsir's and Uncle John Little's pew; Uncle Thurrell's; the Doles'; those of Aunt Sara, Col. Thomas; Mr. Stephen and Enoch Noyes, Deacon Osgood, Mr. Newell, the Emerys, Carrs, Bartletts, Follansbees, Baileys, Uncle John and Deacon Abel Merrill, Dr. Sawyer; the parsonage pew, to the left of the pulpit; those of the Plummers, Woodmans, Chases, Ilsleys, Bricketts, Hills, Adamses, Carletons and Jaques. The pew matching that of the parsonage, to the right of the pulpit, had several owners, and bore the designation of "Everybody's pew". Elderly women in close, black silk bonnets, and thick silks or bright chintzes, quietly seated themselves, with demure, "Sabba' day" faces. More youthful matrons and maidens glided in, radiant in lighter silks, white muslins or cambric calicoes, and silk hats of various hues, gaily trimmed with ribbons, flowers or long, waving plumes. Little folks, like myself, stared about, or twirled the balusters of the pews. The three deacons—Tenney, Merrill and Osgood—entered and took their places beneath the pulpit. Parson Toppan, in his black gown and white bands, accompanied by his wife and family, walked majestically up the broad aisle. There was the clatter of many feet, as the minister's entrance was the signal for the men and boys who had been grouped around the meeting-house, to come in. Tithing-man Tewkesbury, his long pole in hand, took his place amidst the boys in the gallery; Sexton Cooper tip-toed to his seat on the pulpit stairs. Parson Toppan rose and read two lines of a psalm; Deacon Osgood stepped forward and repeated them; mother's cousin, Edmund Little, with a pitch-pipe, set the tune; the choir sang the lines; the two next were given out, and thus the psalm was sung. This was followed by a long prayer and a longer sermon. The benediction pronounced, there was a moment's pause; then the minister descended from the pulpit, took his wife upon his arm, and, followed by his children, proceeded down the aisle, the clerical cortege gracefully returning the respectful bows and courtsies of the congregation. The clergyman's family was followed by the more aristocratic persons from the pews; these by the remainder of the audience. Many people, especially in cold weather, took their dinner, and staid at the meeting-house during the short intermission. In winter we rode in the large, high-backed sleigh. Sometimes, when storm and wind had prevented the breaking of the paths, father and Uncle Enoch walked to meeting on their snow shoes, and Mr. Josiah Bartlett would yoke his oxen and take his large family thither on the sled.

CHAPTER V.

The fourth parish in Newbury, like its predecessor at the river side, and the parent society at Oldtown, belonged to what might be termed, the low church wing of Congregationalism. The Rev. William Johnson had been strongly opposed to the more rigid views of some of his brethren in the ministry. He would not admit the renowned Whitefield into his pulpit, and the great revivalist was obliged to preach in a private house.

I have often heard my great aunt Sara Noyes describe the sensation produced by the eloquent divine. My great grandfather, Deacon John Noyes, fully sympathized in the disapproval evinced by his pastor, and he issued a strict edict forbidding any of his family attending what he termed "those disorderly assemblies." Aunt Sara, then a girl in her teens, entertained, as was natural, a strong desire to see and hear one whose name was on every tongue, and whose words and their effects were the chief topics of conversation on every side. At last, after much fear and trembling, she mustered courage to make a clandestine attempt to satisfy her curiosity. An evening meeting was to be held at a house in the vicinity, and she determined to brave her father's displeasure, if her absence was discovered, and go. It was a dark, cheerless night, when, with a throbbing heart, stealing down the stairs and noiselessly opening the door, she ran lightly down the gravel walk. Her hand was on the latch of the front gate, when a voice, in an authoritative tone, exclaimed "Go back!" Startled, affrighted, she stopped, turned, and peered on all sides into the darkness. No one was in sight. Through the uncurtained window she could see her father and the other members of her family seated around the bright wood fire. Concluding that, owing to the nervous timidity which this disobedience to paternal mandates had caused, imagination had conjured up this voice, with another long and searching look around, she opened the gate. "Go back!" reiterated the voice, even more decidedly than at first, just in her ear. What could it mean? Again she stopped, waited, looked and listened. Nothing unusual could be seen, and not a sound could be heard save the wind sighing through the trees. Sara Noyes was a resolute girl, not easily turned from any purpose she had deliberately formed, neither had she much belief in the supernatural. Thrusting back her fears, with a strong will she stilled her throbbing heart, and with a firm step, she again started forward. "Go back, go back," thundered the voice, in such a powerful and authoritative tone, that, thrilling in every nerve, the astonished girl, completely subdued, hastily turned, and fled into the house. Though she lived to a great age, and could never be reckoned a credulous person, to the last hour of her life she firmly believed that this was a Divine interposition to keep her from evil.

The Rev. David Toppan, the successor of the Rev. William Johnson, entertained even more liberal tenets than his predecessor. A genial, courteous gentleman, ready to sympathize with his charge, in their various phases of weal and woe. Parson Toppan was a universal favorite. His marriage with a towns-woman, Miss Mary Sawyer, the daughter of Dr. Enoch Sawyer, drew him still nearer to the hearts of his people.

The intelligence that their pastor contemplated leaving for a professorship at Harvard, which began to be circulated in the spring of 1792, brought both consternation, and grief. It could not be. A minister ought to live and die amidst the people over which he had been ordained. After many contradictory rumors the matter became at length decided. At the Thursday lecture, Parson Toppan, after a brief summary of the conflicting opinions then agitating the churches, announced the invitation he had received to a professorship at the college at Cambridge, and his intention of accepting it. "This decision had been made after much hesitation and prayerful consideration. Heresy was creeping into the institution, and it was incumbent upon every one to put forth their full power in support of sound doctrine. Neither the honor nor the emolument had borne a feather's weight in this separation from his beloved charge, but what he considered a call to a higher duty, gave him no option but to obey." At these words, up jumped old Mr. Moses Newell, and with ire imprinted on his countenance, shaking his clenched fist at his pastor, he shouted, "you lie, Parson Toppan, you know you lie." Instantly the congregation was in commotion, but the minister by his quiet demeanor and calm tones quelled the tumult; order was restored, Mr. Toppan closed the services, and the audience dispersed with sorrow in their hearts, and grief imprinted upon their faces, but with the firm conviction that their pastor was right; painful as this separation was, it must be made; inclination must be sacrificed to duty. Old Mr. Newell became pacified. His wife and son exerted themselves to this end. The old gentleman apologized, and invited the clergyman and his wife to dine, with a small party of select friends, at his house. There were many parting visits, and a general catechising of the children throughout the parish.

It was the custom to hold these catechisings annually, sometime during the spring or summer, usually on some afternoon in the middle of the week, in a house centrally located in each school district. As Parson Toppan wished to personally bid adieu to every child of his large flock, the catechising was appointed somewhat earlier that year than usual. The children of our district met at my grandfather Little's. Though I was young to attend, being a pet of the parson's, who was a frequent visitor of the family, much to my delight I was permitted to go. With a throbbing heart, clinging to aunt Hannah's hand on one side and uncle Joe's on the other, I entered the large parlor where sat my grandparents and older aunts. Parson Toppan occupied the large arm chair which he drew into the centre of the floor. The children ranged in a line in front. Having taken our places the recitations commenced. With much care mother had taught me the "chief end of man," and one or two of the shortest commandments. Though terribly flustered till my turn came, when it was my time to speak I was so earnest to repeat the lesson right that this self-consciousness passed; thus I was enabled to do myself due credit. The good minister and my grandparents and aunts praised me, the elder children gathered around, petting and caressing the smallest and youngest of the class. Altogether it was as great a triumph as I ever achieved or enjoyed. The catechisings and parting visits were over. The last, sad

Sunday came and a farewell sermon was preached, the last tearful parting had passed, and the upper parish became a society without a pastor.

Candidates began to supply the pulpit. Once a month one of the neighboring clergymen came to preach and administer the communion. The Rev. Barnard Tucker of the Oldtown society died that March. His successor, Rev. Mr. Moore, was not settled until about two years later. At the "Port" at that period there were three societies: The First Church, where Parson Cary had succeeded Dr. Lowell, the first minister; the Old South, where the venerable and saintly Parson Murray still occupied the pulpit; and the North, where the Hopkinsian Dr. Spring poured forth his fiery zeal. There was also St. Paul's Episcopal church, of which Bishop Bass was rector, but with this society ours, of course, had no communion.

I well remember the delight my mother always expressed when Parson Cary preached. He was her favorite minister, but most of her town relations and friends attended on his ministration, and many of the halcyon days of her maidenhood had been connected with this clergyman and his people. This may have induced an undue partiality, still from my childish impression I infer that Parson Cary, until broken by ill health, was both a fine writer and an eloquent speaker.

The Rev. True Kimball was at this time pastor of the Second parish in Newbury, and the Byfield parish had recently ordained the Rev. Elijah Parish, afterwards the distinguished Federalist divine, whose alpha and omega thundered over the land. His eminent talents and commanding eloquence had then just begun to attract public attention. There was also Master Smith, the preceptor of Dummer Academy. He often came over to fill the pulpit when other supply failed. I was greatly amused with this preacher. Short, stout and plethoric, with an abrupt, absent air, and a most singular pronunciation, this gentleman was a never-failing object for merriment amongst the juveniles of the congregation. One of his peculiarities was never closing his eyes when in prayer. People said he had acquired the habit of praying with his eyes open in school, keeping watch and ward over a parcel of unruly boys. Whatever the reason, he used to step forward in the pulpit, clasp his hands on the cushion, and in short, curt tones exclaim: "Ulmitty Gud!" This was the unvarying commencement of his opening prayer. The preceptor had the reputation of being a great linguist. It was affirmed that he knew so many languages that he had partly forgotten his own. Whether or no, the man was a great oddity; one of those isolated beings whose characteristics are wholly originalities.

The neighboring town of Bradford, that part of which is now Groveland, also rejoiced in another somewhat remarkable clergyman. Parson Dutch was what is denominated a smart preacher. He was also distinguished for his equine tastes and jockey predilections. I have often heard my father laugh over an incident that occurred one Sunday about the time of which I am writing. It was a hot summer day, the doors of the meeting-house were wide open. Parson Dutch had come to preach, He had risen to open the afternoon service, when a stranger, mounted upon a superb charger, rode up to the front entrance. Tying his steed opposite the door, he entered the sanctuary. Parson Dutch, from the pulpit, commanded a full view of the horse, and his audience averred that he watched it "all through the sermon." Father said: "If it had not been Sabba' day the parson would have proposed a swap; he knew he longed to bargain. He thought he would, spite of the day and his cloth."

Father Frisby, as he was universally denominated, a much-beloved and venerated old man, was the minister at the adjacent town of Boxford. We had many candidates, amongst whom were young men that in later years became "burning and shining lights."

Year after year rolled past, and still we were without a minister. Like the rest of New England, the parish became divided in sentiment, part adhering to the Arminian tenets, the others going over to what was called the Hopkinsian side.

CHAPTER VI.

The summer I was four years old I began to attend school. The schoolhouse in our district was not erected until some years later, the scholars being accommodated, up to that period, in a private house on the Crane-neck road, a short distance below where the present school edifice is located. My first teacher, Master Zack. Bacon, was a native of Bradford. Female teachers would then have been deemed inadmissible in a district school. It would not have been thought possible that order could be maintained under feminine rule, where often more than half the scholars were unruly boys, many of the eldest men grown.

The school was taught in the larger of the two front rooms, the remainder of the house being occupied by my mother's cousin, Edmund Little. We entered by the front door; the hats and bonnets were hung in the entry. The schoolroom was furnished with a desk and a flag-seated chair for the teacher; a clumsy square board table stood in the centre of the apartment, surrounded by high, wooden benches. Here were seated the older pupils; the younger were placed upon low forms ranged around the walls. The scholars were divided into four ranks: the "Bible," "Testament," "Spelling Book" and "Primer" classes. Dilworth's spelling book was the one then in use. The older scholars studied arithmetic, and wrote. Writing books were a later invention. A strong, coarse paper of foolscap size was then used, either in single sheets or several stitched together in book form. This paper, being plain, was ruled. Lead pencils were then a thing unknown; a plummet of lead supplied their place. These plummets were usually of home construction, and were cut in various devices, to suit the taste of the owner. The arithmetical rules and sums were also copied into books kept specially for that purpose. Master Bacon, a short, slight young man, somewhat of a dandy, and fresh from college, was a little inclined to what is now denominated "fast". Though one of the liveliest and most entertaining of mortals out of school, within he maintained a stern decorum, quite awful to a timid novice, like myself; but, as I had already mastered my alphabet and was exceedingly fascinated by my new primer, I immediately became a favorite with the teacher. With what sadness I used to gaze at that memorable picture of John Rogers at the stake. How many times I have counted the heads, to ascertain whether there were ten or eleven little ones. How my sympathies went out to those poor children and their distressed mother. With what genuine delight I would con—

"In Adam's fall
We sinned all.
The cat doth play,
And after slay."

With what pride I would repeat: "Who was the first man? Adam; Who was the first woman? Eve; Who was the first murderer? Cain; Who was the first martyr? Abel;" and the remainder of the long list of Biblical biography.

The first morning Master Bacon opened the school without prayer. The scholars reported, and in the evening he was waited upon by several of the dignitaries of the district, to ascertain the cause of the omission. The gentleman excused the oversight, with the promise that it should never be repeated. Accordingly we scholars were favored henceforth with an unusually long petition morning and evening, the gentleman assuring his chums that he had as lief pray as do anything else for the money. Master Bacon taught the school for two years, with much acceptance; he then removed to a wider sphere of action. Afterward he emigrated to Vermont, where he became a leading citizen.

His successor was Samuel Moody, from the Falls parish. This gentleman, a very handsome and well-bred young man, besides being an excellent teacher, was proficient as a violinist. His fiddle was a never-failing source of delight. I was a great favorite with Master Sam. He always led me home from school, and as he boarded at my great-uncle John Little's, I was daily favored with a tune.

Master Ned Longfellow, also from Byfield, next taught the school. He soon after removed to Maine, where he became distinguished. It is from this family that the poet, Henry Wadsworth Longfellow, is descended.

The summer I was eight years old a Miss Ruth Emerson, from Hampstead, N. H., collected a select school. There were from twenty to thirty scholars, mostly girls; there were a few small boys. I believe the tuition was but six cents a week. This lady promoted us into "Webster's Spelling Book" and "Webster's Third Part"—books then just coming into use. Miss Emerson was a most accomplished needlewoman, inducting her pupils into the mysteries of ornamental marking and embroidery. This fancy work opened a new world of delight. I became perfectly entranced over a sampler that was much admired, and a muslin handkerchief, that I wrought for mother, became the wonder of the neighborhood.

My father had purchased the portion of the homestead inherited by his brother Samuel, and that gentleman, after much hesitation and deliberation, at length decided upon the arduous undertaking of emigrating to a new country. Several of his wife's relations had recently located themselves upon farms in Vermont. Mrs. Smith was anxious to join them. "She was tired of living in such an old-settled place, where, unless one possessed a large farm, for years they must play second fiddle, screw and scrimp to secure a mere competence. For her part she preferred to go into the wilderness, where, if things were not as nice, one lived as their neighbors. She had rather be at the 'head of the poor than the tail of the rich.' In Vermont, where land was cheap, they could secure a goodly number of acres. The boys would become more useful every year. In time they could get forehanded; be as well off as any one. Then, as her husband possessed fine literary tastes and some culture, it opened a sphere for his ambition. She would not be surprised if he became an influential and distinguished citizen."

Swedenborg affirms that man possesses the understanding, and woman the will. Uncle Sam, after mature consideration, could find no valid reason for insubordination to the feminine will; a tract of land in the town of Berlin was purchased, and the preparations for a removal thither commenced. February was the time set for the flitting, as that month usually gave the best sledding, a great desideratum for the transmission of the household goods. Such a flurry as the whole family and all its collateral branches were in, for several weeks, seldom occurs in a life-time. Clothing for a year or two in advance must be prepared. One sister cut a generous quarter from her web of linen; another from her fulled cloth; a third presented blankets; another relative gave cloth for woolen dresses, and stocking yarn. Several ladies, relatives and friends, clubbed together and bought a number of handsome articles as parting gifts. There was a round of farewell visits, each of which was turned into a sewing-bee for the benefit of the emigrants. A large sleigh was constructed, which was covered by one ofthe check ed woolen coverlets then so much used. A quantity of provisions was provided, cooked meats and poultry, pies, cake, doughnuts, bread, butter and cheese were packed into a wooden box; this, other luggage, a feather bed, bedding and coverlets, were placed in the sleigh, along with the family. It was necessary to thus prepare for the night's accomodation, as the houses of entertainment on the route were few in number, small, and often over-crowded. The furniture was loaded upon two ox-sleds. My father drove his sled, to which was attached a yoke of oxen and a horse. Mr. Bailey, Aunt Smith's brother, drove the other team. Uncle Sam had a yoke of oxen forward of his brother's pair, and another relative drove his four cows. It was a clear, frosty morning when the cavalcade took their departure. A sad parting to all, but especially to me, as my cousin Sally, a girl of my own age, and my other cousins, had been my playmates from infancy. A lonesome fortnight followed; two weeks that, then, appeared as long as two years have since. To add to my discomfort and loneliness, my little brother, like other baby boys, toddling into mischief, contrived, during the momentary absence of mother, to pull over the teakettle, which was standing in the chimney corner, scalding his right arm and hand badly.

Mother went silently about the house with a worried look. Grandmother dozed through the days in her low chair, tipped back against the ceiling by the fireplace. Aunt Sarah was not half as brisk and cheery as usual, and Uncle Enoch grew decidedly surly. Poor little Jim's arm grew worse, Mother and Aunt Sarah became anxious, when one of the neighbors brought in Mrs. Salter's recipe for a burn. Mrs. Salter, a somewhat noted woman at the "Port," had effected many cures. It was concluded to try the prescription. A linen glove and sleeve were fitted over the burn; these were kept saturated with a mixture of olive oil and snow water, beat to a froth. In less than a week the sore was healed and a new skin formed. The sun was just setting, on the twenty-first day of father's absence; I was dragging little Jim across the sanded floor upon his tiny sled, when Aunt Sarah's glad tones reverberated over the house—"Brother Jim 's come; Brother Jim 's coming up the lane." There was a general rush to the back door. Yes, oh joy! there was father, unyoking his oxen at the gate. A regular jubilee ensued. The sirloin steak that had been kept for this occasion was cooked; a plate of the nicest cream toast dipped; the best mince pie, plum cake, doughnuts, cheese and preserves were placed upon the table. Grandma'am, Aunt Sarah and Uncle Enoch joined us at supper. After tea, as the news spread that "Jim Smith had got home," the neighbors flocked in to hear of the journey and the new country which he had visited. The room was soon filled, and a cordial welcome was given to the traveller. We could not but be pleased at the evident satisfaction manifested at father's safe return. I was permitted to sit up till an unwonted hour, to hear a description of the journey; of the slow progress through the long, cold days; and the weary nights at the small, inconvenient taverns, which were often so crowded that the males of the company were obliged to sleep on the kitchen floor, wrapped in their coverlets. At the end of a tedious week the new home was reached. One of Aunt Smith's brothers lived in a log house, roofed with bark; with a stone chimney; the other Mr. Bailey had put up a good-sized frame house. The brick chimney was built, the outside finished, and the floors laid, but the rooms were not partitioned. There was, however, sufficient space. Quilts and coverlets were suspended from the beams. Uncle Sam's family went to housekeeping one side of the chimney, while Mr. Bailey's occupied the other side. A saw mill was near; Uncle Sam immediately began to cut timber and haul it to the mill, and he expected to get up a house and barn that would be tenantable by warm weather.

Father had not caught the emigrant fever; he was a home body, firmly attached to the ancestral acres. "If he left Massachusetts he should prefer to go South rather than North. Still, Vermont was a fine state; a great grain and grazing country." The Baileys had raised a large crop of wheat of an extra quality. Father bought a quantity of the grain, and brought it home in a board chest which he constructed and fastened to his sled for that purpose. This was quite a successful speculation, as he paid only a dollar per bushel and it sold readily at home for a dollar and a half. It must be remembered that the family flour barrel had not then come into vogue. Wheat was raised upon the farm, or bought and ground by the bushel. Bolts had been put into most of the mills, but some families still used their flour unbolted. Indian meal and rye, especially rye, were the staples for daily use in most households. Barley was also raised and ground, but wheat flour was somewhat of a luxury; a housekeeper felt rich with a bushel or two on hand, and it was made to last a long time.

CHAPTER VII.

On July 19th, 1794, occurred one of those catastrophes that send a thrill of horror and anguish throughout the community. My seventh birth-day came a few days previous. Aunt Hannah Little and myself had been for some time anticipating the pleasure of spending the anniversary with my mother's aunt, Mrs. Simeon Chase. This lady still occupied the paternal homestead. The parish, then an infant one just gathered, had not, at the settlement of the Rev. William Johnson, provided a parsonage. The clergyman purchased several acres near the meeting-house, upon which he erected a house and farm buildings. The mansion, a square, double house, with a chimney at either end, stood a little below the meeting-house, on the opposite side of the street, just beyond the brow of the hill. A narrow lawn, shaded by maples, extended in front, a picket fence separating it from the grassy country road from which a gravel walk led up to the front entrance. A carriage drive ran round the end to a side door, and to the barn and other buildings in the rear. Mrs. Chase and another sister, afterwards Mrs. Moody, were unmarried at the time of their father's decease. As the other sisters had each received a full "fixing out," the furniture of the house had been given to these two single daughters. At his marriage, Master Simeon Chase bought the Parsonage, the library and other appertenances: consequently the premises at that time presented nearly the same aspect they had borne during the first pastor's life.

Madame Johnson's father, Dr. Humphrey Bradstreet, had furnished his daughter's new house in a style not frequent in those days. The principal entrance opened into a spacious hall, handsomely furnished in dark wood, from which a highly ornamented staircase led to the story above. The white wall was decorated with the portraits of Lieut. Governor Dummer and his wife, and a view of Harvard College. Under the pictures stood a large, massive dining table. The parlor, a square, pleasant room, was to the left of the entrance. Its three windows commanded a lovely view of the surrounding country and the river, bounded by the rolling hills of its farther shore. This room displayed an unusual embellishment; the walls were hung with a velvet paper, a purple figure on a buff ground.

Papered walls had not yet become common, no paste was used; four polished hard wood convex slats running round the room held the hangings in place. Small, slender brass andirons, and a tiny brass shovel and tongs adorned the tiled fireplace, an antique table, its legs curiously carved and ornamented, stood between the front windows; over it hung a mirror in a black and gilt frame; the chairs were cane seated and a strip of cane was inserted into the high, carved backs. An armchair occupied one corner; opposite stood the buffet, lustrous with rich silver, brightly painted china and glasses of various shapes and graceful device. The library, the opposite front room, had shelves round the two sides, well filled with books, and a study table in the centre. Master Chase kept a private school in this apartment part of the year. The back sitting-room was supplied with more common furniture, and a press-bed that turned up in a recess behind folding doors. The kitchen, the other back room, had been furnished with every convenience then considered requisite for the domestic purposes of a large family; the fireplace was huge, even for those days, and the long dresser shimmered with an array of bright pewter.

Master Chase, a very eccentric person, was his wife's senior by several years, and he was fond of relating how he had never dreamed of marrying little Hannah Johnson when, at her father's desire, she used to draw a tankard of cider for his refreshment upon his calls on the clergyman in his college vacations. The pair were childless for fifteen years of married life; then a little girl was born to them. This event caused such a sensation, was such a wonder throughout the family and the vicinity, that the Master declared the babe's name should be Myra. Myra, therefore, she was christened. Little Myra, on the watch for her expected guests, met us at the gate; Aunt Chase, a slight, black-eyed woman, bade us welcome at the door. After a lunch, Myra took us over the premises. The Master taught one or the other of the district schools in the town during the winter, but through the summer he received pupils at home, youths fitting themselves in the higher branches of learning, for college or mercantile life. School over, we went into the library. How numerous the books looked. Elsewhere I had never found more than a dozen or so in a house, and we were much amused with the plates in illustrated copies of Josephus, and Homer's Iliad. The Master was in the best of humor, and made us laugh through dinner. When he chose he could be one of the most entertaining of mortals, but he was often quite the reverse. His family were accustomed to his oddities, and his pupils were obliged to bear them.

In the afternoon Mr. Parker Chase's daughter Sukey, from the main road, came in. As Aunt Hannah and I took leave, Miss Chase asked me to carry an invitation to our neighbor, Nabby Hale, to join a party, across the river, huckleberrying the next week. Miss Hale, who was on the eve of marriage to Mr. Moses Longfellow, of Byfield, resided with her grandfather Dole, on a farm at the southerly end of Crane-neck hill. The young lady was sewing on her wedding dress, when I delivered the message. She said she should visit her stepfather before her marriage, and if not too busy would join the excursionists.

On the Saturday afternoon of the following week, Aunt Sarah and I went into the pasture to pick berries. It was a hot, sultry day betokening showers. Wandering on into Bradford woods, unheeding the sky, we were startled by a teriffic thunder peal accompanied by a violent gust of wind. Hastily turning, we saw that the west was threateningly black with clouds, and though only a few scattering drops reached us, in the direction of the main road it was raining heavily. The first fright over, I seized my basket, in order to hasten home as fast as possible, but Aunt Sarah said there was no cause for hurry, the shower would not come our way, it would follow the river. Without outstripping my companion I walked fast up the hill. As I neared the stone wall that divided the pasture from the house field, to my surprise I saw mother come from the front door, and run across the newly mown grass in the direction of the bars; I leaped them and rushed to meet her. Tears were streaming down her cheeks, and for a moment her speech failed. Aunt Sarah hurried forward to hear the terrible news, which had been brought by Mr. John Peabody, on his way to Mr. Dole's. The whole of the berrying party, with the exception of Mr. Moses Chase (Nabby Hale's step-father), had been drowned in the Merrimac, by the overturning of the sail-boat during the thunder gust, midway the river, as they were returning to the Newbury shore. Mr. Chase, on seeing the rising cloud, had hurried the embarkation of the company; never dreaming that their safety would be endangered before they could cross. His three children, Polly, Rebecca and Joshua, Nabby Hale, Mercy Pillsbury, Sarah and Mehitable Brown, and Mr. Edmund Kendrick were drowned. Sukey Chase had a singular premonition during the morning, which, as the time for sailing approached, increased to such a degree that, under the plea of headache, she remained at home. My father and Aunt Sarah hastened to Mr. Dole's. The eight bodies were soon drawn from the water, and the remains of the lovely granddaughter were, towards evening, borne to the bereaved home. Words are inadequate to depict the scene! The stricken family and youthful lover were for a time wholly overcome. It was arranged that the seven from the main road should be interred from the meeting-house on the morrow, where Parson Dutch had been engaged to officiate; but, as Mr. and Mrs. Dole were aged and infirm, and it would be more convenient for the Hales, Longfellows, and other Byfield relatives and friends, it was decided that Miss Hale should be buried from her grandfather's house. Father mounted his horse and rode to East Haverhill, to procure the services of the Rev. Mr. Adams, the pastor of the church, for the funeral rites. Until a late hour our house was filled with a sorrow-stricken throng, going and coming from Mr. Dole's. The following day father and Aunt Sarah devoted to the bereaved family, and we all attended the funeral in the afternoon.

The obsequies in the church were solemnly impressive. The seven coffins were placed in the broad aisle, where, amid the sobs and moans, Parson Dutch — his own voice often broken — spoke words befitting the occasion. Then the seven corpses were borne on the shoulders of their friends, a mournful file, followed by a long procession, an immense throng—not only our own people, but from other towns, to the burial place by the river side. Slowly, with uncovered heads, in impressive silence, their burdens were deposited in the seven open graves. Dust was committed to dust, with that hope in a blessed immortality, which is the only source of faith, upbearing the anguish of such an hour. Lingeringly, with many tears, the crowd dispersed, and the dead were left on the picturesque hillside, where the western sun would lovingly linger and the soft breezes play over the grassy mounds, while the river rippled beyond, and the shadows chased each other over field, woodland and swelling hills, and the smoke curled above peaceful homesteads dotting the widespread landscape. Miss Hale's body also rested in a lovely spot; a small, rural graveyard at the foot of Crane-neck Hill; a pleasant, secluded "God's Acre," where the song-birds attune their sweetest melody, and the violets bloom the earliest and grow the largest.

The Sunday following was most memorable to all. Dr. Toppan came early in the week to sympathize with and console his afflicted friends, and former parishioners. The meeting-house was crowded, and when the long list of funeral notes, requesting prayers were read, there was not a dry eye in the assembly. Dr. Toppan preached an extremely appropriate and impressive sermon. Child though I was, the whole scene rises distinctly in my memory. Mrs. Hendrick, in her widow's hood and scarf, with her two little fatherless girls, sat in the next pew, and the other numerous mourners in their sable garb heightened the awe and sadness of the scene.

CHAPTER VIII.

The summer that I attained my ninth year aunt Betsy celebrated her nuptials. Preparations therefor proceeded for some months, and the skill I had acquired in marking and embroidery called my services into requisition.

My grandfather's family presented a perfect type of an orderly Puritan household. A clergyman's daughter, Grandmother Little gave an air of refinement and decorum to her small realm, seldom seen in a farmer's or mechanic's domicile.

Judith, the fourth daughter, had, two years previous, married Mr. Amos Chase, whose residence at this time was in Haverhill. This gentleman descended from Aquila Chase, a mariner from Cornwall, England, who came first to Hampton in 1610, thence to Newbury in 1646. He married Ann Wheeler of Hampton. This pair had eleven children, five sons and six daughters. From these sprung a numerous progeny. Amos, son of Samuel and Sarah (Stuart) Chase, was born in the brick house on the main road nearly opposite that leading to Crane-neck hill, where he resided when first married. A short time previous to Aunt Betsey's wedding, he purchased a farm in Haverhill, about half a mile below Haverhill bridge. In addition to the cultivation of his land, he was largely engaged in the manufacture of shoes.

The Chase arms are:

GULES FOUR CROSSES PATENCE ARGENT, ON A CANTON AZURE A LION PASSANT OR, CREST—A LION RAMPANT OR, HOLDING IN ITS PAWS A CROSS PATENCE ARGENT.

At my grandfather Little's, three daughters, Betsy, Sukey and Hannah, and the three sons still remained under the paternal roof; there were also three young men, apprentices, learning the trade of a shoemaker. Grandsir at that time carried on a brisk business, as business was reckoned in those days, in a shop near the dwelling—this, and the care of a good sized farm, kept every one busy. Family worship and breakfast over, the "men folks" went to their labor, and grandmam' and the girls began the day's routine. The two youngest girls assisting alternately week by week in the housework and spinning. The weaving was usually put out to some neighboring woman, though sometimes an assistant was hired to weave at the house for a few weeks. In the cold weather, the morning work finished, and the dinner put over the fire to boil, grandmam', would seat herself by the window with her basket, and call me to a stool by her side, where I industriously stitched through the day, now and then recreating with a run to the chamber where my aunt, unless the weather was very severe, usually spun, or to the shop or barn with Uncle Joe, my boy uncle, a great rogue, but my very best friend and crony. Company often came of an afternoon, for though my grandmother seldom visited, she was "given to hospitality," and the neighbors, relatives and town's folks fully appreciated and enjoyed the attractions of her house and tea table.

At dark my work was laid aside. Uncle Joe and I occupied the form in the chimney corner of an evening, cracking nuts, parching corn in the ashes with a crooked stick, roasting apples and telling stories or riddles, or playing fox and geese on a board, chalked for the game, with a red kernel of corn for the fox and yellow for geese.

At nine o'clock grandsir and the young men came. Grandsir would seat himself in his arm-chair, before the fire to toast his feet, grandmam' lay aside her knitting and draw her low one to the corner beside our form. The nuts, corn and apples were passed round, and sometimes a mug of flip was made. After all had become warmed and refreshed, the Bible was laid on the stand, a fresh candle lighted, and the old gentleman reverently read a chapter, then a lengthy prayer was offered, through which we all stood with heads bowed devoutly, though I am sorry to say that grandmam's thoughts were sometimes called to this mundane sphere, by that incorrigible Joe, and her low "'sh" could often be detected, as she thwarted some mischief, or prevented some prank, played with the dire intent of making me laugh. With the warmer weather Aunt Betsy transferred our work to her chamber, where it escaped the espionage of the curious eyes and gossiping tongues that during the winter had at times been excessively annoying; but in the long, bright June afternoons I used to steal down to the front entry; seated upon the sill of the open door, my fingers kept time to the murmur of the brook or the song of the birds in the willows bordering the silvery stream just beyond the gravel path, edged by flowers, the perfume of which, mingling with that of the lilacs and sweet briar, filled the air with grateful odor. Grandmam' took great pleasure in her flowers. Though sister Noyes "could not see how she found time for sich fiddle-de-dees," and brother John's wife pronounced "sich things all vanity," and other wise people thought it would be better to raise something useful, grandmam' continued to cultivate her garden to the end of her long life. Her crocuses, tulips and other spring flowers were a rare show; there were a splendid collection of pinks and roses, and a great array of autumnal flowers. Hollyhocks of every variety, French, velvet and double marigolds, asters of all shades, double coxcomb, and a bed of crimson, purple and yellow amaranths. One of my first recollections is sitting on the wide, white door stone, watching the many hued four o'clocks as their petals unfolded to the afternoon sun. Another delight was assisting grandmam', in the autumn to arange in pretty vases of home construction the dried amaranths, which mingled with white-everlasting, milk-weed, bitter-sweet and evergreen, made pretty winter bouquets, to decorate the mantles of the parlor and living room; these, with the wreaths of running evergreen round the mirror and clock, also elicited criticism. "Sich things did very well for some folks. If Miss Little had to delve and drudge like most women, she would'nt want dried posies and greens a littering her house, but she always had contrived to live ladyfied, and with that squad of gals, she could afford to play quality." These and similar speeches often excited the anger of the "squad of gals" but grandmam', in her pleasant way would bid them "never to heed things beneath one's notice." "Recreation was necessary; if she chose to amuse herself in her garden, so long as no duty was neglected, it was no one's concern. As for use she considered flowers of great value. The Almighty had decked the whole universe with beauty. Who was not made happier and better by pretty surroundings? For her part she considered it every woman's duty to make her home as agreeable as possible. She was sure her good sisters-in-law and the other croakers enjoyed a bunch of pinks or a rose, as much as any one, and her mints and sweet herbs were in great demand, especially lavender, to strew in drawers amongst linen."

Sunday was the only day on which I preferred to be at home. Father was somewhat of a latitudinarian, and mother never prohibited my picture books. Of these my town friends and an old lame peddler named Urin who came round five or six times a year, kept me well supplied. Old Urin was quite a character. He would stump in, usually near dusk, with a bag and basket, and sinking into the nearest chair, declare himself "e'en a'most dead, he was so lame!" Then, without stopping to take breath, he would reel off, "Tree fell on me when I was a boy, killed my brother and me jest like him, here's books, pins, needles, black sewing silk all colors, tapes, varses, almanacks and sarmons, thread, fine thread for cambric ruffles, here's varses on the pirate that was hung on Boston Common, solemn varses with a border of coffins atop, and Noble's sarmon preached at his wife's funeral, the 'lection sarmon when the guv'ner took the chair, Jack the Piper, Whittington's Cat, Pilgrim's Progress, Bank of Faith, The History of the Devil, and a great many other religious books." We always kept the old man over night besides purchasing his wares. As I had an eager avidity for books, the peddler's advent was hailed with delight.

At grandsir's the Lord's day was kept in Sabbatical strictness. Every vestige of the week's employment disappeared at sundown Saturday night, no book was permitted save the Bible, some pious treatise and the catechism. Pleasant days, when meeting was attended morning and afternoon, the day was not so tedious, but stormy ones were seemingly interminable. Then that catechism! Though I was quick to learn, this was my one great bugbear. How I used to dread the catechising Grandsir instituted after supper. Sunday evenings, Uncle Joe and I were always falling into disgrace by our dullness, aand unt Hannah frequently could sympathze with us. Then we often unwittingly broke the rules in such a way as to receive a reprimand. Never shall I forget the shame of one memorable Sunday afternoon. It was very muddy riding in the spring, and as it was inconvénient to take us along, Aunt Hannah, Uncle Joe and myself were left at home. We had studied the catechism, read the history of Joseph from the Bible, and played with the cat and kittens till we were tired. Aunt Hannah went into the cellar for apples; there she found some rotten warden pears which she brought above and placed in the sink. Uncle Joe took his jack-knife and scraped out the pulp from one. "Look here," he cried, "see my pail, look at my pail!" "It needs a bail," Aunt Hannah returned, as she brought some strong, blue yarn and proceeded to tie it in. Joe scraped another, Aunt Hannah tied in a second bail. Knowing I ought not to play, I only looked on, an interested spectator. The spring sun was shining brightly in at the open back door, the well curb was near with a trough for watering the horses and cattle. Joe took his pails out to the platform, Aunt Hannah and I followed. We were so intent seeing the little boy fill his novel pails, that we forgot to watch for the close of services as we had intended, and were all caught in the awful crime of playing on "Sabba' day." Such a chastisement as we received! Thereafter I never staid over Sunday at grandsir's if it could be otherwise, and when I did stay, for years I scarcely dared to breathe.

The wedding had been appointed for the last of June. Aunt Sarah, and a famous cook, lent her assistance in baking the cake. Mother cut the bridal dress, a light slate silk gown and skirt, the gown was festooned at the bottom, the neck and the sleeves trimmed with lace. The bridal hat, a French beaver to match, was ornamented with two long, white ostrich plumes. Aunt Sukey and Aunt Hannah had new white muslins, cut square in the neck, and short sleeves; the breadths run the whole length, plaited at the back, and confined at the waist by a ribbon sash. Grandmam's best silk, a blue and red changeable, was newly trimmed, a tasty muslin cap constructed, and her bridal lawn half-handkerchief, richly bordered with broad, thread lace, which never saw the light excepting on high, gala occasions, and sacrament Sundays, was carefully done up.

The important day arrived. The house was swept and garnished, the parlor decorated with white and damask roses. I wore a white muslin, and a blue sash, like Aunt Hannah's. Mother looked beautifully in a white petticoat and brown silk over dress; Aunt Chase wore her bridal silk, a reddish brown; Uncle Bill and his affianced, Miss Sarah Bailey, were groomsman and bridesmaid,—Miss Bailey, a very handsome girl, looked lovely in a peach silk. As we were without a minister, the Rev. True Kimball from the lower parish, performed the ceremony. The wine and cake passed, a merry time was enjoyed.

The Bartletts, with whom the Emerys, Johnsons and Littles have intermarried, are of a family both "Ancient and Honorable." Adam de Bartelot, a Norman knight, accompanied William the Conqueror to England. After the conquest William granted him a large landed estate in Stopham, Sussex Co. Sir Adam de Bartelot died in 1100. He was the progenitor of the Newbury Bartletts. The original grant made by William the Conqueror, with large additions, is still retained by the Bartelots of Stopham. The present representative of the family is Sir Walter Bartelot, Baronet, and member of parliament. John and Richard Bartlett, who came to Newbury in the year 1634, were of the Stopham family, being sons of Edmund Bartelot, third son of William, the then heir to the estate. Another brother, Ensign Thomas Bartlett, accompanied John and Richard to America; he settled in Watertown. Josiah Bartlett purchased a farm in the "West Precinct" Newbury, his son, Josiah, married Prudence Ordway, and succeeded his father on the estate, and, for those days, he carried on a very extensive shoe trade, always employing a half dozen or more apprentices. These youth, for years, bore the designation of "Bartlett's" boys, and a merry set they usually were, up to all kinds of pranks; if any tricks were played, all eyes were instantly turned on "Bartlett's boys." The children of Josiah aud Prudence Bartlett were Josiah, Stephen, Betsey, Samuel, William, John Emery, Prudence, Polly, and Theodore who died in infancy. The arms of the Bartlett family are:

SABLE: THREE SINISTER FALCONER'S GLOVES PROPER, BANDED AND TASSELLED OR.

This without a crest was the family arms for some centuries. Near the close of the fifteenth century one of the present crests, a castle, was granted to Sir John Bartelot, who, in command of the Sussex troops, captured the castle of Fontenoy, in France. In the sixteenth century a swan was added to the crest, to commemorate the right of the family to keep swans on the river Arun, a right granted by William the Conqueror. These were confirmed under the seal of William Segar, Garter King of Arms, October 27, 1616, 14th year of King James, motto "Mature." The bridegroom, Stephen Bartlett, had been in business in Newburyport nearly two years. The year previous Mr. John Peabody had moved thither, with Mr. Luther Waterman, the two gentlemen had formed a partnership, known as the firm of "Peabody, Waterman & Co." Their place of business was a store on the corner of State street and Market Square, running back to Inn street. The front store on State street was devoted to dry goods, the back, entrance on Inn street, had a full supply of groceries, and boots and shoes, the latter being manufactured in the chambers. Stephen Bartlett had purchased the house on State, lower corner of Temple street, and the wedded pair went immediately to housekeeping. As was natural the bride found herself intolerably lonesome in her new home, and a pressing invitation came, that I should pay her a visit. Mother packed my things in her little red, wooden trunk, and I accompanied father the next market day.

I vividly remember the ride down High street, and father's reining in his steed, that I might gaze at the deer in the park at Mt. Rural, and at Dexter's images. Only a beginning of the show had then been made, Washington, Ad-'ams and the Goddess of Liberty adorned the front entrance, and the Lion and Lamb reclined on either side.

We found Mrs. Bartlett fully established, everything in spick and span freshness. The parlor, now the site of Mr. Philip H. Blumpey's store, was a large, pleasant room, the two front windows overlooking State, the two end, Temple street. It was handsomely furnished, for that period, with a mahogany desk and book-case, two mahognay card tables, and alight-stand to match; a large mirror occupied the front pier, two pictures, a marine view, and a landscape ornamented the wall. There were half a dozen dark green, wooden chairs, and two rockers to match. A Franklin stove had been set in the fire-place, in which glittered a highly polished brass fire-set. There was no carpet, floors had not then become generally covered, and, if carpeted in the winter, they were usually bare in summer, carpets being considered hot and dusty. The best chamber was elegant with gay patch hangings to the high square post bedstead, and curtains of the same draped the windows. A toilet table tastily covered with white muslin, and ornamented by blue ribbon bows, stood between the front windows. The case of drawers was handsomely carved, the chairs matched those below, and there was a novelty, the first wash-stand I ever saw, a pretty triangular one of mahogany, a light graceful pattern to fit into a corner of a room. The other chambers, the kitchen, wash room, etc., were in perfect order, and supplied with every convenience. Several newly invented improvements for housekeeping were displayed, amongst which was a tin rooster. Heretofore our meat and poultry had been baked in the brick oven, or roasted on a spit, resting on brackets, fastened for that purpose to the high, iron andirons, common to every kitchen. Sometimes a turkey or goose was depended before the fire by a strong string hitched to a nail in the ceiling. At the "Wolfe tavern," and at the residences of some of the wealthier citizens, a jack turned by clock work had been placed in the wide fire-place of the spacious kitchen. This new "tin kitchen," Aunt Betsey displayed as a rare implement of great value to the culinary art.

After dinner a visit to my aunt Peabody was proposed. I hesitated, and informed my aunt that mother had directed that I should not go anywhere until she had procured me a new bonnet. My aunt laughed, and replied, that she "thought sister Prudy did not expect to have town style like her sisters'. Do not look so sober, little sweet, I knew head-gear was needed, and here it is," she added, taking from a closet a white muslin Quaker-shaped bonnet trimmed with green. Of course I was delighted, and my happiness was enhanced by the information that it was just like my cousin Sophronia's, and hers, of course, was in the tip-top of fashion.

Uncle Peabody had bought a house on Middle street. It was smaller and less pleasant than my aunt Bartlett's, but the furniture was similar. The curtains were white with netted fringe, and the parlor table was decorated with an elegant gilt China tea set in a red and gilt tray. Aunt Betsey wished to embroider cushions for her rockers. Miss Betty Bradstreet was celebrated for designing patterns for such work. Aunt Peabody, learning our intention of calling upon her, summoned Sophronia from school, and with her little daughter accompanied us.

Humphrey Bradstreet, an elder brother, or kinsman, of Gov. Simon Bradstreet, came from Ipswich, England, to Ipswich, America, in the "Elizabeth," in 1634, aged 40, with his wife Bridget, aged 30, and children—Hannah, aged 9, John, 3, Martha, 2, and Mary, 1; had born here Moses, Sarah and Rebecca; was made freeman May 6th, 1635; representative to General Court in 1635; died in 1656.

Humphrey, Rowley, physician, son of Moses, removed to Newbury; there, by wife Sarah, had Dorothy, born Dec. 19th, 1692; Joshua, Feb. 24th, 1695; Sarah, Jan. 16th, 1697; Humphrey, 1700, died young; Daniel, Feb. 13th, 1702; Moses, Feb. 17th, 1707; and Betty, May 16th, 1713. Dr. Bradstreet died May 11th, 1717. His widow, June 9th, 1719, married Edward Sargent. Arms, Bradstreet:

GERRONNY OF SIX GULES AND OR, ON EACH A CRESCENT COUNTERCHANGED. CREST A UNICORN'S HEAD BETWEEN TWO BUNCHES OF LAUREL IN ARLE.

This is the ancient coat. The arms on the seal of Gov. Simeon Bradstreet, born at Kobling, county Lincoln, 1703, where his father Simeon was the minister—are:

ON A FESSE—THREE CRESCENTS—IN BASE A HOUND PASSENT. CREST A DEXTER ARM VAMBRACED EMBOWERED, THE HAND GRASPING A SWORD.

Anne Dudley Bradstreet, Gov. Bradstreet's first wife, was the first "American female Poet," styled the tenth muse. Dr. Humphrey Bradstreet built the second house erected at the water side. It is on Water, upper corner of Lime street, at present a store. His youngest daughter, Betty, married the Rev. William Johnson, and his youngest son, Moses, married, and inherited the paternal mansion. Four out of five of Mr. Moses Bradstreet's children, died within one week from the terrible throat distemper which, in the winter of 1735, despoiled so many households in Massachusetts and New Hampshire. Betty, her aunt Johnson's namesake, alone recovered; but vestiges of the fell disease were carried through a long life in impaired beauty and a weakened constitution. Mr. Bradstreet died in a few years, and Mrs. Bradstreet, upon the death of her children, was thrown into an illness which weakened her mind; though she lived until Miss Betty was well advanced in age, she could never be brought to regard her daughter as other than a little girl. I have been told how touching it was to see the mother leading the grown woman up the aisle of the meeting-house as if she was still a child. Miss Bradstreet had numerous suitors, but till her mother's death her life was devoted to her; afterwards she declared herself too old for matrimony, and in company with her faithful serving maiden, Hannah Brown, she lived a happy, useful and contented life, in the ancestral mansion, an open house to her relatives and friends, while they in turn were often enlivened by a visit from the spinster cousin, whose advent was the signal for a genuine festival throughout the household and neighborhood. To children in particular Miss Betty constituted herself a sort of patron saint, receiving in return a love and devotion never to be forgotten. The Bradstreet mansion had been a pretentious house at the period of its erection, and with its extensive and well kept garden was then a model of neatness and elegance. The windows commanded as exquisite a view as can be found. The beautiful Merrimac broadening to its mouth, Plum Island river pouring in its tributary waters on the right, opposite the picturesque Salisbury shore, terminating in its long, sandy point, the narrow outlet at the bar separating it from the twin point at Plum Island, whose length of sands, marshes and bushy knolls extended into the distance. The two light-houses on its northern extremity gleamed in the afternoon sun, which eradiated the lofty warehouses on the wharves, the wherries, fishing smacks and West India schooners, in the river, and the sails of vessels near and more remote, dotting the waves of Massachusetts Bay, whose blue waters stretched afar, its hues mingling with those of the horizon.

Miss Betty, a tall, prim, rather plain woman of sixty, received us with great cordiality. Her parlor, rich in antique furnishings, if it could be restored, would now become a perfect bijou for an antiquarian. Dark, highly polished tables with claw feet, and high backed, elaborately carved chairs to match; a tall, handsomely ornamented clock ticked in one corner; an elegantly embroidered fire-screen, with mahogany frame, that could be raised or lowered at pleasure, stood opposite. A large mahogany-framed mirror occupied the space between the front windows; over the mantel, which was decorated with tall brass candlesticks, hung the portrait of Dr. Humphrey Bradstreet, in a red coat, buff vest, white wig, ruffled shirt, and delicate ruffles at the wrist, the right hand grasping a lancet. The walls were further ornamented by paintings and embroidered pictures, specimens of the taste and skill of the mistress of the house. The screen, the wrought seats of the chairs, and various other knick-knacks scattered about the room, were also the handiwork of the ingenious and industrious maiden.

Our hostess invited us into the garden, which was gay with a profusion of old-fashioned flowers, besides fruit and vegetables. Each having been supplied with a "bunch of posies," we took our leave. A pressing invitation "to stay to tea," had been givhn, but Uncle Bartlett was to join his wife and myself at Uncle Peabody's, so the visit was postponed until the cushion covers were drawn.

As we returned, my aunts spoke of the terrible distemper, that brought such sorrow to the Bradstreet mansion, as well as to so many other New England homes. Aunt Peabody inquired "if Aunt Bartlett had ever heard of the warning given to Mrs. Stephen Jaques prior to her grand-children's decease?" Aunt Betsey answered in the negative, and inquired what it was. "Mrs. Jaques went to a chamber, the door of which was locked, to get some candles that were in a bushel measure under the bed. She took out the candles, laid them on the bed, and pushed the measure back; as she lifted the quilt, she saw a child's hand and an arm covered witha striped sleeve. She pulled down the bed clothes, and searched the chamber, but no child was there. In a few days her son's children were taken with the throat distemper. OnThursday, just a fortnight from the time she saw the apparition, Stephen's son, Henry, died; the next Thursday, Ebenezer died, and the next Monday his oldest son Stephen, died. "I do not know what to think of such things," Aunt Betsey thoughtfully returned, "you often hear of occurrences that are termed supernatural in times of sickness and distress." I did not know what to think of the story, either. On whispering an inquiry to my cousin, she exclaimed, "Ugh! Don't talk of it, I beg! I shall lie awake all night." I said no more, but the story haunted my imagination. As soon as I shut my eyes of a night, that tiny hand and striped sleeve would present itself, and every time I lifted a quilt it protruded from beneath. I cannot say that I was afraid, but it was a long while ere I lost the vision.

Aunt Peabody told Sophronia she and I might go to the store, and hurry her father and uncle home. I had never visited an establishment of the kind, and I doubt, now, if even Stewart's would appear more spacious and elegant. Sophronia went behind the counter and measuring off two yards of pink satin ribbon, presented me with half of it; I demurred as to the propriety of this proceeding. Mr. Waterman, who was in the front store, told me to take the ribbon, but I was not satisfied until I had informed my uncle Peabody, whom I found in the back store. He said "Yes, Fronie and I were welcome to the ribbon; I am glad to see my little girl generous to her friends." After regaling us on raisins, he led the way back to the front division, and taking down a box of spangled gauze fans, he bade us each choose one. Sophronia took a buff ornamented in silver. I chose blue and gold. Uncle Bartlett came from the shoe manufactory, and invited us up stairs, where he fitted both with a pair of purple kid slippers. Very happy and grateful, we accompanied the gentlemen home to tea. How vividly they rise in remembrance. Gen. Peabody, tall, prepossessing, with a noble figure and courtly bearing, his pleasant face irradiated by smiles as he familiarly chatted with "his little girl." Col. Bartlett of a slighter mould, lithe and active, taciturn and grave, excepting on occasions, when the serious black eye would twinkle, as the thin, firmly cut lips gave utterance to some witticism, or drollery, in a mirth-evoking manner wholly his own.

After supper, Capt. Moses Brown, whose premises adjoined my uncle's, came in to invite the family to visit the ship of war Merrimac, a vessel the town had built and presented to the general government. It had been constructed in an incredibly short period of time, and was the great focus of attraction to the people of that vicinity. Capt. Brown was to command the ship, which, then lay, nearly ready for sea, just back of what is now the City railroad depot.

As there was quite a party of ladies and gentlemen, Aunt Peabody thought Sophronia and I had better go another time. My cousin went to the next house, and returned accompanied by a boy and girl, whom she introduced as my cousins, John and Lydia Kettell. We seated ourselves upon the front door step for a while, then my cousin proposed a run over to the meeting-house. It was a warm, moonlight evening; what is now Market square was soon reached. A large, unpainted building, its heaven-pointing spire, white in the moonbeams rose before us. This, the third Church of Newbury and the first of Newburyport, stood where the city pump is now located. Having run about the meeting-house for awhile, we mounted the steps, and sat down to enjoy the evening and the moonlight, talking the meanwhile as children talk.

The next day Uncle Peabody took us to see the ship, and Mary Smith, a connexion of my uncle's, who resided in his family, invited us to accompany her, in the afternoon, to visit a famous new house then in process of erection on the ridge on High street. Its builder was a Major Shaw. This gentleman failed, and moved from the place ere the edifice was completed. It was purchased and finished, after a while, by Captain Elias Hunt. The following morning I went to school with my cousin. She attended a private school kept by "Marm Emerson," a very good, stout old lady, who taught reading, spelling, the catechism and plain sewing to a flock of the neighboring little ones. In the afternoon Aunt Bartlett took me to call on my father's uncle, Mr. Richard Smith, and at the residences of the two brothers of my grandmother Little, Mr. Daniel and Mr. Bradstreet Johnson; she also called on her cousins, Coombs and Wheelwright. On Saturday I returned home, having enjoyed a most pleasant week. Everywhere I had been welcomed and petted, and I took back an enlargement of ideas, that greatly edified and amused the family, with an enhancement of importance in the eyes of my country mates, which produced a deference due to one cognizant of town elegance and polish.

A short time after this visit the yellow fever, brought from the West Indies, broke out in Newburyport. From the first few cases it rapidly grew to an appalling epidemic; over forty persons died from the disease, amongst them, Doctor Swett, one of the first physicians. Fear and consternation seized the population. Few from abroad ventured into the place, which, as the fever increased, became completely panic-stricken. Many hurried away; others shut themselves in their houses. Business and pleasure were alike suspended. A pall seemed stretched over the summer sky, and death appeared borne upon its soft breezes. Ropes were drawn across Water and other streets, barring off the infected district. It was difficult to obtain attendants for the sick; and the dead, without funeral rites, in tarred sheets and pine coffins, were, at midnight, carried to the grave in a rude vehicle constructed for the purpose of rough boards. Thus, unshrined, unknelled, in all haste, the corpse was covered from sight, and a new mound, that for a time every one would shun, rose on the old burying hill.

When the fever first appeared, before its presence was really known, my uncle Peabody's family received a fright, which happily brought no evil consequences. The eldest daughter, when returning from school, was informed, by a little acquaintance, that a dead man lay in the house they were passing. "Come in and look at him," she said to Sophronia, "he looks real funny. He is just as yellow as saffron." The corpse was laid out ready for burial, in one of the front rooms. The front door was open, and people were passing in and out. Childlike, Fronie peeped in, then tiptoed forward. Sure enough, the dead man's face was of a deep yellow. At dinner she mentioned the incident, inquiring what could have made the corpse so yellow. Her mother could not imagine, but my uncle, who had heard a rumor that there had been cases of yellow fever in the place, too truly divined the matter. Every precaution was instantly taken; Fronie was kept from school, but none of our relatives took the fever. Aunt Bartlett was suddenly and violently seized with a bilious attack, to which she was subject. The family were alarmed, and Grandmother Little was summoned, but she was quickly relieved. The neighborhood was greatly frightened, and the morning after grandmam's arrival ,what was her horror, as she drew aside the curtain in the early dawn, to descry the dread dead-cart drawn up before the back door, awaiting what was supposed to be another victim to the pestilence. She lost no time in sending it away, but it was hours before she recovered from the shock the fell sight had given, and I never heard her recount the incident without a shudder. Frost subdued the plague. The fever entirely vanished, and the "Port" gradually resumed its wonted life and appearance.

CHAPTER X.

The following spring I was prostrated by an illness, the vestiges of which have remained through a long life. My head began to ache, Friday, in school. Master Stephen Longfellow was the teacher. Contrary to my inclination he sent me home. Mother administered camphor, I retired early, and the next morning thought myself well enough to attend school. I loved study, and it was a disappointment to lose a session. Though not feeling strong, I managed to go through the morning creditably. It was the latter part of March; the road was sloppy, the walking tiresome. Just as I reached the lane leading to the house, I was seized with a terrible pain in my right knee. Unable to walk another step, I sank upon a stone by the roadside. My little brother, who was my companion, much frightened, ran for mother; she and Aunt Sarah bore me home. Mother bathed the limb, and I was kept warm and dosed for a cold. The next morning, I was so comfortable, it was not deemed necessary that mother should remain from meeting, and I was left with my brother. A short time after the others had gone, Jim ran in, with the information that the pigs were out of the pen. "They are rooting all over the garden, Sallie. What shall I do? I can't get them back into the pen alone. They will spoil the garden; they have rooted up one bunch of daffies a'ready." Looking from the window, I saw that the little boy was right. The porkers were making sad havoc. I hesitated about venturing forth, but at length decided to go. Putting on my thick boots and wrapping myself up, we sallied forth, and, after a while, managed to get the obstinate animals penned. I was much exhausted by the effort, and when the family came back they found me in a raging fever, stiff, and in pain. Doctor Poore was brought. The worthy doctor examined the case, took a long pinch of snuff, and then pronounced it rheumatic fever. Blisters were applied, and the usual remedies given, but I suffered fearfully. It was three or four weeks ere I could move, and as many more before I could sit up or step. Months passed, and still I remained an invalid. Autumn brought somewhat of the old vigor, but I was obliged to be very careful, and could bear no fatigue nor exposure for a long time. Relatives and friends were most kind in their ministration during this sickness, and at my convalescence every means was used for solace and amusement. It was a perfect boon to be able to read and sew. Pilgrim's Progress and The Arabian Nights were absolutely devoured. Opportunely, Miss Betty Bradstreet paid one of her much prized visits. She devised many sources of relaxation from the dullness of a sick-room. I still have an embroidered pocket, the pattern of which she designed and drew.

Mother was always hurried, and, as I grew stronger, I felt it a duty to assist her; but after I had sewed my seam or knit my stint, I would steal up to Aunt Sarah's chamber, to read, or work upon the border of a skirt which Aunt Sarah, who had a universal genius, had drawn: a lovely vine of roses and leaves. I feared mother would consider this too much of a tax upon my health, so the work was carried on surreptitiously for several weeks. At length it was completed and exhibited in triumph. The flower garden became a source of gratification, and as soon as possible I limped over to our next neighbor's. Mrs. Thurrill was my mother's aunt, my grandfather Little's sister, but her youngest son was only one year my elder; from infancy we were playmates. My little brother used to run, in shouting, "Here's Bill Thuddle, Sallie; Bill Thuddle has come to help you over to his house." Mother would put on my things, and with Bill's and Jim's assistance I would manage to cross the foot-path through the mowing lot, and climb the stile in the stone wall that divided the two farms. Aunt Thurrill was always "so glad to see her leetle gal; she was getting smart, yes indeed real spry!" Then the company loaf of pound cake would be cut and a glass of metheglin presented. Though she would tell the boys to go to the cupboard and get something to eat, that doughnuts and apple pie, and sweetened cider and water were good enough for hearty boys, the urchins never failed to receive a bit of cake and a sip of the honey wine. After I had rested I would crawl up to the spinning room to gossip awhile with Jenny Wheeler. Aunt kept a hired girl through the year. In the summer she helped in the dairy and housework, but her chief employment was spinning.

Uncle Thurrill kept a large flock of sheep. In the winter he fatted wethers, which he slaughtered and marketed; the fleeces the maid spun into yarn which the old gentleman (he was a weaver by trade) wove into cloth, which met with a ready sale. After a hard day's work out of doors, it was no infrequent thing to hear his loom till twelve or one o'clock at night. He was also abstemious in food, rarely eating meat. There was usually a loaf of brown bread, a cut cheese and a pan of milk in the chimney corner; these were his staple viands. Still he was a healthy, strong man, never owning to fatigue. Besides the sheep, he butchered and sold a large number of swine. The first families at the "Port" regularly sought aunt's lard and sausages; and uncle's pork was in great demand. He was also a great orchardist. The best varieties of apple, such as the "Baldwin" and "Russet," were then just becoming known. The "Baldwin" in that region was then called the "Hooper," from its having been introduced by Squire Stephen Hooper, the owner of an elegant country seat on the main road. My father also took great pains to procure the best fruit for his thrifty, young orchard. I have spent many hours helping him graft.

Amongst our near neighbors was a somewhat unique family. Their name was Dole and they lived at the foot of the hill. There were three brothers and four sisters, all unmarried, and, as is often the case with single people, all seven were always addressed by the affectionate appellation of uncle and aunt. Uncle Amos and David tilled the paternal acres; Uncle Moses, a blacksmith, carried on his trade in a shop by the roadside, opposite the dwelling. He boarded with his brothers, paying them the enormous price of one dollar per week. Aunts Jemima, Eunice and Judy attended to the house and dairy, receiving their living, as in their parents' life-time. Aunt Susy, an invalid, was cared for and petted by all. This family, especially Aunt Judy, had been unusually kind during my illness, and they were solicitous that I should take tea with them. As soon as I was able to walk so far, Aunt Sarah took me down. The house, large and commodious, stood a little back from and end to road; a path led up to a door which opened directly into the kitchen or living room. The front commanded a pleasant view of Dole's pond, and a wide stretch of meadow and forest, the Clark homestead, peeping through the woods, being the only house in sight. We were received with great cordiality, and seated in the large, cool room to rest. This apartment had the usual huge fire-place, long dressers, heavy table and flag-bottomed chairs. After awhile we were invited into Aunt Susy's room at the back of the house. The invalid was seated in a chair covered by a coverlet, and the room was hot and oppressive. I was glad to accompany aunt Judy when she went out to begin preparations for tea, which were a source of great entertainment. The good woman moulded a pan of short cake, which she rolled out and placed on six pewter plates ; placing the long iron oven shovel across the andirons, the six plates were deposited before the fire. I distinctly recollect the interest I felt in watching the bannocks ; seeing Aunt Judy turn them, and, when done, split and butter them. They were very light and nice, and eaten with stewed strawberries they tasted deliciously. The three uncles came in to tea ; uncle said a lengthy grace, then we all did justice to the viands. I greatly enjoyed my visit, and on my return made the household laugh heartily with the description of aunt Judy's six Johnny cakes.

That summer our neighbors, the Pillsburys, put up a new house. It was raised in June. This brought a festival. A sumptuous entertainment was provided. Aunt Sarah lent her assistance, and the whole neighborhood were on the qui vive for several days. On the afternoon appointed most of the parish, and visitors from the vicinity, thronged to the place. The stout timbers of the sturdy roof were reared with the usual ceremonies, christened with prime Santa Cruz, then the refreshments were spread. Jollity and sport sped the hours till sun-down, when the crowd dispersed. Notwithstanding every precaution I took cold, and the next morning could not walk one step. Great was my anguish, but nursing and care soon brought the use of my limbs. When I could walk I was invited to spend the day at great-uncle John Little's. His farm lay below, a little farther down the hill. The house, which commanded a pleasant view, stood back from the road, a thrifty orchard extending in front. The two sons and the only daughter had been married several years, and the family consisted of only uncle, aunt and a hired man. I always enjoyed a visit to this quiet domicile. After dinner Ruth laughingly said, "seeing she had distinguished company her weaving should be set aside." Putting on her brightly flowered chintz she took her knitting and called me to join her in the cosy back parlor. We had scarcely become seated when her grandson, David Emery, and his step-brother, Jeremiah Colman, galloped up the lane on two mettled studs. Springing from the saddle the two youth, lads of twelve and fifteen, entered with the information that their father, mother and younger brother were just behind.

Betty Little, at the age of nineteen, had married David Emery. This young man, with his brother Ephraim, left orphans when mere boys, were heirs to a considerable property. They were still young when the Revolutionary war commenced. At the return of the "six months men," called out after the battle of Bunker Hill, another summons for troops came. The militia were drawn up on the training field ; a draft was about to be made, when out stepped young David Emery and volunteered his services. His example was instantly followed, and the quota was obtained without a draft. His older brother, Ephraim, fired with military ardor, also entered the army, in the capacity of fifer, returning, at the disbanding of the officers at the end of the war, with a captain's commission. He afterwards reentered the army with the rank of major, and died at an advanced age, in the enjoyment of a liberal pension. He was one of the foundhawed, drew his fingers through his lank, white hair, then wheeling round facing my poor, trembling, little self, he abruptly asked, "Child, where would you go if you were to die?" I could have truthfully told him, I did not know, but my tongue was palsied, I quaked all over with terror. In a still more severe tone he continued, "Child, do you know the catechism?" I managed to enunciate, "Yes, sir." "Then you know that, as a child of Adam, you were born totally depraved, and unless you are born again in Christ you must be eternally damned. There are many little children in hell, yes, children as young as you, suffering fiery torments." I do not know what farther he might have said, for with an hysterical scream I sprang to my feet, and mother led me from the room, leaving grandmam, who was deaf as a post, to do the parting ceremonies. Father upon learning of the afternoon's occurrence, was positively furious, and he neither went himself nor permitted any of the family to attend divine service through Mr. Clark's ministration. The summer of 1798 the Rev. Leonard Woods came to preach, and after considerable disagreement and hesitation, a call to the candidate was given and accepted, the ceremony of ordination being fixed for the fifth of December. From the first Sunday my father had not been exactly pleased with the new preacher, and as the weeks passed this distrust and dissatisfaction increased. These sentiments were shared by a respectable minority, but with the true democratic spirit, they gracefully yielded to the will of the majority, and the preparations for the ordination were commenced with the accustomed hospitable bountifulness. A few families, zealous for the ancient regime, declaring the pastor elect "a wolf in sheep's clothing, at heart a true blue Hopkinsian," declined to open their houses, or take any part in the festivities or solemnities. Amongst these were my father, the Doles and Master Chase. Aunt Ruth Little was one of Parson Wood's most enthusiastic supporters. She devoted a whole evening to the vain task of bringing my father to a coincidence in her views. Her rhetoric was completely wasted, and, quite angry, she returned home, to wonder at "that obstinate Jim Smith. He was a real Jacobite infidel. Prudy was to be pitied; a minister's granddarter, too; it was scandalous!" Her preparations for the ordination were upon the grandest scale. Mrs. Colman came to assist two or three days prior to it, and quiet Uncle John was stirred up into an unusual interest and activity. The best of viands were procured, the case bottles replenished with choice liquors, and a good supply of New England rum provided for the refreshment of the more humble class of visitors. Grandmother Little had everything in readiness for the exercise of due hospitality, but there was no fuss nor parade. Deacon Tenney, a dignitary of the church, of course, was obliged to keep open house. Aunt Sarah went to help her sister. Our household were habitually in readiness for company, as, living on the old family homestead, we were any day liable to unexpected guests. Our Thanksgiving mince pies and plum cake were fresh; there were plenty of pickles, applesauce and preserves; but mother quietly baked an oven full of pumpkin and apple pies and fried a large batch of company doughnuts, while a nice sirloin of beef was as quietly reserved for the important occasion.

The anticipated fifth of December arrived,—a terribly cold, blustering day. The snow, which had recently fallen to a considerable depth, filled the air, blinding both man and beast, and blocking the roads in such a manner that ox teams were kept going to and fro to keep them passable. Father did have the grace to break a path through our lane in the morning, and mother roasted the beef and baked a plum pudding, but we had only one visitor. Mr. Reuben Pearson, of Byfield, managed to wade through the snow on horseback, but it blew into the avenue as fast as it was cleared, and at night it was level with the boundary walls. In the evening David Emery and William Thurrill came in on snow-shoes. Uncle Thurrill's only daughter married Mr. Jonathan Smith, of Haverhill. Mr. and Mrs. Smith and several friends had come to her father's the night previous upon their return from the services at noon; they found the lane leading to the house impassable, and were obliged to sit in the sleigh until a path was cleared. They were snow-bound, and compelled to remain over another night. David Emery gave a graphic description of the ceremonies at the church. Every one was nearly frozen in the icy building, warmed at that period by nothing larger than the tin foot-stoves, with which most of the women were supplied. The wind whistled and howled as it swept over the summit of the lofty hill, rattling the loose windows and screeching amid the stout rafters of the ancient pile. The lad had called on Master Chase. That eccentric gentleman, having built a tremendous fire in the sitting-room, donned hat and overcoat, muffling himself to the eyes in a huge red bandanna, and drawing on a pair of striped yarn mittens, he mounted guard in the entry, pacing back and forth in a silence which was only broken to inform incomers, of which, as it was the old parsonage, and so near the meeting-house there were many, "that they could warm themselves, but nothing more." David was immensely tickled with the queer oddity. "Oh, you ought to have seen him, Mr. Smith, so grim and glum, but he did pinch my ear, saying that I was my father's own son,—I must come and see him some other day." The youth was not just pleased at the doings at his grandfather's. "Such a crowd! The house had been thronged; he would not have entertained such a gang. The horses had eaten more than half a ton of the best English hay; the pantry was empty, the liquor case ditto, and those Dog-towners had drank a gallon of new rum, and nobody knew how much cider — he drew till he wouldn't draw any more. He thought grandsir had not enjoyed the day, but grandmam said we could not sufficiently rejoice that such a blessed man was settled over us."

As father and others had predicted, the ordination over, a new order of things began to be initiated. During the winter it had been customary for the middle-aged and elderly people to gather at social teas, after which the hours were enlivened by a game of checkers, backgammon or cards; and the young people held evening parties, where the youth and maidens tripped on "the light fantastic toe" to a tune hummed by themselves, or, if any of the number chanced to be musical, to the notes of a fife or flute. Once or twice in the season a ball, over which Fiddler Bailey from the "Port" presided, was held in a hall on the main road. The new pastor soon announced his condemnation of this innocent gaiety. A series of sermons was preached which pretty effectually stopped dancing and card playing; if either were enjoyed it was surreptitiously, but, however on the sly, somehow the malpractice never escaped the minister's knowledge. Fearing "spies from the enemies' camp," other recreations amongst the younger people were substituted — romping, games and forfeits — which even Parson Woods must have admitted were no improvement over the decorous contra dance. The same might have been queried respecting their elders, when, in lieu of their former round game of cards, their only amusement became the discussion of politics, and the scandal of the town and vicinity. Amongst the pastor's favorites, social visiting gave place to a course of evening meetings, which were held at the several school-houses. While many were enthusiastic in praise of these services, they were disapproved by the opposition and the more elderly people. The Sabbath ministrations and the Thursday lecture had hitherto sufficed; they had no faith in these new inventions. "More than half went jest to pass away the time and pick up the news; as for the young folks, it was a nice place to see the gals, and to pick up a beau; they guessed there would be as much courting as godliness."

In the spring another incident caused greater disagreement. During former pastorates every child presented for the rite had been admitted to baptism. It began to be whispered that Parson Woods intended to set aside the "half-way covenant," and baptize only the offspring of church members. A niece of aunt Sara Noyes (recently married) and her husband had come to reside with and take care of the old lady and her farm. In March a son was born to this couple, which Aunt Sara desired christened. As neither Mr. nor Mrs. George were communicants, she thought it proper to ascertain the clergyman's sentiments. Without hesitation, he promised to baptize the infant: "It was too cold to take out such a young babe; when the weather grew milder he would arrange for the ceremony." But Sunday after Sunday passed; the minister could never be made to appoint a day for the rite, some excuse was always ready, till at length it became understood that thenceforth only church members would be permitted to present their children at the baptismal font. Aunt Sara was excessively indignant! The great-granddaughter of the Rev. James Noyes; the daughter of the former senior deacon (one next in dignity to the pastor), and herself one who at all times had been most active, not only in the families of the clergymen, but throughout the parish, whenever her services or money could promote the good of the church, Aunt Sara had come to be regarded, and I think, also (though she would have disclaimed my assertion), to look upon herself somewhat in the light of a lady elect. A slight to such a person could not remain unnoticed. Many were really grieved at this change in the baptismal ordinance; others were angry at what they considered duplicity; many remarked that it was "the cunning, the manœuvering, that excited ire and aversion. The pastor's manner was so arbitrary and domineering that they must regard it as positively insolent. He ought to be taught that he was not a pope to head a hierarchy, but simply a preacher chosen to minister to a congregational society." Several, refusing longer to listen to his teaching, left the society for other parishes; while some, Aunt Sara and Master Chase were of the number, passed the day in private devotion at home. Sometimes the Master joined Miss Noyes, to read aloud a sermon he had written. The Master was proud of his sermons. In his vicinity dwelt another family, of bachelors and maids, by the name of Hills — two brothers and four sisters. The good women were fond of inviting the master in of an evening, to read a sermon to them. One of these sermons became memorable, causing a deal of mirth, from the unique text, which read: "A wonder was seen in heaven, a woman." Father's dissatisfaction was so great that he took a pew in the new church that had recently been built at Byfield.

A disagreement had arisen in that society at the settlement of the Rev. Elijah Parish. The minority separated from the parent Church, formed a new society, and put up a house of worship near where the Depot is now located. Parson Slade, an Englishman, educated under the auspices of Lady Huntingdon, was called to fill the pulpit. Our family continued to occupy their pew in the old meeting-house, but I often rode over to Byfield with my father. This society — consisting of some of the most prominent and wealthy families, the Moodys, Longfellows, Titcombs, Adams, and Pearsons — continued several years. At length the talent and fame, coupled with the genial humor of the celebrated Dr. Parish, drew the seceders back to the old church. Their meeting-house was sold to Deacon Benjamin Colman, who removed it near his residence and fitted it up for a school. A female seminary was established there, which for a number of years enjoyed an enviable celebrity.

The next October, Parson Woods was united in marriage with a Miss Wheeler, a young lady from New Hampshire, and a parsonage was furnished for the young couple on the Main road. Several ladies were active in this service; Aunt Ruth Little was foremost amongst them, and she strenuously exerted herself to incite mother and Aunt Sarah to her own enthusiasm. "Why, the blessed minister 'spake as never man spake!' And it was reported on good authority, that his bride was every way his equal." Though mother made no demonstration she good-naturedly assisted Aunt Ruth in forwarding some of her favorite plans, and Aunt Sarah's services were enlisted at Deacon Tenney's. It had been arranged that the officers of the church, the more prominent members, and the intimate friends of the clergymen and their wives, should meet the bridal party at the Bradford line, and escort them to their new home, where an entertainment was to be given. This programme caused an excessive fluster amongst the feminine portion of the community. Our ladies had acquired a somewhat enviable reputation as cooks, and much anxiety was evinced that on this important occasion their credit should be maintained, no little rivalry being elicited, in both the quantity and quality of the viands. Dress also became a momentous matter; mother, whose skill and taste were unquestionable, was fairly besieged by members of the family, to cut new dresses or remodel old ones. Deacon Tenney brought his wife a new silk dress from Boston, and a fashionable sister selected an elegant hat in Haverhill, that place having even then acquired a prominence for its style and fashion. Our good aunt, a modest, retiring woman, though exceedingly ladylike in manner, yielded, though much against her wishes, to her husband's will in these matters, and much to his and her daughter's delight, Madam Tenney was pronounced the handsomest and best dressed woman in the cortege. On the appointed day, about thirty chaises met at the place of rendezvous, the last house in the parish, and as the clergyman and his bride drove up, after an hilarious welcome, the cavalcade formed in line, the three deacons and their wives in front, and dashed over the road to the new parsonage, where an animated throng awaited them. After the ceremony of introduction to the young madam was over, the crowd repaired to the tables, which were loaded with every luxury. Mirth and good cheer ruled the hour, the bridegroom grew positively gay, and the bride won every heart by her beauty and urbanity. After supper, singing was proposed, there were many good singers in the company, and when several tunes were sung, a prayer was offered, then followed a parting hymn, and the throng dispersed well satisfied with the entertainment. I had been considered too young to attend the party, but I saw Madam Woods the next Sunday. She "walked out bride" in a green silk dress, a white satin bonnet, a white satin cardinal, trimmed with white fur, and a grey fox muff and tippet. She was a tall, handsome lady, and the regard she at first inspired, continued through her sojourn in the parish.

CHAPTER XII.

The farm on which the house was located, where our district school had been kept, belonged to the widow and minor son of the late Robert Adams. Mrs. Adams, a sister of my grandfather Little, had married Mr. Bradstreet Tyler, and moved to Boxford; her young son went with her, but on coming of age, young Robert took possession of the paternal acres, and notice was given, that the district must find other accommodation for their school. Uncle Thurrel had a large back chamber, which, as nothing better offered, was hired for the winter. This was an inconvenient location, on the extreme southerly boundary of the district, too far distant for the girls on the opposite side to reach in cold weather. Singularly, it so chanced that I was the only girl in our neighborhood though there were quite a number of boys, and to my discomfiture I found myself alone, the sole girl amongst a dozen boys. This was so unpleasant that I was permitted to remain from school. The next summer Miss Emerson, after some trouble, secured an unused comb-maker's shop for her private school. The winter following, Deacon Tenney, anxious to secure educational privileges for his daughters, offered a room. This carried the school so far away that a second winter, much to my distress, I was debarred from instruction. Father said things were wrong, something must be done, a school house ought to be built in a spot convenient of access. The subject was brought to public attention and met with general approval, though there was some opposition. A school-meeting was called, and it was voted to build a schoolhouse, as nearly in the centre of the district as possible. Mr. Oliver Dole made a survey, and it was decided to place it on the upper side of Crane-neck road, at the lower corner of the intersecting highway to Bradford, now Groveland, nearly opposite where the present schoolhouse stands. A building about forty feet long and thirty broad was erected, finished and furnished in the best approved style of the period. The entrance at the southerly corner faced the cross road. Passing through an entry, furnished with high and low rows of wooden pegs, you entered the school-room. On the left, extended the fire-place; beyond stood the teacher's desk; in front rose tier after tier of clumsy, unpainted desks, front of these, and around the walls were ranged low forms. Six good sized windows lighted the apartment.

Two long, narrow rocks supplied the place of fire-dogs. The dry kindlings were stored in the entry, but the green logs, the chief fuel, lay conveniently near the door, where it was cut as needed, by the older boys. The new school-house gave general satisfaction, and was regarded as a sumptuous temple of learning, of which the district was justly proud, and the services of Master Chase were secured for the inauguration session. Noted for his eccentricity, great learning and strict discipline, the master was greeted by his pupils, on that memorable morning, with an awe bordering on fear. I had become used to his oddities, and, though never before reckoned amongst his pupils, when visiting at his house I had often been invited into the library, while his scholars were under instruction, and sometimes had participated in the exercises; so with more confidence than the others, I took the desk to which I was assigned. Contrary to the custom, Master Chase never opened school with prayer. "The devotion brought more deviltry than godliness. To prevent mischief, one must pray with open eyes, like Master Smith at Dummer Academy. Let the parents teach the children to pray at home; it was not the province of the school-teacher." At the commencement of his career, this idea had been strongly combatted, but without effect, and his sway had become so indisputable, that now no one thought of questioning it. The school seated, the Bible class was called to read. Books in hand we ranged ourselves before the teacher's desk, when to my astonishment, the master in a loud, authoritative tone, said, "Sallie Smith, take the head of the class, and read the first chapter of Genesis. The others will open their books, and pay particular attention to the reading, especially to the pronunciation and expression." Could I believe my ears? Could I have heard aright? I, read alone—read the whole of that long chapter, with all those scholars, some of them nearly men grown, listening in silence? I could never do it! My inability was signified. "Bosh!" cried the master, "Sallie, take your place and read." I had heard that the teacher's laws were like those of the Medes and Persians; to dispute the point was worse than reading, so, trembling from head to foot, I moved up the class. Encouraging looks were given, Uncle Joe Little managed to whisper, "Don't be scared," and the presence of Nannie Tenney, next to whom I found myself, gave farther reassurance, but the first words were both low and tremulous. "Speak louder," directed the master, in a wonderfully polite and gentle tone, "read as well, Miss Sallie, as you did to your aunt and myself last autumn." This remark expounded the riddle. I could not imagine why he thus called upon me to read. On a recent visit I had entertained my relatives one stormy evening, by reading to them from the "Spectator." Somewhat reassured, I managed to get through the chapter, after which the class read it verse by verse. This finished, we resumed our seats, and prepared to copy the first rule from Pike's arithmetic, in a manuscript book, into which all the rules and our examples were copied. The master having pointed the pens, turned his attention to the younger scholars, those whose acquirements had not advanced beyond Webster's spelling book. At half-past ten a recess of ten minutes was granted, first to the girls, then to the boys. I was thankful to get to the fire, as the sputtering, sizzling green logs gave forth only a doubtful heat, and my desk at the upper end of the room was intolerably cold. Spelling followed the recess. The session closed at twelve with an intermission of an hour and a half. Many of the scholars brought their dinners. The noon was passed in fun and frolic by most, though some of the more studious availed themselves of this time to con their lessons, and some of the older boys chopped wood. The firing was prepared by the boys, who also took turns in kindling the fire, and the girls swept the schoolhouse at noon. The afternoon exercises were opened by the first class, reading from the "American Preceptor;" next the writing books were ruled and the copies set. While the older pupils were thus engaged, the younger scholars again received attention. The afternoon recess over, our spelling books were again taken out. The master having donned his overcoat, red bandanna and woolen mittens, took his big ruler in hand, and commenced a promenade to and fro between the desks and the now smouldering fire. The recitation in spelling, and a second Bible reading closed the afternoon session. A few of the girls, myself included, at Miss Emerson's school had commenced the study of a grammar, styled "The Young Ladies' Accidence." As we were anxious to continue, though out of the common course, the master graciously acceded to our wish, though he would not permit his female pupils to cipher in "Fractions." "It was a waste of time, wholly unnecessary, would never be of the least use to them. If we could count our beaux and skeins of yarn it was sufficient." Those that I have named were the only studies. I was compelled to continue my Bible reading, and the master continued his stern sway. The utmost courtesy was enjoined. He was as exact in the matter of bows, curtseys and other polite formulas as a French dancing master. Occasionally, of a stormy day, perhaps, the grim old fellow would relax for awhile, and become one of the most genial and mirth-provoking of mortals. Having raised an uproarious merriment, he would suddenly thump silence, with his formidable ruler, and the usual routine was resumed. Two or three incorrigible dunces received no mercy. If shakings and spankings could have brightened their wits, they must have become brilliant. Nothing like insubordination ever appeared, but nothing escaped the lynx eye of the teacher, and if a scholar was detected in idleness, or misdemeanor, the Bible or anything handy was launched at the miscreant's head. Mr. Oliver Dole's second son, a lad of twelve, was rather more inclined to indolence, than to either study or play. He had a trick of folding his arms upon the desk, and resting his head upon them, he would doze away the time given for the preparation of the lessons. One afternoon, Diah having become thus comfortably composed, I saw that the master was poising his long ruler in the direction of the lad's head; suddenly it whizzed across the room; as it touched him, the boy gave a quick start, the missile canted sideways, and passed directly through a pane of glass in the window behind. A suppressed titter ran round the room. Without asking permission Joseph Little went and brought in the ruler. As the cold air blew in, I stuffed my hood into the sash. Not a word was spoken, the exercises proceeded as usual, but the next morning, much to our astonishment, the glass was reset. How the master had procured a light, and replaced the glass that cold weather has ever remained a mystery. Amongst the older boys was Samuel Thurrel, Uncle Thurrel's second son. This lad had a somewhat pompous air, was rather too apt to boast of his father's wealth, and the superiority of all his belongings. At New Year he had been the recipient of a silver watch; as no other scholar had acquired to such an appendage, Sam strutted about, to the admiration of the smaller fry, while he excited the scorn of his mates. This disgust had been augmented by the addition of a long silver chain from which was suspended two heavy silver seals, and an immense silver key. This showy ornament was displayed to the greatest advantage, and pains were taken to jingle and jangle it, as the young coxcomb paraded back and forth, between the recitation and his desk. There had been an unusual parade one morning, even the master had shown signs of impatience. The afternoon session had commenced, every scholar but Joe Little was seated. There was the hush which preceded the call to read, when the door opened, and the tardy pupil entered, his face the impersonation of imperturbable gravity, and a long chain, the curb to a bridle, dangling from his pocket; to this chain was attached two seals cut from sole leather, and an enormous key. With a ludicrous imitation of Sam, he made his bow, then strode up the aisle, lifting his foot in such a manner as to jingle the curb chain at every step, while the seals and key swung about most conspicuously. At sight of the youth, the master's face gave a spasmodic twitch, then he was seized with such a fit of coughing, that it was some moments ere the ruler signalled silence, or the general giggle that ran round the room was suppressed, but at length the summons to the class came, and though my uncle continued to strut about, displaying his new ornament, much to the delight of the scholars, especially the older girls, whose merriment was scarcely repressed, he received no reprimand; no notice was taken of the joke, though we all knew that the old fellow was enjoying it hugely. The next morning, Sam appeared minus his watch, and Uncle Joe never again displayed his curb chain. The winter term sped all too soon. Notwithstanding his oddity, and strict discipline, Master Chase had the skill to interest his pupils in their studies, and, though the course was somewhat meagre, it was thorough. We really learned the three studies taught, reading, writing and arithmetic. Few pupils of the present day could surpass our first class reading, our spelling matches must have won the palm, and now we rarely see such penmanship as was common at that period. Some of the arithmetical manuscript were elegant specimens of chirography.

CHAPTER XIII.

On December 14th, 1799, the country was called to mourn the death of Gen. George Washington. Expressions of heartfelt grief were universal. Every one felt that the nation had suffered an irreparable loss, that the family of states was bereft of its head, its father and truest friend. In Newburyport a memorial service was held the second of January, when business was suspended, and residents of the country flocked to the town. While minute guns reverberated on the wintry air, bells mournfully pealed, and flags sadly drooped at half-mast, a long procession bearing the usual insignia of mourning defiled through the principal streets to the Old South meeting-house, where an eulogy was pronounced by Robert Treat Paine. It was a day never to be forgotten, and the crape badge my father had worn was treasured for years as a sacred memento. On the 22d of February, Byfield commemorated the birth and death of Washington by tolling the bell of the meeting-house an hour in the morning, and an oration, delivered by the Rev. Elijah Parish. People from Newburyport and the whole country side thronged the house, drawn thither by the reputation for eloquence which the orator had acquired.

Uncle Samuel Smith had prospered on his Vermont farm. Good buildings had been erected and most of the land cleared and brought under cultivation. His wife's prophecy had been fulfilled. His pleasing address and varied knowledge, enlarged by more studious habits than was usual to a person in his position, had given him a high place in the estimation of his neighbors and townsfolk, and he had been called to fill situations of trust and honor, both in town and county. He usually visited his native place every winter, bringing a sleigh-load of country produce, which was exchanged for dry goods and groceries.

At the end of a bright February afternoon we espied Uncle Sam's team wearily dragging the heavily laden sleigh up the lane, and mother began preparations for an extra nice supper, as our relative was somewhat of an epicure. After the first greetings and mutual inquiries were over, Uncle Sam passed to religious topics, and much to our surprise we learned that he had become interested in the new doctrine of Methodism. An itinerant preacher upon a tour had stopped at his house and claimed hospitality, which had been cordially extended. A clergyman of the strictest Calvinistic proclivities had been recently settled over the congregation at Berlin. Uncle Sam did not coincide with the new minister, but he was immediately impressed by the views which his guest unfolded. It was near the end of the week, and the missionary was invited to stop over Sunday and preach in the schoolhouse. The news circled through the district and the building was thronged. The people were not united respecting the regular minister, and the stranger produced a marked effect. He was invited to prolong his sojourn; Uncle Sam and many others became converted, and a church was formed. The preacher had then gone to new spheres of labor, but Uncle Sam and others conducted a regular Sunday worship at the school house.

Before returning Uncle Sam gave us a specimen of Methodism in a long and singularly well-worded prayer, delivered in the loudest tones of a powerful but finely modulated voice; this petition was followed by a good hymn set to one of the enlivening Methodist tunes. Mr. Smith had a remarkable voice and an exquisite ear and taste, and his singing was superb,—I was enchanted by it. Mother liked the hymn, but father shook his head and gravely declared his sorrow: "Sam's head always would be full of something. He had got over dancing and poetry,—now it was preaching, praying and singing. Well, what was born in the bone could not be beat out of the flesh. He never was cut out for a drudging farmer, and he never would be one; he only hoped he would not let that farm he had got under such headway go all to rack and ruin." Grandm'am was so deaf that it was difficult to make her comprehend the matter; but Uncle Sam was too zealous to leave her long unenlightened. This good woman was positively aghast: "Her son, her son Sam, turned Methodist!"

Grandm'am came of a "first family;" she was as complete an aristocrat as ever trod in No. 2 shoes. "Something must be done; she could not have any such doings. Why, it was a disgrace to the family, and would bring ruin to himself! He had become of some account in that far-away place; he should not subject himself and his friends to ignominy, and mar his bright prospects. Methodists, why they were ranters, gathered from the lower classes! Her son had nothing to do with such people. It was preposterous!" And the sweet, mild little woman put on all the assumption of authority that she could possibly assume, and in the most solemn manner pronounced her ban upon this new spiritual scheme. Aunt Sarah pished and pshawed over the praying and singing, then fidgeted and fussed respecting the business of selling and buying, declaring that "Brother was so full of his new religion that he couldn't tell a cent from a dollar;" and when he brought home a dress pattern of black silk for his wife, and a tasty blue silk bonnet for his daughter, she sat down with a hopeless face, folded her hands, and with uplifted eyes, washed her hands of the whole proceedings. "Sam would never be a forehanded farmer, and she really feared he would become clean distraught. The Lord wasn't deaf, he needn't holler so at prayer as to make the warming-pan ring in the cellar way, or to scare Uncle Thurrel's folks, who couldn't imagine what all that shouting over to Jim Smith's meant. She thought Methody women cut off their hair and made frights of themselves, but then sister hadn't lost her senses, like her husband, as she knowed, and for all his piety, Sam had too much of the old Adam yet, to let his pretty Sally wear anything but the most becoming." A thaw came and Uncle Sam's stay was prolonged. The intelligence of his embracing Methodism, caused no small stir amongst his relatives and acquaintances, and every evening our house was thronged. Some came to hear of the new doctrines from mere curiosity, others from a desire for knowledge, and a few earnestly to combat what they deemed a serious error, affecting both the temporal and spiritual welfare of the convert. Amongst the most forward and zealous of this class, was Aunt Ruth Little. It was vastly amusing to listen to the war of words, and, it must be confessed, Uncle Sam proved more than a match for the contestants. Politics also claimed a due share in the conversation. Parties were in a furious ferment. "Federalist" and "Democratic" (or Jacobin, as the party was usually termed) lines were tightly drawn, each displaying unseemly rancor and bitterness, which had sometimes merged into strife. Father and Uncle Sam were Jacobins, the majority of the visitors Federalists. Uncle Thurrel was a great politician. In the strongest terms he would denounce "that Tom Jefferson; if he was raised to the presidency there would be a second French revolution; the nation would find to their sorrer that they had got a second Robertspear to rule over 'em." Robespierre had for a time been Uncle Thurrel's pet bugbear, and his name continued to be brought forward long after he was mouldering in the grave. Aunt Ruth, with characteristic vehemence, would plunge into the discussion. Her face aglow, and her knitting needles clicking, she would volubly expatiate upon the unsoundness and irreverence of the great Democratic leader. "Why, if he was elected president the country would be turned upside down! Tom Jefferson was no better than Tom Paine. He believed in Voltaire as much as he did in Christ, and put the Age of Reason afore the Bible. Let him get the reins of government and there would be no more 'Sabba' day;' the meetin'-'uses would all be shet, and another rein of terror spread over the land."

At the height of his wife's vehemence quiet Uncle John contrived to change the subject, by some timely question or droll remark. Uncle Sam would tune up in one of his lively Methodist hymns, and the company would disperse in all neighborly friendship, though Aunt Ruth never went without a last word of warning and rebuke.

CHAPTER XIV.

A second surprise came to the family and parish in the engagement of Aunt Susanna Little to her first cousin Robert Adams. This young gentleman had inherited what, at that period, was reckoned a fortune; as he was handsome and prepossessing, he had been riageable daughters in the most favoraregarded by anxious mammas and marble light, and the efforts had not been slight, to win his favor, but young Robert had proved invulnerable. Though he had taken possession of his farm, he had boarded in the family of his cousin Edmund Little, who rented his house, in bachelor content. Now, without the least warning, it was announced that Sukey Little had won the prize, that Mr. Adams was making arrangements to put up a new house, and the marriage would take place on its completion in the autumn.

The Adams families of Newbury claim to have descended from John Ap Adam, who was summoned to parliament as a Baron of the Realm from 1296 to 1307. He descended from a family in Wales whose record runs back several centuries. The genealogy is as follows:

John Ap Adam — Elizabeth Gourney.
Sir John Ap Adam —
William Ap Adam —
Sir John Ap Adam —
Thomas Ap Adam — Jane Inge.
Sir John Ap Adam — Milisccnt Besylls.
Sir John Ap Adam alias Adams — Clara Powell.
Roger Adams — Jane Eliott.
Thomas Adams — Maria Upton.
John Adams — Jane Benneleigh.
John Adams — Catherine Stebling.
John Adams — Margaret Squier.
Richard Adams — Margaret Armager

who had two sons, Robert, who married Elizabeth Shirland, and William, who married —— Barrington. Henry, one of the sons of William, came to New England in 1630, and died in Braintree. He was the ancestor of the presidents John and John Quincy Adams. Robert, the son of Robert, came from Devonshire to Ipswich in 1635, thence to Salem in 1638, and to Newbury in 1640. His wife, Eleanor, died June 12th, 1677. He died Oct. 12th, 1682. His second wife, Sara, widow of Henry Short, he married Feb. 6th, 1678. She died Oct. 24th, 1697. Children: Abraham, born 1639; Isaac, born 1648; Jacob, born April 23, 1649, died in infancy; another Jacob born Sept. 13th, 1651; Hannah, born June 25th, 1650; Robert, Elizabeth, Joanna, Mary and John. Abraham Adams, son of Robert married Mary Pettingell, Nov. 16th, 1670. Children; Robert, born May 12, 1674; Abraham, born May 2d, 1676; Isaac, born Feb. 26th, 1679; Sara, born April 15th, 1681; Matthew, born May 25th, 1686; Israel, born Dec. 25th, 1688; Dorothy, born Oct. 25th, 1691; Richard, born Nov. 22d, 1693. Matthew, the fourth son of Abraham Adams, born May 25th, 1686, married Sara Knight April 4th, 1707, and was the first physician in what is now West Newbury, where he owned a large tract of land. He died Nov. 15th, 1755, aged 69. He had two sons, Matthew and Abraham, and two daughters; one married Joseph Bartlett, of the west precinct, the other, Judith, married my great grandfather, Capt. Edmund Little. Their daughter, Eunice, married her kinsman Robert Adams of the "Farms District," who purchased the farm on Crane-neck formerly owned by my grea-tuncle William Smith. Mr. Adams died young leaving this one son Robert. The Ap Adams arms are

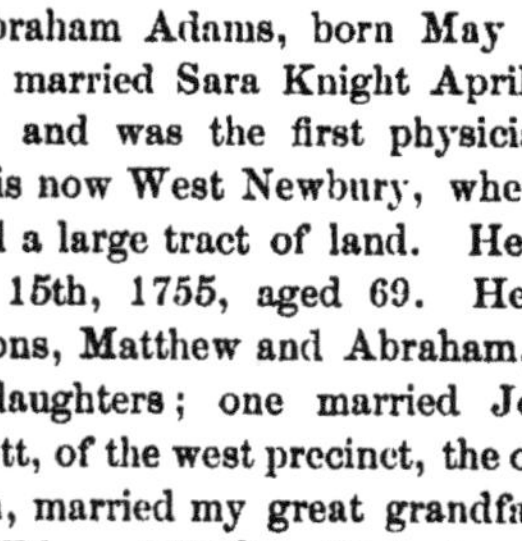

ARGENT, ON A CROSS GULES, FIVE MULLETS OR.

Great was the commotion over the engagement. Suddenly several people made the discovery that gentle, quiet Aunt Sukey "was a sly thing, a real artful piece, despite her demure ways; still waters ran the deepest. They guessed Robert Adams would rue the day he married her, the proud miss, so grand in her airs the ground didn't seem good enough for her to tread on! No good ever came of such marriages, first cousins were altogether too near." A series of visits were vouchsafed us, which we well understood was for the express purpose of gleaning information respecting the pros and cons of the affair. Amongst these visitors were two of the old maid Hills. Joseph, Joshua, Nabbie, Lizzie, Nannie and Hannah Hills, resided on a farm on a cross road beyond Meeting House hill. Out of this family, one brother, Mr. Eliphelet Hills, alone had married. Mr. Joseph and Joshua were pleasant, estimable men. In company with mother's uncle, John Merrill (the great grandfather of Ben: Perley Poore), Uncle Josh, for years, took tea with us in the Thanksgiving holidays, when the jolly pair smacked their lips, joking each other about gormandizing over "Prudy's niceties." The sisters were precise, genteel bodies, in their more youthful days attired in the tip of the mode, greatly exciting my admiration as they followed one another up the broad aisle of the meeting-house with silks rustling and plumes waving. Mrs. Liph. Hills (a Miss Sarah Wyman from the vicinity of Boston) was a milliner. She had a shop in her house on the main road, where she worked at her trade, and kept a variety of wares, and her sisters-in-law were famed for their tasty head gear. They had also become noted for several little, harmless idiosyncrasies. Some ideas respecting housekeeping were especially ludicrous. Though the food was bought in common, each brother and sister provided their own tea and coffee, and each had a separate pot. Uncle Joe drank chocolate, Uncle Josh, coffee, Miss Nabby, strong old hyson, Miss Lizzie liked hers weaker, Miss Nannie preferred young hyson, while Miss Hannah never drank anything but Souchong. It was exceedingly diverting to see the six small pots, like the "four and twenty white pots all in a row," sizzling on six little mounds of embers before the capacious fire. Visitors could take their choice, or have a variety. The girls of the vicinity got a deal of fun, from visiting the maidens, and taking a sip all round. On a wild March day, about one o'clock, in the midst of a smart snow squall, I caught a glimpse of Miss Nannie's red cloak whisking round the corner of the house, while Miss Lizzie, a stout, heavy woman, breathlessly toiled in the rear. I ran to admit the visitors, who came laughing in, Miss Nannie inquiring, "if I thought they snowed down in the squall?" Having rested and gained their breath, they divested themselves of cloaks and hoods, informing us as they did so "that they had come early and must go early; they should like tea in good season." This was an invariable formula, and had passed into a by-word amongst the lively young people. Having become comfortably ensconced before the fire, their fine company knitting in hand, the stream of talk commenced. Aunt Sarah was able to crow over the others, as she had possessed Robert Adams' confidence some weeks before his proposal.

"She saw no hurt in the young couple marrying, although they were near relations. They were wholly dissimilar in temperament, and strongly attached to each other. The Littles were famous for intermarrying; she could not see that any hurt had come of it. Take them as a whole they were a pretty smart lot." The visitors wisely shook their heads, and as wisely concluded that the young couple would take their "ain gate" spite of remarks or remonstrance. The sisters had a deal to tell of the Daltons and Hoopers, two distinguished families, owning two elegant country seats on "Pipe Stave Hill." Mr. Dalton, at that time our senator in Congress, was in Washington, but his family were at their town residence, the fine old mansion opposite the Merrimac House in Newburyport. The Hoopers remained through the year in the country. Several gay sleighing parties had ridden up to the farm during the winter; the spacious residence had been the scene of much convivial festivity. Madam Hooper had also spent some weeks in Boston. A detailed account of the splendor of the wardrobe prepared for this excursion was given and various other on dits of fashionable life, and city and town gossip related. Punctually at four o'clock, tea was on the table; the ladies having regaled themselves, and duly praised the viands, especially the plum cake and the cheese —"Mr. Newell said Prudy Smith's cheese commanded the highest price in the market at the Port"—took their leave in high good humor. Drawing their hoods over their noses, and wrapping their thick, red cloaks about them, they declared that they should be "as warm as toast; the wind would drive them home, and they should get there in grand good season."

A few mornings after this visit, we received a great scare. I went into the garret, and, glancing out of the window, to my amazement and fright, I discerned a dense smoke rising from Mr. Oliver Dole's pasture, at the foot of the hill. I lost no time in hastening down and spreading the alarm. Father, Uncle Enoch, and Uncle Thurrel's folks hurried over to their neighbors. As the wind, which had blown at sunrise, had increased to a gale, the progress of the flames was eagerly watched. How that pasture came to be burning we could not imagine, but the fire soon spent itself, and the return of the gentlemen solved the mystery. The enclosure had grown over to huckleberry bushes; in the season, people came to pick the berries. Mrs. Dole was a Carlton, from the main road, and she had many visitors. Wagonful after wagonful of women and children would ride over, put the horse in the barn, go into the pasture and fill their baskets with huckleberries, then come back to the house to tea. This, in the busy hay season, was somewhat inconvenient, especially as Mrs. Dole was not a very strong woman. Mr. Dole, though neither a morose nor stingy man, lost his patience, and declared a stop should be put to this "huckleberrying visitation." Accordingly, he set fire to his bushes, thinking to totally destroy them; but, instead, the rising wind sent the flames lightly over the brushwood, without touching the roots, and the result was a splendid growth of bushes and an abundant quantity of the largest and most luscious fruit. Mrs. Dole and the neighbors had much sport respecting the result of her husband's destructive efforts. Mrs. Dole said: "Providence did not smile on his inhospitable intent." The children had grown large enough to pick, and the berries were so nice, Mr. Dole marketed them at the Port to much advantage, besides entertaining the visitors. Owners of old huckleberry pastures could take a hint, and, by copying Mr. Dole's mode of culture, improve what in these days has become quite a desideratum in the market.

CHAPTER XV.

One of the great institutions of those days was the spring and fall trainings. There were company musters at the training field on the main road in May and September, and a regimental review at the Plains some time in autumn. The officers of these militia companies alone wore uniforms, the privates mostly turned out in their Sunday suits. The musket in those days was fired by a flint, the spark from which lighted the priming in a little external pan connected with the interior charge through a small vent. A priming wire about the size of a common knitting needle, and a little brush two inches long, which hung by a brass chain to the belt, were used to keep the vent clear and the pan clean. These training days were the occasion for a general frolic, especially the reviews. General trainings drew a motley crowd, venders of all sorts of wares, mountebanks and lewd women; a promiscuous assemblage, bent upon pleasure. Beyond the lines there was always much carousing and hilarious uproar. Many customs were then in vogue, now obsolete in military circles, such as firing at the legs of an officer at his appointment to test his courage, and firing a salute before the residence of a new officer at sunrise on the morning of training day. Of course the recipient of these honors was expected to give a treat. Many a poor fellow became somewhat "onsteady" before the day had far advanced, and more were hors-du-combat ere it had closed. Accidents often occurred. One officer, from the careless loading of a gun, received a severe wound in the leg, and Mr. Oliver Pillsbury had several lights in his new house broken at a salute in honor of his attaining a lieutenancy. At this review there was a large cavalry company, including members from both Newburyport and Newbury. Newburyport had one uniformed company, the artillery. I very well remember how imposing they looked to my childish eyes as they marched onto the muster field at the plains, to the music of fife and drum, with waving flag, and followed by their field pieces. The regimental bands were then unknown. The foot soldiers marched to the fife and drum, the cavalry to the notes of the bugle. Colby Rogers was trumpeter for the troops for many years. The Governor and staff and many distinguished guests were present on the great day I have recalled. A public dinner was given and the festivities were closed by a grand ball in the evening.

I was about seven years old when this militia system was organized, and well do I remember the sensation produced by the officers of our company presenting themselves at meeting, the Sunday preceding the fall training, in their new uniforms. Somerby Chase was captain; Amos Carlton, lieutenant; Paul Bailey, ensign; John Peabody, Josiah Hill, Caleb Chase, and Moses Carr, first, second, third and fourth lieutenants; Mr. Bill Hill was brigade quartermaster. Capt. Goodrich, though he had not then attained that title, was an officer in the cavalry, and he came out in the new troopers' uniform, a red coat, buff vest and pants, black leather cap trimmed with bear skin, and a tall, stiff, straight, red plume. This was a splendid sight for our unsophisticated country folks, and I fear little attention was given to the sermon.

The tedium of the summer work was relieved by the cutting, curing and boating the salt hay from the Plum Island marsh. Every farmer then owned more or less of salt meadow; no one thought of wintering stock without salt hay. Though this brought much heavy labor to both men and women, it was a break in the monotony of the daily round of toil, and for the males, a change of air and scene which my father considered most beneficial.

Our hired help were men from the small hamlet in the woods, beyond the pond, called Dogtown, and good, honest, trusty laborers they were. Uncle Burrel was father's chief factotum, but Joe Gould, Amos Pillsbury, Oliver Goodrich and the Rogerses were also employed. The rate of wages was about fifty cents a day and board, through the six working days; they slept and spent the Sabbath at home. They often preferred to receive their pay in the products of the farm, such as corn, Indian meal, potatoes, pork, and a little butter. This was a mutual convenience, and the best of feelings and the most friendly terms were always maintained between the employer and the employed. Dogtown was two miles distant from Crane-neck, and, after passing Dole's pond, the road ran through thick woods. This, on some dark and stormy nights, was rather bug-a-booish, and on one occasion old Pillsbury got a terrible scare, from which he never became wholly relieved. We were at breakfast when he entered one morning, looking frightened and pale. "What is the matter?" was instantly queried. The old man lisped slightly: "Oh, Mr. Smith, I see a terrible critter in the woods beyant the pond last night."

"A terrible critter, Pillsbury? What was it like?" father inquired.

"Oh, Mr. Smith, it was a terrible big critter, as big as Brindle's calf; its eyes were like fire coals, and it ran past me through the bushes, about a rod from the road, with every hair whistling like a bell. It must have been the wolverine."

"The what, Pillsbury?"

"The wolverine. My old granny used to keep us young 'uns quiet with stories about the wolverine out beyant in the woods. I used to be afeared to stir ten yards from the door o' nights; but, as I had never seen the critter afore, I had begun to think it was one of granny's stories, but I seed him last night, sartin sure; and his eyes were like fire coals, and every hair whistled like a bell."

The old man was so sure that he had met some strange animal that the neighboring men turned out that night, each armed and equipped for a deadly encounter with some ferocious beast, but nothing was found; and, though the quest was continued by the young men and boys for several evenings, no strange animal was ever discovered. But old Pillsbury, to his dying day, used to declare there was "a wolverine in them woods, with eyes like coals of fire, and every hair whistling like a bell," and nothing could ever again induce the old man to travel the road alone after nightfall.

Father's salt meadow was at Hale's cove. Grandsir Little owned one below, in Rowley, and which, as shoemaking was brisk, father cut for several years in addition to his own. The English hay in the barn, the grain reaped and the flax pulled, towards the last of August or the first of September, according to the tides, the salt hay season began. Father and the other mowers — these were neighbors, adepts in mowing, to whom the highest wages, a dollar a day, was paid — rode to Oldtown bridge; the horse having been stabled in one of the adjacent barns, Plum Island river was crossed in a wherry hired for the day, and the work commenced. There was a sufficiency of hands to cut the grass before sunset. Having been left to dry for a day or so, another day was devoted to curing it; then came the boating. This was the grand epoch. Nice food was provided for the mowers and rakers, but boating brought a dog-days Thanksgiving baking. Mince pies, plum cake, rich doughnuts, nice meats, baked beans and other tempting viands were packed in a wooden chest, along with a small keg of cider and a bottle of "Santa Cruz" or "Jamaica." Many farmers would have thought it impossible to get a freight without a gallon or more of rum, but father was a temperate man, and careful not to put any temptation before those in his employ. The gondola laid at the foot of Whetstone lane; if the weather proved auspicious the freight was usually at the landing in thirty-six hours. The neighbors turned out with their teams, and the hay was carted home, a distance of two miles, in a triumphant procession. The mow laid, the supper, a most jovial entertainment, was disposed of, and the weary men separated with the declaration that a "good job, well over," had been completed. Though this hay season gave additional toil to the women of the household, it also brought long leisure days; after the men were finally off in the early morning and the work done, the rest of the day was often devoted to visiting.

Father had been boating Grandsir Little's hay. I was there to assist, when we received an afternoon visit from two neighbors—the Misses Hill—elderly young ladies, very genteel and precise. The conversation turned upon the universal topic, the haying. The visitors expressed much disgust at the whole business. "The toil of cooking in such hot weather was so undesirable, and so much food must be provided, it was not possible to prevent some from being uneaten, but they always threw that away; they never could stomach anything after it had been packed for the meadows." As the family were not noted for an overabundance in their larder at any time, and the "short commons" given to their hired help was proverbial, we were rather diverted at their remarks. It so chanced that when the provision chest had been unloaded the previous evening, a mince pie, a loaf of cake and a plate of doughnuts had been taken out. These with many sly glances to her mother, sister and myself, Aunt

Hannah placed upon the tea table. The visitors enjoyed their supper exceedingly, helped themselves twice to the plum cake—"Mrs. Little's raised cake was always so nice, so much better than they could make; she had the 'knack' for this;" the other edibles were equally eulogized. At early dusk, in time for milking, our visitors left us, without the least idea that they had been feasting on "horrid meadow victuals."

In October Aunt Sukey was married. She had a very quiet wedding, and as the new house was completed, the young couple took immediate possession. The new home was only a few rods from the old one; though so near, still, the bride's absence from the paternal hearth caused a serious vacuum in the household. Uncle Bill married the year after Aunt Betsy; now only Hannah, Ben and Joe remained. Though Sukey was the most retiring and reticent of the family, she had been exceedingly efficient, and she was missed every hour of the day in a multiplicity of matters. Some question respecting the weather had been mooted; it was referred to grandsir: "I do not know, Robert carried away our almanac," was his reply. Much surprised, I cast my eyes to the nail by the fireplace where the family calender always hung. It was in its place. Grandsir caught my look of wonder, and the twinkle of his eyes gave me the hint. Sure enough! Robert had not only carried away the almanac, but a whole treatise of wisdom and prudence beside.

CHAPTER XVI.

April brought the annual "Fast." To overtasked or parsimonious housekeepers this might be a welcome holiday, on which they could sympathize with old Mrs. Tom Pike of Byfield, who declared "she'd ruther have two Fasts than one Thanksgivin'," but to the young folks and children, the day was somewhat of a bug-bear. In some families of the "stricter sort," the children were wont to surreptitiously store a quantity of food against the hungry day. The Perley boys of Byfield always contrived to lay by salt fish and crackers in the hay mow, and other young people of my acquaintance managed to obtain a luncheon between the meetings. The late Deacon Joseph Hale of Byfield, often related an incident of a Fast day of his boyhood. Having accompanied the sons of the Rev. Moses Parsons to the parsonage to spend the noon intermission, somewhat to his surprise, if not horror, those young gentleman stealthily entertained him and supplied themselves with a hearty meal. Having become fairly gorged with good cheer, they seated themselves quietly in the kitchen. As the hour for the afternoon service approached, the good parson, with a kindly regard for youthful stomachs, came into the room and told the boys, "that if they were very hungry he would permit a slight lunch." This the young scamps piously declined, "not wishing to make any infringement on the religious observance of the day," and their clerical papa entered upon the afternoon duties, in the full satisfaction of possessing sons worthy of a sire's confidence and approbation. In most households, the breakfast over, a pot of beans and an Indian pudding were put in the oven; the morning chores done, a sabbatical silence settled over the household. At eleven o'clock every one repaired to the meeting-house; as there was but an hour's intermission between the services, few left the sanctuary. The men gathered round the door steps, discussing local topics or national affairs, the women congregated in the pews, to talk over household matters and the gossip of the neighborhood. If it was a warm day, the girls gathered on the sunny side of the meetinghouse, where many sly glances were exchanged with the group of young men by the horse block. If it chanced to be cold they also sought the pews, and in groups discussed fashion and the beaux, but with a demure air, and in low tones as befitted the occasion.

The clergymen generally embraced this opportunity for some particular theme, some peculiar shortcoming either of a local or political nature. Dr. Elijah Parish was famed for his "Fast" sermons. People used to flock to Byfield meeting-house to hear the doctor's diatribes against Jacobin misrule and French infidelity. The afternoon service over, the hungry multitude hastened home to the beans and pudding which were nicely smoking in the oven. How the gravel stones of the rough road would fly as the impatient steeds sped down the precipitous descent to the peril of life and limb. Supper and milking through, the evening was spent in reading and conversation. I should not have dared to have taken a needle in hand on Fast day. To the horror of the community, one Fast evening, "Bartlett's boys" and some other young men went over to "Gunket," and played ball after supper. One of the number, Enoch Hale, had the misfortune to sprain his arm, and was unable to work for some months. This was regarded as a special mark of Divine displeasure, a signal judgment for a heinous crime.

That spring brought a new fashion in head gear. Straw bonnets came into vogue. Peabody, Waterman & Co. received an invoice from England, and Mrs. Peabody presented one to her sister Hannah. I greatly admired this bonnet, but mother said she could not afford to buy me one that season. Aunt Sarah, noticing my discontented visage, inquired the cause, at which she signified her readiness to teach me to braid straw, and make myself a bonnet. Much surprised, I asked how she had learned. "As I have most things, I taught myself," was the reply. "During the Revolutionary war two British cruisers for two days lay off the mouth of the Merrimac. The inhabitants of the "Port" were greatly alarmed, momentarily expecting a bombardment. Your great-aunt Mollie Noyes packed her effects, and, with her children, came here. Though the men-of-war withdrew without any demonstration, as the news immediately came that Captain Noyes's vessel had been captured, and himself and crew were prisoners at Dartmoor, Mrs. Noyes remained some time. Your father was troubled with headache, and often complained of the heat of his wool hat. One day during haying, Aunt Noyes brought him a straw hat, which she said Captain Noyes had brought from foreign parts. After it was worn out your father missed it so much that the idea struck me of braiding one. We had a field of oats. I cut some straw, took the old hat, and, after patiently unbraiding and braiding for a time, at length succeeded in obtaining the secret. I braided and sewed a hat, which, though not as handsome as the foreign one, did very well. I braided several, and can teach you. When the oats are large enough to cut you can make a pretty bonnet."

Mother tried to dissuade me from this project. She didn't believe I could "make anything decent." I was strong in faith, and my aunt upheld this determination. As soon as the straw was ripe I began to plait, and soon had sufficient for a bonnet. The straw was finer than Aunt Hannah's, but, as no knowledge of bleaching had been obtained, it was not as white; still, it looked very well. Aunt Sarah fashioned it in the prevailing mode, but a difficulty arose respecting pressing. The front was easily managed, but how could the crown be shaped? Aunt Sarah was a person of expedients; I never knew her frustrated in anything she set about. A mortar was turned bottom upward, paper fitted over it, and the crown shaped to the requisite form. I was jubilant over this bonnet, and my aunt Peabody sent a white ribbon to trim it, like Aunt Hannah's. Neither before nor after do I think I was ever so proud of an article of dress as I was of that bonnet. After this we cut a quantity of straw, and I braided father a hat.

This summer was memorable for the dismissal of our district school teacher. Joseph Adams, a young man of nineteen, and nephew of Mrs. Oliver Dole, had been hired to teach the summer school. He professed great piety, and maintained a grave demeanor, which, in school, grew into an imperial sternness, a manner not calculated to win the scholars' affections. Many of the parents became dissatisfied after the first few days. My father declared the teacher wholly unfit for his place; but the summer school was short, and, from respect to Mr. and Mrs. Dole, nothing was said until I rebelled. There were about half a dozen girls in their teens in the school; and, about the third week of the term, Master Adams brought a book, from which he proposed that we should read selections. This exercise was in addition to the regular course. I have forgotten the title of the book, but it was some religious treatise. Having ranged the class before his desk, he took the book, and, standing behind the pupil, he passed his arms around her neck, holding it before her, while he corrected the errors of pronunciation and enunciation. A sentence having been read, he passed to the second, and so down the class. Being the youngest. I was the last. The dresses were at that time cut low in the neck, and I immediately saw that the young man's gaze was not constantly fixed upon the book, and I determined that his arms should not go round me in that manner; I would either hold the book or not read. When my turn came I signified this decision. The master turned as red, and bristled up like a turkey cock; but my resolution could not be shaken, and a compromise was effected, he holding one side of the book and I the other. Father said that I had done right; I might do as I pleased respecting the reading; it was not a regular school exercise, and the master had no right to force me. Accordingly, the next afternoon, I declined to join the class. The master began to threaten, but soon saw he could not use coercion. Thenceforth I was permitted to pursue my own course, but I immediately perceived that I had become a special object of enmity; a spite that was extended to the other and younger members of my family. My brother James was menaced with a whipping for a slight misdemeanor, but the sturdy boy threatened his father's vengeance in such a manner that the master wisely desisted. Still, I could see the smothered wrath, ready to seize the first opportunity when it could find vent. The opportunity was at length taken. My uncle, Enoch Smith, had married, some years previous, Miss Hannah Woodman. Their two sons, Samuel and Moses, attended school. Moses was a poor, little, puny boy of five years, a delicate, sickly child from infancy, but of a quiet and amiable disposition, and, having a wholesome dread of Master Adams, he was the ast one to have made a disturbance. Diah Dole, the great dunce, that Master Chase thumped and shook so unmercifully, was fully double in age. He occupied a front desk; Moses sat on the low form in front of that. One afternoon, soon after the school was called to order, Diah spat upon the floor, and with his toe (he was barefoot) marked out a figure in the aisle, then, contrary to rules, leaned forward and whispered: "Mose, look at my cock; I've made a cock, a biddy." The little boy glanced from his primer, and, with a look of disdain, drew his shoe over the figure. Diah, with an angry push, said: "You have spoiled my cock!" Moses put up his hand and slapped Diah's face. The master flew from his desk, shook Moses unmercifully, and told Diah to mind his book. At recess he directed Moses to bring him a rod from a bush by the roadside. The unsuspecting child obeyed. I thought he was to be whipped then, but the punishment was held in reserve. I had hoped that my suspicions had been groundless, that Moses would not receive chastisement; but I found, when school was dismissed, the little boy was retained. I hurried home to inform his mother. It was such a trivial thing Aunt Smith paid little heed, but I kept an outlook, and after a while I espied Moses creeping up the lane; dragging his little feet wearily along, he sank upon a log just inside the gate. I ran to him. He gazed stupidly into my face, and, with a piteous moan, sank fainting into my arms. My cries aroused the family; the child was taken to the house, and the physician summoned. Consciousness was restored, but the poor little back was shockingly mangled, and vomiting continued at intervals through the night. Dr. Poore looked gruff and glum, and took so much snuff I thought he must choke. After a time he expressed a hope of the little boy's recovery, but his maledictions on the cruel teacher were both loud and deep—"the infernal scoundrel; he would like to seat him in the pillory and thrash him within an inch of his life!" This indignation was universal. There was not time to call a regular school meeting that evening, but the gentlemen of the neighborhood (they all had come in to see Moses) agreed to meet at the school-house the next morning and forbid Master Adams entrance. Accordingly, when the young man opened the door, he found himself confronted by half a dozen of the influential men of the town, who informed him that his services were no longer required; that his presence in that house would not be permitted. The discomfitted teacher for a time was terribly angry and defiant, but at length was obliged to yield. At a school meeting in the evening he was deposed by a unanimous vote. Uncle Enoch sued Mr. Adams, and the case was tried at the September term in Newburyport. The master was sentenced to pay the costs of court and sixty dollars. The money was put in the bank for Moses, and Mr. Adams, unable to procure a school, was obliged to lower his aspirations and obtain a livelihood on the seat of a shoemaker's bench.

I recall an incident that occurred during this trial. Father and Uncle Enoch returned one night from town, declaring that they had that day witnessed a sight that never had been seen before and never would be again. A vessel belonging to the then flourishing firm of Farris & Stocker had arrived from South America, and their supercargo, Mr. Oliver Putnam (since the founder of the Putnam Free School), had brought by it a large sum of money. The Spanish government had prohibited the exportation of bullion, and Mr. Putnam had concealed the silver in the sides of the vessel. Carpenters were set to work to tear off the sheathing, and the Spanish dollars, turned as black as ink, were taken in bushel baskets and carried between two men, to be cleansed in a large cauldron, borrowed from a soap boiler's establishment, which was placed over a fire kindled for that purpose in Market square.

CHAPTER XVII.

Though years had elapsed, the malcontents of the parish had not buried their discontent. Parson Woods had failed to gain either their approval or regard. A printed sermon in which "bawdy French fashions" were severely denounced had given umbrage to a large number of the young people, who declared that the language used in this public reprimand was more indecent than any thing they had ever displayed in dress or manner. The clergyman had become noted for a too large development of the organ of acquisitiveness; he was accused of efforts to serve mammon as well as the Lord. In families where the pastor was held in high regard by the mistress of the mansion complaints were often made by the other members of an undue generosity towards the household at the parsonage. I had a young friend whose residence was near, and she declared she could never have a fresh egg to make cake, and that her mother really denied herself necessaries to supply the minister with luxuries. A story flew like wildfire over the parish, to the effect that Parson Woods had made several calls one afternoon, and at each place asked for a small piece of cheese, as Mrs. Woods had company from out of town; that at each house he had been presented with a whole cheese, and that after the last visit, as he drove from the door, his sleigh tipped upon a drift, when lo! nine cheeses rolled from beneath the checked coverlet which served as a sleigh robe. Another subject of effront was the sale of turkeys presented at Thanksgiving. This autumn the minister declared he could not afford to keep a horse! At the announcement Mr. Josiah Bartlett, Mr. Joseph Newell and Mr. Paul Bailey each sent him a ton of hay, but in a short time both the horse and the hay were sold. The next complaint was a lack of fuel. The usual quantities which had supplied his predecessors was said to be insufficient; consequently two additional loads were drawn. Lieut. Joseph Noyes, an old revolutionary officer, was employed to saw and split the wood. The morning that he commenced work Parson Woods went into the yard, and after looking over the pile he said, "Lieutenant, here are some nice logs, too good for fire-wood, it would be a pity to burn them; here are three or four just right for trunnels, put them aside, they are too nice for fuel."

The lieutenant made no exact reply, but as soon as the minister's back was turned, he fell to work with might and main on those identical logs. After dinner the parson again came out. Gazing hurriedly about, he excitedly exclaimed, "Where are those logs, those nice trunnell logs that I told you to save?"

"Save?" queried the wily old officer, with an air of bewilderment.

"Yes, I told you to put them aside, that they were too good for fire-wood."

"Well, really now! Sometimes I'm a little hard o' hearing, parson. I thought you told me to split them fine logs fust," innocently returned the untruthful old sinner, with a deprecatory air.

"Well, well," said the pastor, "I am sorry, but it cannot be helped now. I was not aware that you were deaf, lieutenant, is that the cause of your absence from divine worship?"

"Why yes, I used to go regerlarly when a youngster, but going into the army upsets people. War is a glorious thing when one is fighting for one's liberties, but it kind of onsettles a fellow. I've had so many bullets whistling round my ears, that half the time it seems as if I couldn't hear anything else."

"If you cannot hear, come and sit in the pulpit; I should be most happy to have you," the parson replied in his most polite manner, as he turned to re-enter the house,

As the Lieutenant had said, the war did unsettle a great many. Good officers made but poor civilians. Lieut. Noyes would not have deliberately performed a bad deed, but his moral sense had become somewhat stretched, and a good joke was the very breath in his nostrils. Though since the end of the war he had led somewhat of a desultory life, he always managed to dress and appear like a gentleman. The next Sunday, to the wonder and consternation of the congregation, just after Parson Woods had taken his place in the pulpit, the lieutenant, in his best suit, his hair elaborately frizzed, powdered and cued, marched up the broad aisle with his most imposing tread, and slowly ascended the pulpit stairs. With a profound military salute he seated himself beside the parson. "What could it mean?" The amazement increased, when, as the clergyman rose to begin the service, the lieutenant rose also; standing a little back with his head slightly inclined forward, and his hand behind his ear, he continued to occupy his post beside the pastor through the long prayer and the longer sermon. As every one knew the old scamp was not the least deaf, they began to surmise that some mischief was on foot, but "what was the mystery?" After two or three Sabbaths, in which the pranky old officer, with the gravity of forty judges, occupied a place in the pulpit, the story of the trunnel logs became whispered about, and his presence there caused such a sensation that the tithing man was compelled to give him a seat on the long bench in front. Aunt Ruth Little and others declared some judgment must fall on the reprobate; but, notwithstanding these menaces, he went on his way rejoicing, getting more treats than ever at the tavern, and a more hearty welcome to good cheer throughout the vicinity.

Parson Wood's friends were zealous in his defence. "A minister had wants of which the common people knew nothing; he had more calls for money. He was a blessed man, a learned man; his thoughts soared above those of the multitude,—they ought not to be lowered by petty cares and the many annoyances of this sublunary existence."

Mrs. Woods' bridal cloak, of white satin, had become somewhat defaced, and a subscription paper was put in circulation the first of the winter to obtain a sum to purchase black satin for another. This gave cause for much remark. It was averred that many gave who could ill afford the outlay; some from a naturally generous impulse, but more from a false pride that would not permit them to omit copying the example of their more wealthy neighbors. Right or wrong, the subscription was made, and a sufficient amount obtained to purchase the satin and a handsome sable muff and tippet. The cloak, an elegant one, trimmed with rich lace, was made by a committee of ladies chosen for that purpose, at the residence of aunt Ruth Little, and on New Year the articles were presented in due form.

A Baptist society had been established in New Rowley. Mrs. Mollie Little, uncle Enoch Little's wife, had been a communicant of this church previous to her marriage, and Mr. Little had accompanied his wife to this ministration. Finding so much division in our parish, the Baptists organized a series of prayer and conference meetings, which were held at Mr. Little's house. My uncle Parker Smith's family also attended the Baptist meetings, and my two cousins, Hannah and Nabby Smith, girls a few years my senior, frequently came to attend the meetings; I accompanied them a few times, but the odd phraseology of some of the speakers—illiterate persons but full of zeal, coupled with the still more singularly expressed experiences, which were nightly related, worked so strongly on my risibles, that it was difficult for me to maintain a proper decorum. Much to the horror of my cousins, that which sent the tears rolling down my cheeks, instead of bringing any sanctifying convictions, merely set me into hysterics from suppressed merriment, and mother declared "I was bad enough anyway, and that she would not have me made worse by attendance at these Baptist gatherings." During the previous summer, one hot afternoon, aunt Sarah ran down stairs with the somewhat startling announcement that "Brother Sam, in his best suit, with saddle-bags across the saddle, was coming on horse-back up the lane." We could scarcely believe she had seen aright. Looking out, we found it was no hallucination, but that Uncle Sam, in the flesh, was leading his horse into the stable. What could it mean? What could have called him from home just in the midst of the

English hay season? To the eager inquiries made on his entrance, he replied in his most imposing style, that he had been to Lynn to be ordained, that now he was a licensed preacher of the Methodist persuasion. Grandmam' groaned over her son's infatuation, and aunt Sarah worried about his grass. "To think of his leaving his farm then! If he must be ordained, why couldn't he have waited for winter when he could be spared." Father laughed; "he had always said Sam never would labor, and he should prove a true prophet." Lifted into a sphere above minor earthly affairs, the gentleman departed for his home on the morrow, wholly oblivious to the prognostications of evil from his course which burthened the minds of his family and friends.

The interest in the Baptist meetings was increasing, when uncle Sam made us his annual winter visit. As soon as his arrival became known he received a pressing invitation to preach at Mr. Little's Sunday evening, which was accepted with evident gratification. He somewhat amused the family by his solicitude respecting his dress. As it was cold weather, and he had not expected to preach, he had come unprovided with a white necktie. A loan of one was solicited, "as it looked more clerical." Father laughingly told his brother, as he handed him the handkerchief, "he saw that he yet retained a piece of the old Adam." Aunt Sarah contemptuously averred, "that he did not live up to his creed—"every earthly pomp and vanity ought to be renounced;" but grandmam' declared she was "glad to see that Sam had some idea of the fitness of things; if he must preach Methody, it pleased her to know that he wished to look and appear like a gentleman, and did not turn himself into an itinerant ranter."

The tidings that Mr. Sam Smith was to expound the novel doctrines of Methodism had called together a crowd, and the ground rooms of the large house were full. After the reading of a portion of the Scripture came a prayer in the usual fervent style; a hymn having been, sung the text was named—Ezekiel 7th chap., 7th verse: "The morning is come upon thee, O thou that dwellest in the land." From these words a powerful discourse in elucidation of the tenets of the new sect was delivered. The speaker had found his vocation; he possessed the gift to enchain an audience, and he held this promiscuous assembly in rapt attention for over an hour. At the close of the sermon up jumped Mr. Silas Moulton, then one of Parson Woods' recent converts, and in a fiery, "Hopkinsonian" prayer, each one of Mr. Smith's doctrinal points was contraverted. This brought on an ardent discussion. The hour grew late; Aunt Enoch Smith and myself essayed to make our exit by the back door. The eager and excited throng barred our progress. David Emery, now a tall youth of seventeen, aided our efforts by raising a couple of chairs above his head, when we managed to squeeze out. The night air was refreshing. One after another the members of the family came home, but it was after eleven when father and uncle Sam arrived. The preacher was completely exhausted. Family prayer was omitted, and aunt Sarah filled the long-handled warming-pan with bright coals, declaring as she went to warm the bed, "that if it was her brother, she must say he was great for argufying, and he had beat Silas Moulton out and out." The morrow brought a severe snow storm, which blocked the road to an unusual degree. In the midst of this storm, much to our astonishment, Mr. Joseph Ames, one of the chief Baptist speakers, came in. He had walked the whole distance from Bradford in that storm to converse with uncle Sam. I became so tired of this discussion, of hearing the changes rung and re-rung upon the conflicting themes, that I kindled a rousing fire in aunt Sarah's chamber, and there sought a respite from the sound of human tongues, and the quiet requisite to an aching head.

CHAPTER XVIII.

The predictions of evil made at the union of Robert Adams and Susan Little had been fully realized. Consanguinity, however, could not be assigned as a cause, but a tendency to consumption, inherited from his father, in the bridegroom. Soon after his marriage Mr. Adams had an attack of hemorrhage of the lungs; the next summer he rallied and hopes were entertained of his recovery, but the bleeding recommenced, and after a season of prostration and suffering, he passed away, some two months prior to the third anniversary of his marriage. One infant had gone before its father, and a second, born after his decease, only entered this world to pass to another.

Aunt Sukey, completely crushed, was thus left alone, the care of a farm devolving upon her. My cousin Nabby Smith had been with Mrs. Adams during her husband's illness, and it was decided she should remain. Uncle William Little sold the farm he had recently purchased in Haverhill, and came to take charge of his sister and her estate. In March aunt Hannah Little was married to Mr. James Stickney, a young man who had for some time resided with the brothers and sisters Dole. A handsome, energetic youth, he had won the regard of the lone bachelors and maids, and they highly favored his match with Hannah Little, and had fitted apartments for the young couple in their large house.

The snow which had fallen during uncle Sam's visit still covered the ground. On the morning of the eighteenth, father and I rode directly over the stone wall dividing the field from the street, on our way to grandsir Little's, but in half an hour the water poured in a perfect torrent down the hill, the brook rose in an unexampled manner, and the roads became nearly impassable. The wedding was appointed at eight o'clock Only the family and nearest relatives had been invited, and it was with extreme difficulty that they reached the house. Mr. Stickney came in looking unusually pale and complaining of a lameness in the back, caused by a fall the day previous. The ladder had slipped as he was descending from the hay-mow, and he fell with great force directly across the machine for breaking flax. The sorrow and concern felt at this accident was expressed, but no one entertained the slightest idea that any serious consequences would ensue, or that it would entail any lasting effect. Parson Woods having sold his horse walked over from the main road. His feet were thoroughly saturated. Dry hose and slippers were furnished, and grandmam' bade me bring the minister a glass of wine, as a preventative against taking cold. but the clergyman said: "if it was just as convenient he would prefer a little rum and molasses." The toddy having been furnished, the company repaired to the parlor. Aunt Hannah looked lovely in a white jaconte muslin; you would have to go a long way, as aunt Judy Dole said, to see a handsomer couple. Travelling was so difficult. the company dispersed at an early hour. The bride and groom remained at grandsir's till the next day. Aunt Sukey and Nabby Smith essayed to walk the distance home, but were obliged to return and don each a pair of men's boots, in order to pass the bridge over the brook, and the next day, when uncle Stickney took his wife and myself home, we were obliged to scramble upon the sleigh seat, the water poured so over the sides of the large, high-backed sleigh.

The previous year had been a sad one to our family, and farther calamity was in store. In April, uncle William Little's only child, a promising lad of five years, died suddenly of croup. This was a severe affliction to the parents; the father for a time was nearly frantic. The first shock of the loss had scarcely passed, when David Eaton, one of Uncle Bill's apprentices was taken sick with the measles. None of the family had had the distemper, every one caught it. Aunt Sukey and Nabby Smith were sick at the same time, and, as I had had the measles, I was obliged to act as nurse. My patients were quite sick, Nabby was insane for twenty-four hours. Uncle Bill's family were all ill one after another. Aunt Little was very sick, fever set in and for several days she was not expected to live. Naturally a delicate woman, it took a long while for nature to rally, and she remained an invalid through the summer. Just as Aunt Little's fever was at its height, the news came that Aunt Bartlett was dangerously sick. Grandmam' Little and my mother hurried to town, but, under Divine Providence, with good nursing. her life was spared.

Uncle Stickney had not recovered from the effects of his fall, as had been anticipated. He took cold while fishing; a cough came on, and, instead of gaining health as the warm weather advanced, day by day he lost both flesh and vigor. Help was hired to do his work upon the farm, and the most serious apprehensions began to be entertained.

With my multifarious duties, I had contrived to plait a new straw bonnet for myself. Aunt Sarah assisted me to make common hats for father and the boys. We also fashioned a cunning bonnet for my little sister Susan to wear upon her first advent at meeting. Upon sight of this head gear, little Joe demanded a Sunday straw hat. Aunt Sarah said that was a good idea. I plaited a fine braid; the hat was made and lined with green silk. Jim thought he should like one, only the braid might be coarser. When father saw this hat, he asked us to make one for him, the light hat was "so comfortable in warm weather." The gentlemen and youth of the neighborhood and vicinity, seeing and liking these hats, came to solicit us to braid some for them. In a short time quite a lucrative business was established. In the midst of the hurry, one of our cousins, Patty Noyes, came in, to beg us to braid her a bonnet; she "must have one for the very next Sunday." "That is an impossibility." "Then sew one from this!" she exclaimed, seizing a roll of the hat braid. "That is too coarse." "That is a matter of taste," she returned; "if I have a coarse straw it may set the fashion. Just sew the braid as I direct."

Remonstrance was useless. The bonnet was sewed. It looked very well, and when trimmed was really pretty. Patty's joke proved a prophecy,—she did set a fashion. Orders came for several similar bonnets. This extra straw work brought a great hurry in the autumn. I was looking forward to a little more leisure in the winter weather, when I was summoned to the Dole place, where with slight intervals I remained for several months. Our worst fears were realized. Uncle Stickney was in a confirmed consumption. Aunt Hannah, feeble from a recent confinement, and worn down by anxiety, watching, and the care of a sickly, puny babe, needed my assistance. The last of December the feeble, wailing infant passed from our tearful care to the arms of the heavenly angels. This was my first experience of the death of a babe, and under the circumstances I felt that it was not a subject for grief, but a beneficent event to both mother and child. Aunt Hannah seemed stunned. She moved about her husband's death-bed like one in a trance. The brothers and sisters Dole were agonized at the thought of the loss of their adopted son; they could not be talked or prayed into submission. "It was hard; oh, so hard, to see that strong, handsome form so fast succumbing to disease." Robert Adams had always been delicate; his illness was more gradual; sad as it was it did not seem so heart-rending as this. Assistance and sympathy were tendered from all quarters, still it was a dark, dark time! Aunt Sukey, naturally of a less buoyant temperament than her sisters, sank into a morbid melancholy, distressing herself with doubts of her late husband's state in the other world, as he had made no death-bed confession. Uncle Sam Smith's visit brought comfort and hope. He cheered aunt Sukey and brought a peaceful submission to the death-stricken household of our neighbors. We began to feel that, though he might not attain to a great worldly wealth, he possessed that pearl of great price, that true riches, before which mere earthly treasures sink into insignificance.

In April, Uncle Stickney left us. His exit had been calm and hopeful. A degree of submission had been attained by those nearest and dearest, and Aunt Hannah returned to the old life, (yet, alas! how sadly different), in the paternal home, bereft of both husband and child in little over one short year,—a childless widow ere she had reached the age of twenty-one.

CHAPTER XIX.

A quantity of straw had been stored the summer before; this spring, orders for bonnets and hats came as fast as they could be filled.

As I have stated, Uncle Thurrel's only daughter had married Mr. Jonathan Smith, the son of the Rev. Dr. Smith, the first Baptist clergyman in

Haverhill. Mr. Smith kept a store in that town. Straw bonnets were becoming so fashionable, Mrs. Smith conceived the idea of our supplying the sale at her husband's establishment. Hitherto our bonnets had remained the natural color of the straw. Straw work had been commenced in Providence, and through some relatives there, Mrs. Smith learned the process of bleaching. We were greatly pleased to become initiated into the mystery, and with her native ingenuity, Aunt Sarah contrived a bleachery. Holes were bored in the head of a barrel, strings were attached to the bonnets and passed up through the apertures, which were then plugged with wooden spiles; sulphur sprinkled over embers put in the dish of a foot-stove was placed beneath; the whole being tightened by an old quilt, not a fume escaped, and the bonnets came forth as white as the imported. To this period the braid had been plaited from whole straw; this year the split straws began to come, and Aunt Sarah finding that she could split straw with a coarse comb, concluded to have some combs made for the purpose. Comb making had been an industry of the town since its first settlement. Mr. Enoch Noyes, my grandmother Smith's nephew, had become noted for the manufacture of combs and horn buttons. He was a great genius, had contrived many inventions and made much improvement in the business. During the Revolutionary war, a Hessian deserter, an adept in the craft, had chanced to drift into the place and was at once employed by Mr. Noyes, much to the advantage of the trade, which immediately increased in extent and importance. Mr. Noyes was a great oddity. He would run half over the parish bareheaded and barefooted. It was no uncommon thing for him to appear at our house, after dinner of a hot summer day, in only a shirt and breeches, having run across the fields two miles, "jest to take a nooning." A great joker and a capital story-teller, his appearance was the signal for a general frolic. He was fond of telling strangers that his father used to say he had "four remarkable children: Molly was remarkably handsome, Tim was a remarkable sloven, John was remarkably wicked, and Enoch was remarkably cunning." To this gentleman aunt Sarah applied. As might have been expected, he entered into the business with characteristic zest, and in a short time we were supplied with half a dozen different-sized straw splitters.

Mrs. Smith, having cut a tiny piece of trimming from an imported bonnet, brought it for me to imitate. How vividly I recall the two long hours which I passed, sitting on the chamber floor surrounded by the litter of straw, patiently weaving and unweaving until the secret was obtained. Having acquired this ornamental cue, I invented several other decorations with which to finish the edge of the bonnets. I also learned to make straw plumes and tassels from examining those on the foreign bonnets. Miss Mary Perkins kept a fashionable millinery establishment in Newburyport. Hearing of our straw manufacture she rode up to see us and immediately ordered bonnets. After a time the plain straw became superseded by diamond and other fancy plaits. These being the ton, Miss Jenkins also purloined a bit from the inside of a diamond satin straw, and brought it as a pattern of a braid. It looked so intricate I nearly despaired of my ability to copy it, but Miss Jenkins would not permit me to demur, and as every one spoke encouragingly I made the effort, and in two or three hours accomplished the task. This was a timely achievement; our bonnets were in great demand, and we continued the business through the warm season for several years until the establishment of straw factories and my approaching marriage curtailed the work; but aunt Sarah continued to braid men's hats and supply her friends' bonnets for a long time.

The year I was seven years old the first incorporated woolen mill in Massachusetts was established at the falls on the river Parker, in the Parish of Byfield in Newbury. The machinery for this factory was made in Newburyport by Messrs. Standring, Armstrong & Guppy, agents; the Messrs. Scholfield and most of the operatives were English. The erection of this mill created a great sensation throughout the whole region. People visited it from far and near. Ten cents was charged as an admittance fee. That first winter sleighing parties came from all the adjacent towns, and as distant as Hampstead and Derry, in New Hampshire. Row after row of sleighs passed over Crane-neck hill, enlivening the bright, cold days by the joyous tones of their merry bells. Never shall I forget the awe with which I entered what then appeared the vast and imposing edifice. The huge drums that carried the bands on the lower floor, coupled with the novel noise and hum increased this awe; but when I reached the second floor where picking, carding, spinning and weaving were in progress my amazement became complete. The machinery, with the exception of the looms, was driven by water power, the weaving was by hand. Most of the operatives were males, a few young girls being employed in splicing rolls.

In a few years the first company was dissolved, and the mill passed into other hands. The Scholfields were succeeded by Messrs. Lees & Taylor. These gentlemen were also English. New machinery imported from England for the manufacture of cotton goods was put in. Mr. Taylor soon left, but Mr. Lees continued to operate the mill for several years. The establishment of this factory brought quite a revolution in the domestic manufactures of the neighborhood. For some time previous, in most families hand carding had been discontinued, the wool having been sent to be converted into rolls to the clothier mills of Mr. Ben. Pearson or Mr. Samuel Dummer. Lees & Taylor made arrangements by which this family carding could be done at their factory both cheaper and better than at the smaller mills. The introduction of cotton opened a new channel of industry. The weaving was still performed by hand; as the business increased this loom power was not sufficient to supply the demand for cloths. Their goods consisted of heavy tickings and a lighter cloth of blue and white striped or checked, suitable for men's and boys' summer wear, aprons, &c. The tickings were woven by men on the looms at the factory, but much of the lighter stuffs were taken into families and woven on the common house loom. The yarns were spun and dyed at the factory; these could be purchased there, and in lieu of the hitherto universal linen and tow, cotton began to be mixed with flax or woven alone. Quite fine cotton fabrics were woven; bleached they looked very nice. Stamps on blocks of wood had been invented, and with home-made dyes, calico was stamped. These chintzes were held in high estimation and many "go-to-meeting gowns" were construct- of them, pieces of which have been handed down, to be cherished as inestimable relics of a former generation. This cotton spinning brought a new occupation to the place. Being prior to Whitney's invention of the cotton gin, the material came just as it had been gathered from the field, and many of the females in the neighborhood of the factory were employed to separate the seed from the cotton. For years one rarely entered a farm house in the vicinity without finding one or more of the inmates busy picking cotton.

A short time prior to the erection of the Byfield factory, Jacob Perkins, the distinguished inventor and the first engraver of bank bills, completed the construction of his first machine for cutting nails. Hitherto every nail in use had been wrought by hand, and this machine became immediately an object of interest, as the community at once perceived its value, and justly took pride in their gifted townsman. Mr. Perkins having hired the old mill house of Capt. Paul Moody in Byfield, commenced business on the same dam as the Factory. This nail factory continued in operation some years, then, as Amesbury presented greater facilities for their manufacture, the business was moved to that town. Mr. Perkins discovered a process for plating shoe buckles, then universally worn: he made improvements in fire engines and hydraulic machines, and machines for boring honey-combed cannon. He was also the most skilful pyrotechnist in the country. He also discovered a method of softening and hardening steel, by which the process of engravings was greatly facilitated. The Bank of England adopted it for their plates. He invented the bathometer, an instrument for measuring the depth of the sea by the pressure of water; and the pleometer, which measured the rate of a ship's sailing. He also demonstrated the impressibility of water. Later in life he went to London, where his experiments on high pressure steam machinery attracted much attention. He contrived a steam gun which could discharge about a thousand balls a minute. Experiments with this gun attracted the attention of the Duke of Wellington and other distinguished military men. These inventions enriched others, but Mr. Perkins died in London in 1840 without the fortune to which, by his labors he was justly entitled.

Mr. Eben Parsons, one of the sons of the Rev. Moses Parsons, the second pastor of the church in Byfield parish, then an eminent merchant in Boston, had purchased an estate contiguous to the parsonage, where he had been born and bred. Neither expense or labor had been spared in improving and ornamenting the grounds and garden of this place, which its owner called the "Fatherland Farm." Now preparation commenced for the erection of a spacious mansion. Raisings at that period were universally a social festival, and this, from the superiority of the building, the elegance of its surroundings, and position of its owner, became an extraordinary fete. Preparations for the occasion were made upon a scale of unusual magnificence. It was arranged that the Rev. Dr. Parish should deliver an address, and a consecrating hymn should be sung. The choir in our parish were invited to join that in Byfield in singing this hymn. As the female singers were to be habited in a uniform of white muslin and blue satin, there was a great stir of preparation, and the whole community was roused into a perfect tiptoe of expectancy. The important day at length arrived. Crowds in carriages, on horseback and on foot thronged to the raising, which was early in the afternoon. Deft hands splendidly did the work; the stout timbers of the spacious building were securely upreared; then the master builder, Mr. Stephen Tappan of Newburyport, appeared on the summit, bottle in hand. Amid profound silence, for a moment he poised himself aloft, then swinging the bottle above his head, with a cheer which was caught up and iterated and reiterated by the multitude, the new roof-tree was duly baptized in pure old Jamaica. The deafening cheers ended, a platform was arranged over a part of the floor timbers, to which mounted the orator, singers and most noted guests. The eloquent divine, inspired by the scene and hour, did himself more than justice, holding his entranced audience in breathless attention for nearly an hour by a perfect rush of eloquence. Next the orchestra took their places. A goodlie company, those stalwart youths and buxom maidens. The bass-viol struck the tune, and the united voices floated forth on the still summer air, and sang

> "If God refuse the house to build
> The workmen toil in vain."

A tremendous crash at this point drowned the last note, and amid screams, cries, and shouts the crowd upon the platform were hurled into the cellar beneath, amidst earth, rubbish and broken boards. For a moment there was the wildest terror and confusion. It was some time ere the semblance of order could be restored, or the extent of injury ascertained. Happily no bones were broken, but there were numerous sprains and contusions. The white muslins were sadly rent and torn, but after repairing damages a degree of equanimity was restored and the sumptuous entertainment was served. This was followed by various pastimes,—wrestling, running and other athletic sports. It was dark before the crowd dispersed, and the great raising formed a topic of conversation for months. Most dire calamities were prognosticated from the accident, by the superstitious. Fatal prophecies foredooming the future of the family at "Fatherland mansion."

Aunt Judy Dole was vehement in her diatribes. A nephew, Mr. Benjamin Wadleigh, who had taken the place of the late James Stickney in the household, received a severe sprain in his shoulder, which incapacitated him from labor for some time. "And served him right," the old woman exclaimed in her most oracular manner. "He'd better have staid at home and minded his business than hyty-titying over to Byfield to sing psalm tunes at such a frolic, and to that great popish stringed instrument of Baal, too. Sposin' old parson Moses Parsons' son was gwine to build a house; because it was bigger than common he needn't make such a fuss, other folks had built big houses. The saying was, destruction went afore a fall; she guessed destruction would come arter, this time. She hoped it would l'arn the young folks sense,—show 'em taint all gold that glittered."

CHAPTER XIX.

Turnpikes were superseding the common roads on the more important routes of travel, and one was projected between Newburyport and Boston. A company was formed, the shares sold and the work commenced. The construction of this road caused considerble excitement in the community. Most were enthusiastic in its favor, while others thought the additional convenience insufficient to repay such an outlay. As several of our family were stockholders, and David Emery assisted on the survey, we were especially interested. David often passed the Sabbath at his grandfather Little's, and he usually dropped in to talk over the work with father. He disapproved of the plan of the road—thought it would have been better to have built it to Salem, to connect with that from Salem to Boston. Then he did not favor an exactly straight thoroughfare if it must be carried over wide morasses and such lofty eminences as the Topsfield hills. Though then a mere youth, I think the verdict of posterity would endorse the young man's ideas. Through the uncounted multitude of obstacles that usually arise to impede a public work, the road was steadily pushed with remarkable energy. Huge hotels and spacious stables were erected at points convenient for relays, and every then modern improvement made for the accommodation of travel. At the time of my first visit to town only one stage plied on alternate days between Newburyport and the capital—going one morning and returning the next afternoon. I well remember my first sight of a stage and the delight with which I gazed at the huge leathern conveyance, with its gaudily emblazoned yellow body and the four prancing white steeds. Soon after relays were established and the stage went out and returned each day. As the travel increased teams were added and the Eastern Stage Company was formed.

On account of ill health, Col. Stephen Bartlett had severed his connection with the firm of Peabody & Waterman. Confirmed consumption had been feared but after a winter passed in Charleston, S. C., Col. Bartlett returned with increased vigor. Active occupation was recommended. The stage company were seeking an agent. The position was offered to Mr. Bartlett, and he immediately entered upon its duties. This appointment was eminently appropriate, and the gentleman remained in the employ of the company until obliged to surrender to the ravages of the fell disease which at last claimed him as its victim. One afternoon, the summer I was sixteen, I rode into town and had just entered aunt Bartlett's parlor when uncle Bartlett drove to the door, on the box of a hack in which were seated my aunt Peabody, and cousin Sophronia. Reining up his pair of spanking bays before the open window, he greeted me: "I am glad to see you, Sally. Put on yonr bonnet and tell your aunt to don hers, and I will give you a ride with Mrs. Peabody and Fronie. The turnpike is graded to the third milestone, and I intend that you shall have the honor of being the first ladies to pass over it." Of course I was highly delighted. We were soon seated. My aunts and cousin were in high spirits, and altogether it was a very merry time. There was a little stir of enthusiasm amid the group lingering about the steps of the "Wolfe Tavern," and we received many polite greetings as we drove forward. It was rather soft wheeling over the freshly-strewn gravel, but that did not signify; our horses were young and strong, their load light, and we dashed forward in fine style. The third milestone soon appeared. After a slight pause to look around, we retraced our steps and alighted at aunt Bartlett's, proud of the achievement of being able to boast that we were the first ladies to ride over the Newburyport and Boston turnpike.

The next year I had another ride with my uncle. The Plum Island bridge and turnpike had been built the previous summer. I was making my annual winter visit in town. That day I had dined at my uncle Peabody's, and we were rising from the table, when uncle Bartlett drove to the door in a double sleigh, to which was attached a splendid span of white horses. He was accompanied by Capt. Stoodley, a brother of Mrs. William Bartlett, jr.,of Portsmouth, N. H. Throwing him the reins, uncle Bartlett ran in, exclaiming: "Come, girls; I have a pair of horses that I wish to prove, and I will give you a ride. Wrap up well, for it is a snapping cold day." Aunt Peabody told us to hasten. "Put on all your furs," she added, as she filled a stove for our feet. We were quickly ensconced on the back seat, well wrapped in buffaloes. Uncle Bartlett turned his horses toward Plum Island. There was not much path, but the powerful steeds dashed lightly along. We had proceeded to the entrance to the bridge, when our further progress was stopped by a huge snow drift. With some difficulty our experienced whip turned his team. Proceeding in the direction of "High street" we soon reached that well-trodden thoroughfare. Though much more sparsely built than now, it was a handsome avenue and a pleasant drive.

In my childhood Frog pond was the center of a tangled wilderness of alder and other bushes, and at the upper end there was a frightful ravine. Near this gully stood the gun house, where the cannon belonging to the artillery company was kept. Back on the heights stood an ancient windmill. Below, near the margin of the pond, stretched a long rope walk. This was removed to give place for the commencement of the turnpike. Back of the pond was located quite an extensive pottery for the manufacture of brown glazed earthern ware. In the year commencing the present century the streets of the town received much improvement, and in the summer of that year the gulley at the head of Green street was filled up, and the mall was laid out, graded and railed. Capt. Edmund Bartlett gave fourteen hundred dollars towards this public improvement, which cost about eighteen hundred. In honor of this munificence, the park received the name of "Bartlett Mall."

In the summer of 1805 the Court house was erected. The building was ornamented by the figure of Justice holding a scale and sword, which surmounted the pedestal. St. Paul's Church was built that same year, and within a short period several handsome private residences had also been erected, adding much to the beauty of the street. Dexter had increased his images; his plan was in full glory; Sentinals mounted guard. Jefferson had joined Washington and Adams over the front entrance. Beneath the Presidents was a bass-relief of the Goddess of Liberty. An half hour's ride brought us to Parsons' tavern on Deer island, at the Essex Merrimac bridge. This was a noted place for pleasure parties. A delightful spot in summer, and a noted rendezvous for sleighing parties in winter, when a supper and dance were enjoyed. At the first snow a rush was made for Parsons', where the first comer was treated to a bottle of wine by mine host. Though our horses had skimmed over the snow like birds, the day was so intensely cold we were fairly benumbed, and the bright wood fire was exceedingly grateful. Capt. Stdooley, according to the custom of the period, politely brought my cousin and myself a glass of wine. Warmed and refreshed we retraced our steps, fully satisfied with the steed, which Col. Bartlett immediately secured for the "Stage Company."

Two other memorable rides fell to my destiny that year. Toward spring father's ox-cart needed new tires. Much to his surprise none could be found in Newburyport. Some one directed him to the store of old Mr. David Howe, in Haverhill, where it was said "every merchantable article could be bought." As aunt Chase resided in Haverhill, father invited me to ride with him. It was a raw March morning and the sleighing poor. Making our way partly in the fields and pastures, partly in the road, we reached "Cottle's Ferry;" there we took the river. The ice was strong but full of seams made by cracks which had been frozen. Our horse, a spirited mare, feared danger, and as she reached one of these seams, with a leap would bound over it, then proceed at a two-forty-pace to the next; then came another bound, and in this way the journey was made.

My aunt resided in a large, old-fashioned brick mansion, picturesquely situated on the right bank of the Merrimac, about half a mile below Haverhill village. The road separated it from the river, and in front a landing led directly to the house. Leaving me at the door father drove to the village, where he procured iron which he lashed under the sleigh. Having dined at Mrs. Chase's we started for home. The rattling of the iron started Kate still more, and the race was greater than in the morning. I never was more thankful than when the Ferry was again reached, and we were once more on terra firma.

My other race was in the autumn. It was customary for the young ladies of the neighborhood to give social tea parties of an afternoon, at which we assembled at an early hour, dressed in our best, with our go-abroad knitting work, usually fine cotton, clocked hose. Some of these clocks comprised the most elaborate patterns. After tea the knitting was laid aside. As the evening drew on the beaux began to appear, then games, or dancing, were enjoyed. At this period the fear of Parson Wood's anathema had in a measure passed and dancing had been generally resumed. We were permitted to indulge in the recreation at my uncle Tenney's when the deacon was from home.

Mr. Benjamin Hill's son, Eliphalet,

had become affianced to Miss Sarah Coffin, of "Scotland," Oldtown parish. The young lady had come to pay Mr. Hill's family a visit, and the Misses Hills gave one of these tea-parties in her honor. Mr. Hill's residence was two miles from ours, and father directed me to go in the chaise. "Liph. Hills will take care of your horse, Sallie, and you can take up the deacon's girls as you go," said he, as he went out, after dinner. We had recently purchased a new "fall back chaise;" our old one had been a square-topped. I was somewhat proud of the new equipage, and of my spirited mare. Trained from infancy to ride and drive, I was a fearless horsewoman. Jim harnessed Kate, and I drove over to uncle Tenney's, where I was joined by my cousins Joan and Lydia. The afternoon and evening were passed most pleasantly. I recollect leading down a new contra figure with my second cousin, Billy Noyes, who was a capital dancer—we two usually headed the set. Fun and frolic ruled the hour till after nine o'clock, when my horse was brought to the door. There were other vehicles, and gentlemen's and ladies' saddle horses, awaiting. My cousins and I sprang into our chaise and I drove forward. We had reached the summit of Plummer's hill when Kate began to prick up her ears and, with a sniff, to gather in her paces. The clatter of approaching hoofs struck my ear, and, before I could realize the situation, William Thurrell and my cousin William Smith rushed past on horseback, the horses going at the top of their speed. One took the right, the other the left of my chaise. As they swept past, Kate gave a snort and, springing forward, joined in the race. Down we went, at a break-neck speed, down the steep declivity, the loose stones of the rough road flying in every direction. As the horse was beyond my control, all I could do was to hold the reins as tightly as possible, but, as they were new, I felt secure. On we dashed, through "Tea street." It was impossible for me to turn to take my cousins home, nor could I stop until the schoolhouse was reached. Here my companions were able to alight, but were obliged to walk back about half a mile, while I proceeded up Crane-neck hill at a more leisurely pace. The young men were somewhat frightened at the escapade, but, upon the whole, enjoyed it vastly, declaring, much to my vexation, that "little Sally Smith can beat the best jockey in the whole country around."

CHAPTER XX.

In contradistinction to the church from which they had separated, our forefathers had established a severe simplicity in public worship, which, as the country grew older, and society increased in liberality and culture, became distasteful to the more youthful portion of the population. Deaconing hymns had become nearly obsolete, and musical instruments began to appear in the singing seats.

Though severe and strict in theological dogmas, Parson Woods was, upon the whole, a progressive man. Through his influence our choir had greatly improved in singing, and when it was proposed to have a viol accompaniment, he made no objection. Accordingly, one fine summer morning, Mr. Ben. Brown, with an important air, marched up the gallery stairs, bearing his bass-viol in his hand. There was a sensational stir throughout the singing seats. Mr. Edmund Little tiptoed to and fro. There were nods and whispers, shuffling of the leaves of singing books; then came the preliminary screams, screeches, grunts, growls, sees and saws from the viol. While this was proceeding, the faces of the congregation were a study worthy of a Hogarth. Amazement subsided into curiosity; the younger portion sat in smiling expectancy, while their elders glanced at one another, disapproval written in every wrinkle of their sour visages, and the children gazed with wide open eyes and open-mouthed astonishment. At the first intimation of the idea of having this instrumental accompaniment, aunt Judy Dole had entered her vehement protest against it. She and her sisters occupied seats upon the women's bench in the gallery. At the first sight of Mr. Brown, the old lady's face grew rigid; stern determination and severe disapproval became legible in every line. Parson Woods and his family came in, and the usual masculine rush followed; the last loiterer had become seated and the last pew door had been slammed. Parson Woods, as was customary, opened the service with a short prayer; then the hymn ,was named and read, and the choir arose, in rustling importance. Mr. Brown, with the air of an emperor, drew his bow across the strings. At the first sound, up jumped aunt Judy, and, with indignant opposition in every creak of the high-heeled channeled pumps, she firmly strode through the gallery and down the stairs, then, passing out at the front door, seated herself on the horse-block, remaining there during the service. At its close she rode home with the rest of the family, but it was a long time ere the prim maiden became sufficiently reconciled to the new fashion to appear in her wonted place on the Sabbath.

The second year of her widowhood, aunt Hannah Stickney married Mr. Samuel Noyes, of the "Farms," Newbury. This gentlemen, a descendant of John, oldest son of Nicholas Noyes, a widower with four children, was a cousin of her first husband. Many wondered that so young a women as aunt Hannah should feel willing to assume the responsibility of rearing and training so many small children. Though the young widow had returned to her father's house, she could not make it the girlish home which she had left with a heart so full of buoyant hope. Mr. Noyes had been most kind in his ministrations during Mr. Stickney's illness, upbearing the fainting souls of the sick man and his family, by his firm faith, and devotional spirit. Through every trial he had been a true comforter to Mrs. Stickney, thereby winning her gratitude and affectionate interest. This good man needed a wife, his children needed a mother, she could supply this need. Cheerfully and lovingly her life's work was assumed. How well this task was performed, the reverent respect and love of her family attested. To no one could more properly be applied the scripture text, "Her children rise up and call her blessed; her husband also, and he praiseth her." The second nuptials were strictly private, the ceremony being performed at the residence of the Rev. Dr. Parish, in Byfield. The little, black doctor, greatly diverted one of his favorite parishioners, Mrs. Moses

Colman, by the information that the day previous he had married the handsomest woman he ever saw, to Mr. Sam Noyes. "Such black eyes, Mrs. Colman, such a complexion, and such a sweet yet sparkling expression. Oh, she is a beauty, Mrs. Colman! I have thought you as handsome as any woman I ever saw, but this one is handsomer; yes," musingly added the divine, as he leaned back in his chair and critically examined his companion's face through half closed eyes, "yes, Mrs. Colman, I must decide that of the two she is the handsomest."

Much amused, Mrs Colman inquired the beauty's name.

"Hannah Stickney; her maiden name was Little."

"Why Doctor, she is my own cousin," the lady replied with surprise.

"Well, you may be proud of your cousin, Mrs. Colman, and I must say your family may be proud of themselves. Such a splendid set of black-eyed queens! Why they are positively regal! Yes, yes, positively regal!" This was too good to be kept private, and the black-eyed queens were duly informed of the distinguished doctor's tribute to their lovliness.

The prostration of grief at length passed, and aunt Adams began to take her wonted interest in the cares and duties of life. As the house was inconvenient for two families, the second year of her widowhood Mrs. Adams took the farm into her own management. Mr. Adams had built a shoemaker's shop when he first took possession of the premises. This was hired by two or three young men, former apprentices of uncle Bill Little. Having come of age, they commenced business for themselves, boarding with aunt Adams, Nabby Smith still being retained as an assistant.

As soon as aunt Hannah had become established in her new home, aunt Adams and myself were invited to pay her a visit. Accordingly, one warm August morning, we set out. We took aunt Adams' chaise and our horse. We had passed the factory and were approaching the "Fatherland Farm," when the pin broke and the right wheel dropped. Luckily, the horse stopped instantly, and I sprang out and held her head while aunt Adams could alight. What next was to be done? Looking around, I espied Mr. Gorham Parsons and some workmen in an adjacent field. I started to gain their assistance, but Mr. Parsons, perceiving our dilemma, came forward to meet me, accompanied by one of the men, who proved to be Joe Gould, who was often employed at our farm. Gould took the chaise to Mr. Moses Dole's blacksmith shop, which was a short distance beyond, and Mr. Parsons escorted aunt Adams and myself to the house, which was now finished and furnished in great elegance, being the most imposing mansion in the vicinity; with its well-ordered stables and other appointments, forming an establishment of which the proprietor might well be proud. The housekeeper, Mrs. Plummer, was called, and we were shown into a parlor. A bell rang above stairs, succeeded by much running to and fro. Next a negro page flung wide the door, and, with a profound obeisance, ushered in Mr. Parsons, supporting on his arm a stout, florid-complexioned woman, habited in a white dimity wrapper, her head adorned by a crape turban, surmounting a frisette of light curls; her gouty feet, encased in velvet slippers, were still further assisted by a gold-headed cane. This lady, Madame Eben Parsons, Mr. Gorham Parsons' mother, was followed by Mrs. Plummer, bearing a fan and scent-bottle, while the rear of the procession was brought up by a young waiting maid, loaded with a footstool, shawl and cushions.

The ceremony of introduction over, after much fixing and fussing, changing from one window to another, arranging and rearranging of footstool and cushions, Madame Parsons at length became seated and at leisure to turn her attention to her visitors. She expressed delight on learning that we were relatives of her friend Mrs. Moses Colman, of whom she spoke in the highest terms. Her sons also received the meed of praise. As they often went on business between the "Fatherland Farm" and Mr. Parsons's estate in Brighton, the lady had made their acquaintance.

I well remembered David Emery's first visit to Boston, then a lad of twelve,—a most remarkable event it then seemed to me, a ten year old girl. How eagerly I listened to every minutæ of the tour which was made in company with his elder brother, Jeremiah Colman. They took two pigs of the famous "Byfield" breed from the "Fatherland Farm" to Brighton, in a spring cart, drawn by a favorite family mare named Dorcas. The journey was made in one day, and they returned on the next. The night was passed at the residence of Mr. Eben Parsons in Boston. This was an ancient structure on Summer street. A flight of steps led directly from the sidewalk to the front door which opened into a square hall that was used as a parlor; in the rear, stood a large stable, and in front stretched a common upon which Mr. Parsons's two cows were pastured.

Cake and wine served we were invited into the garden, which lying on a gentle declivity was laid out in terraces, the walks bordered by trim hedges of box. There was a variety of choice flowers and fruit. Having been regaled with fine specimens of early pears and each presented with a magnificent bouquet; as our chaise had arrived, neatly repaired, we made our adieus amid mutual compliments and hopes of continuing our acquaintance thus accidentally formed. A few moments' ride brought us to "Dummer Academy,"—the Gov. Dummer Mansion House, the same fine specimen of colonial architecture it is to-day. The Academy was the old building, a gambrel-roofed, one-story structure with a low, dome-capped belfry facing the highway. This, the "Alma Mater" of David Emery, the Colman boys and other youthful friends, was to me a spot of much interest.

Crossing the bridge over the river Parker we soon found ourselves in the precincts of the "Farms." As Aunt Adams wished to call upon relatives of her late husband, we stopped at the residence of Mr. Israel and the widow Liffe Adams. We found Mr. and Mrs. Israel Adams seated either side of the wide fire-place, in which smouldered a few embers. Their daughter Polly was knitting by the window. She expressed great pleasure at seeing us, and as she had been a favorite schoolmate of David Emery's, and I had often heard him speak of her, I was happy to make the acquaintance of the belle and heiress of the neighborhood. Mrs. Liffe Adams and her daughter Eunice were weaving in a shop contiguous. Polly having summoned them to the house, a great rejoicing ensued. They were delighted to see their nephew's widow, and I was warmly welcomed. They all spoke with the greatest satisfaction of Mr. Noyes' good fortune in securing Aunt Hannah for a wife. After a pleasant call we took leave with a promise to take tea with them on the next afternoon. A few moments brought us to the Noyes homestead, a large, square house, surrounded by barns and other farm buildings. Maj. Noyes occupied the lower, and his son the upper half. I knocked at the front door, but as no one came I stepped into the hall; as my knock was evidently unheard, I made my way through a back room to the long kitchen and there I found the senior Mrs. Noyes. The old lady was washing the large hearth, exhibiting in the process an excess of neatness, which I never saw either before or since. She had gathered the remnants of the morning fire on a shovel and was washing every brick. I quite startled the good woman, but upon her learning who I was, and that Aunt Adams was waiting outside, she expressed much joy at our coming, and despatched the maid servant for Aunt Hannah, who was in the garden. My aunt came with all speed. As we were the first members of her family that she had seen since her marriage, her greeting was very cordial. The male members of her family were in the meadows, the children at school; as the school-house was at some distance they dined at their uncle Nat Moody's, whose residence was near to it, consequently we had a nice, easy time, all to ourselves. In the afternoon, Grandmam' Noyes and Miss Becky, a single daughter, joined us in Aunt Hannah's room. Between five and six the children came home, a nice girl of ten, quite a little "help" to her step-mother, and two bright boys, whose affections she had evidently won. At dusk the "men folks" arrived. The two gentlemen expressed great pleasure at meeting us. The major, a gallant man of the old school, like his son and the Rev Dr. Parish, was a great admirer of black eyes. He was pleased to be exceedingly complimentary, I saw that Aunt Hannah was a favorite with the old gentleman, as she evidently had become with the whole family. After tea, as it was a bright moonlight evening, we walked out to the family burial place, which was situated on a slight eminence in a pleasant grove back of the house.

The next afternoon, accompanied by aunt Hannah and Miss Becky Noyes, we paid the proposed visit to the Adams family. We enjoyed their company, and were most hospitably entertained. At tea we were joined by Mrs. Liffe Adams' son, Robert, a bashful and eccentric stripling of eighteen. Much to my amusement and that of my two aunts, every endeavor was put forth, by his mother and other relatives, to render the young man companionable to me. Sly promptings were given on every hand to induce him to show his gallantry, but the poor youth was sadly at a loss, completely discomfited. Mrs. Adams, acting, perhaps, upon the principle that children left alone the better facilitate their acquaintance, after tea took the others to look at her cheese. Poor Robert, thus cast upon his own resources, did his best at being agreeable, but his efforts were so ludicrous that, after a vain endeavor to maintain composure, I was obliged to rush into the front yard, under the pretence of looking at the sweet balm, but in reality to suppress my risibles. The rest joined me, and, as aunt Adams thought we had better return that night, we soon took leave. A pleasant ride, without any adventure, carried us home. Our visit had been most satisfactory, and we assured our friends that, however much others might doubt, we were certain that aunt Hannah had not mistaken her vocation.

CHAPTER XXI.

Aunt Susy Dole was a confirmed invalid, and sometimes had ill turns, when a watcher was required. At the period of Mr. Stickney's and the baby's illness I had been so much in the family that the sisters had been in the habit of sending for me at the slightest ailment. One sultry, foggy night, the first of September, a summons came to watch with aunt Susy. Our straw work had been unusually pressing, and I really felt unable to sit up all night. Aunt Sarah declared I should not go, "that Susy Dole no more needed a watcher than a cat needed two tails." Mother, who always considered every one's comfort before her own, thought I had better go. About eight o'clock I went. I found the brothers and sisters seated in the kitchen, the door being ajar into the room where aunt Susy lay in bed. After a little chat, a candle was placed on the round stand, when uncle Amos proceeded to read a chapter from the Bible. The old gentleman was troubled with a cough; he always kept a mug of colts-foot tea handy on the dresser. He would read a few verses and stop to cough; then taking a sip of the tea he would proceed, and in this way, the long chapter was at length finished. Then each rose and bowing over their chair, reverently joined in the long prayer, which, like the reading, was frequently interrupted by coughs and sips of the medicine. Uncle Amos would have been shocked at anything that bordered on ritualism. The bare mention of a liturgy was enough to raise the hair from his brow, yet, by custom, he had brought this daily prayer into a set formula, which scarcely varied from day to day. He prayed for every body and every thing: "The president, vice-president and both houses of congress; the governor, the lieut.-governor, the clergy, the colleges and schools; the aged, infirm and dying; the pensioners, the poor and afflicted; travellers by land and all those that go down to the sea in ships." The lengthy petition ended, the family retired and I entered upon my duty. Aunt Susy seemed very comfortable, said "her abb tea was all that she should need, but that must be kept hot." I added a few sticks to the smouldering fire, and placed a pewter porringer of balm tea on the embers. After inquiries respecting aunt Hannah and her new home, the invalid fell asleep. Screening the candle, I took a pile of "Newburyport Heralds," (uncle Amos was a constant subscriber to that paper), and whiled away a couple of hours; then aunt Susy awoke and demanded the tea; to my chagrin it was not warm enough to suit, and I was compelled to reheat it. When it was ready, my patient was again in sound slumber. Fearing that she might awake and ask for the tea, I kept up the fire until the heat became intolerable.

Tiptoeing into the kitchen, I opened the outer door, but was met by such a swarm of mosquitos, engendered by the vicinity of the pond, that it was instantly closed. I returned to the bedroom and sinking into aunt Susy's easy chair, unintentionally dropped asleep. When I awoke the room was pitchy dark, my head was in a whirl and every limb ached. I sprang for a candle, but was so turned round by the sudden awakening it was difficult to find the table; at length the candle, a small dip with a tow wick, was lightened, the fire replenished, and much to my relief the herb tea boiling when aunt Susy awoke. It suited this time. Dawn began to break, and aunt Judy relieved my vigil. The sick woman bade me good morning, with many encomiums upon my skill as a nurse, declared I had been the best watcher she had had. I arrived at home in time to assist in setting off father and the boys, who were going to Plum Island to rake the last freight of hay for that season. It was an exceedingly sultry morning, but about eleven o'clock a thunder shower came up, after which the wind changed to north-east: a drenching rain set in accompanied by a high wind, which, as the afternoon advanced, grew into a tremendous gale. We were much worried respecting father and the boys, as they did not return, but concluded that they had sought shelter at one of the two farm houses at the lower end of the island.

With some difficulty we managed to get the cows and tie them up in the barn. The milking and other chores done, we tried to pass a cheerful evening, but it did not avail, and a somewhat sleepless night followed. The morning broke cloudy and misty, but the wind had subsided. The cows had been put in a part of the field which had been railed off for fall feed. The bordering wall was lined by apple trees; so many apples had blown to the ground we dared not turn the cows to pasture till they were gathered. The grass and apples were cold and wet, and by the time I had finished picking them, a tooth that had been troublesome was aching excruciatingly. Father and the boys returned that afternoon. They had been subjected to a cold and wearisome experience. In company with numbers of other haymakers, they had received shelter at the "Cross Farm," and slept in the barn under an ox-cart. Happy at their safe return, I bandaged my face and essayed to sleep. It was useless. I tried cold water and hot, cloves, ginger, poultices, and everything that could be suggested, to relieve the pain, but in vain! Two decayed teeth ached with an intolerable persistency that no remedy would relieve, and I came to the conclusion that cold steel would be the only panacea. Tired as he had been, I was in such distress, my young brother Joseph roused himself, and, after an early breakfast, we set forth for Dr. Poore's residence on the main road. The doctor had gone into the pasture to fetch his horse. Mrs. Poore, who was a favorite cousin of my mother's, gave me a most sympathetic welcome. "It was a shame to lose two teeth; could not something be done to save them?" Glad as I should have been to have arrived at a contrary decision, I felt that they must come out, and the doctor, finding that the sight of him did not scare away the pain, concurred in this opinion. I was seated in an arm chair in the centre of the room, and Mrs.

Poore was directed to hold my head. A young lady school teacher, who was a boarder in the family, took a stool, and, placing it at my side, sat down to watch the doctor and the gum. I should have liked to have poked her over, but as neither the doctor nor Mrs. Poore entered any remonstrance at what I deemed an impertinence, of course I remained passive. At sight of the cruel-looking, old-fashioned instruments, my little brother turned pale, and I could not repress a shudder. Mrs. Poore gave me a sympathetic hug, and the doctor applied the cold steel. The instrument was found to be too large, and he proceeded to wind it with his bandanna. I thought of the addiction to snuff, but there was no time for squeamishness. The instrument was again on; a jam, a screw, a twist, a pull, and my molar flew across the room. The good doctor was triumphant — "such a splendid pull; I never had better success!"

My brother heaved a sigh of relief, the school mistress settled herself for another good look, kind Mrs. Poore handed a glass of water, then again pityingly took my head between her hands. More trouble with the instrument slipping, another jam, screw, and a crash that I thought lifted my scalp, and sent sparks flying from my eyes, this second tooth was broken even with the gum. After giving a few moments' rest, the doctor proceeded to pry out the root. He jammed and punched to no purpose, until nature could bear no more, and I sank back almost unconscious. My brother started up, nearly upsetting the school teacher in his eagerness, and vehemently protested against any further operation. Mrs. Poore thought he was right, and the doctor, somewhat reluctantly, desisted from his efforts to extract the root. It would "loosen and come out," he thought, but he feared I would suffer some time. I was too much exhausted to think; all I could do was to endure. The horse had to walk the most of the way home, as the least jar was excruciating. My face swelled fearfully, and my neck and shoulders were so stiff, I could not lie down for two or three nights; all the nourishment I could take was at the corner of my mouth from one of the old fashioned tea spoons. Weeks passed ere I could resume my wonted occupations. I had not fully recovered at Thanksgiving. As Nabby Smith had gone home and aunt Adams felt blue alone, father took me to pass the afternoon with her; David Emery had come to spend the festival at his grandfather's, and towards night he and uncle Joe Little came in with Lewis Hatch and William Smith; the two latter boarded with aunt Adams. The visitors received a cordial greeting, and my aunt insisted that uncle Joe and David should remain to tea. A merry time ensued; David amused us with the description of an adventure that he had experienced that morning. In a hurry to start for "Craneneck," he rose, the first in the house, at dawn. Finding no tinder in the tinder box with which to light the fire, he fixed the kindlings, and taking down the old "Kings Arm" from the brackets over the mantel, placed it across the andirons, and pouring a little powder into the pan, sprang the trigger — a bang, concussion that nearly sent him heels over head, while brick and mortar flew in every direction. Bump, bump, resounded from above, as the snoozers sprang from their beds, while

Mr. & Mrs. Colman rushed from their bedroom on the ground floor en dishabille.

"What is it, David?" shouted the old gentleman.

"My son, what have you done?" screamed his mother, while the remainder of the family rattled down stairs, querying "what is the matter?" The commotion subsided, explanation followed. The gun which David had supposed empty, Daniel had loaded the previous evening in order to fire a Thanksgiving salute in the morning.

"Well, we've had the salute," said his father, "a deuce of a salute; I hope you'r' satisfied;" and amid jokes and laughter the brick and mortar was cleared. The stout, old chimney had well withstood the charge, one jamb was somewhat shattered, but no great damage had been done; but Mrs. Colman concluded "that in future she would ensure a good stock of tinder, that no similar sportsman-like effort should be made in lighting the kitchen fire."

The young man was a good mimic, and possessed considerable theatrical talent, and he related this instance with such inimitable drollery, that the laugh which I was fain to indulge in, fairly took the twist from my jaw, and thenceforward my recovery was rapid.

CHAPTER XXII.

The wealth and superior attractions of Aunt Adams brought her many suitors, but for four years her heart remained constant to the memory of the early loved; then it began to be whispered that she showed an inclination to favor the suit of Mr. John Coker.

Robert Coker, yeoman, born in 1606, came to Newbury with the first settlers, and died May 19th, 1690, aged 84. His wife, Catharine, died May 2nd, 1678. Their children were Joseph, Sara, Benjamin and Hannah,

Joseph Coker married Sara Hathorne April 13, 1665. Children: Sara, who died November 30th, 1667, Benjamin, Sara and Hathorne.

Samuel Coker, son of Hathorne, owned an extensive tract of land at the north part of Newburyport.

Mr. Coker joined the society of "Friends," and his son, Thomas, who inherited the estate and erected several houses in that part of the town, was of the same society. The family burial place was in a lot on Washington, nearly opposite the head of Strong street. Thomas Coker married Sarah Greenleaf. John was their oldest son.

The family arms are:

ARGENT ON A BEND GULES, THREE LEOPARD'S HEADS OR. CREST,—A MOOR'S HEAD, COUPED AT THE SHOULDERS, FULL FACED PPR, WREATHED ABOUT THE TEMPLES.

For some years Mr. Thomas Coker

had cultivated a farm in the lower parish, Newbury, where he had recently died very suddenly. John thus became not only the staff of his widowed mother, but the head of a large family of young brothers and sisters. His filial and fraternal devotion won Mrs. Adams's regard. Handsome, intelligent, highly respected, and a practical farmer, the match appeared exceedingly proper, as the young man was every way qualified for a companion and protector to the youthful widow. The engagement was at length announced, but the marriage was not solemnized until the following October. The wedding was private, but the couple were the centre of observation, the next Sunday. "Walking out bride," was one of the customs of the time. Few finer looking couples ever paced up the aisle of the sacred edifice: the bridegroom with his nicely cued hair, and light drab surtout, the bride habited in a white, dimity flounced dress, a lilac satin; short pelisse, edged by rich black lace, and a salmon colored plush bonnet, surmounted by tossing white plumes.

Mr. Coker took his place most decorously as the head of the household, and he immediately instituted many improvements both within doors and without, the illness and death of the former proprietor having left the new buildings and other appurtenances of the farm in need of care and labor for completion.

I have previously mentioned that amongst the apprentices who came to the place with Mr. William Little was a youth by the name of Lewis Hatch. This young man, left an orphan when a mere child, had purchased his freedom when Mr. Little left his sister's residence, and then a youth of eighteen, he commenced business for himself, working in the shop on the place, and boarding with Mr. Adams.

Politics at this period waxed fierce and furious. John Coker was an enthusiastic "Jacobin," Lewis Hatch as strong a "Federalist." Constant disputes occurred, not pleasant in a household. Mr. Hatch concluded to locate elsewhere, and much as he was respected, Mrs. Coker was pleased at this determination.

Four miles from "Crane-Neck" was a crossing of roads called "New Rowley Corner;" near by resided Maj. Paul Nelson, a smart man, carrying on considerable business. Though a bachelor, he kept house on his estate, upon which was a large tannery. Amongst the appurtenances of the place was a small shoe-maker's shop, which Lewis Hatch hired, and commenced the shoe business on a small scale. In a short time he was joined by my uncle Joe. Little, both young men boarding in the family of Maj. Nelson. The business prospering, my uncle, Ben. Little, joined the firm, which hired the whole premises with the exception of the tannery. A housekeeper was procured, and Maj. Nelson in turn boarded with the young bachelors, who now had also several youths apprenticed to them, besides employing workmen outside.

As a matter of convenience and profit uncle Joe. Little conceived the idea of setting up a small grocery and general furnishing store. One of the front rooms of the house was fitted with shelves and other accommodations, and the goods were purchased. This shop-keeping immediately prospered. The workmen were pleased at being enabled to supply their household needs so easily, and as there had been no store for miles around, custom began to flock to the place, which even then wore a bustling air of prosperity.

It would have seemed but natural, as female cooperation was so necessary, that one at least of this trio of bachelors should seek a wife, and a legend is extant, that uncle Joe did for a time entertain some such idea. Before going to New Rowley, he had formed the acquaintance of a young lady, the teacher of the summer school in our district. The new firm manufactured for merchants in Salem and Boston, and as his grocery business increased, uncle Joe. made weekly trips to those cities, driving his team, which consisted of a two wheeled spring cart drawn by one horse, (four wheeled wagons did not come into use until a few years later).

The father of the young lady teacher kept a tavern on the route; thus my uncle had ample opportunity to renew his acquaintance with the daughter.

The young man from childhood had been addicted to absent fits of introspection, at these times he also had a habit of picking his nails. I have seen him stand ten minutes, wholly oblivious to the outside world, nervously twitching his fingers.

It was reported that one cold afternoon on his way home from Boston, Mr. Little called on the inn keeper's daughter. Unexpectedly opening the door to the private sitting room he briskly entered, but neither the lady nor the room bore the aspect of neatness to have been expected at that hour of the day and from one who had always seemed to pride herself upon her elegance. The story ran that though the young man had entered most cheerily, he suddenly grew silent and glum; refusing the chair offered, he took his stand back to the fire and fell into a brown study, his eyes fixed on vacancy, while his nails were picked most assiduously. A heat at his ankles roused him, and he found that in his abstraction he had burned the heels of his boots.

I never heard that the visit was renewed; every matrimonial inclination disappeared; Mr. Little became wholly immersed in his business, and Miss. Mary Hatch, a sister of Lewis Hatch, took her place as mistress of the bachelor establishment.

The New Rowley manufacturers were often hurried on orders. In the winter season, when the straw work was suspended, I often bound both boots and shoes for them; in an emergency I was their resource.

One afternoon at the period of which I am writing, in the early part of the week, uncle Joe. appeared bearing a hundred pairs of seal-skin boots, which he said must be corded and strapped by Saturday. At first I declared they could not be done in such a limited time, but after some demur, yielding to his ardent solicitation, I promised to do my best, and without the least delay set to work. It was a dirty disagreeable job; only love for my uncle, and a desire to promote his interest could have induced its undertaking. As it was, I stitched and stitched assiduously day after day, and the task was accomplished in the given time. The last stitch was just taken as uncle Joe. entered the door. He was accompanied by David Emery. Smut from head to foot I presented no very attractive aspect. The young man snatched the completed boot from my hand, and tossing it at uncle Joe, vehemently protested against his thus imposing on my good nature. The matter ended in a laugh, but thenceforward only the lighter sort of work was brought to me, and that only upon some sudden exigence.

In a few years the business had increased to such an extent that to better its accommodation a large store was erected exactly on "New Rowley Corner," which thereafter bore the designation of "Little's Corner." A house was also built for the convenience of the bachelor family. In a short time uncle Ben. Little put up a large dwelling house in the vicinity, and some indications of a match between himself and Miss Hatch were thought to be tangible. At this juncture Mr. Lewis Hatch was suddenly prostrated with typhoid fever. After a short illness he died ere he had reached his thirtieth birth-day. His was a short but active life, and his death caused a sad void amidst his limited but choice circle of friends, by whom his memory has been cherished with affectionate respect.

Miss Hatch, a delicate person, was overwhelmed by the death of her brother, and being a victim to disease, and though living to an advanced age, she ever after remained an invalid.

Business at "Little's Corner" rapidly increased, other buildings were erected, a village sprung up, and the nucleus for the now flourishing town of Georgetown was formed. Uncle Ben. and uncle Joe. have passed away, but their mantle has worthily descended to their nephews, Samuel Little and John Coker.

CHAPTER XXIII.

Amidst my first reccollections of the "Port," loom up drear and dread the jail, the whipping post was opposite, and the stocks on Water street just below Market square, and the workhouse on Federal street. Newbury had no poor-house, its paupers were let out in families. In this way most reliable servants for lighter work were often obtained. An old revolutionary soldier by the name of Mitchell resided in the family of Mr. Moses Colman for years. This veteran was held in high estimation by the three boys, to whom he became an unquestionable authority in field sports, the training of horses and dogs, and other masculine accomplishments, besides being a perfect encyclopœdia of knowledge in various departments of natural history, with a never failing stock of humorous anecdotes and tales, mingled with the sterner recital of privation, cold and hunger, battle and siege, with all the details, the light and the shade, the pomp, pageantry, glory and gore of the time that tried men's souls. Later, a woman, always termed "Old Mary," came into the household whom both children and grandchildren regarded as a sort of foster mother, and whose memory is still affectionately cherished.

In my more youthful days the roads were infested by tramps. Ugly looking men and women, begging their way from one place to another. The meeting of such people on my way to and from school was one of the terrors of my childhood. There was an old unoccupied house on the road, and I never passed it alone without accelerated pace and a quaking heart. Then, though the days of Salem witchcraft were ended and old women were no longer hung as witches, in every community there was one or more believed to possess the "evil eye," and in every house could be seen horse shoes above the doors, and other charms against their machinations. I vividly recall the mixture of awe and terror, with which I was wont to regard the large, quaint, red house on the lower corner of Market and High streets, famous in the annals of witchcraft. Here resided Goodwife Elizabeth Morse, who in 1680, "she not having the fear of God before her eyes, being instigated by the Divil, and had familiarity with the Divil contrary to the peace of our sovereign lord the king, his crown and dignity, the laws of God, and of this jurisdiction," was tried in Boston and sentenced to be hanged. Through the firmness of Gov. Bradstreet this sentence was commuted, and though Mrs. Morse lived an exemplary, christian life in her own house for many years, the stigma attached to her character had been transmitted through the succeeding generations. Tales of the "Goody," and the wonderful performances that had taken place at the "Morse House" were familiar legends, which, detailed of a winter's night, by a low burning candle, and smouldering fire, the blast shrieking round the large house and howling down the wide chimney, while the shadows deepened in the spacious room, and the tall clock in the corner ticked a solemn accompaniment to the low, tragic tones of the speaker, had often wrought an effect upon my imagination which time has failed to efface.

It would have been difficult to have ascertained how or why the females thus marked, had received the unenviable notoriety of witches. Generally they were persons of the lower class, some might have lost caste by youthful indiscretion, or by a somewhat dubious means of obtaining a present livelihood, but usually they were hard-working, inoffensive women, possessing a marked individuality, strong intellectual faculties, quick perception and keen wit, united to a firm will and independence of action, characteristics which, in some way, had brought upon them the ban of the community. The witch of the "Falls Parish," was an old woman called "Tuggie Noyes;" her real christian name was Margaret. I never heard how she obtained the nickname of Tuggie. I have only a faint remembrance of her, a dim recollection of stealing behind my mother to peep at the witch, as she bargained for some tobacco which my father had raised. I think this woman gained a livelihood by spinning and weaving, and she was frequently employed by Mrs. Moses Colman. I have often heard David Emery relate an incident of his boyhood by which his disbelief in witches was fully confirmed.

One cold winter morning, David and his chum Nate Perley were on their way to the old school-house at the corners, when they descried Tuggie advancing over the half-trodden path, the hood of her gray lambskin cloak drawn around her face, and a bunch of woolen yarn in her hand.

"There's the witch," Nate exclaimed, lamenting the lack of a sixpence to place in the path to stop her farther progress.

His companion expressed his credulity respecting such an effect, but nevertheless drew a sixpence from his pocket, which he adroitly dropped immediately before the old woman; she passed on directly over it with a curtsy and good day, and David again pocketed his coin, firm in the faith of Tuggie's innocence of any diabolical influence, with a full determination, never to believe in any witch, save the witch of Endor.

When I was six or seven years old, a young man in the neighborhood became insane. For a time he was a complete maniac, necessitating confinement, and a watchful attendance. Disease of the brain was not generally understood; if one became a victim of aberration of intellect, it was universally declared that they were bewitched, and the various charms, most supremely ridiculous, then in vogue, were immediately exercised to dispel the foul fiend. Young Edward Hills, having as it was declared fallen under the influence of the "evil eye," great were the efforts to discover the author of the spell by which he was bound. Suspicion pointed to two or three old women in that and the next parish, over whom a secret but strict surveilliance was instituted, while every test known in the annals of witch lore was put in requisition for the relief of the supposed bewitched youth.

The person held in the greatest distrust was a worthy hard working woman, residing a short distance from Mr. Hill's. Why or how she should have attained to the dubious honor of being considered an equestrienne of the broomstick I never could conceive, unless it was from a shrewd, far-sighted intellect, and a fearless and forcible expression of her convictions, a keen wit, and a somewhat sharp tongue, that usually, to use a familiar phrase, "hit the nail on the head."

Aunt Ruth Little believed in witches as religiously as she did in her bible — the least doubt was considered rank heresy. The supposed witch was employed by the families in the vicinity both in spinning and weaving, and upon learning Edward Hill's situation Mrs. Little commenced a strict scrutiny over her neighbor. One evening that spring a young heifer unused to the process of milking became a little fractious and kicked over the milk pail. Aunt Ruth instantly declared her bewitched, and rushing to the barn armed with her sharp shears, she clipt a few hairs from the animal's tail, which were flung upon the fire. A fortnight after the supposed witch came in with her hand bandaged, she had burned it a few nights previous with the warming-pan. The expression of horror that stole over aunt Ruth's face at this announcement would have established the reputation of a tragic actress. "Sartinly she had had her suspicions, but r'aly they had never amounted to conviction till then; to think that by burning the hair from the heifer's tail the hussy should get her hand scorched by the warming-pan!"

In vain both her husband, the hired man and David Emery, all declared that the incident respecting the heifer took place more than a week prior to the accident by the warming-pan, aunt Ruth was not to be silenced. "She knew black from white, and when her convictions were settled they were settled."

After a time Mr. Hill became perfectly sane. By trade a joiner, he married and settled on the family homestead; years after, a few years prior to my marriage, he was again attacked by insanity. For a time he was extremely violent, so much so that he was chained to the floor of the parlor, which had been denuded of the furniture and the windows boarded to the upper panes. Though this system was rather calculated to enhance than repel the malady, after a time the disease assumed a milder type, and the maniac again took his place in the household, but to the end of a long life, his brain continued clouded. For months he would remain indoors, quiet and silent, then suddenly become the impersonation of activity, brimming over with a crazed wit, that was as humorous as it usually was harmless. At this second period of insanity, the world had sufficiently advanced in knowledge to place the affliction in the appropriate category; only a few, like aunt Ruth, still adhered to the witch doctrine, but the old ideas were held with such tenacity that Parson Woods was called to exorcise the foul fiend, and one watcher was nearly frightened out of his wits at the family cat, supposing her to be some witch's familiar.

As the spring advanced, the young men in the vicinity volunteered to do the ploughing and planting for Mr. Hill. I often went to the Byfield factory on business, and Mrs. Hill told my brother James that she was desirous that I should execute a commission for her the next time I rode thither. Accordingly, one pleasant evening, I went in to receive her orders. Mrs. Hill was milking, the children were with her. Mr. Hill sat before a light fire which was smouldering in the kitchen fireplace. Seeing that he was alone, I hesitated on the threshold; looking up, the lunatic with a pleased expression bade me enter and be seated. "His old woman would be in directly." Squinting up one eye, with a wise shake of the head, he added, "I know what she wants of you, Sallie. She thinks, wonderful woman, that it is a profound secret, but she has sent for you to buy the cloth at the factory for me a pair of breeches, and she has the money laid by to pay for it. Draw up your chair, Sallie, you are not afraid of me. I sha'n't scare you as I did that New Hampshire chap that boarded at Deacon Tenney's last winter. I saw he was scared the moment he came in, and I determined to have a bit of fun. Didn't I kick up a ringtum? The big lout was e'en jest frightened out of his senses; he daresn't stay in the room, but every two minutes he would open the door a crack, and squeak out, 'won't you have a leetle caffee, Mr. Hill—won't you have a leetle caffee?' I got so out of patience, I told him to hold his infernal tongue or I would 'caffee' him with a vengeance! I silenced him, but the darned fool took our old Suke for a witch, declared a strange cat flew into my room through the key hole, when it was only our old cat who pushed in beside him, while he was holding the door and bawling 'caffee.' They say I was bewitched, Sallie. It was sport to make folks think so. Wasn't it fun to make folks' eyes stick out? Aunt Ruth thought she knew. Oh yes, she is the elect lady! She knows; so they sent for Parson Woods. I told him he had such an acquaintance with his Satanic Majesty, his services would have been especially efficacious if needed, but I scarcely thought he would find any divil to exorcise. If he could he was at liberty to pitch him into my pig-sty." Giving me another of his peculiarly knowing squints, he continued, "Between you and I, I think the

Lord was rather hard upon that Gadarene. He must have taken him out of a good round sum. I have been calculating," he added, pointing to some chalk marks by the fire-place, "but as the account only states the number, and not the value per head, I am unable to ascertain the loss. The fact was, Sallie, the Parson came too late, and so I informed him. I told him the witches were dead. I saw them one moonlight night piping and dancing up "Crane-neck road." Old women on broomsticks, and young gals kicking up their heels, old Nick ahead leading the way. Fust they stopped at yer uncle Enoch Little's, but he swore so fast, the Divil gin in, and the gang trooped into uncle John's. Mr. Little was sitting afore the fire toasting fust the palms then the backs of his hands. He looked 'round, held out one hand, then the other, and said, 'yes, yes—yes, yes,' so old Nick struck up again, and on they squirled to your house. Mr. Sam. Smith was down from Vermont, singing Methody hymns so loud they turned over to uncle Thurrel's.

The old man driving up old 'White' in the cider mill, too much hurried to salute his fust cousin, he hollered, 'Terap, Terap,' so lustily, the whole batch scampered off hilter skilter down 'South End,' across 'Crane meadow,' and before they could fetch up, they rushed headlong into 'Crane pond,' and that was the end of the witches."

With this announcement Mr. Hill gravely surveyed the opposite wall in silence, and I indulged in the merriment his apt description of the peculiar traits of the individuals visited by the witches had exacted. Suddenly my companion started from his reverie, and exclaiming that his boot hurt him, drew it from his right foot; having also removed his stockings, part of another stocking foot was disclosed; taking this off, he held up his foot, the toes covered by the thumb and fingers of buckskin glove, and asked, "if I should think that would feel comfortable?"

Answering in the negative, I inquired why he had thus bundled up his toes? Vouchsafing no reply, he slowly and sedately drew off first the thumb and next the fingers, flinging them into the fire with a muttered invocation as each fell upon the coals, and as the last curled upon the embers, he quickly turned, and with a most quizzical look said; "David would get credit in a steeple chase, 'tisn't every one that could leap the wall as he did last winter, but he broke his shaft."

I made no answer, and pretended not to understand.

"You needn't make believe you don't comprehend what I mean. You know last winter when Tea street was blocked up and the path led through my field, David Emery mistook and took a flying leap over the wall above the house instead of going below through the bars. He thought no one knew it. If the windows were boarded up I heard him. He broke his shaft I know. I wanted to go out to help him, but they said no one was there. I was bewitched. There was a line in the sleigh box to tie up the shaft. David tied it together; then I heard the bells as he drove up the hill. David says old Mitchell has taught him to always go armed and equipped. That is a grand horse, and David is a good horseman; not one in a thousand could have cleared that wall as he did. Oh, David's a trump! But you do not know of whom I am speaking! You know nothing of the gentleman nor his proceedings!" and with a prolonged laugh and most emphatic grimaces the lunatic pulled on his stocking and boot. Mrs. Hill came in as she gave me her commission. I repeated what her husband had told me. She expressed great surprise, and said he must have guessed her intentions,as she had never mentioned them. His intuition and cunning were remarkable; she sometimes thought that she must join with aunt Ruth and pronounce him bewitched.

CHAPTER XXIV.

That spring David Emery made his first and last sea voyage. Though this short trip comprised the whole of his sea faring life, it brought that which many a veteran sailor who has circumnavigated the globe has failed to experience — the horrors of a shipwreck.

Business suddenly summoned the young man to Eastport, District of Maine. He expected to be absent a month. In about three weeks I received a letter. It had been long on the road, as in those unsettled regions the mail was chiefly transported in saddle bags by a carrier on horseback. David wrote that we might expect him by the middle of June. Friday, the sixteenth of June, dawned overcast and sultry; scarcely a leaf stirred through the day, and the night came on murky and oppressive. About midnight I was awakened by the wind, a gust struck with great force against the long, sloping, back roof. There was a furious squall for a few moments; while the rain came in a torrent, the wind slightly abated, but a severe north-east storm set in, which continued until noon Saturday.

As we knew David must be near the coast, great anxiety was felt respecting him. Sunday passed without tidings, but Monday morning my brother Joseph learned at the grist mill in Byfield, that he had been cast away on Plum Island, and that his brother, Jeremiah Colman, brought him to his father's on Sunday. Mr. Perley, from whom the news was obtained, reported that no injury had been received to life or limb, "but he did wish we could have seen the figure David cut; his clothes, especially his hat, all filled with lint from the sails, was a sight to behold."

In the afternoon the young man drove over, looking none the worse for his disaster. After father had drawn a mug of his best cider, the traveller gave us a description of his adventures. Though the schooner in which he was forced to take passage was old and dirty, the trip to Eastport was both quick and pleasant; his speculation succeeded, and he was most hospitably entertained by most agreeable people. Business called him to a new settlement up the St. Croix river. The only means of transportation was by a birch bark canoe, paddled by an Indian. The red-skin belonged to a tribe living above Eastport; he had come to the town to procure the wherewithal to celebrate the nuptials of a daughter; an addition to his purse was acceptable, and he readily agreed to take the young man up the river that day and down the next.

His directions as he seated his

passenger in the bottom of the canoe were most strict and emphatic. "Sit straight, keep arms so, keep quiet, canoe go over just like dat," he said, snapping his fingers. "Me drown one white man, me never get no more white man to paddle."

Knowing the nature of the frail bark Mr. Emery comforted himself with such discretion as to win the encomiums of his companion, eliciting grunts of approbation.

The day wore on. Hour after hour they glided up the broad, beautiful stream, bordered by the primeval forest. The grave, taciturn Indian bending to his task, the silence of the still June day unbroken, save by the dip of the paddle, the note of a bird, or the far away cry of some wild animal in the distance.

Hungry and thirsty, weary from the cramped position, near sunset the young man joyfully descried a clearing upon the bank, a little wharf projecting into the river, and a clump of buildings in the back ground.

Upon landing Mr. Emery learned that the gentleman he had come hither to seek was in Boston. A representative from the "District of Maine," he had gone thither to attend the General Court, which at that time commenced its sittings at "Election," which was on the last Wednesday in May. Though the mistress of the mansion expressed regret that her husband could not have the pleasure of entertaining the guest, he received the assurance that she possessed full power to facilitate the errand which had brought him there. Upon Mr. Emery's expressing his fears that his boatman might be an annoyance, she bade him "have no concern, as she often entertained the Indians of the vicinity; had a back room and blankets for their especial accommodation."

The row back to Eastport was made in safety. The Indian had taken a fancy to his passenger, and invited him to his daughter's wedding; press of business prevented the acceptance of this invitation, though it would have given the young man pleasure to have been present at such a novel entertainment. The Indian having made his purchases, a barrel of flour, one cwt. of pork, a keg of molasses, and two gallons of rum, took leave; having been presented with a few trinkets for the bride, the gratified redskin under the influence of gratitude and usquebaugh, affectionately hugged his "white brother," and with grunts of satisfaction seated himself amidst his possessions and slowly paddled homeward.

Upon introduction to a young French priest, the cure of a Catholic mission up the river, Mr. Emery received an invitation to visit the station, which he did the next Sunday in company with a party of ladies and gentlemen. The church and mission house which stood in the midst of the Indian village, were heavy structures of rough stone, the surrounding huts were of slabs and boards, with garden patches showing rude attempt at cultivation. The church was well filled, many of the worshippers having come a long distance through the forest. Several of the women had pappooses strapped on their shoulders in blankets. The men were tall and athletic, the elder women somewhat homely, but the younger ones rather good looking, some of the girls were decidedly pretty. Most of the women were gay with gew-gaws and feathers, their shapely feet showing to great advantage in their elaborately ornamented deerskin moccasins. His companion of the canoe was the first to greet Mr. Emery. His delight at again seeing his "white brother" was warmly expressed, and he hastened to fetch the bride and bridegroom and the other members of his family. The young cure was evidently beloved and respected, his flock were quiet and devout through the service. The party were hospitably entertained by the priest, who in the afternoon, in deference to his guests, preached a fine sermon in English—that in the morning had been delivered in French. This was Mr. Emery's introduction to that church which he had been taught to shun and abhor, but it gave a pleasing impression which ever after remained.

The second week in June the Lucy Ann set sail for Newburyport. The crew consisted of the skipper and three men; there were two passengers beside Mr. Emery, a Mr. Little, an Irishman by birth, and at that time doing business in Boston, and a young man, belonging in Newburyport, by the name of Richardson. Off Boon Island the schooner was becalmed for several days and the passengers took the opportunity to visit a farm-house there. The sixteenth the night closed in dark and foggy. Mr. Emery was awakened by the squall. Amid a terrible pitching, snapping, creaking and flapping, the passengers made their way on deck. The rain poured like a flood, it was difficult to sustain a foothold, everything was flying in every direction. The deck load of wood and bark was pitching hither and thither, pieces of bark being hurled mast high. The squall subsided, but the storm came on fierce and terrific. The skipper thought he was in the vicinity of Portsmouth, and every effort was made to clear the coast. Heavier grew the sea, stronger the blast. Sea after sea swept the deck, the roaring billows dashing to the mast head, raged around the frail craft, phosphorescent crested, one sheet of flame. At length, to everyone's relief, the day dawned, but still the mist and spray shut in the sight. Suddenly came the cry, "a sail ahead;" the fog at that moment slightly cleared, and in affrighted tones, the captain ejaculated, "My God! It is Newburyport lights."

He was an Eastern man, unacquainted with the coast; turning to his passenger, he demanded, "Emery, what am I to do?"

The young man remembering Hampton rocks, replied, "Keep her off, run to the leeward, clear the bar if possible."

The captain "inquired if he could make Cape Ann harbor." Mr. Emery thought not, and shortly a tremendous sea which carried away the main boom settled the question. The weather had begun to clear, Mr. Emery could discern that they were nearly abreast of the Plum Island hotel, and he advised beaching the craft immediately. The helm was turned, she swung slowly 'round and headed for the shore. Those acquainted with the coast in a teriffic northeaster will appreciate the situation. On she went, thrown forward by the waves. A tremendous bump, then she swung back, but the next sea took her and with a second bump and bang, which carried the foremast and mainmast by the board, the Lucy Ann settled into the sand, her aqueous career forever ended.

The storm abated, towards noon the

rain ceased, and preparations were made to get a line on shore. Mr. Clifford, the landlord of the hotel, had espied the schooner, and with his boy was on the beach ready to render assistance, but who was the one to breast that thunderous surf? The lot fell upon a stalwart sailor who had been caught stealing from the passengers. Stripped to his shirt and drawers, a rope secured around his waist, the stout fellow plunged into the swirl of waters, and, after a strenuous struggle, almost exhausted, he at length reached the land. The others prepared to follow. There was valuable property in the cabin; Mr. Little had several thousand dollars on board, the other passengers a considerable sum, all in specie. It was thought that the hull would hold together. Mr. Emery went below to cord his trunk more securely, there he found young Richardson tying up a hundred silver dollars in a bandanna pocket-handkerchief. Mr. Emery vainly tried to persuade the foolish fellow to return the money to his box, but he persisted in taking it on deck, where the first wave burst the frail envelope and a hundred silver dollars were added to the treasures of the deep.

Mr. Little, not a swimmer, was fearful that he could not reach the shore by the line, but being duly encouraged a successful attempt was made, and the whole five reached terra firma without accident.

Refreshed and dried, as the weather had cleared and the tide turned, with the aid of Mr. Clifford's horse and cart the articles were taken from the schooner and brought safely to the hotel. Nothing was lost but Richardson's silver. Mr. Clifford took the skipper to town. Mr. Little was so anxious that Mr. Emery should remain with him over night that the young man somewhat reluctantly consented. The merchant had made arrangements to go into business in Eastport, and he was solicitous to remove all traces of the disaster from his clothes and papers, in order that his wife should know nothing of it, as, if she did, he feared he never would be able to remove her from Boston.

During David's absence, his brother, Jeremiah Colman, had been married to Miss Mary Chute, daughter of Deacon James Chute of Byfield. Mr. Colman had been established in the butchering business in Newburyport for some time, and the young couple had set up housekeeping in half of the Pearson house on Charter street. Learning what had befallen David, Jerry drove to the Island and insisted on taking him to his house, where Mrs. Colman received him with sisterly affection, and every effort was made for his refreshment and comfort.

The hulk after lying some time in the sand was eventually broken up. The vessel had been insured at Newburyport, and at first some had demurred respecting paying the insurance, but upon farther investigation it was promptly handed over.

CHAPTER XXV.

I have stated that Mr. Benjamin Colman purchased "Slade's meeting-house," and having moved it near his residence, which was in the vicinity of the Byfield parsonage, fitted the building for a seminary. The prospectus of the Female Academy, Byfield, published in the "Newburyport Herald," enumerates "Grammar, Arithmetic, Geography, Rhetoric, Composition, Painting and needle-work," as the branches taught. It adds: "It is expected that a gentleman of christian education will, generally, every day visit the Seminary, and if occasion require, lend assistance in teaching the higher branches of study, or give instruction on those topics which may promote the general object of female education." Miss Rebecca Hardy was the first teacher, Miss Rebecca Hazeltine succeeded as principal, and her younger sister, Ann, afterward Mrs. Judson, one of the first American missionaries to India, acted as assistant. A school of from forty to fifty pupils was gathered, young ladies from the wealthier families in the neighborhood and surrounding country, with others from places more remote. The summer of which I am writing there were several from New Hampshire, and the interior towns of Massachusetts. Some of the older pupils were affianced to clergymen, and had placed themselves under Miss Hazeltine's instruction, the better to qualify themselves for the dignified and responsible position of a minister's wife. Amongst these was Miss Lucy Brown, afterwards Mrs. Demond of the upper parish in West Newbury.

The Misses Hazeltine and some half dozen of the pupils boarded with Dr. Parish, a number were accommodated in the families of Messrs. Benjamin and Moses Colman, the others were located in the vicinity. Miss Lucy Brown boarded with Mr. Moses Colman, and she became such a favorite that in after years her sojourn in the family was often referred to with pleasure.

According to the prospectus, clergymen frequented the school to lecture and attend to its interests. To young students about entering the ministry this seminary was a special attraction. The pupils were often in a flutter of excitement over this and that young minister, and several engagements were formed. One morning a very piously disposed youth appeared, whom the principal introduced as the Rev. Mr. ——, adding, "that having determined to consecrate his life to the conversion of heathen in foreign lands, he had come to enquire if any one of the young ladies present could so far deny herself and take up her cross as to accompany him as his soul's partner in his work for Christ and Him crucified. If either of the misses felt that she could do so, put her whole heart into the holy work, she would please rise." As the sound died on the teacher's lips, up jumped every girl in the room. All were ready to be given as lambs to the sacrifice. After much suppressed laughter, some blushes and confusion, the matter was deferred to another time, but in a few weeks the missionary bore away a bride.

From time immemorial it had been the custom for parties to visit Plum Island, in September, when the plums were ripe. Families joined throughout the neighborhood, or the young men and maidens, in as smart turnouts as could be secured, gaily hied, in a long procession, to spend a day or an afternoon in innocent amusement. Several parties of married people in Byfield had made this annual excursion, and as some of the young ladies at the Seminary from the interior towns, who had never seen the sea, had expressed a desire for the ride, the young gentlemen of the parish resolved themselves into a committee to make the necessary arrangements for a Plum Island party. Pains were taken to make it in every respect a first-class affair, the most perfect etiquette being observed in the invitations and arrangements. The intelligence of what was afoot, reached the Seminary a day or two prior to the issue of the invitations, making quite a stir amongst the pupils. The preceptress made no objection to the proposed recreation, but the younger assistant, Miss Ann, or as she was then termed Miss Nancy, set up such a violent opposition that it reached the ears of the gentlemen. Amongst the most prominent of the Byfield beaux, was Joseph Noyes, son of Mr. Lemuel Noyes. Of a wealthy family and liberally educated, with a pleasing person and address, this young man had been selected as the most suitable escort for Miss Nancy Hazeltine, but upon learning her disapproval of the party, he paid his devoirs elsewhere, and several of the girls sought Dr. Parish's advice respecting the propriety of accepting their invitations. The Doctor said go. "He was proud and pleased that the young men of his society had thus given them the opportunity to view the beauty, wonder and sublimity of the mighty ocean." That summer Mr. Moses Colman had purchased a new chaise. This stylish vehicle, the hight of ton, had a square, canvas covered top, with a body painted in bright vermillion, the rest of the wood-work dark brown, the lining and cushions were of drab broadcloth, and an oilcloth covered the floor. David Emery owned a horse; Daniel Colman would take his father's, but which should have the chaise? Poor Mr. Colman puzzled over this problem all one morning. At length a happy idea suggested itself which was made known at the dinner table. Much to his son's astonishment the old gentleman, in his loud, cheery tones, abruptly exclaimed: "Boys the one that carries the best girl to Plum Island shall have the new chaise."

An addition was building to Mr. Colman's house: at the table were two joiners from West Newbury, Mr. Jonathan Chase and Daniel Silloway. Before the disconcerted young men could reply, Mr. Chase exclaimed: "Then David must have the chaise, for he will take Sallie Smith, and she is the best girl in West Newbury." "Good, good," the gentlemen replied with delight. David shall have the chaise. Daniel, as soon you have swallowed your dinner go over to Mose Dole's and hire the best chaise he has."

Chaise making had already become a thriving business in West Newbury, but Mr. Moses Dole of Byfield did most of the blacksmith work. The different artisans often clubbed together to build a lot of chaises, which were divided amongst them; this caused Mr. Dole to usually have a number of these vehicles for sale or to let.

The anticipated morning at length dawned clear and bright, a lovely September day. Mrs. Colman had insisted that I should come over to Byfield and dine. David came for me about ten o'clock. The new chaise was resplendent, and "Bob," a chubby sorrel horse had been groomed to match, and the silver mounted harness was as lustrous as whiting could polish. David in a handsome new suit looked as elegant as his equipage. White cambric or dimity was the fashionable dress for such an occasion. I wore white cambric, and a straw bonnet trimmed with a broad, white, lutestring ribbon.

David was in high spirits. He had just returned from Boston, and entertained me during the ride with a description of his visit. He had dined with his friend, Charles Parsons, at his father's, Judge Parsons' mansion. Charles had greatly diverted his visitor by introducing his youngest brother as, "this is our Thof, a great sarpint, just like pa."

At dinner the judge had been especially entertaining. After minute inquires respecting his boyhood's home, he fell to recounting anecdotes of his school days. The parsonage boys, as is proverbial of minister's sons, had been great rogues.

"One day in mid winter their teacher was invited to dine at the parsonage. He was a self-sufficient, pompous coxcomb, much disliked by his pupils, and the minister's boys determined upon a practical joke. The snow was frozen hard, and the master, to shorten the distance, had come across lots from his boarding place. After dinner, while the pedagogue was sipping hot punch, and smoking a pipe with their father, his hopeful pupils proceeded to crack the ice in a small stream which their teacher would pass on his way home. This accomplished, they hid amidst some alders. It was a tedious while to wait, for the punch and tobacco were good, the minister entertaining, and his parlor warm and pleasant. At length towards dusk their patience was rewarded. The lord of the birch was descried approaching, swinging his cane, full of self-importance and good cheer. Proud of having dined at the parsonage, he strutted forward with an increased assumption of arrogance, dressed in his gold-laced cocked hat, velvet coat and breeches, silk stockings, and gaiters. On he came, his head high in air, his cane twirling from his fingers, on — on — crack — crackle — splash — splurge — kersouse went the discomfitted Dominee knee deep in the brook, much to his chagrin and ire, and to the huge delight of the watchers amid the alders.

There were several sons, and one of the younger boys having inherited all the worn, dog-eared school books of his elder brothers, determined that they should descend no farther; so as fast as a leaf was committed to memory he tore it out and crammed it into a hole in the wall beside his desk, thus at the end of the study the book was minus, excepting covers. Lem. Noyes, a somewhat loutish, dull boy, often became a butt for their jokes. They had excited his wrath, and he had threatened to thrash them. He was larger and stronger than the minister's sons; they knew they stood no chance in an encounter of fisticuffs, so they concocted a plan to get the better of their school-mate. In the vicinity of the school house was a tan yard, and having laid some loose boards over one of the vats, they challenged Lem. to a race. The unsuspecting youth eagerly joining in the sport, of course was permitted to get ahead; proud of his agility, the poor fellow rushed forward with a tremendous effort, to suddenly find himself lying among the hides. Amongst the scholars was a negro boy. Most of the families in Byfield in the olden time held one or more slaves, and there was usually quite a sprinkling of the sable hue amongst the pupils of the district school. The boys under pretence of dressing the darky's head saturated his wool with oil, then they put him up to some prank for which he was sure to receive punishment. The teacher was the one who had received the cold bath, a great dandy, always foppishly attired. Coming up the aisle and noticing the delinquent he gave the little nig a sound cuff in the side of the head which spattered the oil all over his fine clothes. The master in impotent rage glanced over the school house. The parson's boys were the impersonation of serious studiousness, and the other scholars, though wholly innocent of the trick, but many of whom having witnessed the transaction were on the broad grin, received the castigation which was so richly deserved elsewhere.

I was greatly amused at these stories, and the ride seemed unusually short. Some ten years previous Newbury had received an heir, a two years old boy of African lineage. What was to be done with this waif? The overseers of the poor met to decide. It was customary to put such children, to remain until twenty-one, into a family, which received a small compensation from the town until the child was seven years old; after that his services were considered a sufficient remuneration. Somebody must take little Charles Fields, but where could this somebody be found? Mr. Colman's sons always averred, "that father was never satisfied unless he had a parrot, a monkey and a nigger." The black baby with his round woolly head, shining eyes and glistening teeth, fairly won the benevolent gentleman's heart, and as no one else offered, he armfulled up little Charley, and an hour later, much to Mrs. Colman's astonishment, he placed the boy in her lap, with the injunction "to take care of the little rascal." The command was faithfully executed. Charles received every privilege that had been accorded to the sons of the family, with the exception of the academic course at Dummer Academy. I am sorry to say that a poor return was received for this trouble and care. The little black rascal grew up a big rascal, causing much vexation until his decease, which occurred in middle life. At this time he was a stout lad of thirteen. Cap in hand, with a profound obeisance and a great display of ivory, he swung aside the gate at the head of the avenue as we drove up.

Mrs. Colman gave me a cordial, and Mr. Colman a rapturous greeting. "Had he not always promised that I should be David's little wife?" I was introduced to Mr. and Mrs. John Colman. John, the oldest son of Deacon Colman, had married a lady by the name of Danforth. This couple signalized themselves by their migratory life, during which they made thirty-two removals. Some half dozen of these were between Byfield and Maine. Mrs. Colman used to boast that she had crossed the ocean between Newburyport and the District of Maine fourteen times, and she would add, "the happiest time in my life was when I was midway in these removals; at that point I was rejoicing at having left the old place and looking forward with hope to the new."

As was natural, these rolling stones gathered little moss, but always sanguine and cheerful, they passed as happy and contented a life as either of the family. At this time they were paying a farewell visit to their brother prior to one of their flittings eastward.

During the Revolutionary war Deacon Colman had filled an army order for boots and shoes. These with other clothing Moses had taken in mid-winter to New Jersey in a covered cart drawn by a span of horses.

During dinner Mr. Colman gave a graphic description of the ragged and desolate appearance of our troops, on his arrival at Morristown, just at the close of that winter so memorable for suffering, and the joy with which his arrival was hailed.

"Yes," exlaimed old Mitchell, "and the shoes were a good honest make, but the stockings, most of them, were a darned cheat, and the woman that could thus deceive a poor soldier must have a mighty small soul." The hose had been knit loose, then stretched on a board fashioned like a last; when washed they shrunk so as to be scarcely wearable. This was in the good old times; human nature is much alike in all generations.

The rendezvous for the party had been appointed at Deacon Ben. Colman's. From a dozen to fifteen chaises formed in procession, and gaily trotted to the island. Our visit was expected. Mr. Clifford and his waiters were profuse in their attention. We were ushered into the parlor, wine having been served, we proceeded amid much fun and frolic, to make our way to the beach over the loose sand. Joseph Noyes escorted a Miss Parkis, the daughter of Dr. Parkis, a distinguished physician of Hanover; and Daniel Colman, Miss Betsy Smith, a great witch, and the only daughter of a wealthy family in Dover. Miss Parkis and Mr. Noyes were very merry at Miss Nancy Hazeltine's expense. As Mr. Noyes drove up to take Miss Parkis, Miss Hazeltine, glancing from the window, exclaimed, "there's Joe. Noyes, he has come to take me to Plum Island, but he will find I do not countenance such frivolity." To her chagrin Miss Parkis tripped down the stairs, Mr. Noyes assisted her into the chaise, and with a polite salutation to Miss Nancy at the window, drove away.

After a merry afternoon, we returned to the hotel, where an elegant supper awaited us, spread in the upper hall. At its close, as it was near sunset, the chaises were ordered. At Newburyport Mr. Emery and myself bade the others good evening, and took the direct route for West Newbury.

The young ladies at the Seminary were so delighted with their excursion, that girl-like they gave enthusiastic descriptions of the ride. This brought such severe animadversions from the assistant teacher, that her pupils, some of them as old, or older than herself, lost patience. The matter spread amongst the gentlemen, and the big scamps, in the total depravity of their unregenerate hearts, planned a practical joke at the expense of the lady whom they regarded as righteous overmuch. I never knew who originated the plot, but strongly suspect that it might have sprung from the creative brains of Miss Betsy Smith and Daniel Colman. Few that only knew the staid man in after years, could comprehend what a gay fellow he then was.

In Mr. Colman's employ was a young man, the son of a deceased pastor of Rowley, John Jewett, a very clever, but rather simple fellow, who was informed that he ought to invite Miss Hazeltine to go to Plum Island. "She received no invitation at the time of the party; for the honor of Byfield this oversight ought to be repaired. A clergyman's son, he was the one for her escort. He should have the new chaise and David's horse, the most stylish equipment."

At first John demurred, but his courage having been raised by the bribe of a pound of tobacco, an article of which he was inordinately fond, a few evenings after the party, the young man all in his best — and he always dressed handsomely—dashed up to Dr. Parish's door, in the unexceptionable turnout, and inquired for Miss Nancy Hazeltine. Upon that lady's appearance, in his most courtly manner, and he was very well bred, he requested the pleasure of her company on a ride to Plum Island the next afternoon. Miss Nancy drew back in surprise and horror, and with an indignant exclamation, slammed the door in the face of the astonished gallant, who after standing a moment on the door-stone in bewildered astonishment, returned to the chaise, and drove home with curses both loud and deep upon his lips. Miss Nancy sought her room in such an hysterical excitement that it roused the household.

Dr. Parish was subject to slight fits of illness, accompanied by great depression of spirits,— his hypo spells, his wife denominated them. He had been suffering from one of these attacks, had been confined to his bed several days, but upon learning what had occurred he rose, and hurrying on his clothes, summoned the young teacher to his presence. She appeared irate and sobbing. Bidding her be seated, the clergyman exclaimed, "Why, Miss Nancy, I am surprised at this excitement. Do not let your feelings be wounded! John Jewett is a very estimable young man, very estimable. He is a minister's son, Miss Nancy, his father was a very worthy man, old Parson Jewett of Rowley. Dry your eyes, and compose your spirits, my dear, no harm is done, John is a deserving young man, a minister's son, Miss Nancy, a minister's son."

Somewhat mollified, Miss Nancy retired, and the clergyman called for tea and toast, entirely cured of his hypo.

CHAPTER XXVI.

My father had reached his goal. By industry and economy the whole of the ancestral acres had been secured. His heart was in his work; he was a good agriculturalist, and had given great attention to fruit culture. He had planted and grafted some two or three hundred apple trees; there was quite a variety of pears and a thriving peach orchard on the place. Grapes grew spontaneously. The stone walls were covered with vines which bore luxuriantly large, luscious clusters both of the purple and white grapes. There was a difference in the quality of this wild fruit, some being equal if not superior to that produced in our gardens at the present time. The farm on the September of that year presented a tempting array of fruit. The trees never looked finer than on the twelfth of the month. The day was warm and cloudy; at dusk it began to rain. I had a piece of linen whitening on the grass; fearing it might mildew, I went to take it in, and was struck by the sultry stillness of the night. After I went to my chamber, I sat some time at the open window enjoying the quiet rain which was falling steadily. About midnight I was awakened by the unbarring of the front door, and mother screaming "something terrible is coming!" as she hastily opened and closed it. At the moment a strange rush and roar struck my ear, rapidly advancing. I could liken it to nothing but wagons rattling over frozen ground, but it more nearly resembled the noise of a railroad train. Lightning flashed, thunder pealed, and rain poured in torrents. Springing from bed, I seized my sister, a girl of ten, and with the half awakened child descended the stairs, and passing through the front entry, entered the west room. The rush, roar, crash and din are wholly indescribable, accompanied by such dense darkness, that not a thing was discernible. Half way across the front room, we were stopped by a terrible bang and crack, at the same moment a missile was hurled through the broken window, which, striking Susan, fell in the fire-place opposite. The child shrieked fearfully: dragging her by the arm, I rushed into the kitchen screaming, "Sukey is dead, Sukey is dead!"

The whole family had collected in the room. The cry was for a light, but in the fright and confusion not a candle-stick of the number always there could be found. I mustered sufficient composure to bring a candle from the box in the cellar-way; raking open the embers on the hearth it was quickly lighted. Speedily as this had been effected, by the time I had put it in the candle-stick the tornado had passed. As I turned to place the light on the table, the moon burst from the clouds, its beams falling brightly on the white floor. Father opened the back door. With the exclamation, "I am ruined!" he sallied back into a chair and buried his face in his hands. Pale and dismayed, we peered forth. At first nothing was distinguishable but one general wreck and ruin, unroofed buildings, prostrate trees and fences, mixed with the debris of broken farming tools and household utensils. My father was not a man to long succumb to misfortune. Proceeding to dress, he bade the boys get into their clothes. Our first thought was of the cows. As we stepped out to seek them, we met uncle Thurrell, his son and hired man. They were still too much confused to know the extent of the injury done to their premises, but the barn was partly unroofed, the corn barn tipped over, and the cider mill, a large, heavy building, had been lifted from its foundation and carried several rods. The cows were safe, crouched together, a frightened group in the field, and two cossets that had been with them in the cow-yard had taken refuge in the barn, the doors of which had been burst open. The horse had been at pasture half a mile away, but as the men and boys went out she came whinnying towards them. Whether she ran or blew home we never knew, but she evidently had a long story to tell, if it could have been understood.

Nearly half of the roof of our house was gone, and a third of that of the long barn. A large shed had been blown from the end of the barn and flung against the end of the house. The concussion, as this came against the wall, was the cause of my fright as I crossed the room with my sister. From seventy to eighty trees laid on the ground. A cart loaded with hay, that had been left the previous evening front of the barn, had entirely disappeared, not a vestige of it was ever seen excepting one wheel which lay near the back door. Two heavy ox-sleds piled in the yard, had been carried a considerable distance; barrels, boxes, etc. had been taken from the garret with the roof and scattered about the yard, amongst these was a basket of feathers, which had been set down unharmed by the front door. A brass kettle, that had been hanging by the back door, was found some weeks after, battered and bent, in a swamp a quarter of a mile away. The potatoes were blown from the hills. The shed that had come from the barn had shielded the wood-pile, and the milk-pails at the end of the house were found hanging upon the stakes.

Upon examination it was found that about the same number of trees had been uprooted on uncle Thurrell's place as ours; the Doles also sustained some injury to their orchard, but their buildings stood below the track of the hurricane. On Ilsley's hill, the barn doors and the back door of the house were unhinged, and the cow-yard fence was thrown down. Jonathan Ilsley, going home from a party, to his surprise, found the cows in the corn field; as he drove them home, he saw the injury to the premises. Hastening into the house he awoke the family to learn what had happened, but not a soul could tell; their slumbers had been so sound, the storm had not awakened them.

Farther on, the barn of Mr. Daniel Ordway was entirely demolished. Daylight disclosed a straight line of prostrate trees, the path of the tornado as it had passed over Bradford woods, but after leaving Mr. Ordway's, little damage was done; its track was, however, traced to a wharf in Newburyport, where it overturned a small building.

The next morning we learned that a small house, about four miles above us in Bradford had been destroyed, one child killed and the rest of the family injured. The furniture of this house was widely scattered. A bonnet belonging to the mistress of the place being found in the lower parish of West Newbury, some distance beyond Ordway's barn. Before sunrise Mr. Stephen Noyes from the main road coming over Crane-neck street, on his way to the grist mill at Byfield, to his consternation descried the havoc on the top of the hill. Scarcely crediting his sight, he drew rein at Mr. Pillsbury's. The family had just risen; neither they nor that of their opposite neighbor, Mr. Stephen Little, had been awakened by the tornado. In a body these neighbors hastened to our house. At that moment, David Goodrich, a young man residing a quarter of a mile below, rode furiously up the lane. The party that Mr. Ilsley had attended, had been at his house. Dancing had continued till past twelve; in the merriment no one had heeded the shower, and when the company dispersed the sky was, clear, and the moon was shining. Going to the barn in the morning, and chancing to glance up the hill, to his utter amazement and fright, he saw the devastation. Stopping neither for coat nor saddle, he mounted his horse and galloped to our aid. The neighborhood, and ere long, the whole town was aroused; many came from Byfield, and some from Newburyport. Bands were organized, and everybody went to work with a will to repair the damage. Amongst the first and most zealous, was Mr. Edward Hill. By seven o'clock he came in bearing his tools; with a perfectly rational air he quietly inspected the buildings, then set to work with an industry which continued until the premises were again in order.

Derricks were rigged, and the process of resetting the apple trees commenced. The hurricane came Wednesday night; before sunset Saturday evening every tree had been replaced, and the buildings covered. Nothing remained undone, but the repairing of fences, and a general setting to rights of small things about the house and grounds. I believe that every one of those trees lived, some presenting rather a crooked and gnarled appearance, but year by year they bore a goodly burden, and several are still standing vigorous and fruitful.

CHAPTER XXVII.

Prior to my birth there had been an exodus of Newbury people to the wilds of New Hampshire; Littles, Gerrishs, Coffins, Pillsburys, Pearsons and Dodges. These settled in the town of Boscawen. The Littles established themselves on a long and high hill, much resembling " Crane-neck in their native town. There is a legend " that the Littles always settled on high ground, and purchased the land that joined them." Not a lovelier spot could have been selected than "Little's Hill." Kearsarge uprearing its lofty head near by, and the Blackwater meandering in the distance. A tract of land belonging to the estate of the father of David Emery, was located in Boscawen; thither Mr. Colman annually drove a herd of cows for pasturage, the milking and cheese-making being done in the family of Mr. Joseph Little. In this way the sons of the Byfield household became almost domesticated in the place. For several years it had been the custom for these Boscawen farmers, during the winter leisure, to go to Massachusetts and purchase fresh fish, which, in a frozen state, were taken in box sleds drawn by a span of horses, to Montreal in Canada, where they met with a ready sale at renumerative price during Lent. A return load of furs and other articles rendered these trips exceedingly profitable.

Having from boyhood heard the accounts of these journeys, David Emery conceived a strong desire to visit Montreal and try his luck in a venture there. On the twenty-seventh of December, he joined a party consisting of Messrs. Enoch and Joseph Gerrish, Mr. Nathan Carter and a Mr. Clough. After a month's absence, he returned highly delighted with the trip, which had combined both pleasure and profit.

I was making my usual winter visit in town and had gone to pass a day at Mr. Jeremiah Colman's. A shadow darkened the window; glancing up, to our surprise, as he had not been expecting for a week, whom should we espy but David Emery. The dinner hour was enlivened by the young man's graphic account of the journey. His companions were a jolly set, the many little blunders and mishaps inseparable from such a trip, had given amusement rather than annoyance. The inconvenience of the small and crowded houses of entertainment had been received in enterprising man, and both himself and brother were a loss to our community. The preparations for this new home in the wilderness were necessarily upon a large scale, many hands were kept busy for several weeks.

This enterprise proved eminently successful. Each year some of the emigrants visited their old home, and brought glowing accounts of the settlement. Maj. Hill's oldest son, Samuel, had remained in town, but the third year after his father's departure, he concluded to join him. An urgent request was sent to Hannah Bailey, a niece of Mrs. Josiah Hill, to accompany her cousin; her aunt insisted that she should come and stay a year. Hannah was just seventeen, a bright, black-eyed girl, ambitious and capable; fearing nothing, and ready for anything, it was but natural that she should be eager for the expedition. Her father and mother, after a time, gave a somewhat reluctant consent to the visit, but most of the family were vehement in their opposition. Aunt Poll, a maiden sister of Mr. Bailey, was especially exercised respecting her niece. "Brother and sister must be clean distraught, to permit that harum, scarum witch to go sich a jaunt. Why, if she escaped the dangers of the sea, there was rivers to cross, and nobody knew how many miles of woods to ride through afore she could get to Major Hill's. Woods all full of wild beasts, bears, catamounts and sich like, every kind of ravenous animals; she shouldn't be surprised if the Behemoth of Scripter was a roving round in them ere dark, tangled thickets, all full of snakes and other venomous reptiles."

Notwithstanding aunt Poll's and the others' remonstrances, Hannah, not the least daunted at their dire prognostications, sailed in October from Newburyport, with her cousin Sam. Hill, in an old schooner bound for Bangor. The trip was made in safety. Not much troubled with sea-sickness, the novelty was such, Miss Bailey counted the inconvenience of the voyage as nought. The weather became unusually severe for the season, and the ice formed so fast the skipper was compelled to land his passengers twelve miles below Bangor. Mr. Hill had taken his horse, so another must be procured for his cousin, as there was no carriage road to Brownville. Proceeding to Bangor to make arrangements, Mr. Hill unexpectedly found a younger brother, who had come thither to pursue his studies through the winter. His horse was to have been taken home at the first opportunity. It was young and spirited, but Hannah Bailey was an experienced and fearless rider, and it was decided that she should mount the steed, while her cousin rode his own horse. The baggage was taken from the trunks and packed in bags, strapped behind the saddles. Everything made ready, fully equipped, the cousins commenced the journey. The road was only a bridle-path through a dense forest. Streams were to be forded, fallen trees to be leaped, and many other difficulties to be surmounted. Miles apart came clearings, where buildings of logs or slabs uprose amid fields dotted with burned stumps. Rest and refreshment were obtained at these houses. The pair were two days and nights on the road, but arrived safely at their destination, somewhat fatigued, yet highly delighted with the trip. Miss Bailey remained at her uncle's a little over a year, then taking advantage of good sleighing, she came home with two of her cousins. After my return from Newburyport, she paid us a visit. We were greatly entertained with her lively and graphic description of the journeys to and fro, and her life in the forest. The account of the two days ride through the woods, elicited peals of laughter, such queer dilemmas and ludicrous accidents presented themselves. Her young horse needed a firm hand; at the first running stream he hesitated, after a moment's consideration, gathered for a leap, and sprang across; Hannah kept the saddle, and in this way was taken across every brook on the road. The elder horse witnessing his companion's agility, proceeded to copy his example. After Miss Bailey had become domesticated in Brownville, in company with her cousin, Charlotte Hill, she paid frequent visits to the farm houses in the vicinity, but the two horses could never be persuaded to wade a stream; they invariably took them at a flying leap, not a bit to the discomfiture of the gay girls.

Maj. Hill had put up a frame house, but the hearths and the lower half of the chimney were of stone, the upper being topped out with slabs filled in with clay. There was a stone oven, though light could be discerned through a chink in the back, there was plenty of wood to heat it and it baked well.

Bolts had not been set in the grist mill. The wheat flour for the nicest cooking was sifted through a fine hair seive, but the bread for common use was stirred up from the coarse flour, and no lighter, sweeter, or more wholesome bread was never tasted. As there were no apples, in the early summer, before the wild fruit came, pies were made from young sorrel leaves, which were considered very nice.

Though the nearest neighbor was a quarter of a mile away, the winter passed cheerfully. The Indians were frequent guests, and were received with kindly hospitality. Their unique appearance, broken English, original ideas and untutored manners, were a never failing source of interest and amusement.

The next spring, 1809, Maj. Hill built a brick chimney in his house, the brick hearths were the first in the towhship.

The settlement was increased by the arrival of Dr. Wilkins, his wife and five children, from Billerica. The next year the Rev. Samuel May and his family, moved thither from Boston. The clergyman came as a missionary for that part of the District, preaching in Brownville on alternate sabbaths. About the same time a lawyer, Col. Kinsman, with his sons John and Henry came to the place from Waterville.

During the winter Miss Bailey made herself generally useful; in the spring, Maj. Hill fitted a room for a school, and installed his niece as instructress of the children scattered far and wide amid the woods. The giddy young girl proved an excellent teacher, eliciting the affection of her pupils and the respect of their parents. Money was scarce in this primitive settlement, the school-mistress had no regular salary, but she received several handsome presents, amongst which was a nice dress, and a muff and tippett of rich fur.

I recall how the afternoon's mirth was increased at tea, by the wry faces made by my youngest brother, Joseph Little, over a dish of alewives. From its earliest settlement, fishing had been business in the town. Fishing grounds were laid out, which were private property. I have the deed of one that descended to David Emery from his grandfather John Emery.

Our neighbor, Hannah Pillsbury, had some years previous, married Mr. Abraham Brown, of Byfield. Left a widow while her children were still young, Mrs. Brown returned to the paternal roof, bringing with her five sons, two of which were twins. The Brown boys and my brothers were intimate companions.

That afternoon Joe. and his crony, Oliver Brown, had been to the river to look at the fishing, and each had received a bunch of alewives. Highly delighted, Joe. dressed his for supper. Father told him that they were so bony he would not eat them, but to gratify her son, mother fried the fish. The lad sat down to the table with a keen appetite, but soon concluded that alewives were not exactly the thing for a hungry man to eat in a hurry.

In 1808 Dr. Woods accepted an invitation to preside over the Theological Seminary at Andover. This institution had found munificient patrons in two citizens of Newburyport,— Mr. Moses Brown, and William Bartlett Esq. Mr. Bartlett had been enthusiastically zealous in its establishment, an interest which continued to the end of life. Dr. Woods' departure was deplored by his friends, their grief however was assuaged by the pride and pleasure experienced, at their favorite's advancement in place and honor. Aunt Ruth Little could scarcely reconcile herself to the change, but aunt Judy Dole said, "Let him go; he was fitter for a Pope to that new Hopkinsian college, than for a country parson. She was willing to throw all her old shoes after him for good luck." Several years elapsed without a settled minister. The pulpit was mostly supplied from the Andover Seminary. Amongst these young men were the afterwards distinguished missionaries, Messrs Newell and Judson. A great commotion had arisen in the parish respecting the meeting-house. The old building had become dilapidated, almost unfit for use. Every one conceded the necessity of a new house, but its site was the bone of contention. Some, mostly the more elderly members of the society, were desirous to retain the old location,— their plea being that it was exactly in the centre of the parish: the others very wisely objected to climbing the almost inaccessible hill upon which the old structure was perched, urging that it would be better for a few to go a slight distance farther on level ground, than all to climb the high and steep eminence. Agreement could not be reached. The old meeting-house grew worse and worse, snow drifted in at winter, and rain dripped through the cracks and crevices in summer, still the contrary parties could not be brought to agree, people went to meeting because it was customary and considered sinful to remain at home, but there was a sad lack of interest and union in the parish for quite a period.

CHAPTER XXIX.

My ancestors, with the exception of the Johnson branch, came to Newbury either in the band that accompanied Messers Parker and Noyes from Agawam to Quascacunquen in the year 1635, or joined the settlement soon after. From the Noyes grandmother, am descended from the Rev. James Noyes, whose brother Nicholas, tradition asserts, was the first to leap on shore when the emigrants landed. This spot is supposed to be on the north side of the river Parker, near the present bridge, and the colonists located about the lower green, Oldtown, where the first meeting-house was built. Thomas Parker, the pastor, was born in Wiltshire, England, in 1595; he was the only son of Robert Parker, an eminent scholar and an active nonconformist. The Noyes family are of Norman descent; originally the name was spelt Noye. From the conquest the race have been distinguished for influence and scholarship. In 14 and 15 Hen. VIII, William Noyes, of Erchfort, was assessed for the subsidy at £80, and paid £4 yearly. In 1540 he became possessed of the prebend of Erchfort with its dependencies, and died in 1557, leaving a considerable property to a large family, of whom John was M. P. for Laine, A. D., 1600, and Robert the elder, who succeeded to the prebend, having purchased in 1574 for his eldest son, Robert, the manor and estate of King's Hatherdene, in Weghill near Andover. His cousin, Peter Noyes, was also of Weghill and Andover of Berks, in which county, for many generations his descendants owned the estate of Trunkwell, in the parish of Springfield, acquired by a marriage with Agnes, daughter and heiress of John Noyes of that place who died in 1607. Peter Noyes had a second son Richard, and a daughter, Joice, married to the Rev. Robert Wield, D. D. James Noyes, the teacher at Quascacunquen, was born in Choulderton, Wiltshire, England, in 1608. His father was a minister in the same town, a gentleman of superior ability and education. His mother was a sister of the learned Robert Parker. Mr. Noyes was educated at Oxford, and for a time previous to his emigration to America, he was associated with his cousin, Thomas Parker, in teaching at Newbury, where Mr. Parker preached. In honor of these gentlemen, the settlement received the name of Newbury. In 1634, shortly before leaving his native land, Mr. Noyes was married to Sarah, eldest daughter of Joseph Brown of Southampton. He had six sons, and three daughters; Sarah, who died at the age of eleven, Rebecca, and a second Sarah. Through life the cousins, Parker and Noyes, continued in the closest intimacy. They taught in the same school in England, came to America in the same ship, were pastor and teacher in the same church, and as Mr. Parker remained a bachelor, they lived in the same house. For a few years after the settlement of the town their residence was on the west side of the lower green, but on the removal of the meeting-house, Mr. Noyes built a house in 1646, or soon after, which is still standing on Parker street,—a fine old fashioned mansion, still owned and occupied by the clergyman's descendants. A lot of salt meadow, willed by Mr. Parker to his Noyes relatives, has never been bought nor sold, but through the descending generations has successively passed from father to son. The Rev. James Noyes died in the forty-eighth year of his age, Oct. 22d, 1656. His character is thus delineated by Mr. Parker:

"Mr. James Noyes my worthy colleague in the ministry of the gospel, was a man of singular qualifications, in piety excelling, an implacable enemy to all heresy and schism and a most able warrior against the same. He was of a reaching and ready apprehension, a large invention, a most profound judgment, a rare, tenacious and comprehensive memory, fixed and immovable in his well grounded conceptions, sure in words and speech, without rashness, gentle and mild in all expressions, without passion or provoking language, and as he was a notable disputant so he never would provoke his adversary, saving by the short knocks and heavy weight of argument. He was of so loving, compassionate and humble carriage that I believe never any were acquainted with him, but did desire the continuance of his society and acquaintance. He was a most excellent counsellor in doubts, and could strike at a hair's breadth like the Benjamites and expedite the entangled out of the briars. He was courageous in dangers and still was apt to believe the best, and make fair weather in a storm. He was much honored and esteemed in the country, and his death was much bewailed. I think that he may be reckoned among the greatest worthies of the age."

Joseph, oldest son of the Rev. James Noyes, born Oct. 15th, 1637, remained in Newbury, where, for a number of years, he was one of the selectmen. He died in 1717.

James, the second son, born March 11th, 1640; graduated at Harvard in 1659; was a preacher in Stonington, Conn., in 1668; was ordained there Sept. 10th, 1676, and died Dec. 1719, after a ministry of over fifty years.

Moses, the third son, was born Dec. 6th, 1643; graduated at Harvard in 1659; he was the first minister in Lyme, Conn., where he died Nov. 10th, 1726.

John, the fourth son, born June 3d, 1645; was a member of the Ancient and Honorable Artillery Company, Boston.

Col. Thomas, the fifth son, born Aug. 10th, 1648; remained in Newbury where he was a prominent citizen, representing the town in the General Court.

William, the sixth son, born Sept. 22d, 1653, married Sara Cogswell, Nov. 6th, 1685. Children: John, born July 27th, 1686, William, born Sept. 1st, 1688: Sarah, born May 10th, 1691, and died Dec. 3d, 1703; Moses, born Jan. 27th, 1694, and died Feb. 16th; Susanna, born Feb. 25th, 1696; Mary, born May 24th, 1699, and died Dec. 16th, 1703; Sarah, born Dec. 5th, 1703; Parker, born Jan. 17th, 1705.

John, oldest son of William and Sara (Cogswell,) Noyes, married Tabitha Dole, and moved to the West Precinct, Newbury, where he became a leading citizen and deacon of the church; his estate was on the main road near the Bradford line. Children were: William, Sara, Elizabeth, and Parker, who died in childhood. William married Lydia Morse; their children were: Timothy, who married Betty Dean, Enoch, who married Sarah Emery, John, who married Elizabeth Pillsbury, and Molly, who married Webster Bailey.

Sara, the oldest daughter of deacon Noyes, remained single; Elizabeth, the second daughter, married Capt. James Smith of Crane-neck hill — her second husband was Capt. Edmund Little.

Mr. Nicholas Noyes, brother of Rev. James Noyes, was born in 1614; he married Mary Cutting, a sister of Capt. John Cutting who came from London to Charlestown, thence to Newbury about 1642. Their children were, Mary, born Oct. 15th, 1641, married John French. Hannah, born Oct. 31st, 1643, married Peter Cheney, May 14th, 1663. 2d, John Atkinson, born June 3d. 1700, died Jan. 5th. 1705. John, born Jan. 20th, 1646, married Mary Poor, Nov 13th, 1668, died in 1691. Rev. Nicholas, born Dec. 22d. 1647, died unmarried. Cutting, born Sept. 23d. 1649, married Elizabeth Knight; died Oct. 25th. 1734. Sarah, born Sept. 13th. 1651. died Feb. 20th. 1652. Sarah, born Aug. 22d. 1653, married Matthew Pettingel, April 13th. 1674. Timothy, born June 23d. 1655, married Mary Knight, Jan. 13th, 1680; died in 1710. James, born May 15th, 1657, married Hannah Knight, March 31st, 1684; died in 1723. Abigail, born April, 1657, married Simeon French of Salisbury, May 8th, 1707. Rachel, born March 20th, 1661, married James Jackman. Thomas, born June 20th, 1663, married Sarah ——, lived in Haverhill, and died previous to Dec. 30th, 1695. Rebecca, born May 18th, 1665, died Dec. 21st. 1683.

Mr. Noyes was one of the most influential members of the infant settlement, representing it in the General Court, and was also a deacon of the church. He died Nov. 23d. 1701, aged 83.

Hannah, the wife of James Noyes, was the daughter of John Knight, jun., son of John Knight, who with his brother, Deacon Richard Knight, came from Romsey, England, to Newbury, in 1635. Their children were: Rebecca, born Jan. 12th, 1685; Joseph, born Sept. 20th, 1686; Hannah, born March 13th, 1688; Nicholas, born Feb. 9th, 1690, Nathan, born Feb. 5th, 1692; Ephraim, born Nov. 20th and died Dec. 19th, 1694; Lydia, born Nov. 30th, 1695; Ephraim, born Dec. 25th, 1698; Benjamin, born Feb. 22d. 1701; Mary, born March 13th, 1703; James, born Aug. 19th, 1705.

Capt. Ephraim Noyes, fifth son of James and Hannah (Knight) Noyes, settled on the main road, in the West Precinct, Newbury; he married Abigail, daughter of Jonas and Anne Platts, and granddaughter of Deacon Joseph Bailey, of Bradford. Edna, daughter of Capt Ephraim and Abigail (Platts) Noyes, April 7th, 1756, married John, son of David and Abigail (Chase) Emery.

The children of John and Mary (Poor) Noyes were: Nicholas, born May 18th, 1671, married Sarah Lunt, and settled in Abington before 1718. Daniel, born Oct. 23d, 1673, married Judith Knight, Dec. 29th, 1702; died March 13th, 1716. Mary, born Dec. 10th, 1675, married John Noyes. John, born Feb. 19th, 1677, married Mary Thurlow, Jan. 25th, 1703; died previous to Nov. 2d, 1719. Martha, born Dec. 24th, 1679, married Joseph Lunt, Dec. 29th, 1702; died June 26th, 1706. Nathaniel, born Oct. 28th, 1681, married Priscilla Merrill; was in Falmouth, 1733. Elizabeth, born Nov. 11th, 1684. Moses, born May 22d. 1688, died in 1714. Samuel, born Feb. 3d, 1692, married Hannah Poor; lived in Abington previous to 1736.

The children of Daniel and Judith (Knight) Noyes were: Daniel, born

Oct. 16th, 1703, married Abigail Toppan; died April 16th. 1765. Joseph. born Aug. 6th. 1705, married Elizabeth Woodman. Nov. 10th. 1726; died Sept. 15th, 1781. Joshua, born Jan. 26th. 1707, married Sarah Hale. April 7th. 1730; died Jan. 1808. John, born May 9th, 1709, married Ann Woodbridge; died Aug. 13th, 1759. Mary. born Nov. 24th, 1710, died Aug. 1794. Deborah. born May 22d, 1713, married Jacob Knight. Judith. born Jan. 7th, 1715. married Benjamin Poor.

The children of Daniel and Abigail (Toppan) Noyes were: Abigail, born Dec. 28th. 1728. died Aug. 3d 1731. Daniel. born Nov. 7th, 1730, died June 13th, 1735. Zebulon, ——— died June 11th, 1735. Samuel. born April 25th, 1737, married Rebecca Wheeler; died April 1st, 1820. Ebenezer, born in 1739, married Hannah Chase; died Aug. 1767.

Mary and John, twins, born March, 1741. Mary married, first, Samuel Somerby, second, Nathaniel Dole; John married, first, Sarah Little; second. Mary Pierce; died July 18th. 1778. Abigail. born Oct. 5th, 1744, married Joseph Moulton: died Sept. 18th, 1818. Judith. born Nov. 1747. died Oct. 1832.

The children of Samuel and Rebecca (Wheeler) Noyes were: Daniel. born Oct. 22d. 1765. died Dec. 5th. 1768. Samuel, born May 25th, 1767, married, first. Jane Moody, Jan. 22d, 1795; she died Nov. 13th, 1802; second, Hannah, youngest daughter of Joseph Little, and widow of James Stickney, who died Jan. 17th. 1805. Samuel Noyes died July 12th. 1852. and his widow. Hannah Noyes. died March 1st, 1861. Rebecca, born April, 1769. Ebenezer, born April 26th. 1771, died June 16th, 1794. in the West Indies. Judith, born July 13th, 1773, died July 17th, 1777. Daniel. born May 6th, 1775, died Jan. 7th. 1777. Dr. Nathan, born April 3d, 1777. died Sept. 1842. Judith, born Feb. 7th, 1779, married William Moulton; died Oct. 1822.

Rev. Nicholas Noyes, graduated at Harvard 1667, preached in Haddam, Conn., thirteen years, ordained over the first society in Salem, Nov. 14th, 1683, and died Dec. 13th. 1717.

Rev. Edmund Noyes, born March 29th, 1729, graduated at Harvard 1747, was ordained in Salisbury Nov. 20th, 1751, and died July 12th, 1809.

Ebenezer Noyes, born in 1739, graduated at Nassau Hall in 1750, was a physician in Dover, where he died Aug. 11th. 1767.

Rev. Nathaniel Noyes, born Aug. 12th, 1735, graduated at Nassau Hall in 1759, was ordained in South Hampton, N. H., Feb. 23d, 1763, dismissed Dec. 8th, 1800, and died in Newburyport Dec. 1810. Sarah, consort of the Rev. Nathaniel Noyes, died in South Hampton, May 20th, 1771, aged 25 years, 8 months.

Rev. Thomas Noyes, son of Col. Thomas Noyes of the west parish, Newbury, graduated at Harvard in 1795, and died young.

Nathan Noyes, M. D., graduated at Dartmouth. a physician at Newburyport.

Rev. Jeremiah Noyes, graduated at Dartmouth in 1799, ordained Nov. 16, 1803, in Gorham, Maine, and died Jan. 15th, 1807.

Moody Noyes, Harvard, 1800, died young.

Daniel Noyes, born Jan. 29th, 1739,

graduated at Harvard in 1758, was register of probate for Essex, and died in Ipswich March 21st, 1815.

Joshua Noyes, born 1739, graduated at Nassau in 1759; was pastor elect of the church in Kingston, N. H., and died July 8th, 1773, aged 34.

John Noyes, born May 9, 1709, graduated at Harvard in 1753, and died Aug. 13th, 1759.

Rev. George Rappall Noyes, born March 6th, 1798, graduated at Harvard in 1818; was ordained in South Brookfield, Mass., Oct. 30th, 1827; resettled in Petersham Oct. 15th, 1834. Elected professor in the Divinity school, Cambridge, in 1840. Received the degree of D. D. the same year. He died June 3d, 1868, aged 70 years and 3 months. Of Dr. Noyes the late Thomas B. Fox thus wrote:

"His outward life was that of a student and teacher mainly, and so presented but few incidents or events to break the even tenor of its way; but by his Christian character, his learning and his intellectual usefulness to his pupils and to the cause of sacred literature, he won the love, respect and gratitude of all who knew him, as well as the esteem of such as were only familiar with him as an author who had helped them in their inquiries after truth. Dr. Noyes graduated in the class of 1818 which gave fourteen of its members to the ministry. For several years he was pastor of the churches at South Brookfield and Petersham, but the greater portion of his days was spent in the service of his *Alma Mater* as tutor in the college and as a professor on two foundations in the Divinity school. He first attracted public attention by his translation of the book of Job—a work that was followed by versions of the Psalms and the Prophets. Besides these more elaborate productions, he was a contributor of learned and critical articles to the Christian Examiner. He was one of the most diligent and accurate of scholars, and everything that came from his pen showed the conscientious fidelity, the pure, lucid, calm productions of a mind seeking always to be judicially impartial in its investigations and in the statement of its conclusions. His scholarship was large and thorough, and his industry unwearied and unremitted even through seasons of physical weakness and distress.

Up almost to the hour of his decease, he was engaged in correcting with sedulous care the closing proof sheets of a translation of the New Testament. The strength and clearness of his mental powers, the candor and fearlessness of his moral nature, the generosity and justice of his liberality, will be acknowledged by all who had the privilege of listening to his explanatory defence of the Cambridge Theological School, at the last meeting of the Alumni of that institution. His address on that occasion obtained a solemn impression from his bodily infirmity, which had not dimmed the healthful brightness of his mind, or chilled the warmth of his heart. He spoke as it were on the border of the grave, and he spoke as one who humbly but trustfully awaited a judgment more searching than any human judgment can be. We allude to this, his last public discourse, because in it were seen the trained thinker, the honest and catholic man, and the faithful Christian teacher; the culmination as it were, of a life of many virtues and graces, consecrated to learning and to the highest interesst of humanity; a life none the less useful, noble, and brave, because mostly passed in the study, the lecture room, and inthe retirement of comparative privacy, away from the bustle of the world and unattended by circumstances that attract the public gaze. Such a life could not but win the reverent regard of all who witnessed and were benefited by it, and the memory of him who lived it, will be cherished as the memory of a disciple who uniformly sought to use the talents intrusted to him, as one who never forgot that he must give an account of his stewardship."

The following is a tribute from Dr. W. W. Newell. "The death of a worker in the quiet paths of science is scarcely noticed by the world; and yet few men of more active life may have exercised so deep an influence;—so it was with the late George R. Noyes, D. D. For more than twenty years his was the leading mind in the Divinity school at Cambridge. and did more than any other to form the minds of the students, who will always cherish his name with love. It was from him they acquired the scientific spirit, patient, calm. impartial; in him they saw the example of a truly devotional mind, combined with the most searching analysis; they learned to respect his practical wisdom, and to receive his opinions almost as oracles. Such homage from young, free, and independent minds implies great qualities. They were sure no word would fall from his lips not thoroughly weighed and tested. They could trust a moderation which always forbore to dogmatize, and to express even an opinion on doubtful questions, however fascinating the temptation to leap an unbridged chasm. and when he did express an opinion they knew it was no result of individual preference, or of dogmatic assumption but honest fruit of the widest comparison and the strictest inquiry. In his own department, the exegesis of the Scriptures, his scholars believed him unapproached in America. Few could hear him and not admit that Biblical interpretation was now a science whose principles were fixed, and that the vast difference of results arise far more from the different opinions brought to the study, than from the difficulty of the subject. His translation of the poetical books of the Old Testament is, we believe, the best in any language, combining a correct interpretation with the spirit of the original. His lectures illustrated to an even greater degree the high qualities of his mind,—his great shrewdness, profound scholarship, and freedom from prejudice. But opinions, which he arrived at by individual study, and held when they were little supported and indeed almost unknown in this country, have since become widely prevalent among scholars everywhere. With these virtues of the scholar he combined keen wit, and great kindness and tolerance. His students did not admire him more than they reverenced him; and his whole life was in his work. No one could hear him in prayer and not revere his profoundly religious spirit, and wonder at such a union of qualities. No man lives who can fill the place he took in health; and, if in life the general ignorance and prejudice in regard to these subjects prevented general recognition of his merits, in the history of mind his name will stand among the first of American students who brought a scientific treatment to this branch of inquiry. In the minds of his students his memory will always live and his influence always work."

Francis V. Noyes, born Sept. 22d, 1809, graduated at Dartmouth, received the degree of M. D. at Harvard Aug. 1831. He was a physician in Newburyport until 1844, and at present is a resident of Billerica.

Rev. Daniel Parish Noyes, born June 4th, 1820, graduated Aug. 1840, at Yale College. Taught school till 1843; was a tutor in Yale till 1847; student at Andover till 1849; pastor of the 3d Presbyterian church, Brooklyn, N. Y., from April 1849, till Jan. 1854. Secretary of the American Home Missionary Society from Jan. 1854, till June, 1865. Secretary of Home Evangelization in Massachusetts from Jan. 1865, till 1873. While prosecuting this work, he founded a church at Pigeon Cove, Cape Ann, acting as pastor for a time; Oct. 1877 was installed pastor of a church in Wilmington.

Joseph M. Noyes, a distinguished teacher, and Henry Durant Noyes of the firm of Noyes, Snow and Co., publishers, 13½ Bromfield street, Boston. These are grandsons of the Rev. Elijah Parish. Isaac Parsons Noyes, born Dec. 10th, 1822; appointed assistant postmaster at Newburyport, June 19th, 1861; appointed postmaster May 2d, 1877: served on the board of overseers of the poor three years, in the common council one year, secretary of school board six years, re-elected on school committee in 1878 for two years. William Henry Noyes, D. M. D., born in Newbury, July 28, 1825; graduated at Harvard University in dental medicine, March 9th, 1870; married May 14, 1848, Sarah M. Parshley of Strafford, N. H., Children: Ella Ada; Earnest Henry, born Nov. 20th, 1853; graduated at Bowdoin College July 8th 1875, now studying medicine at Harvard.

George E. L. Noyes, D. M. D., son of Geo. W. Noyes, born in Newburyport Aug. 28th, 1850, graduated at Harvard University in dental medicine March 10, 1872; married Nov. 27, 1878, Mary Hill Goodwin of Newburyport, daughter of Daniel A. Goodwin.

CHAPTER XXIX.

"Whence cometh Smith, be he knight or be he
squire,
But from the Smith that forgeth at the fire."

The arms of Smith, granted in some remote age to some meritorious blacksmith, are:

SABLE, ON A FESSE DANCETTE ARGENT SEVEN BILLETS OF THE FIELD. CREST, A SALAMANDER COUCHANT REGARDANT, DUCALLY GORGED, IN FLAMES PROPER.

From the settlement on Crane-neck hill four generations bearing the name of James Smith have succeeded each other on the homestead, and two preceded them at Oldtown, making six in America. The first of this patronymic of whom I have record were Sir James

The Noyes arms are:

ARGENT, GARB OR, THREE MULLETS GULES COUNTERCHANGED. CREST.—DOVE BEARING OLIVE BRANCH.

NOYCE PLACE

Smith, the first baronet of Isfield, who was the eldest son of Sir James Smith Knt., Lord Mayor of London in 1685, who was the second son of Sir Robert Smith, of Upton, Bart., who descended from Robert Smith, citizen and draper of London and Stoke Prior in Worcestershire. This Robert belonged to an ancient family, the Smiths of Cuerdley, in Lancaster. Robert Smith and his descendants Sir Robert, Sir James the Knt., and Sir James the Baronet, bore arms:

AZURE, TWO BARS WAVY ERMINE ON A CHIEF OR, A DEMI-LION RAMPANT ISSUANT SABLE. CREST—AN OSTRICH GULES, IN THE BEAK A HORSE SHOE ARGENT.

This coat was confirmed by Flower Norroy on the 7th of July, 1579, to Thomas Smith, son and heir of Sir Laurence Smith of Hough. Motto: Duriora virtus—Virtue tries harder things.

The same arms were borne by Ferdinando Dudley Lea Smith, esq., great grandson of William Smith of Stoke Prior, County Worcester by the Hon. Anne Lea, his wife, eldest sister and co-heiress of Ferdinando Dudley, Lord Dudley of Halesraven Grange.

Edmund is another patronymic that has descended through the generations. It was derived from the marriage of Margaret, daughter of Thomas Smith of Cockermouth, with Edmund Wilmot of Hampshire. Arms:

SABLE ON A FESSE ENGRAILED OR BETWEEN THREE SQUIRRELS SEJANT ARGENT, EACH HOLDING A MARIGOLD SLIPPED PROPER, AS MANY HERALDIC FOUNTAINS.

Thomas Smith came from Romsey, England, with his wife Rebecca, in the ship James, to Ipswich, Mass., in 1635, thence to Newbury in 1638, and settled on the farm now owned by David Smith. He died April 22, 1666. His children were: Thomas, born in 1639, who was drowned by falling into a clay-pit on his way to school, Dec. 6th. 1648; Rebecca, born Feb. 20th, 1641, married Aug. 4th, 1663, Stephen Swett; Lieut. James Smith, born Sept. 10th. 1645, married July 26th, 1667, Sarah Coker. He was drowned at Anticosti in the disastrous expedition to Quebec, in October, 1690. John, born March 9th, 1648, married Rebecca Poor Nov. 26th, 1667; Matthias, born Oct. 27th, 1652; Thomas, born July 7th, 1654, was killed by the Indians at Bloody Brook in 1696. This was in King Philip's war. As Philip was on the Connecticut river it became necessary for the English to establish an opposing force in some convenient position. As Hadley was selected, an increased supply of provisions in that place was needed. A considerable quantity of wheat being preserved in stacks at Deerfield, it was deemed expedient to have it threshed and brought to Hadley. Captain Lathrop and his company volunteered to proceed to Deerfield and protect the convoy. This company consisted of the flower of the population of Essex —her hopeful young men—all called out of the towns belonging to that county. Of the twenty-three men impressed from Newbury, on the 5th, 6th and 27th of August, to go against the Indian enemy, were Henry Bodwell, who married Bethia, daughter of John and Mary (Webster) Emery, John Toppan, Thomas Smith, Samuel Hills and Jonathan Emery. They arrived safely at Deerfield, threshed the wheat, placed it in eighteen carts, and while on their return through South Deerfield, as they were stopping to gather grapes, which hung in clusters in the forest that lined the narrow road, they were surprised by an ambascade of Indians, outnumbering Capt. Lathrop's company ten to one, who poured upon them a murderous fire; not more than seven or eight of the eighty men in the company escaped. Sergeant Thomas Smith, Samuel Stevens, his brother John Stevens, and John Littlehale were killed; John Toppan, who was wounded in the shoulder, concealed himself in a watercourse then almost dry, and drew grass and weeds over his head, so that, though the Indians sometimes stepped directly over him, he was not discovered. Henry Bodwell had his left arm broken by a musket ball, but being a man of great strength and courage, he siezed his gun in his right hand and swung it round his head, and so forced his way through the Indians by whom he was surrounded. John Toppan brought home the sword of Sergeant Thomas Smith, and it is preserved in the family at the old homestead as a most precious relic. At the recent second centennial celebration of the battle Bloody Brook, it was again borne to the field by Edmund Smith, of Newburyport, where it was the sole memento of that cruel fray. The rapier excited universal attention, being regarded with awe and reverence. Mothers led up their little children to touch the sword of one, whose arm that wielded it, had been mouldering in the dust just two hundred years that day.

"An inventory of the lands, goods and chattels of Thomas Smith, late of Newbury, who was slayne when Capt. Lathrop was slayne, taken by Robert Long and Anthony Somerby, March 22d, 1675: 76

Imprimis foure acres of plowland 3 acres of pasture 4 acres salt marsh & 3 acres of swamp or slow land 55-0-0

A yoke of oxen & a 4 yearf old heifer 16-10-0

His wearing apparrell 5-0-0

A chest a cross cut saw a broad axe 2 augurs A maul 2 addes a rule & a raypier 2-8-0

A gnapsack & a bible & 2 paper bookes 0-3-6

and debts due to him about 1-0-0

Sum is 80-6-6

the deceased was out in the country service about 7 weeks he was at first corporall and after seigent under the said Capt. Lathrop & had all his arms & amunition well fixt which is all lost except the rapier

the debs that the deceased owes is about 10-0-0

Anthony Somerby Robert Long.

This inventory red in court held at Ipswich the 28th of March 1676. As attest—Robert Lord cler."

The children of Lieut. James and Sarah (Coker) Smith were Sarah, born Sept. 12th, 1668, married in 1692, Richard Kelley; James, born Oct. 16th, 1670, married, in 1695, Jane Kent; Thomas, born March 9th, 1673, married March 29th, 1715, Martha Noyes; Hannah, born March 23d, 1675, married in 1695, Joseph Pike. These were the progenitors of Albert Pike the poet. Joseph, born June 8th, 1677, died July 19th, 1677; John, born Nov. 1st, 1678, married Dec. 9th, 1709, Ann Nelson; Benjamin, born Aug. 21st, 1681, married April 19th, 1709, HannahSomes; Mary, born Feb. 27th, 1684, died Dec. 15th, 1685.

The children of James and Jane (Kent) Smith were: Capt. James, born Nov. 25th, 1696, married Dec. 9th, 1719, Elizabeth Moody; Sarah, born June 21st, 1699, married 1728, William Moulton: Mary, born May 23d, 1701, married Feb. 28th, 1724, Moses Noyes; Richard, born March

31st, 1706, died young; John, born June 3d, 1709, married March 3d, 1730, Martha Toppan, and died Sept. 25th. 1734; Moses, born May 16th, 1711, married, Nov. 24th. 1742, Lydia Toppan; James, the husband of Jane Kent, married a second wife, Sarah Ordway, in 1723. Martha Smith, widow of John Smith, married Cutting Moody. She left two children—John Smith, born Nov. 3, 1731, and Abigail Smith, born Nov. 29th, 1732; she married Jonathan Bradbury in 1758. Martha and Lydia Toppan, the wives of John and Moses Smith, were sisters of Rev. Benjamin Toppan, minister at Manchester, Mass., forty-seven years. They were children of Samuel Toppan, who married Abigail, daughter of the Rev. Michael Wigglesworth, author of the Day of Doom. Rev. David Toppan was a son of Benjamin.

Soon after his marriage with Elizabeth Moody, Capt. James Smith, having inherited from his grandfather, John Kent of Kent's island, a hundred acre lot on Crane-neck hill, moved thither. That part of Newbury then termed the "West Precinct," or "Newtown," was a wilderness, with Indians for neighbors. A garrison had been established on the place afterwards owned by Dea. Samuel Tenney. Capt. Smith put up a small house—the back part of the present dwelling; the front was built a few years later. At its erection the house was lighted by casements hung on hinges, with diamond-shaped panes set in leaden sashes. These windows were modernized by his son James, who remodelled the house and built the long barn.

Capt. James and Elizabeth Smith had ten children: Sarah, Samuel, William, James, Richard, Mollie, Jenny, Betty, Stephen and Moses. These ten sons and daughters all grew to man's and woman's estate, comprising a fine family, the young ladies being specially noted for beauty and grace. Sarah married Moody Follansbee and settled on a farm near Meeting-house hill. Samuel married Judith, and William, Mary, sisters of Mr. David Emery at the main road. Capt. Smith gave to each of these two sons a thirty acre lot, upon which they erected houses on Crane-neck road—one above and the other below—where the present school-house is located. Isaac inherited the homestead and married Elizabeth, daughter of Dea. John Noyes. Richard married Abigail, a sister of Moody Follansbee, and established himself in the shoe business in Newburyport, where he built a house on Short, now Independent street. Mollie became the wife of Capt. William Noyes of Newburyport. Fanny died of consumption in early life, unmarried. Betty's first husband was John Emery, son of David; after his decease she married Col. Spofford of New Rowley, now Georgetown. Stephen and Moses moved to Lancaster, where they married. Stephen was a merchant, and Moses cultivated a large farm.

Capt. James Smith, 2d, and Elizabeth (Noyes) Smith had seven children: Parker, Lizzie, John, Samuel, Sarah, James, Enoch.

Parker married Hannah Savory and settled on a farm in Newbury, near the Bradford line. Lizzie became the wife of Deacon Samuel Tenney; John married Mary March, and purchased the Jonas Platts farm in Bradford, now Groveland. Samuel married Sarah Bailey; he became the Methodist preacher; Sarah remained unmarried. James (my father) married Prudence, eldest daughter of Mr. Joseph Little, and succeeded the line of James Smiths on the home farm. Enoch married Hannah Woodman, and purchased the farm of Maj. Hills on Crane-neck road, adjoining that of my grandfather Little. The Smiths of Newbury, West Newbury, and Newburyport, though noted for intelligence, ability, thrift and enterprise, have not been a scholastic race.

Rev. David Smith graduated at Harvard in 1790. I recollect hearing him preach some time during the interregnum between the departure of Parson Toppan and the ordination of Dr. Woods. He was a fine looking man, and an eloquent divine. His record I have been unable to trace.

Daniel Smith, for forty years an apothecary in Newburyport, died Mar. 28, 1878, aged 90 years. Dr. Smith's drug store (now S. A Smith's), was on Market square. He was one of the most upright and genial of men, possessing great intelligence and force of character. The latter part of his life was passed in Lawrence, where he died. His son, Daniel Talcot Smith, born Sept. 17th, 1813, graduated at Amherst in 1831, was assistant instructor at Andover in 1834–6, ordained in Sherburne, Mass., Dec. 5th, 1836. Has been for many years professor in the Bangor Theological Seminary.

Thomas Smith, the first in America, bore the arms of Edward Smith of Hampshire:

SABLE ON A FESSE, ENGRAILED OR, BETWEEN THREE DEMI-LIONS PASSANT, ARGENT, AS MANY FLEUR-DE-LIS GULES.

The ancient arms of Smith of Cuerdley were:

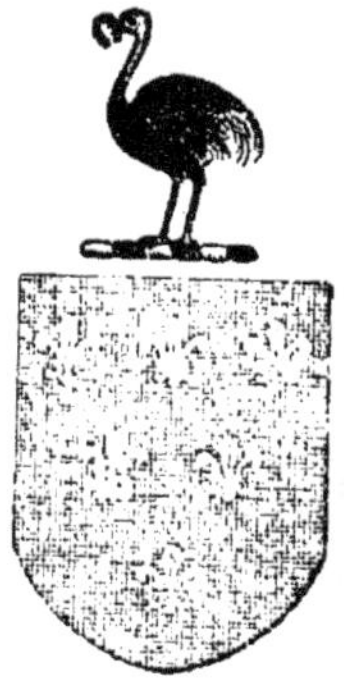

SABLE, SIX FLEUR-DE-LIS, THREE, TWO, AND ONE ARGENT.

Of the English ancestor to whom the arms of Smith were first issued I have no account.

William Smith, Bishop of Lincoln, a descendant of the Smiths of Cuerdley County, Lancaster, was born at Peel House in the township of Widness and chapelry of Farnsworth, in the parish of Prescot County, Lancaster, about the year 1460. In 1492 he was made Bishop of Litchfield and Coventry, and on the 18th of May, 1495, he was translated to the see of Lincoln. About the year 1509, in conjunction with Sir Richard Sutton of Sutton near Macclesfield, he founded a college in the University of Oxford, "commonly called the King's Haule and Colledge of Brazen Nose." He also held the important office of Lord President of the Marches of Wales from the 17th of Henry VII to the 4th of Henry VIII. He made his will on the 26th of Dec. 1512, appointing William Smith, Archdeacon of Lincoln, Gilbert Smith, Archdeacon of Northampton, Thomas Smith of Chester, merchant, and others, his executors. He died at his palace at Buckden on the 2d of January, 1513, and was buried in the nave of

Lincoln Cathedral, near the great western door. Among his other benefactions were a chapel in Farnsworth Church, and a grammar school at the same place. The arms of the Bishop are:

ARGENT, A CHEVRON SABLE BETWEEN THREE ROSES GULES, BARBED AND SEEDED VERT.

He sealed with a W (the initial of his Christian name) between three roses. On the brass to his memory in Lincoln Cathedral, were four escutcheons,—one bearing his arms, two containing those of his two sees—Litchfield and Lincoln, and a fourth blazoned with a soltaire between four fleur-de-lis.

Of the Cuerdley family were Thomas Smith, twice Mayor of the city of Oxford, and Thomas Smith, of Chester, a near relative and one of the executors of Bishop Smith. This Cuerdley family well observed the injunction, "to increase and multiply." Sir Thomas Smith of Hatherton, a descendant of Thomas of Chester, had twenty-two children. Robert Smith, esq., sometime citizen and draper of London, who died 23d of March, 1609–10, had eleven sons and six daughters, all of whom are represented upon his monumental brass in Stoke Prior Church, Worcestershire. His son Robert was the first baronet of Upton. Robert's second son, Sir James Smith, Knt., was Lord Mayor of London in 1685, and his eldest son Sir James Smith was the first baronet of Isfield.

John Smith of St. Giles's, Cripplegate, entered his pedigree in 1663 as the tenth son of John Smith, of "Stoke Priory," and he married two wives and was the father of ten children. Of the same family was William Smith, of Cahir Moyle, Ireland, who had issue, two daughters and co-heiresses—Charlotte, married to Sir Edward O. Brien, Bart, and Harriet, wife of Thomas Arthur, Esq. of Glenomera. The arms of John Smith:

GENTMAN, & CAPTAYNE OF 2d COM. & 50 SOLDIERS. VERT A CHEVRON GULES BETWEEN THREE TURK'S HEADS PROPER, TURBANED OR. CREST—AN OSTRICH OR IN THE BEAK A HORSE SHOE ARGENT.
MOTTO. "VINCERE EST VIVERE."

The exact pedigree of this worthy cannot be traced. It is generally admitted that he was descended from the Smiths of Cuerdley, and he is stated to have been born at Willoughby in Lincolnshire in 1579, and to have been descended by his mother from the Riccards of Great Heck in the West Riding of Yorkshire. He was in the service of Sigismund, brother to Duke of Transylvania, from whom he received in 1623 "three Turks' heads in a shield for his arms by patent under his hand and seal, with an oath ever to wear them in his colors, his picture in gold, and three hundred ducats yearly for a pension." This coat was granted in memory of three Turks, whom with his own sword he overcame, and cut off their heads, in the province of Transylvania.

Captain Smith after various adventures in the old and new worlds, his life being saved by Pocahontas, etc., died in London on the 21st of June, 1631, and was buried in St. Sepulchre's, in the choir, where is, or was, a long inscription to his memory in "fine tinkling rhyme and flowing verse," setting forth his great prowess and many virtues:

"How that he did divide from Pagans three
Their heads and lives, types of his chivalrie;
For which great service in that climated one,
Brave Sigismundus, King of Hungarion,
Did give him a coat of arms to weare,
Those conquered heads got by his sword and speare," etc.

Sir Thomas Smith of Theydon Mount, Essex county, was secretary to King Edward the Sixth and Queen Elisabeth. His family claim descent from Sir Roger de Clarendon, Knt., a natural son of Edward the Black Prince.

Sir Thomas Smith of Hill Hall, Essex, was created a baronet in 1661, his arms were:

SABLE, A FESSE DANCETTE ARGENT, BILLETY OF THE FIELD, BETWEEN THREE LIONS RAMPANT, GUARDANT OF THE SECOND, EACH SUPPORTING AN ALTAR OR, FLAMING PROPER. CREST—A SALAMANDER IN FLAMES, DUCALLY GORGED, REGUARDANT PROPER.

Some have supposed this crest indicative of the escape of Sir. Thomas from being burned in Queen Mary's reign, but the fiery crest is rather allusive to the "Smith that forgeth at the fire" of honest Verstegan.

Thomas, second son of John Smith of Corsham County, Wilts., settled in London and became farmer of the Customs to Queens Mary and Elizabeth. He purchased the estate of Ostenhanger (now called Westenhanger) and other property, in Kent, and died in 1591, aged 69. By Alice, his wife, daughter and heiress of Sir Andrew Judde, Lord Mayor of London in 1550 (son of John Judde of Yurnbridge, by Margaret, daughter and co-heiress of Valentine Chiche, which Valentine married Philippa, daughter and co-heiress of Sir Robert Chichele, Lord Mayor of London 1411 and 1421, by Agnes, his wife, daughter and heiress of William Apuldrefield, brother of Archbishop Chichele, founder of All Souls), he had seven sons. It is said that Smith farmed the Customs, at first, for £12,000 a year, and that they were then raised, time after time, until he paid £55,000 a year, and, £60,000 being afterward demanded, he relinquished the contract. He gave his eldest son Thomas (who was made a Knight of the Bath by King James) £8,000 a year, and upon each of his other sons he bestowed not less in estates than £6,000 a year. He had six sons, who were sheriffs of six different counties.

The surname of Smith is of great antiquity in Scotland, and of old was variously written Smyt, Smyth and Smith, and sometimes they have been called Gow, which is Gaelic for Smith. The traditional accounts of their origin is, that they are decended from the Clan Chattan: that Niel Croomb, third son of Murdoch of that clan, who lived in the reign of William the Lion, was their progenitor. The sejant cat is the device of the Clan Chattan, the motto "Na beau d'on chat gan lamhainu."—Touch not the cat without a glove. "The Clan Chattan, who gave the name to the county of Caithness, bore as their chief cognizance the wild mountain cat, and called their chieftain the Earl of Sutherland, Mohr an Chat, the great wild cat."

CHAPTER XXX.

On the maternal side my first ancestor in America was George Little, who came to Newbury, from Unicorn street near London bridge, in 1640. Though a young man, it appears as though he brought a considerable sum of money, as he made an extensive purchase of land, which now comprises some of the finest farms in Oldtown, most of this estate being still retained by his descendants. He was a man of honesty and ability, often appointed to fill places of trust and honor. He married Alice Poore, who sailed for New England from Southampton in May 1638, together with her younger brothers, Samuel and Daniel, in the party of Mr. Richard Dummer. She died in 1680, aged 62. His second wife was Eleanor Barnard, widow of Thomas Barnard of Amesbury.

George and Alice Little had five children—Sarah who died in infancy, Joseph, John, Moses, and a second Sarah. Capt. Joseph Little married Mary, daughter of Tristram Coffin, Esq. Their children were Judith, Joseph, (who died at the age of thirteen), George, Sarah, Enoch, Tristram, Moses, Daniel, and Benjamin.

Ensign Enoch Little married Elizabeth, daughter of John Worth. Ensign Little took his bride to a farm recently granted on Crane-neck hill; this comprised the lower end of the hill; Capt. James Smith's was above; Mr. Ezra Pillsbury's place lay on the northern, and that of Dr. Adams on the southern slopes. The bridegroom mounted his horse, with his young wife on the pillion, and with their effects packed in saddle-bags, they rode over the bridle-path through the woods to their new home. No shelter had been provided. It was pleasant summer weather, and the young couple on the first day dined upon a large, flat rock, which is still preserved as a memorial; at night they sought the protection of the garrison house. A small house and suitable out-buildings were built, trees were felled, and fruitful fields soon replaced the ancient forest. This pair had seven children: Joseph, Elizabeth, John, Edmund, Enoch, Daniel, and Benjamin. Five of these—Joseph, John, Enoch, Daniel and Benjamin, died of the throat distemper, which at one time committed such fearful ravages throughout the colony. The only daughter, Elizabeth, married Abel Huse. Capt. Edmund Little married Judith, daughter of Dr. Matthew Adams of Crane-neck hill; their children were Elizabeth, Judith, Joseph, John, Sarah and Mary, (twins), Enoch, Eunice, Prudence and Hannah. Elizabeth married Abram Day, and moved to Bradford. Judith married twice—first Abram Adams, at the "Farms;" second, Capt. Joseph Noyes of Newburyport. Joseph (my grandfather) married Betty Merrill. Within one year from her nuptials Mrs. Little died of consumption; his second wife was Mary, third daughter of the Rev. William Johnson. John married Ruth, daughter of Ezekiel Hale; and Enoch, Mary, half-sister of Ruth: Sarah married Samuel Thurrell, or Thurlow. Mr. Thurrell resided some time at the "Farms." In the year 1788 he purchased the Dr. Adams place and moved to Crane-neck hill. Mary became the wife of John Merrill; their only child, Lydia, married Dr. Daniel Noyes Poore; these were the great-grandparents of the present Indian

Hill family. Eunice married Robert Adams at the "Farms." Prudence died when a child. Hannah married Samuel Dole; this pair resided some years in Oldtown: afterwards Mr. Dole purchased the March Farm in Newtown, and moved thither.

Capt. Edmund Little apportioned to his son Joseph about seventy acres. He erected a house and barn at the foot of Crane-neck hill, just beyond the brook. This was then a considerable stream, with sufficient power to turn the wheel of a grist mill which accommodated the neighborhood. Capt. Little had erected the present large and commodious mansion, now owned by his great-great-grandson, Edmund Little, and here he resided, his son Enoch occupying half of the house. A smaller one was built for John, farther up the hill. The homestead was divided equally between these two, who cultivated the place, annually paying their father one-third of the income.

To avoid confusion I have spoken of my father's mother as Grandmother Smith, and have not mentioned her leaving the Smith homestead. In the year 1787 Capt. James Smith died. At that time Capt. Edmund Little was a widower. Two years later widow James Smith married her neighbor Capt. Edmund Little. Her son Enoch and daughter Sarah still occupied her part of the house, and cultivated the land. Prior to her marriage, settlements were drawn up by which, if Mrs. Little survived her husband, in lieu of the widow's dower, she was to receive a certain sum of money, and return to the home of her first marriage. This aged couple lived a most pleasant and contented life for fourteen years; then great-grandsir died quite suddenly, and "little grandmother," as I used to style her, returned to her former home. Uncle Enoch Smith bought the Major Hill farm and moved thither, while grandmother sank into her former routine, with her daughter Sarah for housekeeper, Uncle Enoch tilling the land as before. This marriage brought some queer relationships into our family. Prior to his mother's second union her son James had married Prudence, granddaughter of Capt. Edmund Little. Thus my father became son-in-law to his wife's grandfather. The stone erected at the grave of my father's mother bears this inscription:

ELIZABETH,
WIFE OF CAPT. JAMES SMITH,
AND RELICT OF CAPT. EDMUND LITTLE,
AGED EIGHTY-SEVEN.

The first ancestor in America of Elizabeth Worth, the wife of Ensign Enoch Little, was Lionel Worth, who married Susanna Whipple. Her father John Worth, married Elizabeth, daughter of Israel Webster, the second son of John and Mary (Shatswell) Webster of Ipswich. Mrs. Webster's second husband was John Emery of Newbury, who emigrated to this country from Romsey, England.

The arms of Worth are;

ARGENT, AN EAGLE IMPERIAL SABLE, MEMBERED OR.
CREST—A LION RAMPANT PPR.

The Rev. Daniel Little was born July 18th, 1724. He married in 1751, Mary, daughter of Rev. Joseph Emerson, who died June 2d, 1758, aged 32, and Sarah Coffin, June 6th, 1759. Though Mr. Little did not pursue a collegiate course, he spent several years in teaching, and the degree of A. M. was conferred by Harvard College in 1766. He studied theology with Rev. Joseph Moody of York, District of Maine, and in March, 1751, was ordained pastor of the second parish in Wells, in that district. Mr. Little was one of the most distinguished and influential clergyman in that region, enjoying a most successful pastorate of over fifty years. In 1772 he was appointed for missionary service in the eastern portion of the district of Maine. This work led during the succeeding years to be a series of arduous tours and he became styled the Apostle of the East. He established a school for the Indians on the Penobscot, and prepared a full vocabulary of their language. Mr. Little was much interested in the education of youth, and when far advanced in years, was selected as one of the trustees of Bowdoin College at its establishment. He died suddenly of paralysis, on the 5th of December, 1801, leaving several children and grandchildren; one of the latter became the leading partner in the firm Little, Brown & Co., Boston.

Col. Moses Little, born in Newbury May 8th, 1724, married, June 5th, 1743, Abigail, daughter of Joshua Bailey, twin sister of Judith, who married his brother Stephen, also sister of Gen. Jacob Bailey, a distinguished officer in the French and Revolutionary wars. She died Feb. 6th, aged 91.

During Col. Little's early manhood there was much activity in settling townships; large tracts of land had been granted to the officers and soldiers of the French and Indian war; many wealthy people were also securing grants. Col. Little obtained the appointment of surveyor of the King's lands. In 1750 he was one of a company who acquired from Gov. Benning Wentworth a large grant of the unoccupied crown lands lying within the present limits of Vermont. A few years after he purchased a large tract of land in the township of Apthorp, N. H., which was divided into two towns, one being named in his honor, Littleton, and the other Dalton, from his townsman, Hon. Tristram Dalton. His possessions in this region were increased by subsequent purchases, with Maj. Samuel Gerrish and Col. Jonathan Bailey. He acted as agent for the proprietors of Bakerstown, and succeeded in obtaining for them from the General Court of Massachusetts a township of land in Maine in lieu of the one granted in 1736, which was subsequently decided to be within the borders of New Hampshire. By purchasing from time to time the rights of the original proprietors he became the owner of the greater part of the grant, which comprised a large part of what is now Androscoggin county. In 1768 the Pejepscot Company granted to him and Col. Bailey a still larger tract in the same county, on the eastern side of the Androscoggin, on condition that they would settle fifty families there before June 1st, 1774, and build certain roads. These conditions being only partially fulfilled the amount of land deeded was diminished. Though over fifty years of age, the war of the Revolution found in Col. Little one of the most active and patriotic of his country's defenders. Being senior captain, at the news of the British expedition to Concord, which found him ploughing, he unyoked his oxen, and rallying his company, marched to the American head-quarters at Cambridge. At the battle of Bunker Hill he commanded a regiment. Forming his men in Indian file he led them across Charlestown Neck under a terrible fire from the British batteries and ships of war, arriving at the scene of conflict just prior to the third and final charge of the enemy. Though unhurt, Col. Little had several narrow escapes; comrades falling on either side bespattered his black velvet clothes with blood. In August he returned home to attend the funeral of two of his children, and rejoined his command after an absence of only two days. After the evacuation of Boston he accompanied the army to New York, his regiment forming a part of Gen. Greene's brigade.

On the 4th of April Washington left Cambridge for New York. Expecting him at Providence, Gen. Greene, who had been detained there, ordered two regiments, Hitchcock's Rhode Island and Little's Massachusetts, to appear in their best form, and escort the General into the city. The minuteness of Greene's directions on the occasion depicts the personal appearance of the early Continental soldier. The following has been preserved amongst Col. Little's papers:

"Providence, April 4th, 1776.
Col. Hitchcock's and Col. Little's regiments are to turn out to-morrow morning to escort his Excellency into town, to parade at 8 o'clock, both officers and men dressed in uniform; and none to turn out except those dressed in uniform; and those of the non-commissioned officers and soldiers that turn out to be washed, both face and hands, clean, their beards shaved, their hair combed and powdered, and their arms cleaned. The General hopes that both officers and soldiers will exert themselves for the honor of the regiment and brigade to which they belong. He wishes to pay the honors to the Commander-in-Chief in as decent and respectable a manner as possible."

Upon Washington's arrival at New York he arranged the army into five brigades, under Heath, Spencer, Sullivan, Green, and Stirling. It becoming necessary to despatch Gen. Sullivan with six regiments to the northward, on the 29th of April the troops were anew formed into four brigades. —Green's third brigade being assigned to Long Island. Owing to bad weather it did not cross until the third of May. These troops consisted of Col. Edward Hand's Pennsylvania Riflemen, two Rhode Island regiments under Cols. James Mitchell Varnum and Daniel Hitchcock, and Col. Moses Little's regiment from Massachusetts. These ranked as the first, ninth, eleventh and twelfth of the Continental Establishment, and were as well armed and under as good discipline as any in the army. Hand's regiment numbered four hundred and seventy officers and men, the others having an average of about three hundred and fifty each. These troops occupied the water front to keep the enemy's ships out of the river, and to secure themselves from an attack by land. To hold the Brooklyn peninsula a chain of works was thrown up across the neck. Three forts and two redoubts, with connecting breastworks, were thrown out. These forts were named Green, Box, and Putnam. The command of Fort Green was assigned to Col. Little, who describes it as the largest of the works on Long Island, and he resolved it never should be surrendered while he was alive.

Washington's army at the opening of the campaign of August 27th consisted of twenty-eight thousand five hundred officers and men. Of these Massachusetts furnished seven thousand three hundred. Greene having been advanced to the rank of Major-General, his brigade had been placed under the command of Brigadier-General John Nixion,—a sixth regiment from Massachusetts, under Col. William Prescott, having been added to the force.

On the 22d of August the British troops crossed from Staten to Long Island. When tidings of the enemy's landing reached Washington the troops were immediately put under arms. Col. Little expecting that morning would bring on a battle, and remembering his promise to defend Fort Greene to the last extremity, wrote the following letter to his son Isaiah:

AUG. 22, 1776.

I have thought fit to send you my will. You will take all charge necessary, &c. The enemy this day landed on this island and marched within three miles of our camp. Three or four regiments lodge within two miles of the enemy. I expect morning will bring us a battle.

Below is Col. Little's account of the battle:

IN CAMP, NEW YORK,
Sept. 1st, 1776.

The enemy left Staten Island and landed on Long Island the 22d, and encamped on a large plain five or six miles aross, at Flat Bush, four miles distant. In the morning at two o'clock, the enemy attacked our right wing; a smart engagement for some time. The enemy also advanced on our left. Lord Stirling reinforced the right wing and defended himself till 12 o'clock, when our wing gave way. My regiment was in the centre on guard. The enemy's right wing almost encircled two or three regiments, and as they were not together they were not able to defend themselves and retreated with about twenty wounded. Our people came in about eleven o'clock. The enemy at the same time with their light horse and English troops attempted to force our lines, but soon retreated, being met with a smart fire from our breast works.

Two deserters informed us that the number of enemy's dead and wounded was upwards of five hundred—I wish ours may not be more. On the morning of the 28th, the enemy were encamped on the heights in front of our encampment. Firing was kept up on both sides, from the right to the left. Weather very rainy; 29th, very rainy. Firing by both sides in front of Fort Putnam. About sunset the enemy pushed to recover the ground we had taken (about one hundred rods) in in front of the fort. The fire was very hot, the enemy gave way and our people recovered the ground. The fire ceased and our people retired to the fort. The enemy took possession again, and on the morning of the 30th, had a breast work there sixty rods long and one hundred and fifty rods distant from Fort Putnam.

Two ships of war had got up the sound as far as Hell-gate by this time. The general ordered each regiment to be paraded on their own parades at 7 o'clock p. m. and wait for orders. We received orders to strike our tents and march with our baggage, to New York. Our lines were manned until day-break. The reason of the retreat was, that we should have no chance to retreat if the ships came up. I am not certain we shall be able to keep the city of New York. You may hear of our being at King's bridge. A great battle I think will be fought here, or near King's bridge. I am in a good state of health.

I am your affectionate father,

MOSES LITTLE.

To Mr. Josiah Little.

Adjutant Josiah Adams, Lieut. Samuel Huse, Moses Pillsbury, Samuel Smith, Chase Colby, Richard Short, and David Emery, were seven of the soldiers from Newbury in this battle. The two latter stood shoulder to shoulder in the fray. Mr. Short ever cherished a tender memory of his deceased comrade,—an affection extended to his son. To the latest day of his long life his first words of greeting always were, "David, your father and I faced death together."

The following is taken from Col. Little's order book:

"REGIMENTAL ORDERS.

(Col. Little's.)

Officers for fatigue to-morrow—Capt. Gerrish, Lt. Kent, and Lt. Atkinson."

"Regimental Orders for the 12th Regiment of Foot:

James Holland, a fifer in Cap. Dodge's Company, is appointed fife-major to this regiment, and is to be obeyed as such. Com'd officers for picket to-night—Lt. Atkinson and Lt. Fiske.

May 21st, 1776. Field officer for picket to-morrow night—Lt. Col. Crary, Adj. from Col. Little's regiment."

GEN. GREEN'S ORDER.

May 25, 1776.

Capt. Silas Talbot of Col. Hitchcock's regiment, Cap'n Frazier of Cap'n (Col.) Wayne's regiment, Lt. Noel Allen of Col. Varnum's regiment, and Lt. Samuel Huse of Col. Little's regiment, are a committee to inspect the provisions for the troops of this bridage.

June 21, 1776.

Lt. Huse is requested to oversee the well-digging in Fort Green.

July 18, 1776.

Field officer of the day to-morrow, Lt. Col. Henderson, Adj. from Col. Little's.

Aug. 16, 1776.

The gin shops, and houses selling liquor, strictly forbidden to sell to soldiers, excepting near the two ferries. The General is determined to have any soldiers punished that may be found disguised with liquor, as no soldier in such a situation can be fit for defense or attack.

The General orders that no sutler in the army shall sell to any soldier more than 1 gill of spirits per day. If the above orders are not adhered to, there shall be no more retailed out at all.

List of killed and missing at the battle of Brooklyn, Col. Little's, Twelfth Continental (Mass.)

Captain Parker's Company.

Killed—Peter Barthrick.

Capt. Wade's Company.

Missing—Archelaus Pulsifer.

Capt. Dodge's Company.

Missing—Elijah Lewis.

After the battle of Brooklyn, Col. Little was entrusted with the command of an encampment at Peekskill, where he was detained by illness during Washington's retreat through New Jersey. At the battles of Trenton and Princeton his troops were commanded by Lieut.-Col. Henshaw, but he rejoined the army in time for efficient service. His health being seriously impaired, he returned home in 1777. In 1779 he was appointed by the Commonwealth to take command of the naval armament, which was designed to dislodge the enemy at Penobscot, but declined on account of ill health. He lost his speech in 1781, from a stroke of paralysis, and died May 27, 1798, aged 74.

Col. Little was characterized by sagacity, strength of mind, and a self-possession which in the most trying situations never deserted him. He made the acquaintance of Washington early in the war, who held him in high esteem, and often relied upon his judgment. An autograph letter from the latter, with the sword worn at the battle of Bunker Hill, and other relics, are still in the possession of his descendants.

Col. Josiah, son of Col. Moses Little, born Feb. 16, 1747; married, Nov. 23, 1770, Sarah, daughter of Edward Toppan, of Newbury. Like his father, Col. Josiah Little was noted for energy and activity. Until far advanced in years, he annually visited the lands he inherited in Maine, New Hampshire and Vermont, driving over the rough roads alone, even after he had lost one hand by a premature explosion while overseeing the blasting of a passage through some rapids on the Androscoggin. He had charge of his father's real estate for many years. As the agent of the Pejebscot Company, whose claims were not very readily acknowledged, he was often brought into unfriendly relations with the squatters, who were numerous in Maine at that time. Tradition has handed down many laughable adventures, but frequently his personal safety was in jeopardy. In Newbury, Col. Little was both influential and popular, representing the town in the General Court for nearly thirty successive years. In addition to his other business he was largely engaged in shipping. At his death he left a fortune valued at several hundred thousand dollars. He died Dec. 26, 1830, aged 83.

Michael, oldest child of Col. Josiah Little was born March 14, 1772; graduated at Dartmouth in 1792; married, Oct. 19, 1800, Sarah Stover, who died July 28, 1801. His second wife was Elizabeth Ricker, of Somersworth. He died March 16, 1830.

Hon. Edward Little, the second son of Col. Josiah Little, was born March 12th, 1773. Graduated at Dartmouth College in 1797; married, Jan. 10th, 1799, Hannah, daughter of Captain Thomas Brown of Newbury. She died Aug. 1st, 1828, aged 56 years. His second wife was Hannah, widow of Tappan Chase of Portland. He studied law in Newburyport in the office of Judge Parsons; practised his profession for several years with success; was county attorney and publisher of law reports for the Commonwealth. After the fire of 1811, by which he lost nearly all of his property, he removed to Portland, and in 1826 to Auburn, where he continued to reside during the remainder of his life. The owner, by inheritance, of the larger part of the surrounding territory, he had great influence in directing and promoting the growth of the place. He endowed an academy which continued in successful operation for forty years. After the formation of the high school system the grounds and a portion of the funds were transferred by the trustees to the town, which now maintains an Edward Little High School. He died Sept. 21st, 1849.

Josiah, the third son of Col. Josiah Little, born Jan. 13th, 1791, graduated at Bowdoin in 1811; married, Jan. 24th, 1814, Sophronia Balch. He was an extensive land owner, and engaged in manufactures; a member of the Maine Historical Society, and an Overseer of Bowdoin College, where he established a professorship of Natural Science, and founded the Public Library of Newburyport, where for many years he occupied the residence of the late Dr. Edmund Sawyer on High street. He died Feb 5th, 1860.

Josiah Stover, only child of Michael and Sarah (Stover) Little, born July 9th, 1801, graduated at Bowdoin at the head of the class of 1825; married Abby Chamberlain, Sept., 1833. He was President of the Atlantic and St. Lawrence Railroad, and Speaker of the Maine House of Representatives for several years. He died April 2d, 1862.

Josiah, second son of Hon. Edward Little, born April 29th, 1801, was a graduate of Bowdoin, studied law with his father, practiced his profession for several years, afterwards engaged in manufactures. He married, Sept. 2d, 1822, Mary Holt Cummings of Norway, Me., who died at Minot, Oct 6th, 1829, aged 25 years and 6 months; March 30th, 1830, Nancy Williams Bradford, who died at Auburn, Nov. 20th, 1834, aged 26 years and 7 months; May 26th, 1835, Sally Brooks, of Alfred, who died at Auburn, April 15th, 1849, aged 41 years and 11 months, and May 20th, 1850, Charlotte Ann Brooks, who survives him.

After an absence of many years he returned to his native place, Newburyport, where he resided until his death. As a man of business he posessed excellent judgment. As a citizen he was the firm friend of good order and good morals, furthering to his utmost the well-being of the community. For many years he took a deep interest in the church and Christian institutions. He died Aug. 9th, 1863.

Edward Toppan, third son of the Hon. Edward Little, born Dec. 29th, 1809, studied law with his father, represented his town in the State legislature for several years, and was Judge of Probate for Androscoggin county. For many years he was a director in the Maine Central Railroad and of the First National Bank of Auburn. His reputation as an upright and able lawyer gave him an extensive practice. He married, Oct. 2d, 1839, Melinda C., daughter of the Rev. W. B. Adams, who died at Auburn, Sept. 30th, 1842; and June 9th, 1846, Lucy Jane, daughter of Zeba Bliss. He died November, 1805.

Hon. Moses, the youngest son of Col. Moses Little, born Jan. 20th, 1767, married, Aug. 6th, 1786, Elizabeth, daughter of Shubael Dummer, who died Oct. 22d, 1840. He held the commission of justice of the peace for fifty years, represented the town of Newbury in the Legislature nineteen years, was a member of the convention for altering the constitution of Massachusetts, and a deacon of the Belleville church for thirty years. He died April 28th, 1857.

Moses, son of Moses and Lydia (Coffin) Little, born Feb. 26th, 1691; married Sarah, daughter of Sergeant Stephen and Deborah Jaques, Feb. 12th, 1716. He died Oct. 17th, 1780.

The following epitaph is taken from stone in the upper burying ground, on the Plains, at Newbury:—

MR. MOSES LITTLE DEPARTED THIS LIFE
OCT. 17TH, IN THE 90TH
YEAR OF HIS AGE.
HE WAS TEMPERATE IN ALL THINGS.
INDUSTRIOUS, HOSPITABLE, YET FRUGAL.
A KIND HUSBAND AND TENDER FATHER.
A GOOD NEIGHBOR AND GOOD CITIZEN,
AND WHILE LIVING JUSTLY SUSTAINED THE FIRST
OF CHARACTERS—AN HONEST MAN.

"A wit's a feather, a chief's a rod,
An honest man's ye noblest work of God."

Deacon Stephen, oldest son of Mr. Moses Little, born May 19th, 1719; married, Aug. 5th, 1743, Judith Bailey, who died 1764, aged 40, and afterwards Mary Long, who survived him, dying in 1798, in her 75th year;

Deacon Little died Aug. 30th, 1793.

Jacob, the youngest child of Deacon Stephen Little, born 1763; married Hannah, daughter of Moses and Hannah Sawyer, Sept. 28th, 1786. Their seventh child, Jacob, born March 19th, 1797, in Newbury, Belleville, was one of the most prominent of New York brokers. His father, Jacob Little, was a man of wealth and distinction, but commercial disasters swept away his property, and the war of 1812 nearly completed his financial ruin. In 1817 Mr. Little secured a situation for his son Jacob in counting-house of the renowned Jacob Barker, and at once he became a favorite with that successful merchant. After remaining with Mr. Barker five years, he began business on his own account as an exchange specie broker, in a small basement office on Wall street. During the next twelve years, working eighteen hours a day in his little office, he promptly and shrewdly executed every order, and his success was due no less to his integrity than to his talent. In 1834 Mr. Little stood at the head of the leading financiers and bankers of the city, but commercial disaster overtook him. Thrice Mr. Little was carried down, but he was never dishonored. He recovered himself, and paid up his contracts in full. On his first suspension, though legally free from liability, he disbursed nearly $1,000,000, paying every creditor in full with interest, so that it was a common saying among moneyed men, that Jacob Little's suspended paper was better than the checks of most merchants. He closed his long career without a stain upon his mercantile reputation. He died March 28th, 1865, leaving a widow and one son. The newsof his death startled the great city. Merchants congregated to do him honor. Resolutions of enduring respect were adopted, and the Stock Board adjourned to attend his funeral. He was borne to his burial in Greenwood Cemetery with all honor.

Paul, the youngest son of Mr. Moses Little, born April 1, 1740; married, May 20, 1762, Hannah Emery, who died in September, 1771; widow Sarah Souther of Ipswich, Aug. 30, 1772, who died Sept. 26, 1797, aged 54; and afterwards widow Sarah Emerson of Boxford, who died May 25, 1817, aged 55. He moved from Newburyport to Portland in 1761; was a goldsmith by trade, but engaged in commercial business to a considerable extent. After the destruction of the town by the British in 1776 he removed to Windham, where many of his descendants still reside.

Silas Little, born in March, 1754; graduated at Dartmouth in 1792; married his cousin Lucretia, daughter of Joseph and Elizabeth Hazen Little, and died in 1845. Squire Little was a prominent citizen, and owned a fine farm in Oldtown. Among other public offices, he was one of the selectmen, and a representative to the state legislature for several years.

Moses Little, born July 3, 1766; graduated at Harvard in 1787; was a physician in Salem, Mass., and died Oct. 13, 1811.

William Little, born Oct. 14, 1825; married Ellen M. Carlton, of Haverhill, Oct. 6, 1864. Town clerk of Newbury for over twenty years, and president of the Antiquarian and Historical Society of Old Newbury.

David Little Withington, born in Newbury, Feb. 2, 1854; graduated at

Harvard in 1874. A practicing lawyer in Boston and Newburyport.

Lothrop Withington, born in Newbury, Jan. 31, 1856; educated at Dummer Academy and Putnam Free School, graduating at the latter in 1872. Since 1873, has resided a large part of the time in England and France. Edited and published "The Ocean Wave," a daily evening paper, in Newburyport, from October, 1878, to April, 1879, and was lately on the staff of the Newburyport Herald.

Russel Moody Little, born in 1858; a student at Amherst.

The exact pedigree of George Little, of Unicorn street, London, I have been unable to learn; the family descent can be traced by the coats of arms. The first granted are: Little—Sable, a saltire or (another or). The next record of these arms are: Little, Meichledale, Scotland—Sa, saltire, engr. or; Little, Liberton, Scotland—the same arms, with a crescent for difference. Crest, a leopard's head or; motto, Magnum in parvo.

At some period between 1698 and 1731, a William Little, of Liberton, county Edinburgh, a gentleman of ancient family, which had been in possession of the barony of Liberton for over a hundred years preceding, married Helen, daughter of Sir Alexander Gilmour, of Craigmillar in the same county. Next in order comes George Little, esq., of Llanvair Grange, county Monmouth, Wales. Arms:

SA, A CHEVRON ENGR. ARGENT. CREST—LEOPARD'S HEAD PPR. MOTTO—"MAGNUM IN PARVO."

There was a family of Littles, of Kilnrea, Yorkshire, England, recorded as "long time resident in this parish," in 1671, but the arms are a lion.

The arms transmitted by the descendants of George Little in America are:

OR, A SALTIRE, OR ST. ANDREW'S CROSS, ENGRAILED SABLE. CREST—A WOLF'S HEAD. MOTTO—"MAGNUM IN PARVO," GREAT IN LITTLE.

The arms of the family of Alice Poore, the first wife of George Little, are:

OR, A FESS AZURE, THREE MULLETS GULES. CREST—LION'S HEAD OR. MOTTO—"PAUPER NON IN SPE," POOR NOT IN HOPE.

CHAPTER XXXI.

The Amery's (or Emery's) first ancestor in England was Gilbert D'Amery, a Norman Knight of Tours, who, in

1066, fought at Hastings with William the Conqueror. The Roll of Battle Abbey, where the names of the Conqueror's chieftains are recorded, gives the name as "Damery."

Gilbert D'Amery received large landed estates from William the Conqueror. He owned Thackingdon, and half a dozen manors, near Oxford, which were held by his descendants until 1376, when the third Baron Richard D'Amery died. They long dwelt at Berkwell manor, ten miles from Oxford, where still stands the church they built. The property went by heiresses to other names, but John represented the county in parliament as late as 1423. Another John settled in Devon, and his heir held the mânor of White Chapel at Bishops Nympton, which Frances, the heiress of William, carried to Edward Gibbon, whose tablet, at Tiverton, is dated 1707.

Thomas Emery, citizen and upholder, of London, left a will, dated March 11, 1533, proved June 2, 1534, bequeathing his soul to God, the Virgin Mary, &c., and desiring to be buried in the churchyard of St. Michael, Cornhill, London.

Edward Emery, of Mary at Rooting, County Essex, gent., will dated Oct. 30, 1637, proved Jan. 15, 1641, names elder brother Thomas Emery, and appoints his younger brother, Anthony Emery, his executor.

The Herald's Visitation of Essex, 1634, contains the following:

"Thomas Emery als Amery of Little Baddow co. Essex, Thomas Emery of Little Baddow eldest sonn, mar. Mary dau. of Folliett of qu Filliot, Oldhall in Rayne. Thomas Emery of Little Baddow co. Essex 1634, mar. Jane, daughter of Bayley of Wadesmill co. Hertford; children, Edward, Anthony, Mary, Elisabeth."

Thomas Amery, son of Robert and Miss Elliot, held estates near Bristol. He married the daughter of the nineteenth Lord Kerry. His brother Jonathan came to Carolina as advocate-general and treasurer. His daughter Sarah married Gov. Arthur Middleton. His son Thomas settled in Boston.

Edwards, in his Life of Sir Walter Raleigh, quotes a letter from John Hooker to Sir Walter:

"Your ancestor, Sir John de Raleigh, married the daughter of D'Amerie, D'Amerie of Clare, Clare of King Edward the First, which Clare, by his father, descended of King Henry the First."

In a volume of French history it is said that when Napoleon had resolved to negotiate "avec Rome pour retablir' L'ancien culte," his first advances were "sous la direction religieuse du respectable abbe Emery, superieur general de Saint Sulspice."

Anthony and John Emery, the first in America, came from Romsey, England, in the ship James, to Ipswich, thence to Newbury, in June, 1635. Romsey is a rare old town in Hampshire (Hants), on the river Esk (the Auton of the Roman period). The broad, but winding and shallow vale is indescribably beautiful, with its manors and cottages amidst the slumberous foliage, its wheat meadows, green slopes, and crystal "Auton water." Flocks of Southdowns dot the pasture swells, and myriads of sparrows sweep around the ripening grain acres. Towards Southampton stretches the superb park and forest of "Broadlands," the seat of Lord Palmerston. Beyond is the old mediæval town; the great square tower of the abbey church of St. Mary's towering above the quaint buildings, with the walled and buttressed bridge of high arches spanning the gleaming river. In the churchyard of the old abbey (one of the oldest in England, a part of the walls having been erected in the twelfth century, by Henry De Blois, bishop of Winchester) repose the dust of successive generations of Emerys, and within its time-honored walls Anthony and John Emery were baptised. In the churchyard were interred my Smith ancestors. Thomas Smith came from Romsey. It was from the worship in this ancient pile that the forefathers seceded to join the sect of the Puritans. The Emerys are still represented in Romsey. A John Emery recently deceased there, who counted his descent from an ancestor in the middle ages.

Anthony Emery, with his wife Frances, and son James (born in England), went to Dover as early as 1644, where he occupied land which he purchased of Stephen Goddard in 1643. In 1646 he had a grant of land of the town, and was one of the selectmen of Dover. He kept a tavern, but, having trouble with the authorities respecting his license to sell wines, &c., in 1648 he assigned his land to Thomas Layton, and moved to Kittery, and settled in what is now called Elliot. He signed the submission to Massachusetts, in 1652, and was elected as one of the townsmen or selectmen for that year, and also for 1654. He received from the town, in 1650, grants of land of two hundred acres. He was the first ferryman between Kittery and "Strawberry Bank"; a prominent citizen, holding several local offices; a smart, enterprising man; and many of his descendants are notable persons. The time of his death is unknown.

James Emery, born about 1630; came to this country with his father; went to Kittery, and signed the submission to Massachusetts in 1652. He had grants of land from the town of Kittery from 1652 to 1671 of four hundred and ten acres; was one of the selectmen of Kittery for several years, and was a representative to the General Court at Boston in 1676. His wife was Elizabeth. Children: James, born about 1658; Zachariah, born in 1660; Noah, born in 1663; Daniel, born in 1666; Job, born in 1670.

James Emery, son of James, married Margaret, daughter of Richard Hitchcock, Dec. 18, 1685. Children: Margaret, born Dec. 18, 1686; James, born Feb. 18, 1688; Lydia, born April 28, 1891; Frances, born Dec. 17, 1694; Rebekah, born March 7, 1697 (the latter married Daniel Smith, of Saco, Jan. 1, 1719, and Matthew Ladd, of Falmouth, May 7, 1755); Samuel, born Sept. 2, 1700; Elizabeth, born March 7, 1703; Thomas, born Dec. 2, 1706; Lucretia, born March 6, 1709.

Zachariah Emery received from the town of Kittery in 1665 a grant of fifty acres. His wife was Elizabeth. Children: Elizabeth, born Nov. 24, 1687; Zachariah, born Oct. 5, 1690.

Noah Emery had a grant of land from the town of Kittery, in 1885 and 1699, of one hundred acres.

Daniel Emery married Margaret, daughter of William Gowen, March 17, 1695. He died Oct. 15, 1722. He had a grant of twenty acres of land in 1694. He was an original member of the church in South Berwick in 1702, a deacon in 1703, and an elder in 1720. He and his brother James were selectmen of the town in 1707, and for several subsequent years. He was also noted surveyor of land. His farm in Elliot is still owned and occupied by his descendants. His children were: Daniel, born June 25, 1697; Noah, born Dec. 11, 1699, settled in Exeter, N. H.; Simon, born Jan. 6, 1702; Zachariah, born March 12, 1704; Margaret, born March 3, 1707; Caleb, born Oct. —, 1710; Ann, born March 19, 1712; Joshua, born June 30, 1715; Tirzah, born Sept. 19, 1717 (married Dudley James, of Exeter, Jan. 12, 1753); Huldah, born Aug. 4, 1720.

Job Emery had grants of land from Kittery, in 1694 and 1699, of thirty acres. His wife was Charity. Children: Job, born Jan. 29, 1697; Charity, born April 24, 1699; Sarah, born Feb. 4, 1700; Joseph, born Feb. 4, 1702 (married Mehitable Stacy, Oct. 10, 1727; she was born Feb. 4, 1705); Jonathan, born Feb. 27, 1709; Elizabeth, born July 8, 1711; Mary Abigail, born Nov. 17, 1713; Miriam, born April 8, 1716; Jabez, born July 13, 1718; Mary, born Dec. 4, 1720.

John Emery secured a grant of land on the southerly side of the main road leading to the bridge over the river Parker, a short distance above the "Lower Green," Oldtown. He had been accompanied from England by his wife (whose maiden name is unknown), a son, John, born about 1629, and a daughter, Anna, born in 1631. The record of the third child, the first born in America, is: "Ebenezer, a daughter, 16 Sept., 1848, being Monday morning, two hours before day." "*Ebenezer*: Hitherto hath the Lord helped us." Evidently this daughter was named from hearts overflowing with thankfulness. Though Miss Ebenezer might not have exactly fancied her christian name, I doubt not it gave her Puritan sire the keenest satisfaction. Mrs. Emery died the April following the birth of this daughter. The 29th of October, 1650, John Emery married Mary (Shatswell) Webster, widow of John Webster, of Ipswich. They had one son, Jonathan Emery.

John Emery, jr., Oct. 2, 1648, married Miss Mary Webster, a daughter of the widow Mary (Shatswell) Webster. Children: Mary, born June 24, 1652; Hannah, born April 26, 1654; John, born Sept. 12, 1656; Bethia, born Oct. 15, 1658; Sarah, born Feb. 26, 1661; Joseph, born March 23, 1663; Stephen, born, Sept. 6, 1666; Abigail, born Jan. 16, 1669; Samuel, born Dec. 20, 1670; Judith, born Feb. 4, 1673; Lydia, born Feb. 19, 1675; Elizabeth, born Feb. 8, 1680; Josiah, born Feb. 28, 1681. John Emery died in 1693. Mary, his widow, died April 28, 1694.

Anna Emery married, Nov. 23, 1648, James Ordway, who, tradition says, came from Wales to Newbury. He was born in 1620, and died after 1702. Anna, his wife, died March 31, 1687. Children: Ephraim, born April 25, 1650; James, born April 16, 1651; Edward, born Sept. 14, 1653; Sarah, born Sept. 14, 1656; John, born Nov. 17, 1658; Isaac, born Dec. 4, 1660, and died Jan. 16, 1669; Jane, born Nov. 12, 1663; Hananiah, born Dec. 2, 1865; Anne, born Feb. 17, 1670.

Jonathan Emery, second son of John, senior, married, Nov. 29, 1676, Mary, daughter of Edward Woodman, jr. Children: Mary, born Sept. 24, 1677; Jonathan, born Feb. 2, 1679; David, born Sept. 28, 1682; Anthony, born Nov. 13, 1684; Stephen, born Jan. 13, 1687, and died in Oct., 1688; Sara, born Dec. 18, 1688; Stephen, born

June 24, 1692; Edward, born Nov. 10, 1694, and James.

Eleanor Emery, a sister of Anthony and John, married John Bailey, jr., who came to Salisbury, thence to Newbury, in 1650. Children: Rebecca, born 1641; John, born May 18, 1643, and died June 22, 1663; Joshua, died April 7, 1652; Sarah, born Aug. 17, 1644: Joseph, born April 4, 1648; James, born Sept. 12, 1650; Joshua, born Feb. 17, 1653; Isaac, born July 22, 1654; Rachel, born Oct. 19, 1662; Judith, born Aug. 3, 1665, and died Sept. 20, 1668.

Ebenezer Emery married, April 21, 1669, John Hoag. Children: John, born Feb. 20, 1670: Jonathan, born Oct. 28, 1671; Joseph, born Jan. 10, 1677; Hannah, born Jan. 3, 1683; Judith, born April 20, 1687.

John, oldest son of Jonathan and Mary (Woodman) Emery, married, March 1, 1705, Hannah Morss. She died Oct. 4, 1732. In 1733, Mr. Emery married Rebecca Walker. Children: Hannah, born June 19, 1706, married Edward Holman, May 19, 1726; Joshua, born March 21, 1708, married Sarah Smith, March 28, 1728; David, born Jan. 24, 1710, married Abigail, daughter of Deacon Daniel Chase, Jan. 27, 1732. She died Aug. 29, 1753, aged 38. His second wife's maiden name was Mary Pillsbury; she first married John Hills, in 1728, second, Enoch Hale, Feb. 1, 1750; Sarah, born Dec., 1711, married David Chase, Nov. 24, 1729; Dr. Anthony, born Sept. 5, 1713, married Abigail Leavitt, of Hampton, N. H., May 10, 1738; Mehitabel, born Oct. 12, 1718, married Nathan Morss, Oct. 20, 1742; Judith, born Jan. 10, 1722, married Samuel Smith, Dec. 2, 1742; Mary, born Dec. 8, 1726, married William Smith, May 20, 1747.

David, second son of John and Hannah Emery, obtained a grant of land in the "West Precinct" of Newbury, on the main road in the upper parish, and became one of the wealthiest citizens in that part of the town. His children, all by his first wife, Abigail Chase, were: David, born Jan. 23, 1734, died Feb. 14, 1734; John, born Jan. 16, 1735, married Edna Noyes, April 7, 1756; Abigail, born June 2, 1737, married Ephraim Boynton, Feb. 19, 1756; Hannah, born Feb., 1739, married Daniel Hills, May 15, 1757; Martha, born March 1, 1741, married Nathaniel Bailey, August 6, 1761; Sarah, born June 24, 1744, married Enoch Noyes, Oct. 30, 1765; Moses, born Jan. 13, 1748, married Sarah Hale, Sept. 27, 1770 — children, Abigail, John, Jacob, and Moses; Thomas, born 1750, married Ruth March, Oct. 10, 1770, and died Nov. 21, 1770. His widow married John White, 3rd, May 7, 1772.

David Emery and his second wife died from dysentery, a short time from each other. Their gravestones read:

MARY,
WIFE OF DAVID EMERY,
DIED SEPT. 16, 1778,
AGED 66.

DAVID EMERY,
DIED OCT. 29th, 1778,
AGED 69 YEARS.

John, son of David and Abigail (Chase) Emery, married Edna, daughter of Capt. Ephraim Noyes, for his first wife. Edna (Noyes) Emery, a great-granddaughter of Mr. Nicholas Noyes, and great-grandneice of Rev. James Noyes, also descended from a noteworthy family on the maternal side, her mother being Abigail, the second child of Jonas and Anna (Bailey) Platts, and granddaughter of Dea. Joseph Bailey, of Bradford.

Dea. Joseph Bailey was the only child of Richard Bailey, who came from Yorkshire, England, to America, when he was fifteen years old, with Richard Dummer, in the ship Bevis, 150 tons, Robert Batten, master, in April, 1638. At that early age, young Bailey was noted for piety; and, during a violent storm on the voyage, he was called upon by the ship's company to pray for their safety. He married Edna Holstead, and purchased an estate in Rowley. He was one of a company to set up the first cloth mill in America, which was in Rowley, on the site of the present "Dummer's (Glen) Mills." Richard Bailey died in 1647 or 1648. In 1619, Edna, the widow of Richard Bailey, married Ezekiel Northend, of Rowley, who probably took possession of the homestead, as it has been in the possession of the Northend family from that time.

When Dea. Joseph Bailey obtained his lot, and built his house, the homestead was included within the ancient precincts of Rowley, that part bordering the river bearing the designation of "Merrimac Land." This was soon incorporated as the town of Bradford, and in 1850 the east part of Bradford, in which his farm was situated, was set off as a separate town under the name of Groveland. Deacon Bailey was one of the leading men of Bradford, in civil, military and ecclesiastical affairs. He was one of the selectmen twenty-three years between 1675 and 1710, and one of the deacons from the formation of the church until his death, Oct. 11, 1712.

The Bailey arms are:

OR, ON A FESS BETWEEN THREE MARTLETS GU, A BEZANT. CREST—A DEMI-LADY, HOLDING IN HER DEXTER HAND A TOWER, AND IN SINISTER A BRANCH OF LAUREL.

The children of John and Edna (Noyes) Emery were: Ephraim, born Feb. 28, 1758; David, born April 20, 1763; Hannah, who died in childhood. Mrs. Emery deceased soon after, and Mr. Emery married Betty Smith, of Crane-neck hill. He lived but a short time after this union, and his widow married Col. Spofford, of New Rowley.

Ephraim, oldest son of John and Edna Emery, married Mary, daughter of Peter Russell, of Bradford. Children: Mary, Thomas, Sohn and Hannah.

David Emery, the second son, born April 20, 1763, married Betty, only daughter of John and Ruth (Hale) Little. He died Oct. 21, 1785. Their son, David, was born Dec. 22, 1785. The third year of her widowhood, Betty (Little) Emery married Moses Colman, of Byfield.

Stephen, third son of John, jr., and Mary (Webster) Emery, born in 1666, married Ruth Jaques in 1692, and settled on a farm, on the "river road," in what is now the first parish in West

Newbury. Children: Anna, Sarah, Ruth, Mary, Judith, Abigail, Elizabeth, Stephen, Hannah, Miriam, and Lydia.

Lydia, born in 1717, married her kinsman, Moses Emery. Their children were: Lydia, Mary, John, Moses, Josiah, Nathan, Sarah, Anna, Amos, and Michael.

Amos, born in 1757, married Anna Moody in 1784. Children: Hannah, Anna, Ebenezer, Lydia, Miriam, Moses, Amos and Jacob Moody.

A part of the farm is still the residence of the widow and daughters of the late Jacob Moody Emery. A clock that had ticked in its corner at the homestead, for nearly one hundred and fifty years, has recently been taken to Portland, Maine, by a grandson of Amos Emery, Amos Emery Howell, where it has been rejunevated, looking even betetter than in its palmiest days, over a century ago.

Michael Emery was one of the first carriage builders of Amesbury. John Emery, senior, must have been a man of consideration and education, as we find his name bearing honorable mention, in the earliest annals of the settlement. February 1st, 1638, the town ordered that "John Emery shall make a sufficient pound for the use of the towne, two rods and a halfe square, by the last of the present month if he cann." On the following 17th of May, Anthony Emery was fined "twenty shillings for a pound breach, and to give thirteen shillings and fourpence to Thomas Coleman for his charges." Dec. 18th, 1645, a committee of seven men was appointed "at a publique meeting for to procure a water mill for to be built and set up in said towne (of Newbury), to grind theyr corne." And they agreed to give John Emery and Samuel Scullard £20 in merchantable pay, to give them ten acres of upland, and six acres of meadow, and that the said mill is to "be free from all rates for the first seven years, and to be a freehold to them and their heirs forever, they on their part agreeing to sett up said mill between Nicholas Holt's point and Edward Woodman's bridge, ready for the town's use, to grind the town's grists, at or before the twenty-ninth of Sept. 1646."

This was the second grist mill established in Newbury — the first was erected at "the falls," on the river Parker, by Messrs Dummer & Spencer, in accordance with the grant from the General Court, and an agreement with the town in 1635.

May 18th, 1647, the town, for three pounds, granted to John Emery "that parcell of land called the greene, about three akers, being more or lesse, bounded by the half-acre lots on the west, the hyeway on the south-east, and his own land on the north, being in a triangle, only the twenty rods is reserved in said land for a burying place as it is bounded with stakes with a way to it from the east."

This burying place is situated east of Oldtown hill, and is still called the "Emery lot." At a short distance may be seen the site of the first residence of John Emery with the well near by.

At the court in Salem, May 5th, 1663, John Emery was fined four pounds for entertaining Quakers. His offence consisted in granting food and lodging to two men and two women, who were travelling together farther east.

In George Bishop's "New England Judged," will be found this narration:

"Edward and George Preston, and

Mary Tompkins and Alice Ambrose, alias Gary, passed eastward to visit the seed of God in those parts, and in their way through Newbury, they went into the house of one John Emery, (a friendly man), who with his wife seemed glad to receive them, at whose house they found freedom to stay all night, and when the next morning came the priest, Thomas Parker, and many of his followers came to the man's house, and much reasoning and dispute there was about truth; but the priest's and many of the people's ears were shut against the truth. And in the time of their discourse, the wind striving in Mary Tompkin's stomach, making some noise, she having received no sustenance for the space of near forty-eight hours, one Joseph Pike, after they were departed the town said 'she had a devil in her.' After a while the priest perceiving that the battle might be too hard for him, rose up, and took the man of the house and his wife out of doors with him, and began to deal with them for entertaining such dangerous people. They replied they were required to entertain strangers. The priest said it was dangerous entertaining such as had plague sores upon them. Which the women hearing, began to take the priest to do for saying such false, wicked and malicious words, but he hasted away. Mary Tompkins called him to come back again, and not to show himself to be one of those hirelings that flee and leave their flocks behind them, but he would not."

It appears by the following, that John Emery was not completely over-awed by the good but mistaken Parker:

"The testimony of Henry Jaques aged about 44 years, saith, that I heard Joseph Noyes say, that after that time that the Quakers had their meeting at John Emery's, that he saw two Quakers at John Emery's house, and John Emery bade them welcome, and further saith that I heard Joseph Noyes say, that John Emery had entertained Quakers, both to bed and table, after the time they had their meeting at John Emery's house, and this he testified before the church at Newbury, and farther I do testify that I heard John Emery and his wife say that he had entertained Quakers and that he would not put them from his house, and used argument for the lawfulness of it.

HENRY JAQUES.

Sworn in Court, May 7, 1663,
Before Robert Lord, Clerk."

[This Henry Jaques was a constable of Newbury.]

"The Deposition of Joseph Noyes, aged 26 years:

This Deponent saith yt as he was agoing to Goodman Emerie's sen., he overtook two women Quakers, and supposing they would call at ye house of ye forementioned Emmery, he desired him not to entertain ym. But whilst he was in discourse, they came into ye house, and staid until he went away. Goodman Emmery was in ye chamber, (as he knows, because he ym upon an occasion called out to his wife) his wife being in ye same room with ye Quakers, at his house wn Mr. Parker was yr. Farther he had understood by those yt wr eye-witnesses, yt two men Quakers wr yr entertained very kindly to bed and table, & John Emmerie shook ym by ye hand and bid ym welcome. Ye substance of ys he or his wife in his presence told him and owned it, (according to his best remembrance) more yn once. This also ws severl days after ye meeting above said.

Taken upon Oath 24, 4th, 67,
before me, Simon Bradstreet."

At this period one can scarcely depict the commotion such an incident must have caused in the secluded and quiet settlement of Quascacunquen, on the banks of the winding Parker, or appreciate the courage evinced by John Emery and his wife in thus rising above popular prejudice, and fanatical bigotry and intolerance.

The Quaker guests, Mary Tompkins and Alice Ambrose, came from England to Boston, with George Preston in 1662. These women in company with a third, Anna Colman, on their visit to the "seed of God" in New Hampshire, aroused the indignation of the authorities, and Capt. Richard Waldron of Dover was impowered to act in the execution of the laws against "the wicked errors of Quakers," upon which he issued the following proclamation:

"To the Constables of Dover, Hampton, Salisbury, Newbury, Rowley, Ipswich, Windham, Lynn, Boston, Roxbury, Dedham, and until these vagabond Quakers are out of our jurisdiction."

"You and every one of you are required in the King's Majesty's name to take these vagabond Quakers, Anna Colman, Mary Tompkins, and Alice Ambrose, that they be stripped naked from the middle upwards, and make them fast to the cart's tail, and drawing the cart through the several towns, to whip them upon their naked backs not exceeding ten stripes apiece on each of them in each town, and so convey them from constable to constable till they are out of this jurisdiction, as you will answer it at your peril and this shall be your warrent.

Per me,
RICHARD WALDRON,"

Dover, Dec. 22, 1662.

This order was executed in Dover, Hampton, and Salisbury; but through the intervention of Walter Barefoot, Deputy Governor of New Hampshire, Newbury escaped the disgrace of such an act of cruelty. On pretence of delivering the persecuted females to the constables of Newbury, Gov. Barefoot took them from the New Hampshire constables, and secured them from further molestation by sending them out of the Province.

In October, 1657, the General Court had ordered that the penalty for entertaining Quakers should be forty shillings. In 1659, Thomas Macy, one of the first settlers of Newbury, but at that time a resident of Salisbury, was summoned to appear before the General Court, for violating the above law. Instead of complying, he sent a letter of which the following is a copy:

"This is to entreat the honored court not to be offended because of my non-appearance. It is not from slighting the authority of this honored court, nor from feare to answer the case; but I have bin for some weeks past, very ill, and am so at present, and notwithstanding my illness, yet I, desirous to appear, have done my utmost endeavor to hire a horse, but I cannot procure one at present; I being at present destitute have endeavored to purchase, but at present cannot attaine it, but I shall relate the truth of the case as my answer should be to ye honored court, and more cannot be proved, nor so much. On a rainy morning there came to my house Edward Wharton and three men more; the said Wharton spoke to me saying that they were travelling eastward, and desired me to direct them in the way to Hampton, and asked me how far it was to Casco bay. I never saw any of ye men afore except Wharton, neither did I require their names, or who they were, but by their carriage I thought they might be quakers, and told them so, and therefore desired them to pass on their way, saying to them I might possibly give offence in entertaining them; as soon as the violence of the rain ceased (for it rained very hard), they went away, and I never saw them since. The time that they were in the house was about three-quarters of an hour, but I can safely affirme it was not an houre. They spake not many words in the time, neither was I at leisure to talke with them, for I came home wet to ye skin immediately afore they came to the house, and I found my wife sick in bed. If this satisfie not the honored court, I shall subject to their sentence; I have not willingly offended, I am ready to serve and obey you in the Lord.

THO. MACY."

Notwithstanding this explanation and apology, Mr. Macy was fined thirty shillings, and was ordered to be admonished by the governor. Tradition informs us that Thomas Macy, immediately after his sentence, with his family repaired to Nantucket in an open boat, being one of the first English settlers on that island, where he passed the remainder of his life. This incident, Whittier has woven into one of his most charming ballads.

Two of the Quakers who received shelter in Thomas Macy's house, William Robinson and Marmaduke Stephenson, were hung at Boston, December 27, 1659.

There is more "truth than poetry" in Jay's "Innocency's Complaint," where he writes, "The making laws for to ensnare the just of God, is hated and to be accurst. The Massachusetts is alike for crime unto Judea in Christ Jesus' time. Here laws are extant that doth terrify well-meaning men and Liberty deny. Here innocents are fined, whipt and branded, ears cropped, some sold for slaves, some lashed, some hanged. Whoever is contrary to them found, tho' in his spirit, their fine must be five pounds, or else three days in jail ere a discharge, and with a ten-lashed whipping be enlarged."

The following, respecting the entertainment of Dr. Henry Greenland, Newbury's earliest physician, has been found among the Massachusetts archives:

Copy of the Petition of John Emery, sen., of Newbury to the Massachusetts General Court, in relation to his fine for "Entertaining Strangers," 1663.

May 21, 1663.

To the honord Generall Court now assembled at Boston — the Humble petition of John Emery humbly showethe That your Petitioner dwelling in Newbury, It so fell out by Providence of God that a certain Gentleman (named Mr. Henry Greenland) coming from England upon his occasion was by reason of his acquaintance with Capt. Barefoot &c. inclinable to settle in ye Country if hee liked, and to make use of his practise of Physic and Chirurgery amongst us; But being as yet unsettled & oncertanie where to fix untill his wife (whom hee hath sent for) did come By Reason of some employment by ye Providence of God presented itself to him; hee was necissarily put upon it to reside neer such Patients as had put themselves into his hands for Cure: Among which one being more than ordinarily disordered Hee Desired entertainment. And your Petitioner did for Reason above mentioned Receive and entertain him this winter past for which I am fined four Pounds by ye hon'rd Court at Ipswich for Breach of a Law; not having [at first] License under the hand of a magistrate: hee himselfe being a stranger and not knowing the Law, nor your Petitioner — the Humble request of your Petitioner is; That this honobl Court would bee Pleased to remit ye saide fine (it being not done in Contempt but only as necessarily occasioned as above sd.) wherein ye Gentleman hath by God's blessing been furthered & been of much good by his calling; Both in Physick and Chirurgery and your pore Petitioner shall ever Pray.

We the Selectmen & such others as are subscribed, Considering the usefulness of Mr. Greenlands in respect of his practice in our towne, do humbly desire the same if this hon'd court please.

John Pike,	Abraham Toppan,
Richard Thurlo,	John Bayley,
Thomas	Sam Pore,
Peter Godrie,	Edw. Richardson,
James Ordway,	Robere Coker,
Lionel Worth,	Richard Fits,

Stephen Swett,	John Cheney, Jun.,
Anthony Morse, sen.,	Robert
Willi	John Wilcutt,
	Robt Adams,
Richard Loell,	Lanslet Granger,
Anhony Sumerbee,	Will
John Mearell,	Anthony Short,
	John Knight,
Abell Huse,	John
John Cheney, sen'r,	Rich
James Jackman,	Brown,
Joseph Plumer	Peter Toppan,
John Parker, Senior,	Jeremy Gutridge,
John Jun.,	William
Thomas Brown,	
William Titcomb,	Stephen
Richard Bartlet,	Saml
Thomas	Thomas Hale, Jun.,
Wilum Morse,	John Poore, Senor.
Josif Tainey,	

2, 3, 63. The Magts have considered the grounds of this Petr; & consent not to any reversion of the coun. Court's sentence.

THO. DANFORTH, P. E. R. S.

Consented to by ye depety provided they may have ye ten shillings agayne.

WILLIAM TORREY, Clerk.

The Magists Consentyes,

EDW: RAWSON, Secry."

This ancient document being much worn, some of the names are in part, or wholly illegible.

In 1669, the ecclesiastical difficulties by which the town had been for some time agitated, arose to such a height, that an appeal to the civil authority was considered necessary. The cause of this disturbance was a change of sentiment, which Messrs. Parker and Noyes manifested respecting church government and discipline.

Johnson, in his "Wonder-working Providence" says:. "The teaching elders of Newbury have carried it very lovingly toward their people, permitting them to assist in admitting of persons into the church society, and in church censure, so long as they act regularly, but in case of maladministration they assume the power wholly to themselves."

Johnson very well expressed the principles of church discipline held by Messrs. Parker and Noyes, principles which engendered a controversy that was not settled until a short time prior to Mr. Parker's death in 1677. A majority of the church demanded as a right, what the pastor and teacher "lovingly permitted" as a favor, and believing that the church in its corporate capacity had a right, and therefore were under a sacred obligation to manage its own affairs, they contended most strenuously against their elders assuming the powers wholly to themselves.

October 22d, 1656, "Mr. Noise, the blessed light of Newbury, died." Of his uncle, the Rev. Nicholas Noyes thus writes: "They who differed from him in smaller matters as to discipline, held a most amicable correspondence with him." During Mr. Noyes' lifetime, there was no serious difficulty in the church. After the return of Mr. John Woodbridge from England in 1663, he was employed by the town to assist his uncle Parker in preaching, at a salary of sixty pounds per annum, until 1670, when the town agreed to dispense with his services. From 1665 to 1669, the church and town were in a most excited and unconciliatory state, being about equally divided, one party adhering to Mr. Parker, while the opposition were led by Mr. Edward Woodman, a man of talents, influence, firmness, and decision, and from him were styled Mr. Woodman's party. This gentleman affirmed "that Mr. Parker would set up a prelacy, and have more power than the pope, for the pope had his council of cardinals." Both John Emery, sen., and his son, John Emery, jr., joined Mr. Woodman's party. The following is extracted from the records of the court at Salem :—

"I. John Pike, do testifie that I was present at the gathering of the church at Newbury, and I did hear our reverand pastor preach a sermon on the eighteenth of Matthew, seventeenth verse, 'and if he neglect to hear them, tell it unto the church; but if he neglect to hear the church, let him be unto thee as an heathen man and a publican,' wherein he did hould forth that the power of discipline belonged to the whole church, yt the matter of the church ought to be visible saints joyned or gathered together, that the manner of their joyning together ought to be by covenant, yt the end of it is for the exereisinge and enjoyinge of the ordinances of Christ togeather. He strongly proved his doctrine by many places of the Scripture, both in the old and new testament. The which sermon togeather with the Scriptures did much instruct and confirme us in that waye of church discipline which as I understood he then preached for, namely the congregational waye. some noates of the said sermon, which I then took from his mouth, I have here ready to shew if you please. The sermon being ended the brethren joyned together by express covenant, and being joyned they chose their pastor Mr. Parker, who accepted the call, and joyned with them according to the covenant aforesaid; and those that afterward joyned to the church, consented to the said covenant explicit. The brethren of the church acted in these admissions of ye members, expressinge their voats therein by lifting up the hande, and soe continued together lovingly a considerable number of yeares untill other doctrine began to be preached amongst us.

Per me, JOHN PIKE.

Sworne in court 30 March, 1669."

"Robert Pike also testifies that the meeting was on the Sabbath in the open air under a tree."

"At the same time that Mr. Parker was chosen pastor, Mr. James Noyes was chosen teacher."

Similar testimonies were give by John Emery and Thomas Browne.

Tradition asserts that the tree under which this first sermon was preached was a majestic oak, which stood on the north bank of the river Parker, about a hundred yards below the present bridge.

After a series of trials and appeals, and a council of the neighboring elders and churches, which was convened Nov. 3d, 1669, the controversy was finally settled at the court at Ipswich, May 29th, 1671, "which adjudged the said Mr. Woodman, and party adhering to him, to pay the several fines underwritten, with the charge of the witnesses, and fees of court, and that they all stand committed till the said fines, charges and fees be satisfied and paid.

Mr. Edward Woodman, twenty nobles; Mr. Richard Dummer, Richard Thorlay, Stephen Greenleaf, Richard Bartlet, and William Titcomb, four nobles each; Francis Plumer, John Emery, sen., John Emery, jun., John Merrill, and Thomas Browne, a mark each; Nicholas Batt, Anthony Morse, senior, Abraham Toppan, William Sawyer, Edward Woodman, junior, John Webster, John Bartlet, senior, John Bartlett, junior, Joseph Plumer, Edward Richardson, Thomas Hale, junior, Edmund Moores, Benjamin Lowle, Job Pilsbury, John Wells, William Ilsley, James Ordway, Francis Thorlay, Abraham Merrill, John Bailey, Benjamin Rolfe, Steven Swett, and Samuel Plumer, a noble each; Robert Coker and William Moody were not fined."

A noble is six shillings and eightpence; a mark, thirteen shillings and fourpence.

The following are the names of Mr. Parker's party:

Mr. John Woodbridge, Capt. Paul White, Mr. Henry Sewall, Richard Kent, John Kent, Henry Short, Daniel Price, senior, Richard Knight, John Kelley, John Knight, Henry Jaques, Thomas Hale, senior, Robert Adams, Abel Huse, George Little, Samuel Moody, William Chandler, Mr. Nicholas Noyes, Nicholas Wallington, Capt. William Gerrish, Mr. Percival Lowle, James Kent, Robert Long, Richard Pettingell, William Morse, John Davis, John Smith, James Smith, James Jackman, Joseph Muzzey, Richard Dole, Anthony Somerby, Nathaniel Clark, Tristram Coffin, Nicholas Noyes, senior, Thomas Tarvill, Mr. John Gerrish.

Though during this controversy, George Little adhered to his pastor, in company with Philip Squire, Nathaniel Cheney, William Sayer and wife, Benjamin Morse and wife, Mr. Edward Woodman and wife, John Sayer and Abel Merrill, he joined the Baptist church at Boston, and in 1682 that church assented to the formation of a Baptist church in Newbury. This church never gained many converts, and it was too few in numbers to long maintain a separate existence.

In 1654, "John Emery was chosen to answer at the next court at Ipswich, concerning the presentment about the way to Andover."

April 10, 1644. "There was laid out to John Emery, jun., four-score akers of upland, bee it more or lesse joining unto Merrimacke river on the north, and running from the mouth of Artichoke river, unto a marked tree by a swampe on the north-west corner, being about one hundred and thirty-two rods long at the head of the cove, thence about a hundred rods to the south-east corner, thence running a strait lyne about a hundred and fifty-six rods to Artichoke river on the east about eighty rods broad."

March 3, 1679, the town granted to Sergeant John Emery twelve acres of land on the west side of Artichoke river, "provided he build and maintain a corn mill, to grind the town's corn from time to time, and to build it within one year and a half after the date hereof," and so forth. This farm is still owned by the descendants of John Emery, jr. John Emery, senior, passed the latter part of his life there; he died Nov. 3, 1683, aged 85.

A portion of the estate of David Emery, above, on the main road, is still in the possession of his descendants, and there is a wood lot owned in my family which was purchased with money inherited from that ancestor.

Jonathan Emery, the youngest son of John Emery, senior, fought through King Philip's war, with the renowned "Flower of Essex." He belonged to Major Appleton's company, which was considered the crack company of the Small army. In the archives at the state-house, Boston, is the original muster-roll of the company, and it is there recorded: "Jonathan Emery, wounded in the neck." This wound, from an Indian arrow, was received at the capture of the fort in Narraganset, Dec. 19, 1675.

This was a terrible battle, the most sanguinary of the campaign. The Indians had built a fort in the Narraganset country. Within a strong palisade of timber were nearly five hundred wigwams, sheltering nearly five thousand persons, with great store of provisions. The cold was intense, and the air filled with a frosty rime, as our brave little army drew near to the great swamp.

Around the fated hamlet, outside the palisade, was a high barricade of felled trees, almost or quite impossible to climb, and a nearly impenetrable thicket of swamp wood; surrounding these defences was a broad moat filled with water, which could only be crossed by passing over a large tree placed by the Indians for a bridge. At about one o'clock p. m. our bold men began the attack. Though they were obliged to pass over that tree trunk single file, in the face of a terrible fire from the enemy, which sent many a man instantly to his death, they persisted, again and again. Six of our captains were killed and a proportionate number of men, before a few of the brave soldiers effected an entrance into the five-acre enclosure of the Indians. Here the slaughter was hand to hand, with horrible odds against the invaders. Never-the-less, they won the day. The cry that the Indians were flying rallied our men outside, who had recoiled somewhat from the death-line of the tree. The Indians were left dead in heaps "upon ye snow." The wigwams were soon in flames, and several hundred of the hapless children of the forest perished in the fire; other hundreds were taken prisoners, while the great Philip barely escaped. Our army lost about eighty killed and nearly one hundred and fifty wounded. The total loss of the Indians was computed at about a thousand. After this fearful combat our people marched seventeen or eighteen miles "in a most horrid and boisterous night," before the wounded could be cared for. Several of our dead were left in the burning ruins of the fort. The sufferings "of the English after this fight have hardly a parallel in history." What, then, must have been the sufferings of the Indians? The English lions won their victory, at great cost of pain and blood, over the Indian tigers.

Jonathan Emery after his return from the war used this seal, which he probably had engraved to commemorate his deeds and sufferings. The Lion representing the bold Briton inspiring terror, the arrow seized by the rampant beast, the emblem of Indian warfare, which from its position indicates the Lion's victory, The decendants of John jr. and Jonathan Emery have become widely scattered, Many have been, and are still counted amongst the prominent men and women of the country. The name has been, and still is, well represented, amongst the clergy, at the bar, in the medical profession, in the military, literary and mercantile walks of life. Some of the family have excelled in mechanics, and in an unusual degree as a race. they possess the talent of a "ready writer."

The spirit of emigration decended from the sires. Several of the family pressing into the wilderness, founded, what are now flourishing towns. Moses Emery, a great grandson of John Emery jr. was the first settler at Minot, Maine. Edward Emery, seventh son of Jonathan Emery, married a Miss Sarah Sibley and settled at Contoocook (now Boscawen, N. H,) in 1734 or thereabouts. In 1740 he was one of a committee there to secure a minister for the plantation. He was killed by the Indians while hunting beaver at Newfound Lake, in 1756. Ezekiel Flanders his companion was also slain by the savages. Anthony Emery, third son of John and Hannah Emery, graduated from Harvard College in 1736. He was surgeon in the English army at the capture of Louisburg, and was the first physician at Chelmsford, Mass., then at Hampton N. H.. where he died. Aug. 19th, 1781, aged 67. Dr. Emery was one of the proprietors of Andover N. H., which for some time bore the designation of "Emery Town." His son William settled on his father's land, being the third settler in the town. His son, Captain Anthony Emery succeeded on the paternal acres, where he was distinguished as a sheep-grower. He kept more sheep, sold more mutton, and procured the manufacture of more of the old-fashioned coverlets, than any three men in his county.

Rev. Samuel Emery, born in Newbury Dec. 20th, 1670, graduated at Harvard in 1691, and was ordained in Wells, Me., the 29th of October 1701, he died Dec. 18th, 1724.

Rev. Stephen Emery was born in Newbury, graduated at Harvard in 1730; was soon after settled over the society in Nottingham, N. H.

Thomas Emery, son of David Emery, sen., graduated at Harvard in 1768, and studied medicine; he died Nov. 21st, 1772, aged 22, leaving one son, Thomas Emery, who married first a daughter of the Rev. Moses Hale of the lower parish, by whom he had three sons, Flavius, Charles and Moses; his second wife was Margaret, widow of Joseph Coffin, of Oldtown.

Rev. Samuel M. Emery, son of Moody and Abigail Emery, of Newbury, now West Newbury, born April 10th, 1804, graduated at Harvard in 1830, received the Master's degree at Trinity college, Hartford, Conn., and several years after the honorary degree of D. D., from the same. He was ordained Deacon in Trinity church, Boston, in July, 1835, and soon afterwards receiven a call to Trinity church, Portland, Conn., where he was ordained priest. He remained rector of that parish until August, 1870,—nearly thirty-five years. Since then he has retired from the active duties of the ministry. He married Mary Hale, only child of Eliphalet Emery, Esq. of the Artichoke river farm, and granddaughter of the Rev. Moses Hale.

Rev. Samuel Hopkins Emery, born Aug. 22d, 1815; graduated at Amherst in 1834; at Andover Theological Seminary in 1837; was ordained at Taunton, Mass., Nov. 23d, 1837; pastor at Quincy, Ill., and Bedford, Mass.; stated supply at Chicago, Providence, Bridgeport, Ct., and North Middleborough, Mass.; now city missionary, and minister of Cedar street chapel, Taunton, Mass.; married, March 7th, 1838, Julia Reed of Taunton.

Rev. Joshua Emery, born in Newburyport Aug. 1807, graduated at Amherst in 1831; at Andover Theological Seminary in 1834; was ordained pastor of Calvanistic Congregational Church, Fitchburg Mass., May 13th 1835; was called to First Church (old North) Weymouth, Mass., Dec. 1837, and installed pastor Jan. 25th, 1838; retired from active service in 1873. He married May 19th, 1835, Hariet, daughter of Jacob Peabody, of Salem, Mass.

Horace Brown, son of Hayden and Hariet (Emery) Brown, and grandson of Moses Emery, born in West Newbury Aug. 31st, 1851, was fitted for college at Phillip's Academy, Exeter and graduated at Harvard in 1872, and the Harvard Law School, in 1874. He began the practice of his profession in the office of Ives & Lincoln, Salem.

Mass., July 7th, 1874; was admitted to the United States Supreme Court Jan. 1878; was elected to the State Legislature, to represent the city of Salem, Nov. 5th, 1878; is a member of the Essex Institute, and of the American Association for the Advancement of Science.

Samuel E. Emery D. D. S., son of Rev. Samuel M. Emery, D. D., was born at Portland, Conn., April 10th 1852. Graduated at the Boston Dental College 1876. A practising dentist in Newburyport.

Flavius Emery, son of Thomas and Elizabeth (Hale) Emery, married Elizabeth Emery, daughter of Moody and Abigail Emery, of West Newbury, Nov. 1 1826. Their son, Rufus Emery, born July 25th, 1827; graduated at Trinity college, Hartford, Conn., in 1854: was tutor in the Institution from 1855 to 1857. He graduated at the Berkley Divinity school in Middletown, Conn., in 1858; took charge of the church in Southport, Conn., where, Aug. 5th, he was ordained priest, remaining over the society about twelve years. He married Adelaide, daughter of Erastus and Mary W. Brainerd, of Portland, Conn., Nov. 17th. 1858. Having resigned the parish of Trinity church, Southport, he officiated some two years in Calvary Church, Stonington, Conn., when he accepted a call to the rectorship of St. Paul's Church Newburg, N. Y.

Emery is both an ancient and an historic name. In the "Doom's Day Book," 1086, those of the Norman French family D'Amery, who followed the Conqueror to England, are recorded as landed proprietors in Oxford and Devon, in the mediæval Latin as Haimericus. At present the Emerys of England, as a rule, use the orthographic form, most prevalent in the United States, though some as here, prefer Amery or Amory. From the old records, it is seen that the first settlers here, as was then common, spelled the name in a variety of ways. John Emery of Romsey, in old age, spelled his name Emerry, but his will, now on file among the Essex county, Massachusetts court papers, exhibits his signature as John Emry. The name is not rare in France; there its usual forms are Amory, Emery, and D'Emery. The name does not appear in France previous to the Norman invasion of Gaul. It was brought with the fierce followers of Rollo, gathered from Norway, Sweden, Denmark, and some of the North German provinces, who in the early part of the tenth century invaded the beautiful land of Neustra, and wrested it from Charles the Simple, changing the name to Normandy. It has been claimed that the practice of giving "Sir" names originated in Normandy, and was transported to Great Britain at the time of the conquest. The name Emery, or its equivalent, however, appears in Europe as early as the fourth century, where it is found in Switzerland, Spain and Italy, and it is well known in Germany, Emmerich, an ancient fortified town of Germany, derived its name from Count Embric or Emeric.

Autograph of John Emery of Romsey.

Anderson (Sir Names) Edinburgh, 1865, says, "From Amalarich (exalted ruler)—Gothic—has come descended in regular transformation, Amalric, Almaric, Amaury, Aimery, Ermenrich, and Emerich, the English names Amory, Damery, Damer and Emery."

Though of historic interest, it is not generally known that this western continent, in a slightly modified form bears the name under notice. Columbus never doubted that the lands he had discovered were parts of the East Indies or Asia; but, after extended exploration, Americus Vespucius (or Amerigo Vespucci, as his name appears in Italian) became assured that they were no other than a second or western continent. His written accounts of the climate, people and productions, obtained a corroboration of this idea among the inhabitants of the old world. The honor of having his name applied to the extent of the mainland of South America, by him visited and described, was not sought by the daring Florentine. The suggestion of his name came from Matthias Ringman, the poet, and a few friends, students at the College of St. Die in Lorraine, among the Vosges mountains, in a corner of France. In 1507 they put forth a little work entitled "Cosmographiæ Introductis," in which the suggestion was made that the New World should be named America, after a man, inasmuch as Europe and Asia had been named after women. The suggestion was adopted, and America finally became the name of the whole western continent. Thus was Americus Vespucius honored in the use of that part of his name which then had been known for more than ten centuries.

Dixon, in his "Sir Names," says:

"Emmery (F), Armanarciks (Go:). 'Most exalted or universal ruler.' The Gothic name became changed to Armanarich, Ermanarich, Ermenrich, Emmenrich, etc.; and from it were probably derived the English Sir names, Emerich, Emeryke, and sometimes Emery. The forename of the Italian Vespucci was also a corruption of the name of a king of the Goths in the fourth century."

Americus is not properly a corruption of the original Gothic, but rather its legitimate Latinized form. Another author (M. A. Lowe, Patronymica Britannica) writes:

"From the personal name Emeric or Almericus, equivalent to the Italian Amerigo, Latinized Americus, whence the name of the great western continent. It seems to have undergone the following changes: Emeric, Emery, Amery, Amary, Ammary, and, in the Domesday Book, Haimericus. It is asserted that the family of D'Amery came to England with the Conqueror, from Tours."

The following statement appears in "English Sir-Names: their Source and Signification," by Charles W. Bailey, A. M., London, 1875:

"Emery, though now utterly forgotten as a personal name, may be said to live only in our Sir names. It was once no unimportant sobriquet. Americ, Almeric, Emeric, and Eimeric, seem to have been original spellings in England, and thus, at least, it is more likely to remind us that it is the same name to which, in the Italian form of Amerigo, we owe the title of that vast expanse of Western territory which is so indissolubly connected with English industry and English interests."

While it is true that Emery is not now used as a personal or given name in England, it is frequently so used in the Eastern States of America. All things considered, the name in question may fairly claim to rank amongst the most remarkable in the whole range of personal nomenclature.

The arms of Amery, or Emery, are:

ARGENT, THREE BARS NEBULÉE, GULES; IN CHIEF, AS MANY TORTEAUX. CREST—OUT OF A MURAL CROWN, A DEMI-HORSE ARGENT, MANED OR, COLLARED GULES, STUDDED OF THE FIRST.
THE LEGEND, "FIDELIS ET SAUVIS."

Shatswell, Shotswell, Satchwell, or Satchell. John, Ipswich, 1633; died in 1647. His will was proved March 30. It names wife Joanna, son Richard, brother Theophilus, brother Curwin, and sister Mary Webster, widow of John. The widow Mary (Shatswell) Webster, with her children, John, Thomas, Stephen, Israel, Nathan, Mary, Hannah, Elizabeth, and Abigail, removed to Newbury about 1642. On October 29, 1650, she married John Emery. She died August 28, 1694. John Emery was very fond of his step-children, and they reciprocated the affection. Israel and Nathan, the one eighteen and the other fifteen years of age, with their mother, soon after her marriage, petitioned the General Court to consent to their choosing their father-in-law, John Emery, senior, and brother, John Emery, jr., as their guardians. All of the Websters were remembered in Mr. Emery's will, where they are styled "his dear children." Hannah Webster married Thomas Emerson; her daughter Hannah Emerson, married Thomas Dustan, and became the famous Indian slayer, to whose memory a monument has been erected in Haverhill.

CHAPTER XXXII.

Thomas Colman, born in 1602, came from Marlboro, Wiltshire, England, to Newbury, in the party who landed with Messrs. Parker and Noyes. His first wife Susanna, died the 17th of Nov. 1650. The same year he removed to Hampton, and married Mary, widow of Edmund Johnson, July 11th, 1651, who died in Hampton Jan. 30th, 1663. His third wife was Margery ——. After 1680 he moved to Nantucket, where he died in 1685, aged 83 His children were Benjamin, Joseph, Isaac, Joanna, John and Tobias. Tobias, the last child of his third wife, was the ancestor of the Byfield family. Deacon Benjamin Colman, born in 1724, married first, Ann Brown, from the Brown's Spring Farm on the main road. This lady was a decendant of John Brown of Turkey Hill, whose dwelling was attacked by the Indians in 1695. Their children were John, Dudley, Thomas, Samuel, Benjamin, Moses, Caleb, William and Mary. Deacon Colman's second wife, was widow Sarah Stickney, whom he married Oct. 27th, 1778. John, born 1774, married a Miss Danforth. This was the migratory couple I have mentioned.

Dudley, born Aug. 13th, 1745, graduated at Harvard in 1765. He married Mary, daughter of John and

Mary (Whipple) Jones, and established a tavern in Oldtown on the old Boston road. The house is still standing on High street, now styled the old Ilsley house. He was town clerk for Newbury, and at the commencement of the Revolutionary war entered the army, where he attained the rank of colonel. Mrs. Colman, a tall, dignified woman, possessing a superior education, and much elegance of manner, during her husband's absence, conducted the public house with great success. Col. Colman removed to Boston, where for several years he was landlord of the "Bunch of Grapes Tavern." His health failing he purchased a farm in Brookfield, N. H., where he died Nov. 16th, 1797.

The following items of Col. Colman's military career are of interest. The first is taken from the order book of Col. Moses Little, the October succeeding the battle of Long Island:

FORT CONSTITUTION,
Oct. 13th.

It is Gen. Greene's orders that my Brigade move over the Ferry immediately. The regiments to leave a careful officer & 12 men each to bring forward their baggage to King's Bridge, who is to take care that none of it be left behind or lost. When the Reg'ts are over the ferry, they will march to Mt. Washington & remain there till further orders. You will hurry the march as fast as possible, as they must cross the ferry this night.

JNO. NIXON, B. C.

To Dudley Colman, A. B. M.

EAST CHESTER, Oct. 16th.

The several reg'ts in this Brigade are to draw 4 days provision & have it cooked immediately. The Q. M. will apply to the assistant Q. M. Gen'l for carriages to transport their provisions. Col. Varnum's Reg't to relieve Col. Nixon's at Frogg's Point this P. M.

Oct. 16th.

Sir:—You are to order Col. Varnum's reg't to march immediately to Frogg's Neck to relieve Col. Ritzema's or Col. Malcom's reg't (which of the two you find there not relieved). You will get a pilot from Col. Nixon's reg't to direct them thither.

JNO. NIXON, B. C.

To Dudley Colman, Brigade Major.

MILES SQUARE,
EAST CHESTER,
Oct. 18th.

Sir:—You will have a working party of 300 men & officers ready to go to work as soon as the tools arrive, which I have sent for, & you will see that suitable guards are mounted by each regiment.

JNO. NIXON, B. C.

To D. Colman, B. Major.

Subjoined is a copy of a letter from Col. Dudley Colman to Col. Moses Little, of Turkey Hill:

CAMP ALBANY,
Oct. 28th, 1777.

Dear Sir:—I have the pleasure, though late, to congratulate you on the surrender of Gen. Burgoyne and his army. Some of them doubtless you will have the pleasure of seeing before this reaches you. It may I think be reckoned among the extraordinary events history furnishes us with to have 5000 and upwards of veteran, disciplined troops, besides followers of the army surrounded & their resources & retreat so cut off in the field, as to oblige them to surrender prisoners of war, without daring to come to further action, is an event I do not recollect to have met with in history, much less did I ever expect to see it in this war. I confess I could hardly believe it to be a reality when I saw it, the prospect was truly extremely pleasing to see our troops paraded in the best order, and to see them march as prisoners by after they had laid down their arms, who but a few days before had pretended to despise (although at the same time I believe they did not think so lightly of us as they pretended) afforded a most striking & agreeable prospect. I can but mention the good order observed by our troops on seeing them march by, no laughing or marks of exultation were to be seen among them, nothing more than a manly joy appeared on the countenances of our troops, which showed that they had fortitude of mind to bear prosperity without being too much elated, as well as to encounter the greatest hardships & dangers. It has likewise been observed to me by several of the British officers, that they did not expect to be received in so polite a manner, & that they never saw troops behave with more decency, or a better spirit on such an occasion.

We have I think for the present restored peace in the northern quarter & although for a little time past viewed the evacuation of Ticonderoga as a misfortune, we may now see it has proved a means of destroying this enemy.

Gen. Clinton has of late made an attempt to come up the river & has destroyed several places in order to make a diversion in favor of Gen. Burgoyne, but he was too late. We expect orders to strike our tents every day, as we have been under marching orders these three days, & part of the army are gone. I know not where we are to march to, but suppose it to be down the river, when if we can get between the enemy & their ships, we shall endeavor to convince them that they are not to proceed in the way they have done, of destroying the property of our fellow-countrymen. Please to give my best regards to Mr. Gray and family, & all friends, & I should be happy to have a line from you.

I am, dear Sir,
Your most obedient,
humble servant,
DUDLEY COLMAN.

To Col. Moses Little, member of the House of Representatives.

The following letter, dated Newbury, July 19th, 1792, was written by Dea. Benjamin Colman, soon after the death of his second wife, to his son, Col. Dudley Colman, in Boston. The latter part refers to Col. Colman's having embraced more liberal religious views than those in which he had been educated. I omit an account of the sickness of Mrs. Colman; after announcing her departure, Dea. Colman writes:

"In the time of her sickness, as well as before, I used to put questions to her that I might know the state of her mind. She used always to entertain a hope that God had given her a gracious turn of mind, but she was pressing after that full assurance of an interest in the favor of God, whereby she might be actually ready for the summons of death & meet it with an holy confidence. I can't say that she did attain to that full assurance which she wished & longed for, but about three days before she died, which was the last time I could understand what she said, I ask'd her about the state of her mind, how it was as to her hopes & fears, and she answered me as near as I can repeat in the following words, viz: 'Mr. Colman, I am conscious to myself of many failings, infirmities and shortcomings, I have no righteousness of my own to plead for my justification before God, my only hope of salvation is in the atoning blood, and righteousness of the great Redeemer, the Lord Jesus Christ.' Some other things she spake at the same time to the same purpose, after that conversation her speech failed, so that I could understand but little she said, though she continued near three days, I hope and trust she was sincere and sound in the faith, so that she is received to the mercy of eternal life thro' Jesus Christ our Lord. And now in my old age, God has a second time deprived me of a companion, my prayer is that God will grant me his quickening grace that I may double my diligence in preparing to follow my deceased wives to that world of spirits to which we are all hastening. And now my dear child, what shall I say to you. You and I

20

dailey see that death is the end of all men and women. and the wise man tells us the living will lay it to heart, i e, we should do so, & if we are rational we shall do so. if we act wisely for ourselves we shall consider ourselves as we are, probationers for that final state of retribution & judgment after which there will be no change—consider my dear child, you and I are near this change of states, by which unconceivable happiness or unconceivable misery will take place on us. I beseech you to allow yourself a little time, if it be but a quarter of an hour in a day, to retire from company to your closet or chamber to look into the state of your immortal soul, and think with yourself if you had a large estate in prospect, even in this world, if you doubted as to your title to the same, if you feared you should lose all & be a beggar in misery & distress, how solicitous would you be to secure a good title to that estate which you could keep & enjoy but for a short, limited time,—but alas, what a faint similitude is this to set forth the favor of God, & an interest in Christ, and an interest in that kingdom, where you may enjoy all that heart can wish or tho't conceive, consider if you lose your soul. 'twill be an infinite loss, an irreparable loss, therefore your all is at stake. I beseech you lay to heart Christ's own words viz: 'what will it profit a man if he gain the whole world & lose his soul,' these are the words of him that is Wisdom itself & truth itself, they are the words of him that laid down his precious life a ransome for mankind — sinners; that will be the final Judge of all the world, both Angels & men, for God the father has constituted the Son, as God man, Mediator to that office, and has given assurance of it to all men in that he has raised him from the dead, declared him to be the son of God, with power by his resurrection. Set him at his own right hand, exalted him for this very purpose, to give repentance & remission of sins. This Jesus will be our Judge at the last day, inspiration tells us he will come in flaming fire to take vengeance on them that know not God, and that obey not the gospel of our Lord Jesus Christ, who shall be punished with everlasting destruction from the presence of the Lord & from the glory of his power. Dreadful words, and more dreadful day, when this exalted God man shall assume his throne, appear in his robes of majesty, to take vengeance on his enemies, on all contemners, & sliters of gospel salvation & mercy, which he has tendered to lost, perishing sinners, in & through that precious blood of his, which he shed for the remission of our sins, how can we endure to hear that dreadful sentence, depart from me ye cursed, you have slited offered mercy, abused my patience, resisted & grieved my spirit, and now the door is shut. This my dear child, will inevitably be the doleful doom of all that set light by Jesus Christ & neglect the great salvation, purchased by the blood of him that was God as well as man. But am I saying all this to an Infidel—a Socinian who denies the Divinity of Jesus Christ,—or to a Universalist, who hopes & expects that all men will be saved at last, tho' they have no gracious principle wrought in them in this life of probation & trial, or am I writing to a fatalist that presumes on the decrees of God, and argues thus with himself: if I am elected I shall be saved let me do as I will, and live as I list; and if I am not elected, 'tis impossible for me to be saved, let me do all that I can in a way of means, and take ever so much pains for the salvation of my soul. because God's eternal decrees stand against me. These pernicious tenets, and a thousand more artfices the malicious Adversary of our precious souls suggests to us to wheedle us along by his artful devices, till the summons of death arrests us and then he will be sure of us. O, my dear child, resist and shun his devices, flee to Christ by faith now while the door of mercy & hope are yet open, make God in Christ your refuge, & believe God's word, whatever his secret decrees are (which you can not know at your pleasure), his word &

on the south side of the river Parker. He died December 21, 1682, aged 78. She died January 30, 1683. Children: Thomas, born 1633; John, born 1636; and Samuel.

Thomas Hale, jr., married Mary Hutchinson of Danvers, May 26, 1657. He died October, 1688. Children: Thomas, born February, 1658; Mary, born July 15. 1660; Abigail, born April 8, 1662; Hannah, born November 29, 1663; Lydia, born April 17, 1666; Elizabeth, born October 16, 1668; Joseph, born February 20, 1671; Samuel, born June 6, 1674.

Capt. Thomas Hale married Sarah, daughter of Ezekiel and Edna (Holstead) Northend of Rowley, May 16, 1682. Children: Thomas, born March 9. 1683; Edna, born November 21, 1684; Mary, born April 28, 1687; Ezekiel, born May 13, 1689; Nathan, born June 2, 1691; Sarah, born March 9, 1693; Ebenezer, born April 21, 1695; Daniel, born February 22, 1697; Hannah, born June 7, 1699; Joshua, born March 17, 1701.

Ezekiel Hale purchased a farm in the west precinct, and married Ruth Moody of Pipestave hill. She died, leaving two daughters, Ruth, and Elizabeth who died in childhood. Mr. Hale next married Mary Sargent of Amesbury. She died, leaving a daughter Mary. His third wife was Sarah, daughter of Parson Balch of Bradford. She died, leaving a daughter Sarah. The fourth wife was Mary (Poor) Spofford. She had one son, Ezekiel, and three daughters; one of these married Mr. Buttrick, the second Mr. Hildreth, and the third Squire Farnum of Dracut. Ruth, the oldest daughter, married John, second son of Capt. Edmund Little, of Crane-neck hill. Mary, the second daughter, married Enoch, the third son of Capt. Edmund Little. Sarah, the third daughter, married Mr. Moses Pillsbury, of Crane-neck hill. From the son, Ezekiel, descended Joshua Hale, born in Dracut, August 27, 1777, who died in New Orleans, of yellow fever, August 29, 1817. He went to Worcester, where he was a clothier and builder of machinery, and was the first who built a wool-carding machine in New England. Rev. Christopher Sargent Hale, Brown University 1820, and Hon. Ezekiel James Madison Hale, Dartmouth 1835, now of Haverhill, Mass.

Daniel, fifth son of Capt. Thomas Hale, married Judith Emery. He commanded a company in Col. Samuel Waldo's Massachusetts regiment in the expedition against Louisburg in 1745, and was killed at the head of his company, in the trenches before that fortification, May 21, 1745. His descendants are numerous in Essex county, Mass., and elsewhere. Among them are the late Francis Pickard Hale, Bowdoin 1845, of Charlestown, Mass., and Daniel Harris Hale, esq., of Rowley, president of the Rowley Historical Society.

Rev. Moses Hale, born July 10, 1678; graduated at Harvard in 1699; ordained in Newbury, Byfield, October, 1706; and died in January, 1743, aged 66 years.

Rev. Moses Hale, born in Newbury in 1703; graduated at Harvard in 1722; was ordained in Chester, N. H., October 20, 1731, and dismissed June 4, 1735.

Rev. Moses Hale, born January 18, 1715; graduated at Harvard in 1734; settled in Newbury, west parish, February 20, 1752; and died January 15, 1779, aged 64.

Rev. Moses Hale, son of the preceding, born in Rowley, February 19, 1749; graduated at Harvard in 1771; was ordained in Boxford, and died May 26, 1798.

Nathan Hale, born in Newbury, March 1, 1720; graduated at Harvard in 1739, and died in Newbury.

Samuel Hale, born in Newbury, August 24, 1718; graduated at Harvard in 1740. In 1745 he commanded a company of provincials at Louisburg, and for more than thirty years was a distinguished teacher of youth in Portsmouth, N. H. He died July 10, 1807, aged 89.

Thomas Hale of Newbury, May 25, 1797, married Alice, the eldest daughter of Col. Josiah Little. Children:

Rev. Benjamin, D.D., born November 23, 1797, graduated at Bowdoin College in 1818, studied theology at Andover, was professor of chemistry and mineralogy at Dartmouth College, president of Hobart College, Geneva, N.Y., for over twenty years, and the author of various educational works. He married, April 9, 1829, Mary Caroline King. Dr. Hale died July 15, 1863.

Moses Little, born April 7, 1799. An eminent business man of Boston, deacon of the Bowdoin street church, and the occupant of many responsible positions. He married Mary Lane, youngest daughter of the Rev. James Miltimore, first pastor of the Belleville church. He died June 22, 1874.

Thomas, born October 13, 1800; married Caroline Charlotte Jordan October 7, 1836. He died May 28, 1854.

Sarah, born March 29, 1802; died April 9, 1834.

Josiah Little, born December 9, 1803; entered the office of the Merchants Insurance Company, of Boston, at the age of eighteen, where his fidelity and courteous manners soon won him promotion. In 1825 he became secretary of the Washington Marine Insurance Company, and in 1828, on the opening of a branch office, he went to New York as its manager. After a year of marked success in this position, he joined with the late Walter R. Jones in establishing the Atlantic Insurance Company of New York. To do this he had to raise $150,000 of the capital stock, and his Boston friends proved their confidence in his character and ability by subscriptions to twice that amount. In this position he remained for twenty-five years, in which time the Atlantic became the leading marine insurance company in the country. He was compelled, by continued ill health, to resign his office in 1854. In the resolutions of respect and regret then adopted, the trustees refer to the company as established essentially through his active instrumentality, and as having under his administration enjoyed a course of uninterrupted success. Mr. Hale held with an intelligent and firm conviction the great doctrines of grace, but without bigotry or sectarianism. The Bible was his constant companion, and doing good his constant delight. He died February 26, 1875.

Edward, born November 8, 1805; married widow Elizabeth L. Brown January 30, 1837.

Mary, born July 5, 1807; died March 13, 1859.

Dr. Ebenezer, born April 28, 1809; graduated at Dartmouth in 1829; married Sarah Bannister June 13, 1844. He died August 2, 1847.

Alice Little, born April 15, 1811;

married, April 23, 1832, Rev. John Charles March, second pastor of the Belleville church, who died September 26, 1846.

Capt. Joshua, born December 14, 1812; married Sophia Cutler Tenney January 4, 1844.

Alice, wife of Thomas Hale, died July 27, 1819. On September 17, 1822, Mr. Hale married Mary, fifth daughter of Col. Josiah Little. Their only child was James White, born September 8, 1827, and died October 11, 1832.

Mr. Thomas Hale died August 14, 1836. Mary, widow of Thomas Hale, died January 26, 1871.

Benjamin, oldest son of Dr. Benjamin Hale, born October 31, 1827; graduated at Hobart College in 1848; October 29, 1855, he married Lucy Balch Hale, only daughter of Col. Ebenezer Hale.

Thomas, the second son, born July 11, 1834; graduated at Hobart College in 1853: vice-president of the Pacific Mutual Insurance Company, New York; February 24, 1870, married Lucy F. Searcy.

Cyrus King, third son, born March 17, 1838; graduated at Hobart College in 1858; May 9, 1866, married Alice Little, only child of Capt. Joshua Hale; died June 6, 1874.

Dr. Josiah, fourth son, born April 1, 1841; graduated at Hobart College in 1860; studied medicine at Harvard Medical School and in Europe; April 24, 1873, he married Annie Skinner Pierce.

Eben Thomas Hale, only son of Col. Ebenezer and Lucy (Balch) Hale, born May 9, 1842; graduated at Yale College in 1862. That year he enlisted in Forty-fifth Massachusetts regiment for nine months' service, under General Foster. Stationed at Newbern, N. C., the regiment did provost duty; was in the engagement at Whitehall and Kingston, returning home in June, 1863. Afterward he studied law at the Harvard Law School. His health becoming impaired, he went to South America in 1866, visiting Rio Janeiro and other places of interest. After his return he became a partner in the firm of Lowell & Brett, stationers, Boston, continuing in the business until his death, which took place September 7, 1868.

Moses Hoyt Hale, born May 24, 1829; married C. Adeline Preston, of Danvers, January 29, 1852; represented Salem in Massachusetts legislature in 1868 and 1869. Since February 14, 1870, a special agent of the United States treasury department. He died at his home in Danvers, in 1879.

Albert Hale, born September 13, 1839; graduated at Harvard in 1861; principal of the high school in Fairhaven, Mass., from January, 1862, to April, 1864; principal of female high school at Newburyport, Mass., from May, 1864, to November, 1865; private tutor in Cambridge and Boston in 1865 and 1866; teacher in the English high school, Boston, from 1866; since 1875 a master in said school. August 18, 1869, he married Katherine, daughter of Albert and Katherine (Davenport) Wood, of Newburyport.

Frank A. Hale, born January 8, 1854; received the degree of M. D. March 1, 1876, at the Boston University School of Medicine.

The arms of the Hales of King's Walden, are:

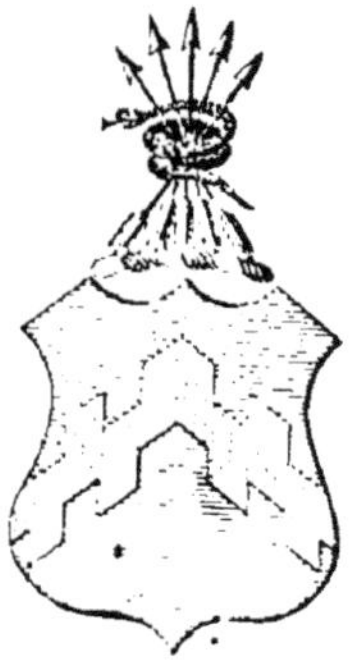

AZURE, A CHEVRON EMBATTLED, COUNTER-EMBATTLED OR. CREST—A SNAKE PROPER, ENTWINED AROUND FIVE ARROWS OR, HEADED SABLE, FEATHERED ARGENT, ONE IN PALE, FOUR SALTIRE.

William Moody came from Ipswich, England, to Ipswich, America, in 1634, and to Newbury in 1635. His wife was Sarah. Children: Joshua, Caleb, William and Samuel.

Caleb Moody married Sara Pierce, who died August 25, 1665. Children: Daniel and Sara. His second wife was Judith Bradbury. Children: Caleb, Thomas, Judith, (born September 23, 1669, and died at Salisbury, January 28, 1679), Joshua, William, Samuel, Mary, and Judith.

Joshua Moody married Mary Greenleaf in 1696. Children: Mary, born June 26, 1697; Elisabeth, December 4, 1698; Joshua, born Nov. 11, 1700; Abigail, born September 30, 1703; and Judith, born October 26, 1705.

Elisabeth, second daughter of Mr. Joshua Moody, married my great-grandfather, Capt. James Smith, the first owner of the Crane-neck hill farm.

Caleb Moody, married Ruth Morse, Dec. 9, 1690, and settled on a farm at Pipestave hill, now known as the Ridgway place. Their daughter Elisabeth, married Mr. Ezekiel Hale, whose daughter Ruth, became the wife of John Little, of Crane-neck hill.

William Moody, of Ipswich, Eng., settled on a farm in Oldtown, which is still retained by his descendants; the son of Mr. N. Warren Moody, being the ninth generation born on the place.

William Moody married Mehetabel Sewell, November, 1684, and settled on a farm in Byfield, where his descendants became prominent citizens. It was from one of these, Capt. Paul Moody, that the company which founded the first woolen factory in the state, purchased the water power at the falls of the river Parker. Perkins's cut nails were first manufactured in the mill house previously owned by Capt. Moody. By such surroundings his sons from youth, became initiated in mechanics.

Paul Moody, jr., and Steven Kent, manufactured the first broadcloth in the United States, at the factory in Byfield. Afterwards Mr. Moody was engaged on the mills at Waltham, then in company with John Dummer, another Byfield genius, and Kirk Boot; he was prominent amongst the founders of the city of Lowell, ranking as the first machinist in New England.

David Moody, a younger brother, superintended the construction of the Boston mill dam, and for several years was the sureintendent of the iron works there.

The two oldest sons of Capt. Paul Moody, Nathan and Samuel, after graduating at Dartmouth college, with another son, Enoch, went to Hallowell, Maine, where Mr. Enoch Moody founded the Hallowell bank. Afterwards he returned to Massachusetts and became a resident of Newburyport, where he died.

Rev. Joshua Moody, the oldest son of William, of England, born in 1632, graduated at Harvard in 1655; was ordained at Portsmouth, N. H., 1671; was minister of the first church in Boston, from May 23, 1684, till 1692, and died in Boston, July 4, 1697, in his 65th year. This divine was distinguished for his vehement opposition to the witchcraft delusion, in which he stood nearly alone amongst the New England clergy, at the imminent risk of himself becoming a victim to the popular frenzy.

Caleb, the second son of Mr. William Moody, represented Newbury in the General Court, where his plucky resistance to the tyrant, Sir Edmund Andross, caused him to be imprisoned for treason.

Rev. Joseph Moody of York, the father of the renowned Master Moody of Dummer Academy, was known throughout the colony as "Handkerchief Moody," from his wearing, for many years, a handkerchief over his face in the pulpit, or in any public place. This monomania was induced by the idea that he was responsible for the death of an intimate friend; to expiate his sin he veiled his face forevermore from the sight of his fellow mortals. This pious maniac was a man of superior ability, which was manifested in various civil offices, including that of county judge, which he held previous to entering the ministry. His son, Samuel Moody, a graduate of Harvard in 1763, became the first preceptor of Dummer Academy, Master Moody was a stout, stalwart man, odd and eccentric, but few teachers have been more revered and beloved by their pupils, amongst whom he lived to count with some of the most eminent men in the country. To dunces he showed as little sympathy or mercy as Master Chase. He was wont to mingle in the sports of his scholars, whom he encouraged to become good swimmers, for which exercise the vicinity of the river Parker gave ample opportunity. He also, to the horror of the Puritan community, introduced dancing as a school exercise, a French dancing master being hired to give the boys instruction. I think the dancing hall was in the loft of the school-room, in the gamble roof, which was well lighted by end windows, and dormer ones in front. This project, which no one but the omnipotent and favorite Master Moody could have carried out, caused a great commotion. Mrs. Daniel Chute, who had two sons in the school, wrote a long poem, commencing:

"Ye sons of Byfield, now draw near;
Leave worship for the dance;
Nor farther walk in wisdom's ways,
But in the ways of France;"

and Dea. Benjamin Colman, as long an essay, in which he vehemently protested against this innovation, holding forth in the strongest terms its foolish frivolity, and the enormity of promiscuous dancing in general.

For thirty years Master Moody held undisputed sway over the academy; then the infirmities of age became so evident that the appointment of a new teacher was deemed a necessity. To effect this it was expedient to obtain an act of incorporation, which gave the trustees greater control over the establishment. It was a delicate and painful task to ask the resignation of such a man as Master Moody, and he did not readily resign the sceptre he had so long wielded, but at length was induced to do so, on March 25, 1790. He lived until 1796, spending most of his time amongst his old pupils, at whose homes he ever met a cordial reception. He died at Exeter, N. H. The following is the epitaph on his tombstone, in the graveyard at York, Me.:

"*Integer vitæ celerisque purus.*
Here lies the remains of SAMUEL MOODY, Esq., Preceptor of Dummer Academy (the First Institution of the kind in Mass.). He left no child to mourn his sudden death (for he died a Bachelor), yet his numerous pupils in the U. S. will ever retain a lively sense of the Sociability, Industry, Integrity and Piety he possessed in an uncommon degree as well as the disinterested, zealous, faithful and useful manner he discharged the duties of the Academy for 30 years. He died at Exeter Dec. 17, aet 70."

Rev. Samuel Moody, born January 4, 1675; graduated at Harvard in 1697; was ordained in York, Maine, December 20, 1700, and there died November 13, 1747. Parson Moody was chaplain in the army at the reduction of Louisburg. So confident was he of the success of our troops that he took with him a hatchet to cut the images in the Catholic churches.

Samuel Moody, born in 1700, commanded the fort at Pemaquid, then Fort George; was a physician in Brunswick, Me., where he died in 1758.

Rev. John Moody, born in 1705; graduated at Harvard in 1727; was ordained in Newmarket November 25, 1730, and died October 15, 1778, aged seventy-three.

Rev. Amos Moody, born November 20, 1739; graduated at Harvard 1759; was ordained in Pelham, N. H., Nov. 20, 1765; dismissed in 1792, and died March 22, 1819, aged seventy-nine.

Rev. Silas Moody, born April 28, 1742; graduated at Harvard in 1761; was ordained in Arundel January 9, 1771, and died in April, 1816.

Stephen Moody, Harvard, 1790, was a lawyer in Gilmanton, N. H., where he died.

The arms of Moodye (Ipswich, Co. Suffolk, Eng.) are:

ARGENT, ON A CHEVRON, ENGRAILED SABLE, BETWEEN THREE TREFOILS SLIPPED VERT, AS MANY LOZENGES OR; ON A CHIEF AZURE, TWO ARMS ISSUING FROM CLOUDS PPR, VESTED BENDY OR, AND GULES, HOLDING IN HANDS A ROSE OF THE LAST. CREST—TWO ARMS EMBOWERED IN SALTIRE, THE DEXTER VESTED GULES, THE SINISTER VERT, EACH HOLDING A CUTLASS ARGENT, HILTED OR.

Richard, senior, and Stephen Kent, brothers, with their wives, came to Ipswich in 1635, thence to Newbury the same year, in the party of first settlers, with Messrs. Parker and Noyes. Stephen Kent went to Haverhill, thence to Woodbridge, N. J. His second wife, Ann, died in 1660. He then married Eleanor, widow of William Scadlock, May 9, 1662. Children: Elisabeth, Hannah, Steven, Rebecca and Mary.

Richard Kent, senior, had three sons — Richard, jr., and James, born in England, and John, born in Newbury— a daughter, Rebecca, who married Samuel Scullard, then John Bishop; Sarah, whom he left in England, and other daughters. Richard Kent, senior, maltster, was a large landholder; his house and malthouse were at the foot of Kent street.

Richard Kent, jr., and his brother James owned Kent's Island, and land in Oldtown extending to Oldtown hill. Richard Kent, jr., married Jane——— who died June 26, 1674. He married his second wife, Mrs. Joanna Davidson, Jan. 6, 1675. He died Nov. 25, 1689, leaving no heirs.

James Kent died Dec. 12, 1681, leaving one son, John, who inherited the whole estate. He married Mary Hobbs Feb. 24, 1665. He made his will the first of January, 1712, in which he gave his dwelling-house, barn, shop, and two orchards, half of his island, household goods, a horse, etc., to his wife, Mary, for her use and comfort during life, and "to give, sell or dispose of as she shall think fit among her children and grandchildren at her decease or before as she may have occasion. Also I give my said wife all money I shall have in possession at the time of my decease. To my son Richard Kent, I do confirm the gift of my uncle Richard Kent, late of Newbury, aforesaid, deceased, of eight score acres of land upon said island given by my said uncle to my said son, so as that he may enjoy the same. I do give him my said son the other half of sd. Island both meadow and upland & appurtenances thereunto belonging, together with all my housing & orchards thereon, & all my common privileges & rights in all the common undivided lands for pastures where I have rights within the township of Newbury aforesd & my wood lot, with all my right in the lands where the sd. wood lot is made, with all other of my estate both real and personal wheresoever & whatsoever it may consist, excepting what is before given to my wife, & that which I do hereby give to the rest of of my children, on condition that he my sd. son Richard Kent do perform the trust I shall repose & commit unto him as my executor to this my last will.

I give to my daughter Jane Smith, the wife of my son-in-law James Smith five pounds, together with what she has already received & has been given her.

I give and bequeath to my son-in law Jacob Toppan four pounds, to be divided among the children of Sarah Toppan his late wife deceased.

I give unto Sarah Thing, who was the wife of my son James Kent, late of Newbury aforesaid deceased, twenty shillings.

I give unto Elizabeth Kent widow & Relict of my son James Kent of Newbury deceased twenty shillings.

I do ratify and confirm my late conveyance of my land in the upper commons made to my grandson James Smith jun, according to the tenor of the deed & on the condition thereof whereby I have conveyed the same to him."

The bequest in the "upper commons," was the James Smith farm, on Crane-neck hill, West Newbury. As the house was built in 1707, James and Elizabeth (Moody) Smith had been in possession five years, when this will was written.

Col. Richard Kent married first, Mrs. Sarah Greenleaf; second, Mrs. Hannah Carter of Charlestown, whose mother was a daughter of Daniel Gookin, a preacher much valued in his day. Col. Kent by his will, entailed Kent's Island to his son Richard, and after his decease to his oldest son, and to the oldest male heir forever. He was a prominent and influential man in the town. His monument on the old burying hill bears the following inscription:

HERE LIES INTERRED
THE BODY OF
RICHARD KENT, ESQ.,
LATE COLONEL OF THE
SECOND REGIMENT IN THE
COUNTY OF ESSEX, WHO DEPARTED
THIS LIFE MAY THE 8TH, 1740,
IN THE 68 YEAR OF HIS AGE.

Col. Kent's son, Richard, came into possession of the whole of Kent Island according to the entail, but the birth of twins, his first sons, Stephen and Joseph, on May 9, 1741, brought an unexpected difficulty, as the nurse could not or would not say which was the first born. This question has never been decided, though a long and troublesome lawsuit ensued, which at length was ended by an equal division of the property. I give a copy of the final decision by the court.

"COMMONWEALTH OF MASSACHUSETTS.

In the year of oue Lord One Thousand Seven Hundred and Eighty Four, an act for apportioning and Establishing the Posession of the heirs at Law of Richard Kent, son of Richard Kent, late of Newbury deceast, to a certain Island called Kent's Island in Newbury aforesaid.

Whereas the said Richard Kent the Father, by his last will and testament bearing date the sixth day of May, in the year of our Lord, One Thousand Seven Hundred and Forty, among other things, did devise that his son Richard above said, should have and enjoy the whole of the Island aforesaid during his natural life, and after his decease his oldest Son should have and enjoy the same, as an estate tail to his, and the heirs male of his Body Forever. Which last will and testament was afterwards duly proved and approved—and the said Richard the son, on the death of his father, entered into possession of the premises devised as aforesaid, and thereof died siezed, leaving issue Joseph Kent and Stephen Kent twin brothers, and Moses Kent, a younger brother, his sole heirs, and thereupon the sd. Joseph & Stephen entered into the possession thereof, and still hold the same, and by reason of some singular, and extraordinary circumstances attending the birth of the said Joseph and Stephen, it remained uncertain which is the oldest son, although a suit at law, and the verdict of two juries, have been had to determine the question. By which uncertainty great difficulty and contention may further arise among the heirs of the said Richard to the utter ruin of the improvements, and cultivation of so valuable an an Island, and to the Disgust of divers others good citizens, from preventing of which :—

Be it enacted by the Senate and House of Representatives, in General Court assembled, and by the authority of the same, that the Justices of the Supreme Court, on the application of the said Joseph, Stephen and Moses, or on the application of either of them, his or their heirs, shall cause partition of the said Island to be made, and by like Process as is provided for dividing of other Real Estate on application to the said Court:

One third part of the said Island shall be set off to the said Joseph Kent or his heirs, one third to the said Stephen Kent or his heirs, one third to the said Moses Kent or his heirs."

The island is now in possession of the heir of Stephen Kent, Joshua Noyes Kent, he and his brother, John Kent, being the seventh in descent from Richard Kent, jr., and Mr. Joshua N. Kent's sons, and grandson, are the eighth and ninth generations on the island, and tenth in descent from Richard Kent, sen. The Kents have been esteemed and influential citizens. In 1636, Richard Kent, sen. was chosen among the first "seven men," to conduct the town's affairs. First called "seven men," then "town's men," finally "selectmen." Stephen, the brother of Richard, sen., was one of the four, who with Mr. Edward Rawson "contradicented" the order for moving the meeting-house from the lower green. In 1640 Richard Kent, jr., "in ye name of nine others," petitioned the General Court, to grant that Newbury should hold the whole of Plum Island, "to relieve our pinching necessities." During the trouble in the church, the names of Richard, John and James Kent are among those adhering to Mr. Parker's party. In 1683, with ten others, Capt. John Kent petitioned that Newbury might be made a port of entry as well as Salem. This Capt. Kent commanded the brig Merrimack, which was taken by pirates in Martha's Vineyard sound, Aug. 22, 1669. In 1788, Richard and Abel Kent gave the location to the town of the lower part of Kent street; a lane led thence through the Coker estate to High street, which was called Coker's lane.

Amos Kent, graduate of Harvard, 1795, was a lawyer in Chester, N. H.

Moody Kent, graduate of Harvard, 1801, practiced law in Concord, N. H.

The arms of Kent are:

ARGENT, LEOPARD'S HEAD OR; THREE MULLETS VERT, TWO AND ONE COUNTERCHANGED.
CREST—GRIFFIN'S HEAD OR.

Joseph Atkins, born in 1680, came from Isle of Wight to Newbury, with his wife, and sons, William and Joseph, and William's wife, about 1728. Tradition asserts that he had been a lieutenant in the British navy, in the service of Queen Anne. Mrs. Atkins, whose maiden name was Strover, died soon after her arrival, and the widower married a second wife, Mary (Dudley) Wainright, widow of Francis Wainright, daughter of Gov. Joseph Dudley, and sister of Katherine, wife of Lieut.-Gov. Dummer. Captain Atkins, as he was styled, built a house which is still standing on the lower side of Strong street. At its erection it was surrounded by extensive grounds reaching to High street, a garden handsomely laid out stretched in front to the river, and a broad avenue shaded by trees led to the mansion. Capt. Atkins was prominent both in the town and church, being vestryman and warden at Queen Ann's chapel, and a warden at St. Paul's. The erection of the church by the "water side," was first suggested by him, and towards which he gave fifty pounds, and at the first sale of pews he headed the list by taking four, his son William taking a fifth. In 1738, permission was granted Joseph Atkins, esq., and sixty-four others, to build a wharf at the foot of Queen, now Market street. His tomb in the St. Paul's church yard bears this inscription:

"This stone is erected to the Memory of Joseph Atkins Esquire. One of the Founders and A Generous Benefactor of this Church. Formerly an Eminent Merchant in this Towne, and Highly Esteemed by those who knew him. He departed this life Jan. 2d, 1773, Aged 92.

And of Mrs. Mary Atkins:

The Virtuous and amiable Relick of Joseph Atkins, Esq., And Daughter of His Excellency Joseph Dudley. She died November 12th, 1774. Aged 82.

Joseph and Mary Atkins had one son, Dudley, born in 1731; he graduated at Harvard in 1748.

Prior to the decease of Col. Richard Kent, of Kent's Island, Col. Richard having entailed the estate to his oldest son, Richard, by his first wife, and to the oldest male heir forever, the family had removed to a residence owned by Col. Kent in Newburyport, where he died, and where his widow, formerly Hannah (Gookin) Carter, and her children, one son and two daughters by second marriage, continued to reside.

Madam Kent was a superior woman, possessed of a sound understanding and great benevolence, and although a most sincere and pious christian, her religion had nothing in it of austerity or bigotry. On winter evenings it was her custom to collect her children around her to read to them from some instructive book, while she earnestly strove to imbue them thoroughly with the principles and precepts of the Bible.

Madam Kent was a neighbor of Capt. Atkins. The society of this interesting family must have been most congenial to young Dudley Atkins; on May 4, 1752, he led to the hymenial altar Miss Sarah Kent. Their children were Mary Rapell, born August, 1753; Joseph, born April, 1755; Hannah, born April, 1957; Katherine, born Oct. 1758; Dudley, born Sept., 1760: Rebecca, born March, 1767.

Dudley Atkins was a prominent merchant and a leading citizen of the town, a warden and active member of St. Paul's church.

Oct. 21, 1765, Newburyport held a town meeting to instruct their representative, Dudley Atkins, esq., "relating to his acting in the General Court," respecting the Stamp Act. These instructions expressed the most loyal sentiments toward the king, but the Stamp Act was esteemed a peculiar grievance, and he was directed to use his influence to his utmost ability "that the rights and privileges of the province may be preserved inviolate." A long list of resolutions ends with abhorrence of all seditious and mobbish insurrections, of all breaches of the peace, and "that you will readily concur in any constitutional measure that may be necessary to secure the public tranquillity."

The troubles with England increased, but Dudley Atkins remained loyal to King George. On one occasion his house was surrounded by a mob; Mr. Atkins being indisposed, several gentlemen went to his assistance, but his wife, the courageous Sarah (Kent) Atkins quelled the infuriated populace. Contrary to the remonstrance of friends, she opened the door, and addressed the throng, telling them, "that her husband was ill in bed, might not live to see them again; they had always respected him, and they ought not to molest her and her small and helpless children." The evil spirit was laid. Promises of security were given, and the mob retired with cheers for Madame Atkins. Dudley Atkins, esq., died Sept. 24, 1761, aged 38 years. His widow went to Amesbury where she resided for a time. Feeling the necessity of making some exertion towards the support of her young family, she determined to open a store on State street, Newburyport. This was in the building now occupied by Mrs. Altar. It was mid-winter when the removal took place, the furniture and the family, with the exception of Mrs. Atkins and a man-servant, had gone, when a violent snow storm so blocked the roads that it would be impossible to travel by the usual mode of conveyance for some days. Unwilling to remain thus separated from her new home, where her presence was so imperatively demanded, infusing her spirit of enterprise, as was her wont, into those around her, she obtained the willing consent of her own man, and another belonging to the farm, to draw her to Newburyport on a hand-sled, which they accomplished without any great difficulty. Passing the house of a friend, where a large party were assembled at dinner, upon seeing her unique equipage they rushed out with ludicrous expressions of surprise and congratulation, while the contrast between their situation and pursuits and hers were vividly striking. Friends in Boston supplied Madam Atkins with fine goods, the store prospered, and became the fashionable emporium of State street.

Gov. Joseph Dudley married Rebecca Tyng. Their son, Edward, brother of Mrs. Joseph Atkins, left a large estate in Tyngsborough to his daughter, Mrs. Winslow. This lady, a childless widow, proposed to adopt young Dudley Atkins, and make him her heir if he would add Tyng to his name. As there was the oldest son Joseph to transmit the name of Atkins, this offer was accepted, but Joseph Atkins, an enterprising ship-master, died unmarried. His vessel was wrecked on a return voyage, in a winter storm, and the whole crew perished. The body of Capt. Atkins, found frozen to the mast, was brought to the bereaved home for burial amongst his kindred in St. Paul's church yard. The stone erected to his memory bears this inscription:

"Here are interred The Remains of Capt. Joseph Atkins, who (with his whole Ship's Company) perished by Shipwreck on Cape Cod, Feb. ye 8th, 1787. Aged 31 years.
He that goeth on his way weeping & beareth good Seed shall doubtless come again with Joy brigning his Sheaves with him."

Mary Rapell Atkins married George, son of George and Catherine (Gore) Searle, in 1779. This lady was named for a Wainright, daughter of Mrs. Joseph Atkins, who married Judge Rapell, an Englishmen, judge of the Superior court, and judge of the Admiralty for these Provinces, in the time of George 2d. It is said he never had but one decision reversed during forty years.

Hannah Atkins died Sept. 25, 1771, in the 15th year of her age.

Katherine Atkins married Samuel Elliot of Boston; she was the ancestress of Samuel Elliot, president of Harvard University, and other distinguished persons.

Rebecca Atkins died June 23, 1842, unmarried.

In 1788, Dudley A. Tyng, esq., purchased the present Tyng estate on High street for his mother, to which she removed with her daughter Rebecca.

Mrs. George Searle, having become a widow with ten orphan children, took her mother's store on State street, which she kept until after the fire of 1811. Mrs. Margaret Curson of Curson's mill was her daughter.

Dudley Atkins Tyng fitted for college at Dummer academy, graduated at Harvard in 1781, and studied law with Judge Parsons in Newburyport. In 1795, he was appointed by Adams, Collector of the district of Newburyport. For some years he was Recorder of the Supreme Court of Massachusetts; during this period he resided in Cambridge, but Newburyport was his favorite abode, and most of his summers were passed here. He first married Sarah, daughter of Stephen Higginson of Boston; second, her sister Elisabeth. Madam Sarah (Kent) Atkins died on the 16th of October, 1810, aged 81. In 1821, Squire Tyng built the lower of the two Tyng houses for his sister Rebecca, and having remodelled and enlarged the other mansion, in the autumn of that year he returned to Newburyport, which was his permanent reisdence until his death on Aug. 1, 1829, aged 69. Dudley A. Tyng. like his father and grand-father, was an active and beneficent member of St. Paul's church, filling the office of warden for some years. He gave a silver paten for the communion service, which bears this inscription:

PRESENTED BY HON. D. A. TYNG, ESQ.

In 1790, Hon. T. Dalton and D. A. Tyng, esq., were chosen lay delegates to a convention at Salem, to prepare an Ecclesiastical constitution for Massachusetts, which was adopted by St. Paul's church, Jan. 16, 1791; the same delegates with Hon. Jona. Jackson and Mr. Lewis Jenkins were a committee to ratify the same at the next convention in Boston.

Dudley A. and Sarah Tyng had eight children: Sarah, who married first, Charles Head; second, Joseph Marquand. Susan C, married Edward A. Newton; Dudley, who died in infancy; a second Dudley, who took the name of Atkins.

Dr. Dudley Tyng Atkins graduated at Harvard in 1816, and studied medicine. He married Ann, daughter of Judge Bowman of Wilksbarre, Pa. For a time was practising physician in Newburyport, afterwards went to the city of New York, where he died April 7, 1845.

The Rev. Stephen Higginson Tyng. graduated at Harvard in 1817; was professor at Jefferson college, settled in Philadelphia, but for more than forty years had been the distinguished rector of St. George's Church, New York. He has now retired from the active duties of the ministry. He married, first, Anna, daughter of Bishop Griswold; second, Susan, daughter of John Mitchell, of Philadelphia.

Charles died June 20, 1879, aged 78. He was a successful ship master, and merchant; was for many years established at Havana, Island of Cuba, where he endeared hinself, by his hearty sympathy, and benevolence, to his countrymen there. He married, first, Anna Selina Anold, who died July 5, 1831, aged 25; second, AnnaA., daughter of John H. McAlpine, of New York. The McAlpines are of the oldest of the Highland Clans, dating back to Kenneth McAlpine, Feb. 6, in the year eight hundred and thirty six.

Mary, married Robert Cross, esq. She died some years since.

James, graduated at Bowdoin in 1827, studied for the ministry, for many years was a rector in New York. He married Matilda Degan, and died April 6, 1879.

George Tyng, graduated at Harvard in 1822, and died April 2, 1823, aged 25.

Many of my readers will remember the genial, and hospitable Miss Rebecca Atkins, aunt Becky, as she was usually styled, and her pleasant home. Her house, and that of Squire Tyng have been modernized, but most of the ancient heir-looms, that formely graced them, are still retained. Amongst these are fine portraits of Joseph Atkins, esq. and Mary Dudlev, his second wife, and a painting, representing the visit of Queen Ann and the Royal Family to the man of war, of which young Atkins was Lieutenant, a new vessel, then considered a model craft. This picture Capt. Atkins brought to America, and he held it in such estimation as to bequeath it in his will, as a special legacy to be transmitted from his son, and son's son, through the generations.

Capt. Joseph Atkins, the second son of Joseph Atkins, esq., died a bachelor, Feb. 6, 1782, aged 76.

William Atkins, esq., the oldest son, was a prominent merchant and citizen, and an active member and warden of St. Paul's church. His name stands first on the list of two hundred and six of the "water side" people who signed the petition to be "set off from Newbury, and incorporated as a town by themselves," and, in direct contradistinction to his half-brother, Dudley, was an active Whig, and enthusiastic Revolutionist, being one of the Committee of Safety and Correspondence appointed by the town on the 23d of September, 1774. Before leaving England, he had married Abigail Beck, by whom he had one son and four daughters. He built a house near where the present custom house now stands, a handsome Colonial mansion, with wainscotted rooms, deep window seats, broad stone hearths, and fire-places decorated with Dutch tiles depicting Scripture scenes. At his death this house was purchased by the father of Captains John and Benjamin Harrod; there they and their sisters were born. It was burned in the great fire of 1811, then known as the Harrod house. The Atkins family and their widowed sister, Mrs. Dr. Samuel Colman, and her children, at that time resided opposite; their house was also burned.

William Atkins, esq., died Aug. 27, 1788, aged 77.

Mrs. Abigail Atkins died Dec. 5, 1786, aged 68.

Miss Mary Atkins died Aug. 31, 1802, aged 64.

Hannah C. Atkins died June 6, 1811, aged 57.

Elisabeth Atkins died July 30, 1838, aged 88.

Susanna (Atkins) Colman died in Salem, July 9, 1827, aged 65.

William Atkins, the only son, was lost at sea.

The Atkins arms are:

OR, A CROSS QUARTERLY PIERCED FLORY AND COUNTER FLORY, AZURE; BETWEEN FOUR MULLETS SABLE; CRESCENT, GULES, IN CHIEF. CREST—TWO GREYHOUNDS HEADS ENBOSSED, COLLAR DOVETAILED, PER PALE OR AND AZURE, COUNTERCHANGED.

Dudley and Tyng per pale. Dudley—Or, lion rampant. Tyng—Argent, on a chevron sable three martlets proper. Crest—a martlet.

Motto—"Esse quam videri."

CHAPTER XXXIII.

At the trying period of the Revolution, Newbury and Newburyport displayed great heroism. At the first intelligence of the battle of Lexington, four companies immediately marched to the scene of action. Those from Newbury were commanded by Colonel Samuel Gerrish and Colonel Moses Little. The Newburyport companies were led by Capt. Ezra Lunt and Colonel Benjamin Perkins. On a stormy day, as we sat at our work, grandmother, aunt Sarah and mother often recalled those stirring times, and of a winter's evening my father and other friends frequently talked over the events of the war. My father was an excellent singer, and he was often invited to sing the songs that had then been popular. Two of these "The Vision" and "Burgoyne's Lamentation," I will note; would that I could give the voice, expression, and enthusiasm of the singer.

THE VISION.

"I was an old farmer,
  Was born in the woods,
Of late had a vision
  From one of the gods.

"Last Saturday night,
As I slept on my bed,
The following dream
  Came into my head:

"I thought I was towering
  Aloft in the air,
Then rambled to Boston
  To see what was there.

"First viewing the troops,
  Which were tired of intrenching,
Then going to see Tom,
  Who was giddy with drinking.

"For of wine, gin and ale
  So freely he drank,
That he was scarce able
  To visit his rank.

"His friends were all round him,
  And if you think fitting,
I'll tell you the posture
  The club was now sitting.

"There were Tim, Dick and Will,
  And several more;
I thought in the whole,
  They would make nigh a score.

"Sat round a large table,
  But all at a pause,
To think of a plan
  To enforce these new laws.

"I wondered at this,
  And asking old Beetle,
For knowing the villain
  Was apt for to tattle;

"He honestly told me
  What was the reason,
The Devil, says he,
  Has gone for a season,

"To help his friend North
  Project a new plan,

And when this is done,
  We expect him again;

"But if he should choose
  For to tarry all winter,
We think it not safe,
  Out of Boston to venture.

For the Congress has met,
  And passed such votes,
That all our old plans
  Are now come to nought.

"And the governor says,
  So well do unite,
He believes the devilish villains
  Determined to fight,

"And think it not best
  To provoke them to blows,
Lest in a cold winter,
  The harbor gets froze;

"And if they should come over us,
  Our fleet could not save us.
Of consequence,
  The Devil must have us.

"Many such stories
  He did me detain,
Till Tom got so well
  He could stagger again.

"And laying his course
  For crossing the hall,
He luckily met
  With an impudent fall,

"Which brought him at last,
  Two yards on the floor,
Which tickled me so,
  I dreamed no more."

BURGOYNE'S LAMENTATION.

"Ye powers look down and pity my case,
For the once great Burgoyne is now in distress.
For I am surrounded by a numerous foe,
Who, I fear, my whole army will soon overthrow.

"Oh, cursed be the villain who did us much hurt,
Who carried to England so false a report.
For it is commonly reported in fair England,
That the sight of a Briton would make Yankees run,

"That the report of a cannon would make Yankees fly,
"Oh, were they as numerous as stars in the sky.
To my woful experience I found it was false,
For of two, the Yankees are better than us.
"They will fight with great valor when in the open field,
Take them in the forest, then Britons must yield,
For they will shut up one eye, and squint at the gun,
And we are surely dead as soon as that's done.
We stand no more chance among Yankee paws,
Than to fling an old cat into hell without claws."

On the arrival of the "courier" with news of the Lexington fight, the minute men of the upper parish quickly gathered at the training field on the main road. The company having been formed, boards were thrown over an ox-cart; from this hastily improvised rostrum, Parson Toppan spoke a few words of patriotism and encouragement, then invoked the Divine blessing upon the gallant band. Meantime individuals were going from house to house, collecting food and other necessaries. The news came at midnight, and soon after sunrise the company commenced its march; the rations, baggage, etc., being conveyed by two ox-teams. One can imagine the sensation throughout the usually quiet country side. The sorrowful faces and anxious hearts, prayerfully striving to bear the worst bravely, for the sake of country and liberty.

By order of the selectmen on the following day, a further supply of provisions was forwarded to the troops. Every household contributed, and the donations were most generous. The day had been a busy one at Craneneck; the large and small ovens had been filled and refilled; beef, pork, hams, flour, meal and a small supply of groceries and medicines, been packed; lint been scraped and bandages rolled. This was sad work, but provision must be made for the worst. It was near sunset when aunt Sarah, (then a girl of sixteen,) on her way to the well, espied a horseman coming at a furious pace up the road, swinging his hat and shouting: "The regulars are coming! They have landed at Plum Island, have got to Artichoke bridge, are burning and killing all before them!" For an instant the maiden stood in frightened bewilderment, then she ran to communicate the news. The neighbors flocked in, a terror stricken throng, to counsel respecting further measures. Most of the able bodied men armed themselves and went to seek the foe, if foe were there. After the first excitement had passed, doubts of the genuineness of the tidings arose. Neither my grandfather Smith, nor grandsir Little credited the story, and they advised every one, after the men had marched away to stay quietly at home until further intelligence could be obtained. A few did so, but most, in a perfect frenzy of fright, sought every means for safety.

Uncle Thurrel's farm at that time belonged to the family of the late Dr. Adams. This gentleman had been the first physician to settle in the town; he acquired a wide spread practice in the surrounding infant settlements, and at his decease left a reputation for superior knowledge and skill. The house was occupied by his grandchildren, and their aged and feeble widowed mother. This household passed the night in the greatest anxiety and alarm. Having hidden their choicest effects, the horse was harnessed to the chaise, an uncovered vehicle on two wheels, at that time the stylish equipage for ladies, which was drawn up before the door through the night, while the old lady, wrapped in a coverlet sat through the long hours in her large arm chair, in readiness to be conveyed down "South End," a rocky, steep declivity at the southerly side of the hill, a descent from which one might have expected as dire a catastrophe, as from a raid of any number of "regulars."

Old Mr. Joshua Bartlett, commonly designated "Uncle Vun," yoked his oxen to the cart, and took his family to the Platts place, a lone, unoccupied farm-house, remote from the road. Several families sought the same refuge. Col. Stephen Bartlett was an infant just weaned; in the flurry the jug of milk had been left behind, and the hungry babe demanded his food so lustily, that some one in the distracted throng proposed to kill him, lest his cries should disclose their hiding place.

Hannah Eastman, an old, asthmatic woman, breathed so hard, she was wrapped in a blanket and buried in the leaves under a stone wall, at some distance from the house. After a sleepless night, at sunrise the croud ventured home. One young fellow, instead of marching to meet the "regulars," skedaddled into the pasture, having armed himself with a junk of salt pork, and half a loaf brown bread, in addition to his gun and powder horn; he climbed into an oak, and quakingly awaited events. The night wore on, day dawned, the sun rose, ascended higher and higher, noon passed, still the young hero durst not venture from his sylvan retreat, until his absence having created a general alarm, he was descried by a squad of relatives and neighbors who had instituted a search.

One gentleman hid his papers in a hollow tree from which they were extracted with much difficulty; his wife lowered her silver spoons into the well, and the servant girl, beside herself with fright, pulled the "nubs and drops" from her ears and flung them into the same receptacle. The spoons were recovered, but the ear jewels could never be found. It was an anxious and sleepless night for all. I have often heard Mrs. Moses Colman, then Betty Little, a girl of nine, relate how she fancied the wind in the chimney, and the sizzling of the wood fire, were the drums and fifes of the enemy. Towards morning the men and boys returned, without sight or hearing of "regulars." How this scare arose was never known, but it was supposed to have been a strategem to try the mettle of the people.

Anxious weeks, which had brôught but few tidings from the army around Boston, had glided away. The morning of the seventeenth of June dawned, a hot summer day. The spring had been uncommonly warm, and vegetation was unusually forward. In those days it was the custom to have men's garments made at home. Tailor Palmer, a veteran of the old French war, came to Capt. Smith's that day to fashion the go-to-meeting coats and breeches for the summer. Aunt Sarah was sewing with the tailor, when her ear caught a rumble. "Did it thunder?" She rose and looked from the door. Not a cloud was in sight. Again and again she caught the sound as of distant thunder. The men came from the field to luncheon, but paused to look and listen. "I'll tell ye what 'tis," said the tailor, "its big guns, cannon. There's a battle." The noise increased, and it was evident the old soldier was right. Soon smoke was discerned on the southern sky, which momentarily increased in volume. It was thought that Boston was burning. Higher and higher rose the smoke, louder thundered the cannon, work was forgotten, the dinner remained untasted. People began to flock up the hill, in groups they watched and listened. Slowly the lurid sun sank in the sky, gradually the boom of the guns ceased, the smoke cleared, and all was over. Nothing could be done but to await intelligence, with what calmness and patience could be summoned. The news of the battle of Bunker Hill, and the burning of Charlestown was received the next day, but the full particulars did not come for more than a week. I believe no one in our companies were killed, a few were wounded. Col. Joseph Whitmore and Sergeant Amos Pearson of Newburyport were wounded, and several men killed. Capt. Ezra Lunt's company, acting as rear guard, suffered severely.

Quite a number from the four companies that fought at Bunker Hill joined the disastrous expedition against Quebec, the September following. This force consisted of eleven companies of musketmen and three companies of riflemen, amounting to eleven hundred men, under the command of Col. Benedict Arnold, Lieut.-Colonel Christopher Green of Rhode Island, and Major Timothy Bigelow of Massachusetts. The Newbury and Newburyport men were in Capt. Ward's company. The riflemen were commanded by Capt. Daniel Morgan. The Rev. Samuel Spring, afterwards the distinguished pastor of the North church in Newburyport, acted as chaplain. . Many noted men accompanied this band; Matthew Ogden, Aaron Burr, John I. Henry, afterwards Judge Henry of Pennsylvania; Captain, afterwards Gen. Henry Dearborn of New Hampshire; Major Keturn I. Meigs, Captains William Kendricks and Matthew Smith, with others whose names have descended amongst the Revolutionary heroes. The detachment arrived in Newburyport Saturday, Sept. 16th, and embarked at 10 a. m. on Tuesday, the 19th, in eleven transports, sloops and schooners. The troops were quartered in the ropewalk of Edmund Swett, which extended from Fair to Federal streets; the riflemen bivouacked at the head of Rolfe's lane, now Ocean avenue, and the officers were entertained at the spacious and hospitable mansions of Nathaniel Tracy and Tristram Dalton.

This was a notable epoch for Newburyport. The short sojourn of the army was made a season of gaiety. The sunny side, with all the pomp and pageantry of war.

On Sunday, the troops, with drums rolling and flags flying, marched to the Old South meeting house. This had been completed but a few years, and was the largest and one of the finest places of public worship in New England. The high pulpit and elaborately-ornamented sounding board were celebrated specimens of the style of the period. To the right of the sacred desk was a high seat for the sexton, and before it the "elders' seat," a square pew, raised a few steps, with a table in the centre. In front of this came the "deacon's seat." To this was attached the communion table, which was swung back when not in use. A broad aisle and two side aisles ran through the house. The pews were square, with seats all around and a chair in the centre. Spacious galleries ran around three sides of the house, the "singing seats" being opposite the pulpit, and at either end there were large porches.

The troops, having halted in the aisles, presented arms as their chaplain, a keen-eyed, stalwart young fellow, six feet high, passed through. The guns having been stacked in the aisles, the soldiers were seated in the body of the house, the galleries and every other available portion being packed by a crowd of citizens. The clergyman preached fromt he text, "If thy Spirit go not up with us, carry us not up hence." The eloquence and power of the preacher made such an impression on his audience, that before he left, a promise had been secured that he would return to the town, at the end of the war. This promise was redeemed, and the South church and the Rev. Dr. Samuel Spring, became watchwords upon the hill of Zion. The following morning there was a grand review, in which the men appeared to great advantage, their spirits being raised by the presence of hundreds of sympathizing spectators, drawn thither from far and near. The officers were entertained at dinner and evening parties, at which majestic matrons and lovely maidens, in their richest brocades, and choicest gauzes and laces, conversed most graciously and smiled their sweetest, using every exertion for the amusement of the gallant men, about to risk their lives on the altar of liberty. In friendly courtesy, glass clinked to glass with fervent wishes for honor and success. Gracefully the stately minuet was danced.

Enthusiastically, patriotic songs were sung to the accompaniment of the spinnet or harpsicord. On the morning of the nineteenth, amid cheer upon cheer from the assembled multitude, the troops embarked. In a perfect whirlwind of patriotic excitement, flags flying, drums beating and fifes playing, the transports weighed anchor, their sails gleaming in the bright sunlight; they slowly glided down the broad, beautiful Merrimac, and with aching hearts, but a brave front, the citizens dispersed, to pursue again the even tenor of life.

CHAPTER XXXIV.

From the settlement of the town, ship-building had been one of the chief employments of the "water side people." Prior to the revolution, this business had been very lucrative. Though many of the vessels launched at our yards were owned and fitted for sea by the "Port" merchants, others were built expressly for the English market. The British merchants purchased our ships and lumber; in return we received their manufactures, and the produce from their possessions in the West Indies. As Newburyport was the centre for the trade of a wide agricultural district, it had become one of the most thriving of the sea-board towns.

Partnerships often existed between our merchants and individuals in England. Mr. Benjamin Harris and an English gentleman, Mr. Witter Cummings, built a ship at Samuel Moggaridge's yard, shortly before the war. At the commencement of the troubles, much of our merchant marine was sent out as privateers. Some of these were most successful, fully repaying their owners for the business lost by the war. So many prizes within a few days were brought in to Mr. Joseph Marquand, that in the press of the occasion, that gentleman hastily exclaimed, "Oh Lord! Thy servant has enough; stay thy hand." His prayer was answered, for with subsequent losses, and the great fire, the rich merchant died a comparatively poor man.

Many of the vessels cleared from the port were either lost at sea or taken by the enemy. The fate of several with that of their crews was never known. The loss of one, the "Yankee Hero," carrying twenty guns, commanded by Capt. James Tracy, brought mourning throughout the town, as out of one hundred and seventy men, fifty were from Newburyport and vicinity, volunteers from some of the first families.

Those so unfortunate as to fall into the enemy's hands, suffered great hardship in the loathsome English prisons and prison ships. The crews of the brig Dalton, fitted out by Stephen Hooper, and the brigantine Fanny, were confined between two and three years, in the Old Mill prison in Plymouth.

Many of the privateers were of small burthen, and but poorly armed; still this hastily improvised navy did good service, making many notable captures, and carrying havoc to the enemy's fleet.

The following is the commission of the commander of one of these vessels:

COLONY OF MASSACHUSETTS BAY.

The Major of the Council of the Massachusetts Bay, New England. To John Wigglesworth, Gentleman, Greeting.

You being appointed to take the

James Bowdoin	Winthrop, Command
Rich'd Derby jr.	of the armed Sloop
J. Cushing	called the Swift, of the
S. Holton	burthen of thirty-five
Jabez Fisher	tons, or thereabouts,
Moses Gill	mounting four swivels
B. White	& one carriage Gun,
Benj. Austin	and navigated by ten
Henry Gardener	men, fitted out at the
W. Phillips	expense, & for the
Dan. Davis	service of this Colony.
B. Lincoln	By virtue of the pow-
Dan. Hopkins	er vested in us, we do

by these presents (reposing special trust and confidence in your ability, courage, and good conduct,) commission you accordingly, and give you the said John Wigglesworth, full power with such persons as shall engage to your assistance, by force of arms to attack, seize, and take the Ships, and other Vessels belonging to the inhabitants of Great Britain, or any of them with Tackel, Apparel, furniture & Lading on the high seas, or between high water and low water mark, and to bring the same to some convenient Port in this colony, in order that the courts, which have been, or shall be hereafter appointed to hear & determine maritime causes, may proceed in due form to condemn the said Captaines if they be adjudged lawful Prize, the said John Wigglesworth having given bonds to the Treasurer of this Colony with sufficient Sureties that nothing be done by the said John Wigglesworth or any of his Officers, Marines, or Company of the said Vessel contrary to, or inconsistant with the usage and customs of Nations, and the instructions that are or may be given to him by order of the Great and General Court. And we will, and require all our officers to give Succour and assistance to the said John Wigglesworth in the premises. This commission to continue in force until further orders.

Given under our hands and Seal of the said colony at Watertown, the third day of June in the year of our LORD, one thousand seven hundred and seventy-six.

By their Honor's Command.

Of the Newburyport vessels, a large number were sent out by Messrs. Nathaniel and John Tracy. Their ships captured one hundred and twenty sail, which, with their cargoes, brought three million, nine hundred and fifty thousand dollars. Of this sum, one hundred and sixty-seven thousand, two hundred and nineteen dollars, was devoted to the army and other public exigencies. Out of one hundred and ten merchant vessels, twenty-three of which were letters-of-marque, only thirteen, and of twenty-four cruisers, but one, remained at the close of the war; all the others had been lost or captured. The ship Friends, Capt. Bowie, of London, bound to Boston with provisions for the British army, having mistaken her course, on the morning of the 15th of January was discovered off the "Bar." Three whale boats manned by armed men, commanded by Capt. Offin Boardman, immediately put out to her. Captain Boardman, representing himself as a pilot from Boston, was taken on board. Whilst the unsuspecting English captain was conversing with the supposed pilot on the quarter-deck, the crews from the three boats, seventeen in number, quietly ascended the gangway. Seeing all was ready, Capt. Boardman in stentorian tones ordered the English flag to be struck. Overcome by astonishment, neither the commander nor crew made the least resistance, and the prize was brought in triumph to the wharf.

The ship Hibernia, owned by Captains Joseph and John O'Brien, and commanded by the latter, was very successful. On her first cruise she captured three brigs, a ship, and two schooners, in less than four weeks. In this cruise she met with a sixteen-gun ship, with which she had an engagement that lasted nearly two hours, but from which she finally escaped, with the loss of three men and several wounded.

Capt. William Russell, in the Gen. Ward, a small vessel, mounting one light swivel, with about a dozen men, each armed with a musket, captured two brigs and a schooner. Only two men could be spared to be put on board the schooner, and she was retaken, but the brigs were brought safely into town. The privateer Hawk, Captain Jack Lee, sent in an English brig from Oporto, loaded with wine, and a large amount of specie. Captain Moses Brown, in the privateer Gen. Arnold, took several rich prizes, but was at length captured by the British brig Experiment, of fifty guns. Capt. Brown was for some time confined on board a prison ship at Savannah, Georgia, but was exchanged, and returned to Newburyport.

On May 19, 1780, occurred that phenomenon, commonly called the "Dark day." There had been extensive fires in the woods, and for several days previous the air had been thick, and the sky murky. On the memorable nineteenth, the sun rose as usual, but soon clouds began to appear and the whole sky became overcast; about ten o'clock there was a slight shower. My mother, then thirteen years of age, had gone to the garret to give it the spring cleaning. At first she thought a thunder shower was rising, but the increasing darkness, and the singular aspect without, caused her to leave her work, and in somewhat of a panic join the family below. Dense, black clouds overspread the heavens with a lighter gleam at the horizon; the fowls went to roost, and the birds flew into the trees. The darkness was the most intense between twelve and one o'clock. Candles were lighted for the dinner table, and the meal was shorter and more silent than usual. Both grandsir and grandma'm Little were quiet, firm people; there was no undue excitement in their household, still it was a strange, and somewhat solemn day. Many families were in a perfect frenzy. "The Judgment Day had come," and amid tears and piteous lamentations and confessions, with prayer and Bible reading, the frightened creatures tremblingly passed the hours, momentarily expecting that the dread trump would sound. The darkness continued into the night, but the following morning the sun rose bright and the air had resumed its usual clearness.

A while after, the inhabitants of the upper parish had another fright. Mr. Enos Bartlett, at the Training Field, had a load of bricks to draw to Byfield. The weather was intensely hot, and he started soon after midnight. The cart wheels were dry, needed greasing; they soon began to creak. The noise increased, until it blended into a series of unearthly creaks and grinds. Along the route every one was aroused, half unconscious, and unable to understand the diabolical sounds, most were terribly frightened. As it was a still night, the noise reached quite a distance, and what it was could not be imagined. Some thinking the last day had come, fell to praying and reading their bibles. When Mr. Bartlett reached the brook above grandsir Little's, he drove through the water, thus ending the noise and commotion. I have often heard aunt Hannah describe the fright of herself and the other children, roused from sound sleep, but grandma'm having ascertained the source of the discord, went about and quieted her flock, and thereafter she would never permit her girls to laugh at their more credulous neighbors, bidding them, "to so live that at any moment the judgment might find them ready to give a good account."

The depreciation of the paper money issued by congress to meet the exigencies of the war for a time caused general disorder in monetary affairs, and in some instances great distress. By 1780, the continental money had driven nearly all the gold and silver out of circulation, and this paper currency lessened in value with such rapidity that in remote places, and where people were unacquainted with the money market, fraud could be easily perpetrated. In this way Gen. John Peabody's mother was cheated out of a large part of her late husband's estate. She sold the homestead for a good price, and received in full payment a whole trunk full of money, which to her utter amazement and dismay she learned was in reality not worth more than a third of its nominal value. When I was a child, I had several of these continental bills, with which I used to play shopping, and for years my father kept one in his wallet as a memento, laughingly averring that so long as this bill was in his pocket he was not devoid of money. Aunt Sarah had a calico dress, which cost a one hundred dollar bill, and a set of knitting needles for which she paid a dollar. Mrs. Moses Colman, then Betty Little, paid one hundred and fifty dollars for sufficient black silk to make a short cloak, a sort of mantilla, then fashionable for summer wear. She often laughingly boasted of her one expensive garment.

In 1789, Washington on his eastern tour visited Newburyport. He came Friday, Dec. 1, and remained until the next morning.

In my childhood I often heard descriptions of the grandeur of his reception, and on a stormy Sunday I often conned the volumes of the "Essex Journal and New Hampshire Packet," of December fourth, which contained a full account of the proceedings. This was the first paper printed in the town, a Republican sheet, first published Dec. 4, 1773, by Thomas and Tinges, and continued by Ezra Lunt and John Mycall. The President came by the old Boston road, over the Parker river bridge, and through Oldtown. At the upper green he left his carriage, and mounted his horse. He had been met at Ipswich and escorted hither, by Marshall Jackson, the High Sheriff of the county of Essex, the Hon. Tristram Dalton, Maj. General Titcomb, and other officers and gentlemen from Newburyport and the surrounding towns, and two companies of cavalry from Ipswich and Andover. As the cortege moved on to High street, it was met near South, now Bromfield, by a long procession. The Artillery fired a Federal salute, and a company of young men sang the following ode:

"He comes, He comes! The Hero comes!
Sound, Sound your trumpets, Beat, Beat your Drums.
From port, to port, let cannons roar,
His welcome to New England's shore.
Welcome, welcome, welcome, welcome,
Welcome to New England's shore!

Prepare! Prepare! your Songs prepare,

Loud, loudly rend the echoing air;
From Pole to Pole, his praise resound,
For Virtue is with glory crowned.
Virtue, virtue, virtue, virtue,
Virtue is with glory crowned."

The lines in the first verse, which call for the beating of drums and roaring of cannon, were instantly obeyed, after the pronunciation of each word, and to the vocal was joined all the instrumental music in both choruses, which were repeated. Washington was exceedingly pleased with this novel reception, moved even to tears. Next the President, preceded by the several companies of Militia and Artillery of the town, the Musicians, Selectmen, High Sheriff and Marshall Jackson, passed the Ministers, Physicians, Lawyers, Magistrates, Town officers, Marine Society, Tradesmen and Manufacturers, Captains of Vessels, Sailors, and School Masters with their Scholars, who had paraded, and opened to the right and left, each of whom as the President passed closed and joined in the procession, which was terminated by four hundred and twenty scholars, all with quills in their hands, headed by their Preceptors. Their motto, "We are the free born subjects of the United States." This procession passed through High to State street conducting Washington to the residence of Nathaniel Tracy, esq., where he was entertained in princely style. On his arrival he was greeted with the following address, written by John Quincy Adams, then a student at law in the office of Theophilus Parsons, esq., who had been appointed by the town to prepare it.

To the President of the United States:—Sir: When, by the unanimous suffrages of your countrymen, you were called to preside over their public councils, the citizens of the town of Newburyport participated in the general joy that arose from anticipating an administration conducted by the man to whose wisdom and valor they owed their liberties. Pleasing were their reflections, that he who, by the blessing of Heaven, had given them their independance, would again relinquish the felicities of domestic retirement, to teach them its just value. They have seen you, victorious, leave the field, followed with the applause of a grateful country; and they now see you, entwining the Olive with the Laurel, and, in peace, giving security and happiness to a people, whom in war, you covered with glory. At the present moment, they indulge themselves in sentiments of joy, resulting from a principle, perhaps less elevated, but exceedingly dear to their hearts, from a gratification of their affections, in beholding personally among them, the Friend, the Benefactor, and the Father of their Country.

They cannot hope, Sir, to exhibit any peculiar marks of attachment to your person; for, could they express their feelings of the most ardent and sincere gratitude, they would only repeat the sentiments, which are deeply impressed upon the hearts of all their fellow citizens; but, in justice to themselves, they beg leave to assure you, that in no part of the United States are those sentiments of gratitude and affection more cordial and animated than in the town, which, at this time, is honored with your presence.

Long, sir, may you continue the ornament and support of these States, and may the period be late, when you shall be called to receive a reward, adequate to your virtue, which it is not in the power of this country to bestow.

The President replied as follows:

"To the citizens of the town of Newburyport:—

Gentlemen: The demonstrations of respect and affection which you are pleased to pay to an individual whose highest pretension is to rank as your fellow-citizen, are of a nature too distinguished not to claim the warmest return that gratitude can make.

My endeavors to be useful to my country have been no more than the result of conscious duty. Regards like yours, would reward services of the highest estimation and sacrifice; yet, it is due to my feelings, that I should tell you those regards are received with esteem, and replied to with sincerity.

In visiting the town of Newburyport, I have obeyed a favorite inclination, and I am much gratified by the indulgence. In expressing a sincere wish for its prosperity, and the happiness of its inhabitants, I do justice to my own sentiments and their merit."

A *feu de joie* was fired by the militia companies, and in the evening there was a display of fireworks. Saturday morning the President started for Portsmouth, under the escort that conducted him into town, with the addition of a large number of military and other gentlemen of Newburyport, who accompanied him to the New Hampshire line, where he was met by Gen. Sullivan, Governor of the State, with four companies of light-horse, who conducted him to Portsmouth. This was previous to the erection of the Essex Merrimac bridge, and Washington crossed the river at the Amesbury ferry. The Marine society fitted and decorated a barge for that purpose, which was commanded by one their members, the bargemen being dressed in white. As the boat came midway the stream, a ship from Teneriffe, gaily adorned with flags and commanded by Captain Joseph A. de Murrietta, fired the salute of his nation, twenty-one guns. In Amesbury and Salisbury the militia were paraded, and saluted the President as he passed.

CHAPTER XXXV.

The French Revolution, and the general confusion which reigned in Europe after the decapitation of Louis XVI, brought a large carrying trade to the seaports of the Union. American shipping was protected in the Texal, and the Empress Catherine granted us the freedom of the Baltic. A brisk trade was opened with the English, French, Spanish and Dutch possessions. Though Newburyport prospered from her foreign trade for a number of years, yet many heavy losses occurred, and much annoyance was experienced from the divers decrees of the belligerent powers. Under the pretext of recovering English deserters, Great Britain claimed the right of search. In the exercise of this disputed right, frequent seizures were made of what were called enemy's goods — goods shipped from some nation with whom she was at war. Under such pretexts, vessel and cargo were confiscated, or subjected to such delay and loss that the whole profits of the voyage were absorbed. In addition to the English insults and injuries, the French, aggrieved at the refusal of the United States to form an alliance with them, at the same time affirming that we permitted British to take French goods out of our ships, adopted retaliatory measures, and French privateers were fitted out to prey on our merchantmen. In 1793, the allied powers decreed that no exportation of provisions to France should be allowed, and they engaged to unite to prevent neutral nations from supplying her directly or indirectly. The Empress Catherine also requested the king of Sweden not to allow his ships of war to convey merchantmen destined for France. Thus our commerce met with a continuation of entanglements.

For several years war had been waged between Portugal and Algiers. Hitherto, by a powerful fleet, Portugal had confined the Algerine cruisers to the Mediterranean, but in September, 1793, a truce was concluded between the Dey of Algiers and the King of Portugal. Thus the whole Algerine fleet was let loose to prey upon the commerce of the Atlantic. Many American vessels were captured, the crews robbed and reduced to slavery, with no hope of release unless ransomed.

In the summer of 1793, the brig Polly, commanded by Capt. Samuel Bayley, a son of Mr. Samuel Bayley, one of the wealthiest merchants of Newburyport, was taken by an Algerine cruiser, while on a voyage from Baltimore to Cadiz. Several of the crew also belonged in the town and vicinity, and the news of their capture created a great sensation. Though I was then only six years old, I vividly remember the heart-rending tales which my father, on his return from town, market days, used to relate, as from time to time tidings of the suffering captives reached their friends. A large sum was raised for their ransom. The families and friends of the prisoners contributed generously, and appeal was made in their behalf from the pulpits of the various societies, and a contribution taken, the Sunday preceding the Thanksgiving after their capture.

The Dey of Algiers, thinking that our government, in its anxiety for the release of the prisoners, would acquiesce in any demand, set such an exorbitant price as their ransom that Congress, not wishing to encourage his piracy, demurred as to its payment; but in the December following their enslavement, this crew, with those of other American vessels, were furnished, through Mr. Skjolderbrand, the Swedish consul, with money and comfortable clothing: each captain and supercargo receiving eight Spanish dollars per month, the mates six, and the sailors three each.

Meantime negotiations for the release of our countrymen were continued through Daniel Humphreys, esq., and Joseph Donaldson, jr., esq. At length, in July, 1796, through the zealous efforts of these gentlemen, and of Joel Barlow, esq., consul-general of the United States to Algiers, negotiations were closed and the prisoners set at liberty, but young Capt. Bayley was not permitted to return to his native shores. On the second day of his homeward voyage he was attacked with the plague, from which he died, after an illness of two days.

One of the mariners of the brig Polly was John Foss, a native of Byfield. After his return he published an account of his captivity, which was exceedingly interesting. At that time I had never seen a geography — "Morse & Parish's" was a later production — and Mr. Foss's delineation of foreign places, the Mediterranean and Algiers, was my introduction to a knowledge of that part of the world. His descriptions of the bagnio where the men were confined, and the cruelty shown to the prisoners, who were treated as slaves and compelled to perform severe tasks while heavily ironed, and subjected to the bastinado and other barbarities for the slightest offence, were touchingly graphic. After three years' servitude, on the 11th of July, the prisoners were called from the bagnio and conducted to the Dey to receive their passports, and at 9 a. m. they embarked on a ship belonging to a Jew, Mr. Baccri. On the 12th, received provisions and got ready for sea; on the 13th, stood to sea. On board were forty-eight Neapolitans that had been ransomed: that night one of these was taken sick with the plague; this man was taken on shore by the harbor master. On the 14th, another Neapolitan was taken sick; he died on the 16th. On the 15th, Capt. Bayley was taken ill, and died on the 17th. Finding the plague raging to such a degree, the ship put into Marseilles. On the 8th of October, Mr. Foss shipped as first mate on board the ship Fortune of Philadelphia, commanded by Capt. Michael Smith. On the 17th, sailed from Marseilles, bound to Bona in Algiers, where the vessel arrived on the 7th of December. On the 15th of January, 1799, again sailed for Marseilles; on the 24th, was boarded by his Britannic Majesty's ship Pallas, treated politely, and permitted to proceed. February 5th, about nine leagues from Marseilles, the ship was captured by his Britannic Majesty's ships Inconstant and Blanche, and ordered to Porto Ferrajo in the island of Elba, where they arrived on the 15th, and were sent on shore on the 16th, and not allowed to stay on board the frigate unless they would enter his Britannic Majesty's service. None were willing to do so. One man was impressed on board the Inconstant, and three others entered on board the Union, a British transport; the rest procured a passage for Leghorn, but having been robbed of their money and part of their clothes, they found it difficult to subsist until the vessel was ready to sail. They sailed for Leghorn on the 23d, and arrived the next day, were kept in quarantine until the 5th of March, on which day Capt. Smith arrived from Porto Ferrajo, and sailed for Marseilles the 10th, with all the crew but Mr. Foss and Moses Brown of Newburyport, who were left sick in the hospital. On the 20th, Mr. Foss sailed from Leghorn in an open boat for Piombino in Naples. On his arrival he met Mr. Donaldson, the American consul, who had been instrumental in his deliverance from Algiers. In his company he sailed for Porto Ferrajo, arriving the same evening. On the 24th, they sailed for Leghorn, arriving on the 26th.

On the second of April, Mr. Foss embarked as passenger on board the Mandonna del Rosario e san Vincenzo Sceraro, of Ragusa, bound to Philadelphia; sailed on the 4th, and on the 11th, was captured by a Spanish privateer and carried into Barcelona; was cleared on the 12th, and again sailed, but on the 20th, was again captured by a French privateer, and carried into Almeria, treated politely, and sailed on the 22d. On the 29th, the wind having been contrary for several days, they ran into Malaga, where they remained until the 21st of May. Again sailed on the 22d. On the same day was boarded by his Britannic Majesty's ship Petteral, treated well, and permitted to proceed. On the 23d, at 6 p. m. was boarded by two Spanish privateers and carried into Ceuta. Mr. Foss having struck one of the privateer's men with a sword, and wounded him on the arm, was put into a dungeon, ironed hands and feet, where he was kept about an hour and a half. That same evening the vessel sailed for Philadelphia. On the 28th, was boarded by another Spanish privateer, and robbed of a quantity of provisions, and the greater part of the clothes of the crew and passengers. On the first of July was boarded by his Britannic Majesty's ship Woolwich, were treated politely, and permitted to proceed. Being short of provisions, endeavors were made to procure a supply from the Woolwich, but she being also short none could be obtained. On the 24th, spoke the brig Jefferson from St. Croix, bound to Philadelphia, from whom provisions were obtained which were most thankfully received, as for nearly forty days they had subsisted on one biscuit per day, with oil and wine. On the 25th, Mr. Foss arrived in Philadelphia, where he was detained by indisposition until the 11th of August. He then took passage in the schooner Jay, belonging to Edgartown, bound to Boston, David Smith commander. He arrived in Boston on the 17th. On the 23, he reached Newburyport, and after such a terrible and varied experience, was restored to his family at Byfield.

I have made this extract from Mr. Foss' journal, to show the peril and annoyance to which at that period our marine were subjected.

Out of the nine persons who left Baltimore on the brig Polly, only four returned besides Mr. Foss. These were Michael Smith, the first mate, Benjamin Edwards, the second mate, and Moses Brown, mariner. The others all died of the plague. Capt. Samuel E. Bayley, whose ransom had been forwarded by his father, was a young man of much promise, universally beloved and respected, and his sad fate was greatly deplored. Subjoined are some lines written by Capt. Bayley while a prisoner in Algiers. They were addressed to a young lady to whom he was betrothed:

"To you, my friend, these lines I send,
Though distant far from me;
Though we're apart, my aching heart
Is ever still with thee.

To let thee know my grief and woe
Is far beyond my art;
I can't express the sore distress
That racks my pained heart.

I mourn and weep while others sleep,
My nights are turned to day;
While time runs on, and hope forlorn,
And rest goes far away.

I think of thee where'er I be,
Of thy unhappy state:
My thoughts and care are always there—
On thee I contemplate.

Though hard my fate and wretched state,
I pray for a relief;
That God would bless me in distress
And mitigate my grief.

Without neglect I shall respect
My parents till I die;
Their tender care for my welfare
Lives in my memory.

I trust in God who holds the rod
And doth chastise in love;
He can relieve the captive slave,
And hear him from above."

At this time imposters were often met, tramping from place to place, begging money, under the pretext of raising the ransom of a son or brother held in captivity at Algiers. For years such persons were an annoyance everywhere, and often a terror to solitary people in lone country houses.

CHAPTER XXXVI.

The conflicts of the French Revolution reached the French West Indian colonies with even more intense cruelties than in the mother country. One day one party was in power, the next the opposite. On all sides persons in authority were imprisoned and guillotined, their property confiscated, and their children outlawed. Many of the most wealthy and influential citizens became fugitives. As Newburyport had a large West Indian commerce, many of these exiles came thither. In Guadaloupe the blood-thirsty mob poured out upon the noble families the brutal passion of wild beasts. The atrocities committed almost surpass belief. Many met the most horrible deaths; a few were enabled to escape to neighboring islands in boats; and about twenty succeeded in getting on board of a brig belonging in Newburyport, which lay off the island, which arrived at that port in March, 1792. Among these exiles was St. Sauveur de Poyen. His eldest and youngest sons, Robert and St. Sauveur, were killed by the brutal mob of republicans; but the father and three sons, Joseph Rochmont, Montrape, Dupiton, and two daughters, escaped, and succeeded, after great suffering, in getting on board the Newburyport brig.

St. Sauveur de Poyen was a direct descendant from the Marquis Jean de Poyen, who emigrated to the island of Guadaloupe in 1658. He inherited all the instincts and pride of the aristocracy of France, the class to which he belonged, and when the troublous times of the French Revolution came, they found him a staunch royalist and an ardent defender of King Louis XVI. The loss of home, change of climate, grief and anxiety, was too much for the exile; he passed away only a few months before Louis was beheaded, the king to whose cause he was so strongly attached, for which he sacrificed a home of luxury and ease.

"Habitation Piton," five miles from the romantic village of St. Rose, is the point at which the French discovered the island. The plantation borders on the sea. A romantic ride by the shore brings the "Habitation" to view on a small plateau, a little distance up the side of the mountain. Turning from the shore the road runs direct to the "Habitation," through a valley filled with sugar-cane. A broad avenue terminates the valley road, with rows of lofty palms on either side; a winding way leads to the dwelling. This point presents a panorama of great beauty. The valley, widening as it recedes, is filled with luxuriant cane, which also covers the mountains far up their sides. About a mile from the shore, a circular rock called "Englishman's head," rises from the water to the height of one hundred feet, and is the only object that breaks the surface of the broad ocean to the horizon; in the distance two shadowy forms appear, the islands of Montserrat and Antigua, so indistinct and misty as not to break the horizon line.

In a low, narrow valley in the old graveyard on burying hill, in Newburyport, is a stone bearing this inscription:

SACRED TO THE MEMORY OF
MR. POYEN DE ST. SAUVEUR,
WHO FOR A LONG TIME WAS
AN INHABITANT & A REPUTABLE
PLANTER ON THE ISLAND
OF GUADULOUPE.
DIED OCTOBER 14TH, 1792,
AGED 52 YEARS.

After a few years, when affairs had become settled, several of the surviving exiles returned to their homes. Amongst those that remained were Joseph Rochemont de Poyen, de St. Sauveur, (St. Sauveur indicated the branch of the family to which he belonged).

and a sister who died in Baltimore. This land of refuge had many attractions for young Poyen. He never wearied of wandering up and down the shores of the beautiful Merrimac. Some twelve years were spent in careless, easy living, dividing his time between the town, and the romantic villages along the river's bank. At one of these, Rock's Bridge, (East Haverhill), he at length passed most of his time. It is a singularly picturesque spot, and its natural beauties attracted the artistic eye of the sensitive young Frenchman. Here also he met the guiding star of his life, Sally Elliot, a handsome, brilliant girl, a daughter of one of the oldest families of the place, and with the impetuous character of his race, he carried off and married his willing bride, in spite of the protest of her parents. In this village they settled, and children were born to them. Years passed, and grandchildren also came, and grew up to love the dear old man, whose delight it was to play and dance with them; he grew old in years but not in elasticity of spirit, and his life went out in glorious fullness, at a ripe old age. I well remember Sally Elliot; she made Rochemont de Poyen a most excellent wife; and I vividly recall the genial Frenchman; a lithe, active man, a great fancier of horse flesh, always ready for a trade; he and my grandsir Little frequently had dealings together. His fiddle was also ever at the service of the young folks. The beaux and belles of the main road were often indebted to Mr. Poyen for the music at a social dance. Though irascible and impatient, he was the soul of wit and good humor, happy in making all around him happy.

The Poyen arms are:

GULES, A CHIEF AZURE, PEACOCK ON TERRACE VERT. THREE MULLETS PROPER CREST—MARQUIS' CROWN, SUPPORTED BY TWO SAVAGES, DEXTER CLUB AT GROUND, SINISTER CLUB AT SHOULDER.

With the family of St. Sauveur de Poyen came his nephew the Count Francis de Vipart, the son of a Count of the same name, and a grandson of the Marquis de Vipart. This young man remained in America, accompanying his cousin Joseph Rochemont de Poyen in his wanderings upon the banks of the Merrimac, and with him located at the "Rocks." There he married another of the village belles and beauties, Mary Ingalls. The Ingalls family through the Bradstreets, were connections of my grandmother Little. Mary Ingalls possessed uncommon personal and mental attractions. Of medium height, hair in long golden curls, violet eyes, fair complexion and rosy cheeks, "none knew her but to love her." In a house nestled between the hills, since for many years owned and occupied by the late Dr. Kennison, the French lord wooed and won the Puritan maid. Their moonlight sails, and saunterings upon the pleasant Newbury shore, with the sweet strains of the Count's violin, are still remembered by a few aged inhabitants.

The wedding created a great sensation in the quiet village. The bride looked supremely lovely in a dress of pink satin, with an over dress of white lace, and white satin slippers.

Though it was the delight of the Count to lavish every luxury upon his young wife, she continued the same unpretending, modest person as before marriage. A few short weeks of bliss, and a shade fell over the sunlight of the new life of the wedded pair. Naturally delicate, continuous care and attention to a sick mother, had planted the germs of New England's scourge, consumption, by which the Countess de Vipart rapidly declined. In this illness she is described as presenting an almost seraphic loveliness. Reclining in an easy chair, draped in white, her appearance was that of a being of a higher world than earth.

Not a twelvemonth from the joyous bridal eve, the village bell pealed the funeral knell, and the remains of the lovely Mary Ingalls, Countess de Vipart, were deposited under the turf of the quiet rural burial place on the hill side, "beneath the locust bloom." A low, slate stone, the style of the period, marks her grave, it bears this inscription:

MARY,
WIFE OF FRANCIS VIPART,
OF GUADALOUPE.
DIED JANUARY 5, 1807,
AGED 21 YEARS.

This incident of the union of the exiled nobleman and the New England maiden, Whittier has woven into one of his most pleasing ballads, and in his "Countess" it will be perpetuated to future generations—

"The Gascon lord, the village maid,
In death still clasp their hands;
The love that levels rank and grade,
Unite their severed hands."

Overwhelmed with grief, the stricken husband soon after his wife's death, returned to his West Indian home. Several articles that had belonged to the Count and his bride, are still cherished as sacred mementoes, by relatives and friends, in the vicinity of the home of their brief wedded life.

Time having in a measure healed the heart wound, Count de Vipart again married in Guadaloupe, where he died and was buried. His descendants still reside at their homes on the island, ranking high in the order of nobility.

The retired valley on the old burying hill, Newburyport, contains the remains of several French exiles, who died during the years from 1792 to 1812. Doubtless the whole number were Catholics, and as at that period no ground had been consecrated in the Puritan town, this quiet spot was chosen in a Protestant burial ground, to lay their bodies apart from others, when their spirits had departed—a spot doubly consecrated by the tears and prayers of surviving relatives and friends. Most of these graves were marked by head stones; some of these have been broken; those that remain are inscribed as follows:

CI GIT
MAPIE FELICITTE NADAU,
NEE A LA BASSETERRE GUADALOUPE
DECEDE LE 19TH FEVRIER, 1812,
AGEE DE 25 ANS ET 6 MOIS.
ESPOUSEDE MR. PIERRE MORLANDE,
HABITANT AU QUARTIER DE ST. ROSE,
DE LA DITTE ILE.

JOHN BAPTISTE DATOUR, ESQ.,
FORMERLY OF GRANTERRE IN THE ISLAND
OF GUADALOUPE.
DIED APRIL 24, 1797,
AGED 74.

HERE LIES
A GOOD SON,
JAQUE MESTRE,
WHO DIED
AUG'ST 2ND, 1793,
AGED 21 YEARS.

HERE LIES
A GOOD SON,
LOUIS EN MESTRE,
WHO DIED
DEC'R 9TH, 1792,
AGED 17 YEARS.

M. MEDERIC DUMAS,
NATIF DE BORDEAUX,
HABITANT DU FORT DAUPHIN,
ISLE ST. DOMINIQUE,
DECEDE A NEWBURYPORT,
LE 9TH OF MAR., 1792,
AGE DE 49 ANS.

In 1795, Nicholas Cools Godefroy, from Castrie in the island of St. Lucia, in the West Indies, came to Newburyport in a vessel commanded by Capt. John Coombs. He was accompanied by his youngest son, Moise Jacques Dupree Cooles Godefroy, who was born in Bordeaux, France, in 1785, and about twenty negro slaves, house servants, and families from his plantation. The oldest son, Jacques Mane Cools Godefroy, had previously come to Baltimore. This family of exiles commenced housekeeping in a house near the head of Federal street; but, aged and infirm, torn from home and friends, the exhausted fugitive turned his face to the wall and died, surviving scarcely a week from the day of his landing. A will is on record in Salem, which was proved Dec. 28, 1795, by which the plantation in the island of St. Lucia was bequeathed to the eldest son, and a large sum of money to the youngest, to whom Capt. Coombs was appointed guardian, and in whose family he found a home. The negroes, now free, went to service in Oldtown, where the jovial faces, woolly heads and glistening ivory of the little darkies, and their frolicsome pranks, attracted much notice. They and their parents are still remembered by some aged persons. Owing to a wrong translation of the will of his father which was written in French, the lad, Moise Cooles Godefroy, was defrauded of a portion of his inheritance; the household effects were sold—plate engraved with the family arms, clothing and linen. Nothing of this personal property has descended in the family, with the exception of one solitary counterpne, made from a dress of Madam Nicholas Cooles Godefroy, who had died some years previous to her husband's exile. In 1810 Jacques Mane Cooles Godefroy, visited his brother previous to his return to the plantation in St. Lucia. He presented Moise with nearly a thousand dollars to stock his store on State street, and made a will in his favor, which was deposited with Bishop Chevereux in Boston, who was appointed the executor. He died a few years after, at his home in St. Lucia. A short time after, to his surprise, Moise Cooles Godefroy received a notification from Bishop Cheveraux, purporting that a priest and a lawyer had arrived in Boston, bringing with them a second and later will made by Jacques Cooles Godefroy shortly before his decease, by which his estate was willed to the church. Proof was wanting to controvert this second will, which the descendants have supposed forged or obtained from a mind weakened by disease. Sam L. Knapp, esq. was employed by Moses Cooles Godefroy, but nothing was effected, and the despoiled heir, under the plain English name of Moses Cole, continued his business on State street. He married Miss Sally Avery from York, Maine, and reared a large family. Mr. Cole possessed a fine talent for portrait painting, which he delighted to cultivate. His sitters were counted amongst our most prominent citizens, and many of his portraits are extant. I have mentioned that he was an adept in framing the paintings and wrought pictures of the young ladies of Newburyport. On Monroe's visit to this town, unknown to the president, Mr. Cole sketched a fine likeness of him while he was at the dinner table. This artistic talent descended in his family; three of the sons chose art as a profession. Joseph and Charles, both deceased, were noted painters, and Mr. Lyman Cole's pictures are well known in this vicinity. Mr. Moses Cole was a sufferer by the great fire of 1811, losing both his dwelling house on Middle street, and his store on State street. He died in 1819, aged 65. His widow, Sally (Avery) Cole, survived many years, dying Oct. 23, 1874, at the advanced age of 92 years.

The Godefroy arms are:

THREE PELICANS' HEADS VULNING THEMSELVES. CREST—A DEMI SARACEN PPR, HOLDING IN THE DEXTER HAND A CROSS CROSSLET FITCHEE A.

The remains of Nicholas Cooles Godefroy lie with his countrymen, in the valley on burying hill, but no stone marks the grave.

Anthony and Mary Le Breton were born in the city of Nantes, France. They had thirteen children. Stephen Le Breton their eldest child emigrated to the West Indies, and settled in Guadaloupe.

Pierre Le Breton was born in Nantes. Oct. 17, 1745, being the youngest of thirteen children, receiving his name from his paternal grandfather. When he was about fifteen years old, he took French leave of his parents and home, and went to join his brother Stephen, of whom he was very fond. His brother sent him immediately back to France. As a punishment for this escapade, his father placed him an apprentice to a cabinet maker; here he learned the use of tools, which ever after was a source of pleasure to him. When they thought him sufficiently punished, his parents consented to his joining his brother. At the age of twenty he was the owner of a large plantation and a number of slaves When about twenty-one he became very ill, pronounced in a consumption, and his physicians, for a change of air, advised a trip to New England. Capt. William Noyes, the husband of my great-aunt Mollie Smith, was at the island in a fine new ship, and with him young Le Breton took passage. This Capt. Noyes had lost one of his hands: he was the one so long confined in Dartmoor prison during the Revolutionary war; it was his hat that furnished the braid by which my aunt Sarah Smith learned to braid straw. Capt. Noyes and his passenger became firm friends, and upon their arrival in Newburyport, the captain took the young Frenchman home to his house on Liberty street, where he remained boarding in the family until he entirely recovered his health. Pierre LeBreton often accompanied Captain and

Mrs. Noyes in their visits to the Smith homestead on Crane-neck hill. I have often heard my aunt Sarah speak of his appearance as most striking. A pale, fair complexion, deep, blue eyes shaded by long, black lashes, and dark, chestnut hair waving in curls about his face and neck. A large garden was attached to Capt. Noyes' house, and there Pierre delighted to resort. In an adjoining garden, belonging to a Mr. Pearson, the young foreigner often observed a young lady busy among the flowers; he soon formed an acquaintance, and became deeply interested in her. This interest combined with his friendship for the Noyes family, and his strong liking for the town of Newburyport, induced him to dispose of his plantation in Guadaloupe and settle here. This was done against his parents' and brother Stephen's advice and entreaties. Not being acquainted with business, he had not been long in the country before he lost all his property. This event was such a surprise that ever after he lived in a state of expectancy and preparation for a similar occurrence.

He had now to commence life anew, and went to his old friend, to whom he was very strongly attached, for advice. This turned his attention to navigation. He sailed with Capt. Noyes until he became both ship master and owner. Having secured a competence, again become a rich man, he built the house on Middle street, on the corner of Fair, opposite the Universalist church, with a shop attached, that in case he should lose property he might in some measure be prepared for it. This calamity, so greatly feared, never occurred. The great fire of 1811 burned to his house and there stopped.

Having accumulated a fortune, and built his house, he determined to marry. All this time he had entertained an interest in Miss Elisabeth Pearson, and having ascertained that this affection was mutual, after great opposition from her parents on account of his being a foreigner, they were married in 1776. Their children were Peter and Elisabeth LeBreton. Mrs. LeBreton died, of typhoid fever, taken from her husband, Dec. 27, 1781, aged thirty-six years.

After remaining three years a widower, Mr. LeBreton married Miss Elizabeth Sawyer, on the 20th of March, 1784. They had one child who died in infancy. At the time of this marriage, a sister of Elizabeth, Eunice Sawyer, was taken into and made one of the family, and on his decease, Mr. LeBreton bequeathed to her a sufficient maintenance during her life. This property Eunice willed back to the LeBreton family, but, by some informality in the will, it went to the Sawyer relatives. Mr. and Mrs. LeBreton adopted the daughter of her eldest sister Eunice Couch; they also adopted the first grandchild, Peter LeBreton, when he was two years old. Capt LeBreton was a generous, genial gentleman, the soul of hospitality and good humor.

One morning, Mr. Moses Colman was called to his door, where he found a strange woman whose home he failed to enquire, offering a pig for sale. She was on horseback, her wares in pannier baskets. Mr. Colman did not need the pig but the little fellow looked so cunning, peeping from the basket, that the old gentleman, fond of pets, concluded the bargain, and the small porker was placed in the pen, where he became the distinguished sire of the famous Byfield breed of swine. This caused Mr. Colman's pork to be in great demand. Capt. LeBreton having purchased a pig for family use, David Emery, then a lad in his teens, took it to the house, where it was carried to the kitchen to be cut up. Through his father Colman, David had formed the acquaintance of Capt. LeBreton, with whom he was a favorite. One o'clock came, the dinner bell sounded. A summons was sent for David; the youth hesitated; he wore only his common suit under his frock: to dine with Capt. LeBreton he ought to be dressed in his Sunday best, but the old gentleman stepping into the kitchen, in his most peremptory manner ordered David to take off his frock and follow him. The bountiful repast over, wine was served with dessert, and little Peter, then scarcely able to talk plain, was told to drink to the guest. The little fellow bashfully demurred, at which the old gentleman exclaimed, "Peter, mine grandson, be a little gentleman, and drink Monsieur Emery's health directly. The tiny glass was filled, and little Peter drank with due etiquette. Mr. Emery was so much amused that he often related the story.

Capt. Le Breton was exceedingly liberal to his workmen. Every Saturday night those in his employ received a piece of meat for their Sunday dinner. For years the Captain bought his meat of Mr. Emery. Amongst the stevedores was an Irishman by the name of Murray. The master always superintended the giving out of the meat to his men, and in his funny way he would say: "Cut dat for Murray, David, he 'ave one hard tooth."

This Murray had a wife, a most worthy woman, who worked for me for years on Monday, for a quarter of a dollar and a basket of cold victuals: and on Saturday she scoured the brasses, candlesticks, stairs and floors, did the day's cleaning, receiving therefor, with much gratitude, her bundle of edibles, and the coffee grounds which for a long period were daily poured into a pitcher for her use.

Capt. LeBreton's good humored generosity was often subjected to imposition. One day he came to the shambles, and with a jovial face and in gay tones, said, "David, yesterday, I gave one leetle boy a pair of shoes; dis mornin' half a dozen leetle boys come shoof, shoof, shoof, after me. What did it mean? Wanted shoes, hey! Too moosh, too moosh, David, but I shod the rogues, I shod every garcon, David," ending his recital with a hearty laugh, rubbing his hands together in great glee.

In 1807, Etienne LeBretagne, Capt. LeBreton's eldest and best beloved brother, Stephen, made him a visit, and was much pleased with the country and people, and declared, "if he had been a younger man he would remove himself and family, and finish his days here with his brother." Two other brothers visited him, one of whom settled in the city of New Orleans, the other in some part of New Jersey.

Capt. LeBreton was a Catholic. In performance of a vow he presented the First Religious society of Newburyport with the pair of tall silver tankards, used in the sacramental service.

Pierre LeBreton died in Newburyport, from gout in the stomach, February 24, 1813, aged 67 years.

Peter LeBreton, the only son of Capt. LeBreton, married Tabitha Lewis of Marblehead, Sept., 1800. Their oldest son, Peter, adopted by his grandfather, at his death received property independent of his father. Peter LeBreton 3d, married in 1823, Sarah E., daughter of Tristram Chase, of the Chase farm, Meeting-house hill, West Newbury.

Elisabeth LeBreton, the oldest daughter, married Henry Johnson in 1825. This lady died at the age of twenty-one, leaving an infant ten days old.

Mary Anthony, the second daughter of Peter LeBreton, jun., named by her grandfather for his father and mother, Marie Antoine LeBretagne, married Henry Johnson, May, 1826.

Edmund Lewis LeBreton, the second son, married Lucy Oliver, daughter of Dr. Prescott, September, 1829.

Stephen LeBreton, the third son of Peter LeBreton, jun., died unmarried, Nov. 4, 1834.

Caroline Lewis, the third daughter, married John Stephen Bartlett, July, 1832. John Stephen Bartlett, M. D., died in Marblehead, March 6, 1840: his widow married Capt. William Hammond of Marblehead, May, 1842.

The fourth son, George Washington LeBreton, was shot by an Indian in Oregon, and died from inflammation, March 6, 1844, aged 32 years.

Charlotte, youngest daughter of Peter LeBreton, jun., married John James Coombs, August, 1835.

Elisabeth LeBreton, only daughter of Capt. Peter and Elisabeth (Pearson) LeBreton, was born Nov. 28, 1786. Her mother died when she was but two years old. Her grandmother and aunts who lived in the next house, cared for her until her father's second marriage, in 1784, to Elisabeth Sawyer, who made herself beloved, not only to the father, the children, and the Pearson family, but to all who knew her.

Elisabeth LeBreton married Captain David Stickney, in 1802. They had four children; Elisabeth LeBreton, Hannah Lee, Peter LeBreton, and Mary Thurston Stickney. Capt. Stickney died February, 1820. The widow Stickney married the Rev. Henry C. Wright, then pastor of the society in first parish in West Newbury, in 1826.

Eunice Couch, the niece adopted by Captain and Mrs. LeBreton, married David Rogers. She died in Cincinnati, aged 30 years.

Mrs. Elisabeth (Sawyer) LeBreton died May 4, 1822, aged 74 years.

CHAPTER XXXVII.

The first meeting-house in Newbury was built on the lower green in Old-town, but in 1642, a majority of the population having moved farther up on the Merrimac, a new house of worship was erected. This removal caused much opposition and contention, but in 1642 "there was granted to Mr. James Noyes, four acres of land upon the hill, by the little pine swamp, upon which to set the meeting-house." Of this structure I have no record, excepting that the canopy of the pulpit was presented to the new society in the west precinct, after the erection of their meeting-house, the first parish having built a new sanctuary, in the year 1700.

I distinctly remember this building, the spire and high pointed roof being plainly visible from Crane-neck hill. It was a square edifice of two stories, with front and side entrances, the high four-sided roof terminated at the apex in a dome-shaped belfry, surmounted by a high, pointed spire, crowned by a copper weathercock. The principal entrance opened into a broad aisle, which led to the high pulpit, with the sounding-board above, the deacon's seat beneath, and the communion table in front. Two short cross aisles led from the side doors. Galleries ran round three sides of the house. The "singing seats" were opposite the pulpit; the side galleries were filled with benches, and a larger part of the lower floor. Space was appropriated for pews, and permission granted to about twenty persons to build them. It was voted, "that a pew be built for the minister's wife by the pulpit stairs: that Colonel Daniel Pierce esquire should have the first choice of a pew and Major Thomas Noyes the second, and Colonel Daniel Pierce esquire, and Tristram Coffin esquire, be impowered to procure a bell of about four hundred pounds weight."

The inscription on this bell, was "let us love as brethren. Mathew Bayley fundet 1705." It was ordered "that this bell be rung at nine o'clock every night and the day of the month be tolled."

As the belfry was just above the centre of the ceiling, the bell rope depended therefrom, and the bell-ringer stood in the broad aisle to perform his duty.

The Rev. John Woodbridge, the successor of Messrs. Parker and Noyes, died in 1695. The next clergyman was the Rev. John Richardson; his succescessor, the Rev. Christopher Toppan, who died in 1747; he was followed by the Rev. John Tucker; the last clergyman to minister through his pastorate in the old meeting house was the Rev. Abraham Moore, a fine speaker and a man of superior literary attainments; he died in 1801, and the Rev. John Popkin was ordained in 1801. In 1806 a new house was built: this structure many of our readers still remember. On May 4, Dr. Popkin preached for the last time in the old building; May 6th, it was torn down.

On the 16th of June there was a total eclipse of the sun; the obscuration commenced about ten o'clock, and in half an hour stars were visible: the birds flew to the trees, and the fowl sought their roosts. On this day the sills of the new meeting house were laid, and it was dedicated on the seventeenth of September. The raising and dedication were days of jubilee, in which great crowds thronged to Oldtown.

By the year 1685, what was termed the west precinct, or the new town, had acquired so large a population, that the inhabitants, being such a distance from the meeting house, began to consider the expediency of forming a second parish, and erecting a house of worship in a more convenient locality. March 10, a petition was sent to the town of Newbury, "the humble request of some of the inhabitants of this town, doe desire and entreat, that you would be pleased to grant us your consent, approbation and assistance in getting some help in the ministry amongst us, by reason that we doe live soe remote from the means, great part of us, that we cannot with any comfort and convenience come to the public worship of God; neither can our families be brought up under the means of grace as christians ought to bee, and which is absolutely necessary unto salvation; therefore we will humbly crave your loving compliance with us in this our request." This petition commenced a contest which lasted for several years, which shows that the men of "ye good old times" were subject to like passions and prejudices as those of more modern days.

In 1688, Joseph Moring bequeathed, in his will, twenty pounds to the "new town" in Newbury, to help build a meeting-house. The next year, 1869, sixteen persons erected a meeting-house about thirty feet square, at the plains. In the February following, the town appointed a committee of eight persons to confer with the Rev. Mr. Richardson respecting the propriety of the west-end people calling a minister. Mr. Richardson, anxious not to give offence, declined to express his opinion or give his advice. The committee reported, "that considering the times as troublesome, and the towne being so much behind with Mr. Richardson's salary, the farmers and the neck men being under great disadvantages upon many accounts, do desire and expect, if such a thing be granted, that they should have the same privilege to provide for themselves, which we think cannot conduce to peace, therefore desire the new towne to rest satisfied for the present."

At the town meeting in March, fifteen men belonging to the west end, "after stating that it was well known how far they had proceeded as to a meeting-house, left two propositions with the town; one that the town would agree to support two ministers, so that one could preach at the west end meeting-house, or that the town would consent to have the ministry amongst them upon their own charge, and that the town would lovingly agree upon a dividing line between them so that they might know what families may now belong to the west meeting-house."

The summer following, the inhabitants of the "new towne" began to consider respecting the calling of Mr. Edward Tomson to minister to them in spiritual things. This elicited a vote by the town "against the settlement of Mr. Tomson or any other minister until ye church and towne are agreed upon it, looking upon such a thing as an intrusion upon ye church and town." In October the people of the west end petitioned the general court, "to be established a people by themselves, for the maintenance of the ministry amongst them."

In December, the town voted against this petition being granted, and chose a committee to present a counter petition to the general court. In 1692 the west end people again made a petition and proposition about calling a minister. Dec. 20, the town voted that they would call another minister at the west end. On the 27th, a committee was chosen "to enquire after a suitable person to preach at the west end and to keep schoole." In May, 1693, the town voted that Mr. John Clark be called to assist Mr. Richardson at the west end, and to keep a grammar school." This vote caused much dissension, as most of the west end people felt bound to adhere to Mr. Tomson. June 15, another petition was forwarded to the general court, in which they request the governor and council, "to pity and help them, to ease them of a heavy burden of travel on God's day." July 5th, "the town in their votes for the choice of a minister for the west end of the towne, in order to a full settlement in the work of the ministry, and Mr. John Clark was then chosen and not one vote against him." Twenty-five persons of the west end entered their dissent against calling Mr. Clark, "for the reason that the new towne have a minister already." Mr. Clark declined the call, and Mr. Christopher Toppan was invited to preach at the "new towne." Mr. Toppan declined to settle, but expressing his willingness to help in the work of the ministry for a year, the town voted to give Mr. Toppan forty pounds in money, and four contributions a year.

Oct. 22d, 1694, "the towne brought in theyr votes by papers, for a minister for the west end of Newbury, and Mr. Christopher Toppan had sixty-five votes and Mr. Tomson seventeen. Jan. 1, 1695, the town met and voted "that Pipestave hill near Daniel Jaques' house shall be the place for the meeting-house, and those that live nearest to that place shall pay to the ministry there, and those that live nearest to the old meeting-house shall pay there: the inhabitants of the west end to choose a minister for themselves, only Mr. Tomson excepted, and the meeting-house to stand where it do, until the major part of them see cause to remove it."

Jan. 3d, Tristram Coffin, Henry Short and Abraham Merrill, divided the town into two parishes.

June 5th, "Town voted to give Mr. Christopher Toppan 20 pounds yearly in money, and three hundred pounds in good country pay, so long as he carries on one half of the ministry among them, and thirty pounds a year so long as he shall keep a grammar and a writing school, the scholars to pay as they did to Mr. John Clark Mr. Toppan accepted these proposals July seventeenth.

Dec. 18th. The town, "on the request of the inhabitants of the west end of the town of Newbury, granted them five acres of land on the east side of Artichoke river for a pasture for the ministry, and one acre of land near the west meeting house, and when the major part shall see cause to remove the said meeting house, the land shall be at the disposal of the town to procure land for the ministry, near the west meeting house when removed."

Feb. 28th. 1696. A rate was made for payment of building and furnishing the west end meeting-house and ministry house. The expense was twenty-two pounds and three shillings in money, and two hundred and eighteen pounds, eighteen shillings and two pence in pay. This was due from sixty-four persons. Of this number twenty-four objected to the continuance of the meeting-house on the plains, being desirous that it should be removed farther up to Pipestave hill. These were Benjamin and Joseph Morse, Thomas, Daniel and Moses Chase, John senior and John jr., and Abial Kelley, Mr. Abraham Annis, Isaac and Joseph Richardson. Abel Huse, Caleb Moody, Benjamin Low, Tristram Greenleaf, Daniel Morrison, Edward Woodman, John Hoag, Hanariah Ordway, Thomas Follansbee, Lieut. John Emerson, Thomas Williams, Francis Willet and Samuel Sayer jr., This dissent continued for years, the subject of strife thereafter being the site of the west end meeting-house.

In April the Rev. Mr. Richardson died, and in September Mr. Christopher Toppan was ordained his successor. That same year the Rev. Samuel

Belcher with his family came to the west precinct. In October, 1698, a church was gathered and the Rev. Mr. Belcher was ordained on November 10th. In January, 1706, the precinct voted "that they either would remove the meeting-house and build an addition to it, or else build a new meeting-house." February 28th, it was voted "that ye inhabitants of ye west end of the town of Newbury will build a new meeting-house upon Pipestave hill, fifty-four feet long, and thirty-four feet broad, within ye space of five years at ye furthest, and to meet in the old meeting-house five years, and not to force any person to pay any money or pay till three years be expired, and then to pay one-quarter part yearly until ye whole be paid." From this vote twenty persons dissented. Captain Hugh March, Caleb Moody, and sergeant John Ordway were chosen a committee to build the new meeting-house, and the foundation was laid in 1709. In February the opposition at the plains petitioned the general court for relief, showing that only twelve years before they had built a meeting-house, and those now calling themselves the majority had been since planted in the upper part of the precinct, yet the majority had proceeded to levy a tax, and to employ a collector to take away their goods for the furtherance of their design to erect the more remote house; that the expense of another building would be a heavy burthen, necessitating them to lose the charge to which they had been put, besides frustrating the enjoyment of the means of grace for themselves and their children. If no other relief offered, they prayed to be set off, to maintain a minister and a ministry amongst themselves. This document was signed by fifty-five persons,—eleven Bartlets, six Sawyers, three Merrills, four Browns, three Baileys, Charles and Joseph Annis, two Thurstons, two named Rogers, three Littles, and nineteen others. In the March town meeting of the next year, the inhabitants of the precinct voted "that they accepted of what was already done, and authorized the major part of the committee (who were chosen in 1706, February twenty-eighth) to proceed and finish the meeting-house according to the time mentioned in said vote."

On June 2d, a notification from the general court was served on the town of Newbury, by some of the west end petitioners. June 7th, the town chose Col. Thomas Noyes to act in their behalf. This gentleman decided that the major part could not be aggrieved by putting down the old, or putting up the new meeting-house; he concluded by saying, "the whole of the western precinct, assemble in a house not above thirty feet square, and yet rather than not have their wills they would have two churches."

This produced a reply from the minority, in which they state that they "have one hundred and thirty families, seventy of which do not live two miles from the old meeting-house." They confess to a desire to have their wills, in so far as they are not sparing of their purses for the propagation of the gospel for themselves, and particularly for their children, and if it is more convenient to obtain this good end, they had rather have two churches and two meeting-houses, and they petitioned the court to this end. This petition was not granted, and it was resolved in council, that Pipestave hill was the most convenient place, and a committee was appointed to wait upon the Rev. Mr. Belcher and acquaint him with the desire of the court, that when a meeting-house should be erected there, and convenient dwelling house, with suitable accommodation of land, he be content to remove thither.

Determined not to worship in the meeting-house on Pipestave hill, twenty-seven of the petitioners signed the following:

"July ye 12th, 1710.

We whose names Are hereto Subscribed doo Agree And oblidge ourséalves to each other to mayntain the publick ministry At the old meeting-house in ye west precinct in Newbury. Although we are forsed to pay Elsewhere what shall be lavid upon us."

On the next day the inhabitants of the west end held a meeting, and voted to "observe the direction and resolve of the general court." On July 17th they held another meeting, in which they voted to "levy a tax of four hundred pounds to defray part of the charges of building a meeting-house, ministry house, and so forth, to pay back all they had taken by distraint, and to confirm all that the building committee chosen in 1706 had done, and gave them full power to finish."

On the 19th of April, 1711, the precinct had another meeting, and, as the time of five years during which they had determined to meet in the old meeting-house had expired, the majority proceeded to carry the remainder of the vote into execution. A committee of three was chosen, to dispose of the ministry house and land near the old meeting-house, and obtain a house and land near the new meeting-house at Pipestave hill. It was also voted "to take the seates and boards and glass out of ye old meeting-house to be improved in the new meeting-house, and also to remove the old meeting-house and sett it up att Pipestave hill to be improved as a barn for the ministry in convenient time."

Of course this vote but added fuel to the flame. The minority firmly resisted every attempt at removal of "the Plains" meeting-house. One night in the first of the summer, a party came down from the upper part of the parish, and in a disorderly and riotous manner tore down the old meeting-house and carried it off. The minority, being as determined not to submit as the majority were to govern, immediately began the erection of another house of worship. To frustrate this undertaking, in July a committee of six persons petitioned the general court to stay the proceedings. The court directed that the "raysing of the meeting-house be delayed until there be a hearing of the matter before the court."

No attention was paid, by the minority, to this order. This caused another petition against them, in which it was stated that the minority had "raised and part covered a meeting-house, and set it near the dividing line, notwithstanding the advice and direction of the court."

The court immediately ordered "that Samuel Bartlet, John Ordway, Deacon Joshua Brown, Joshua Bailey, Skipper Lunt and Penuel Titcomb, be anew served by the sheriff with a process and order of this court, strictly forbidding them and their associates proceeding in the work of their intended meeting-house, and that said persons be summoned to attend the fall session of the court."

On the 23d of October, 1711, the

minority again petitioned the court for leave to go on with their meeting-house. "That the farthermost of forty families, and about thirty more of our neighbors are not above one and a half miles from the meeting-house we are about to erect, and that we deem it a duty to maintain the Rev. Mr. Belcher, (for whom we have a peculiar respect), until he may be orderly dismist." They also requested the court "to set them off as a precinct, making Artichoke river the dividing line, as there are now ninety-six families above Artichoke river." The court considered that there was no present necessity for this new precinct and church, and ordered that the building of the house be no further proceeded with. No regard being paid to this order, the court sent an express to forbid the work. Several gentlemen went to Boston to show their grievances, but obtained no relief; there they met a Mr. John Bridger of Portsmouth. This gentleman was "surveyor of the king's woods," and a churchman. He informed the Newbury party that the Church of England would protect them if they would put themselves under its control. He visited Newbury, and told the "plains" people that if they would convert their intended meeting-house into a church, he would ensure them the protection of the governor.

Some were somewhat acquainted with the church; after the perusal of several Episcopal books, a consent was given, and the Rev. Henry Harris, who had been sent from England to minister at King's Chapel, Boston, came and preached to them. This gentlemen was the father of Mr. Benjamin Harris for whom Harris street is named. At the time of his coming, when a ship arrived from England it was customary for persons expecting friends to go to the wharf to meet them on their landing. Amongst the throng assembled on this occasion was a young lady, whose glance riveted that of the handsome missionary ere the ship reached the landing. This "love at first sight" was soon followed by the marriage of the youthful pair.

Mr. Harris sent a Mr. Lampton, the chaplain of a station ship, to preach at the Plains. Some went to the meeting at Pipestave hill, but the majority embraced the doctrines of the Church of England. Thus the Episcopal society was formed, and the church completed, under the designation of Queen Ann's Chapel. In May, 1715, the Rev. Henry Lucas, of London, was appointed their rector. The bishop of London presented a bell to the society. This bell afterwards became memorable as an object of contention between the society at Belleville and that of St. Paul's. A large silver christening basin was presented by Capt. Richard Brown, a native of England, who came to Newburyport from the West Indies. He married a Miss Hudson. Capt. Daniel Marquand married his widow, from whom are the descendants of that name and one family of Jenkins. He was interred in the cemetery on the Plains. The communion service consisted of a flagon, inscribed: "The gift of K. William and Q. Mary to the Rev. Samuel Myles, for the use of their Majesties' Chappell in New England, 1694," and a chalice with the inscription: "Ex dono Johannis Mills 1693." This plate, in good preservation, is now in use at St. Paul's church. In 1720 Mr. Lucas died, and the Rev. Matthias Plant, a graduate of Jesus College,

Cambridge, England, succeeded in the rectorship.

As early as 1725, the church people dwelling at the water side formed the idea of building a new church, but the "Plains" people being unwilling to join them, nothing was done until 1738. Then, the Rev. Mr. Plant and Joseph Atkins, esq., each having offered to present fifty pounds towards building a new church at the "Port," the foundation of one was laid at the head of Queen, now Market street. The church was not completed until 1740. It was arranged that Mr. Plant should officiate at both churches. This caused some difficulty, which was happily settled. In 1751 Mr. Edward Bass was chosen to assist Mr. Plant, who died in 1753. For a while a monthly service was held in Queen Ann's Chapel, but, as time passed, this gradually became discontinued, and the building fell into decay.

The Rev. Edward Bass, though advanced to the bishopric of Massachusetts, still continued to officiate at St. Paul's church. He died the 10th of September, 1803, and the Rev. James Morse was settled the November following.

In 1800 the present church was built. I have a recollection of the old building, which was small and painted light yellow. This church had been furnished with an organ, the first in the town. This organ is a noted instrument, being the oldest in America. It was built by J. Preston, in York, England. Having been detained in his workshop, it escaped destruction at the time of the pious raid upon organs in the churches by Cromwell's soldiers. At the commencement of the last century it was brought to Boston by Thomas Brattle, and presented to King's Chapel in that city, but so strong was the feeling in New England against anything savoring of popery that it remained a long time in the packing case in the porch. At length, in 1714, it was set up, and used for forty years, when it was bought by the society of St. Paul's. In that church it sent forth its melody for more than two generations. Some years since, a larger organ having been procured, the venerable relic was purchased by the society of St. John's church, in Portsmouth, N. H. When a girl, my mother attended St. Paul's to hear the novel instrument. She was highly delighted with the music and much impressed by the service, and the grandeur of the Daltons, Atkins, Cutlers, Hoopers, Jacksons, John Tracy's, and other families of *ton* who worshipped there.

The corner-stone of the present church was laid with masonic ceremonies. The altar, aisles and gallery are as when built, but the first pews were roomy compartments, with high, paneled sides. The pulpit was peculiarly graceful, rising from a pillar and spreading like a wineglass. Above it hung a sounding-board, equally elegant in design. Before the reading desk was a lower one for the clerk. Either side of the entrance to the broad aisle were two small pews, with high, ornamental partitions; from the front corners of each to the right and left, uprose two tall, brightly-painted poles, terminating at the top by gilded balls. These pews were the seats for the church wardens, and the rods were the warden's poles, which in those days played no unimportant part in the ceremonies of the service, being borne in state by the wardens, as, with majestic step, they preceded the bishop up the broad aisle upon his entrance into the church. They also did good service in the discipline of the more youthful worshippers — the fear of a rap on the pate from these emblazoned poles being inculcated with becoming seriousness by the matrons of the society, as they marshalled their bright, frolicsome troops of boys and girls across the portals of the sacred edifice.

CHAPTER XXXVIII.

The Rev. Samuel Belcher having become aged and infirm, returned to Ipswich, his native place, where he died March 12th, 1715, universally mourned and esteemed.

The Rev. John Tufts was ordained over the society at Pipestave hill in 1714. Mr. Tufts possessed a fine taste, and, for those days, superior skill in music. To improve the singing in his choir and those of other churches, the year after his settlement he published a small work on music, which was sold for sixpence a copy or five shillings per dozen. Few tunes were then used — York, Hackney, St. Mary's, Windsor, and Martyrs, were the principal. In most congregations the singing was entirely by rote, which was considered papistical by the more rigid; and Mr. Tuft's attempt to improve sacred music was a daring innovation that for a time met much opposition.

In January, 1716, the church in the west precinct kept a day of humiliation and prayer, to petition that God would "prevent the spread of errors in the place, especially the error of quakers." The causes that had driven some into episcopacy had led others to join the "Friends." The sons of Mr. John Hoag having embraced the doctrines of that sect, others became interested and meetings were held at private houses. The first of these gatherings was at the dwelling of Mr. Samuel Sayer. A society was formed, which, in the summer of 1744, erected a meeting-house on a site nearly opposite the present Belleville church.

On Feb. 26th, 1738, a council was called, in the west parish, to consider "the distressed state and condition of ye second church of Christ in Newbury, by reason of the reverend pastor, Mr. John Tufts, being charged by a woman, or women, of his indecent carriage, also of his abusive and unchristian behavior towards them at several times, and so forth."

This council consisted of ten clergymen and twenty delegates. Mr. Tufts refused to unite with the council and opposed the swearing of witnesses, and immediately asked his dismission, which was granted, the church refusing to give him a recommendation elsewhere. He was succeeded by Thomas Barnard, who was dismissed in 1751. The Rev. Moses Hale was ordained the same year. He married Mehitable Dummer, and was the only pastor, amongst the long list of those that have been ordained over this society, who spent his life among his people. He died in 1779.

The meeting-house on Pipestave hill had become somewhat dilapidated; by the setting off of the fourth parish, it was no longer in a central locality; then, many objected to climbing the long hill. As expensive repairs were necessary, it was proposed to move the building a quarter of a mile below on the main road, at the corner of the one leading to the river. This raised a storm of objections, but finally, in 1758, the seventh year of Mr. Hale's pastorate, the plan was effected. The house, which was a good-sized structure, without a tower, was repaired and remodeled. The parsonage, which lay below on Pipestave hill, was retained by the parish for some years. It is still standing in good preservation.

The Rev. True Kimball was settled in 1782, and dismissed in 1797. His successor, the Rev. Samuel Tomb, was ordained the next year. He was dismissed in 1808, the same year that Dr. Woods left the fourth parish for the seminary at Andover. Great scandal had been raised in the parish respecting Parson Tomb's ill treatment of a little girl, bound as a servant in his family. It was alleged that, being unmercifully whipped for every slight offence, to screen herself, the child became an adept at deceit. To punish her for lying, the minister, it was said, tied her tongue to her great toe. Such discontent was aroused that the reverend gentleman asked a dismission, which was granted, though many of the society discredited the stories about him. My father would not accept Dr. Woods' ministry; after the Slade meeting-house at Byfield was closed he attended service at the lower parish.

After Mr. Tomb's departure the pulpit was for a time supplied by a Mr. Hull. A part of the society, in which my father was included, were much pleased with Parson Hull's preaching, declaring it to be good Arminian doctrine, but the more Calvinistic portion, who were a majority, pronounced it tame and unsound. Old Mr. Ben. Poore (father of Dr. Poore) in his most emphatic manner, declared, "His name is Hull and he was *hull* indeed." In consequence Mr. Hull did not receive a call, and the Rev. Ebenezer Hubbard was ordained in May, 1809. Persons at that time were assessed for the support of the gospel according to their property. My father had paid the year's tax at the lower parish. Towards spring, to his surprise, the collector of the upper parish also presented a bill. Father produced the one he had paid, but the collector, Mr. Bailey, said: "The law required every one to pay in his own parish unless they attended on the worship of a different sect. As the lower parish was Congregationalist, as well as the upper, he must pay a tax to the society in the parish where he resided." Father refused to comply with the demand, and Mr. Bailey took two of our best cows from the barnyard and drove them down the lane. Mother cried, but father laughed and sat down to dinner. When the meal was over we saw the cows standing by the cowyard bars, and nothing more was done about the tax bill. Uncle Enoch Little invited father to take a seat in his pew at the Baptist meeting-house in New Rowley, which he did. As, after Parson Woods left, the services in our parish were irregular, mother or some of the family generally accompanied him. After a while it became the settled place of worship, and, in later years, my mother united with that church.

As the service in Queen Ann's Chapel became gradually discontinued, a new Congregationalist society was formed in that quarter. For a time, with the permission of the Episcopal society, they occupied the old chapel, but after a while a small, plain build ing was put up, a little above Queen Ann's, and on Sept. 1, 1762, the Rev. Oliver Noble was ordained. Father Noble, as he was commonly styled, was a somewhat eccentric character. With a quick eye and ready wit at barter and sale, he could turn an honest penny with any one; and, as his congregation was small, and it was not easy to raise even the limited stipend to which he was entitled, it was convenient to eke out a living by his own exertions. Some few years after his settlement his wife died, and the bereaved husband preached her funeral sermon, which he had printed. Stuffing his saddle bags, he mounted his old horse, known as "Noble's frame," and proceeded to peddle his sermon over the country. My father, then a lad, in after years used to give a laughable description of his visit at Crane-neck. He rode rode up one warm afternoon, habited in a long, flowing, black flannel gown, and, with tears and piteous sighs, told his grief, ending by the presentation of the sermon, which was purchased, with sympathetic condolence, while, at the same time, warning glances were threateningly cast to Jim and the other boys and girls who were snickering in the background.

At the time of the depreciation of the continental money, two gentlemen in Bradford having obtained an inkling of the probable state of the market, held a consultation respecting the best method of ridding themselves of a quantity of bills which they held. It was suggested by one, that they should ride down to Father Noble's, and trade off the currency for some land that the clergyman had for sale. "Grasshopper plains" was warm, dry land, very suitable for early crops, and especially good for corn. This plan was carried into effect. The Parson received his visitors with great urbanity; he was not the man however to be behindhand in knowledge respecting public events, or business in general, and the trick which the gentlemen intended to play, was instantly divined. Though the land on the plains had all the good qualities the Bradford man had mentioned, every one at all conversant with that locality knows that there are several acres back from the river consisting of sandy knolls, a somewhat singular conformation, which are almost worthless, would scarcely subsist a small number of the insects from which the plains derive their name. The Parson at that time had quite a lot of this land which he was desirous to put into a more profitable investment; he was therefore willing to bargain, not too eager, but to accommodate the gentlemen, after a time the purchase was effected. Father Noble, shaking with inward chuckles, received the condemned bills, which before the news of their loss of value became general he disposed of very satisfactorily. At the time of the purchase the land was covered with snow, and the gentlemen anxious to get rid of the notes, took but a cursory look, and had not been particular in enquiries respecting it. As the spring advanced somehow the story of the sale became bruited about, and the would be biters were informed that they had been unmercifully bitten. Accordingly they rode down to take a survey of the land. Scarcely liking the lay of it they went with their protest to the Parson. Father Noble was all fair and square. "He should be sorry to do anything wrong, he was to exchange the next Sunday with Parson Dutch: he would remain in Bradford over night, and Monday morning the gentlemen might call upon him and talk the matter over" Accordingly, on Sunday Parson Noble appeared in the pulpit of the Bradford meeting-house. The morning service passed as usual, but in the afternoon the congregation were favored by a specimen of pulpit eloquence which caused a universal sensation. The house was crowded, and knowing what was pending, an unusual expectancy was felt. The psalms and prayer over, the preacher with peculiar emphasis named his text: "I have bought a piece of ground, and I must needs go to see it." To see it was the pith of the discourse, which was so apt, and the would be deceit of the complainants was so deftly shown, that they turned all colors and writhed in their pews, while the rest of the audience had much ado to preserve the decorum proper for "Sabba' day." The next morning the two gentlemen rode over to the parsonage. As was customary, Parson Dutch produced the liquor case, sugar, hot water, pipes and tobacco. The quartette drank healths, smoked, conversed upon the weather, the crops, and the state of the country, but not a lisp was made respecting the land sale. Towards noon Father Noble in his most genial manner, with fervent wishes for the temporal and spiritual welfare of his friends, bade them good morning, and wended his way down the main road, in high esteem with himself and his grasshopper land speculation.

A man like the Rev. Oliver Noble could not be expected to remain in a small parish like that at the Plains, neither was it probable that as a spiritual guide he gave universal satisfaction. He resigned his charge April 7, 1784. Afterwards he was settled in New Castle, N. H., where he died in 1792, aged fifty-six.

After his departure, preaching was for a time held irregularly in "Noble's meeting-house," but at length was wholly discontinued, and the old building fell into decay; finally, one stormy winter night it blew down.

In 1807 a new society was formed in that locality, a new meeting-house erected on High street, and the Rev. James Miltimore was settled in April, 1808.

In 1702 the parish, afterwards called Byfield, was incorporated. This was taken from the towns of Rowley and Newbury, and at first was designated Rowlbury. Two years later it was named Byfield in honor of Judge Nathaniel Byfield. The first pastor of the new parish was the Rev. Moses Hale; he was succeeded by the Rev. Moses Parsons, who died in 1783. The Rev. Elijah Parish was ordained in 1787.

The pastorate of the Rev. Mr. Parsons was memorable for a contest between the clergyman and one of the church officers, Deacon Benjamin Colman, on the subject of slavery. At that time nearly every family owned one or more negro slaves. My great-grandfather Noyes had a man named Primus, of whom the grandchildren were especially fond. He was a church member and very much respected. As Dea. Noyes' favorite servant, Primus considered himself somewhat of an important personage, and always comported himself with suitable dignity. My great-grandfather Smith owned a black maid; great-grandsir Little a man; this couple were married. The husband usually came to great-grandfather Smith's to sleep, but on very pleasant evenings the wife would go over to great-grandsir Little's to visit her husband. The agreement at their marriage, between their owners, had been, if there were children to divide them. Two or three were born, but they were swept away with those of their masters, by the throat distemper, the year it made such ravage in New England.

As Violet, the Rev. Mr. Parsons's woman, like most head servants in a large family, literally "ruled the roast," being a perfect autocrat in the kitchen, and a presiding genius in every department of the household, holding an affectionate but unquestioned sway over the bevy of bright, roguish boys that were reared in the parsonage, the zealous deacon could not have founded his complaint upon any but conscientious scruples. The principle of slavery was the sin against which he contended, thus unwittingly becoming pioneer in a cause which has produced such momentous results. Church meeting after church meeting was held. The deacon was suspended for indecorous language respecting his pastor, and the discussion continued until after the clergyman's decease, when at a church meeting on the 26th of October, 1785, Deacon Colman, after having acknowledged, "that in his treatment of the Rev. Moses Parsons, the late worthy pastor of the church, he urged his arguments against the slavery of the Africans with vehemence and asperity, without showing a due concern for his character and usefulness as an elder, or the peace and edicfiation of the church," he was restored to the church and the deaconship.

In 1762 an academy building was erected, and a committee chosen in Byfield parish to appoint a grammar school master, according to the will of Gov. Dummer. The academy was opened on Monday, Feb. 27, 1763. The Rev. Moses Parsons preached a sermon on the occasion from the text, "The liberal soul deviseth liberal things." The first preceptor, as previously stated, was Mr. Samuel Moody. The school, by the Governor's will, was made free to the boys of the parish; those from abroad paid the usual tuition. This academy immediately took rank with the first in the country — a reputation which has been ably sustained.

April 27, 1778, the inhabitants of Byfield were startled by a phenomenon usually termed the "Flying Giant." The following description is from the diary of Deacon Daniel Chute:

"Yesterday, being the Lord's day, the first Sunday after Easter, about five of the clock in the p. m., a most terrible, and as most men do conceive supernatural thing took place. A form as of a giant, I suppose rather under than over twenty feet high, walked through the air from somewhere nigh the Governor's school, where it was first spied by some boys, till it past the meeting-house, where Mr. Whittam, who was driving home his cows, saw it, as well as the cows also, which ran violently bellowing. Sundry on the whole road from the meeting-house to Deacon Searles' house, saw and heard it, till it vanished from sight nigh Hunslow's hill, as Deacon Searles saw. It strode so fast as a good horse might gallop, and two or three feet above the ground, and what more than all we admired, it went through walls and fences as one goes through water, yet were they not broken or overthrown. It was black, as it might be dressed in cloth indeed, yet were we so terrified that none observed what manner if at all it was habited. It made continually a terrifying scream, 'hoo, hoo,' so that some women fainted."

The majority of the people, the Rev. Moses Parsons included, believed this spectre to be the devil taking a walk to oversee his mundane affairs. Deacon Benjamin Colman published an account of this occurrence in the Essex Journal and New Hampshire Packet. This was in the midst of his controversy with Mr. Parsons on the slavery question, and he attributed the diabolical visitation to the heinous sin of slave-holding by the pastor of the parish, followed by quaint theological speculations, in the deacon's strong and fearless style.

CHAPTER XXXIX.

In 1725 the Third parish in Newbury erected a meeting-house at the water side, fronting on Fish street. Many entertained serious doubts of the desirability of this church. Mr. William Moody, writing to his brother, Judge Sewell in Boston, says: "Our people at towne are going to build another meeting-house, but intend to set it so nigh to Mr. Toppan's, that I fear it will make great contention."

The new house was dedicated the 20th of June; the Rev. John Tufts preached the sermon. On January 19, 1726, the Rev. John Lowell was ordained, the sermon was by the Rev. Thomas Foxcroft of Boston.

The Lowles or Lowells are a very ancient family, dating back to the reign of Richard the Second. Mr. Percival Lowle, born in Yardley county, Worcester, a merchant of Bristol, England, in 1639, with his two sons, John and Richard, came to Newbury, where John married his last wife, Naomi Sylvester; their youngest son, Ebenezer, went to Boston and became a merchant; he married Elisabeth Shale: their oldest son, the Rev. John Lowell, was born in Boston, March 14, 1704; Dec. 23, 1725, he married Sarah Champney. After his ordination, Parson Lowell commenced housekeeping on Greenleaf's lane, now State street. After the clergyman's decease, the estate having been purchased by Mr. Nathaniel Tracy for the site of a new mansion, the house was moved to Temple street. Two sons were born to the young couple; one died in infancy, the other, the distinguished Judge Lowell, and his noted descendants, have a world wide reputation.

The posterity of the other children of John and Richard Lowle are still numerous within the precincts of Old Newbury and the towns adjacent, prominent and respected citizens, while others of equal worth are settled in different sections of the country.

Both Parson and Madam Lowell were assiduous in advancing the spiritual and intellectual welfare of the parish.

Notwithstanding the expense of building a new meeting-house, the parish duplicated the town's appropriation for educational purposes, and in 1731 hired Mr. John Woodbridge to teach Latin to the youth of the parish, at sixty pounds a year; scholars out of the parish were to pay fourpence or six cents a week.

At that period the minister's lady was preeminently the head of feminine society. Her position was much more marked, and her duties far more onerous than at present. As chief lady in the parish, and mistress of a household distinguished for hospitality, Madam Lowell won encomiums from old and young, rich and poor. Possessing tact, quick perception, and decision of character, united to great skill and notability in domestic affairs, with rare culture and accomplishments for those days, her precept and example was well calculated to raise the standard of female character in her husband's parish. My great-grandfather Johnson and his wife held Parson and Madam Lowell in the most affectionate esteem and reverence. Called to the ministry a few years later than Mr. Lowell, Mr. Johnson often spoke of the interest manifested and the assistance rendered him by his pastor while he was pursuing his studies. Madam Johnson, the daughter of Dr. Humphrey Bradstreet, though younger, was a dear friend of Madam Lowell. I have frequently heard my grandmother Little speak of the gratitude her mother often expressed for Madam Lowell's advice and sympathy, when, young and inexperienced, she assumed the responsible position of a clergyman's wife. Madam Lowell died in 1756; my great grandfather was one of the pall bearers. In those days it was customary at the funeral of persons of note, to present in addition to the usual crape bands and silk gloves, a gold ring as a memorial of the departed. My grandfather's mourning ring descended to me. It is a thick, plain ring of the old fashioned yellow gold; on the outside is engraved the then usual insignia of death, a skull and cross bone; within is inscribed: "Sarah Lowell ob. 28 of June, 1756, Æ. 52." The Rev. John Tucker was also a pall bearer, and a similar ring has been preserved by his descendants.

Parson Lowell married as a second wife, Elisabeth, widow of the Rev. William A. Whipple, of Hampton Falls. Mr. Lowell died 15th of May 1767, in his 64th year. His loss was keenly felt by the bereaved parish. The Rev. John Tucker in the sermon preached at the funeral, says of him, "He was endowed with good natural powers, which he improved by study, under the advantages of a liberal education. He was not only acquainted with those polite arts, and sciences, which distinguished him as a scholar and a gentleman, but was well furnished with that kind of knowledge, which was requisite to forming his character, and enabling him while young, to appear with advantage as a minister of the gospel. In his domestic and social connections and behavior; in his private conversation, both as a christian and a minister, he maintained a good reputation. He was a lover of good men though of different denominations and differing sentiments, and much given to hospitality."

Over the fire-place in the dining room of Parson Lowell's residence was a painted panel representing a group of clergymen seated around a table, on which were a punch bowl and tobacco dish. Above this he had inscribed in Latin the motto "In essentials, unity; in non-essentials liberty, in all things charity."

The arms of Lowle, Somersetshire and Yardley, are:

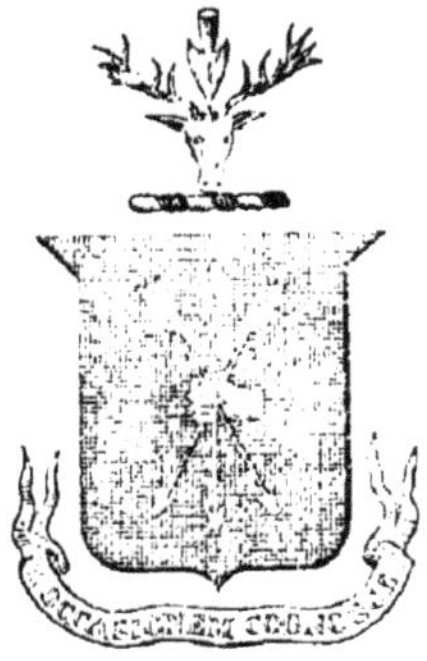

SA, A HAND COUPED AT THE WRIST, GRASPING THREE DARTS, ONE IN PALE AND TWO IN SALTIRE AZ. CREST—A STAG'S HEAD EMBOSSED OR, BETWEEN THE ALTIRES A PHEON AZ.

Two candidates supplied the pulpit of the Third church for several months, the Rev. Christopher B. Marsh of Boston and Thomas Carey of Charlestown. Both of these young gentlemen were graduates of Harvard, but Mr. Marsh had embraced more rigid — in the parlance of the time, "Hopkinsian" views — while Mr. Carey followed in the footsteps of the fathers. Mr. Carey, having received the votes of two thirds of the parish, was ordained on the 11th of May, 1768. The other third amicably separated from the Third parish, receiving their share of the church plate, and formed a new society. They erected a meeting-house on Titcomb street, and the Rev. Mr. Marsh was ordained the 19th of October, 1768. He died in 1773, and was succeeded by the Rev. Samuel Spring in 1777.

Parson Carey was stricken with palsy after the morning service on Sunday, March 9, 1788, and a colleague was appointed. The Rev. John Andrews, born at Hingham, March 3, 1764; graduated at Harvard in 1786: married, Sept. 8, 1788, Margaret, oldest daughter of Rev. Prof. Edward and Margaret Wigglesworth; was ordained over the First society, Newburyport, Dec. 10, 1788; received the degree of D. D. at Harvard College in 1824; resigned his pastoral charge May 1, 1830. He died in August, 1845.

Through the preaching of Whitefield and the influence of the "great awakening," several persons became dissatisfied with the doctrines in which they had been reared. These "new schemers" were vehemently opposed by Mr. Toppan, and as firmly by Mr. Lowell, both denouncing their meetings as "irregular and disorderly." Rev. John Tucker having been settled colleague with Mr. Toppan, the opposition strengthened, and in 1743 the "Separatists" held their first public assembly in a barn near the upper green, in Oldtown. A small house of worship was soon after erected on Norfolk, now High street, just below Federal street, Mr. Joseph Adams, a young graduate of Harvard University, officiating as minister. The "Separatists" having anathematized the parent church as "Old Dagon," in retaliation the new one received the soubriquet of "Young Dagon." The new house, which was never entirely finished, blew down in a severe thunderstorm, a catastrophe that brought exceeding satisfaction to the opposition, who piously regarded it as a just judgment sent by the indignant hand of an outraged Deity.

On January 3, 1746, nineteen persons withdrew from the First church and formed a new church. Thirty-eight, three years previous, had withdrawn from communion with the Third church. As their petition for dismission from that church and a recommendation to the new church was denied, they were admitted to that body without a recommendation. On the 22d of the same month, acting on the advice of Whitefield, the "Separatists" extended a call to the Rev. Jonathan Parsons to become their pastor. This invitation was accepted, and the installation took place on the 19th of March. This church, not being yet united to a Presbytery, was styled "Independent." The installation services were conducted entirely by the people and the pastor-elect. Having mutually pledged themselves to support each other in the work of the gospel, Mr. Parsons offered prayer and preached a sermon. On the 7th of April the organization of the church was completed by the choice of six ruling elders, and the September following it united with the Presbytery of Boston. Much trouble arose respecting the assessment of taxes, as the first and third parishes insisted upon the right to tax the seceders. An appeal was made by the Presbyterians to Gov. Shirley, and various other methods used, for years, to obtain redress, but without effect, until the different societies became distinct corporations, which act was passed Feb. 22, 1794. The Presbyterian society erected the church on Federal street in 1756. On Sunday morning, Sept. 30, 1770, George Whitefield died, at the residence of Rev. Jonathan Parsons, and his remains were interred under the pulpit of that church. Mr. Parsons died in 1776, and the Rev. John Murray was ordained in 1781. He died in 1793, and was succeeded by the Rev. Daniel Dana, Nov. 19, 1794.

January 28, 1764, that part of Newbury now called Newburyport was incorporated as a separate town, and the Third church of Newbury became the First of Newburyport. As the old meeting-house on Fish street had become time-worn, and too small to accommodate the large congregation, in 1801 the church on Pleasant street was erected. This edifice, built by Daniel Spofford and Amos Palmer, was the most splendid in the vicinity, and a model of architectural beauty. Its erection created a great sensation. The Rev. Mr. Carey was able to preach the last sermon in the old house, which was on Sept. 27th. This sermon showed that, though weak in body, the clergyman's mind was wholly unimpaired.

The next morning a vast crowd assembled to witness the demolition of "ye ancient meeting-'us." I have often heard David Emery, then a lad of sixteen, and my cousin, Sophronia Peabody, describe the scene. The supports, excepting at one corner, having been removed, a hawser was placed around the post, and a band of sailors, with "a long pull, a strong pull, and a pull all together," brought the large building to the ground, amidst clouds of dust and the huzzas of the multitude. Gen. Peabody entertained the ladies who had gathered in the chambers of his store with wines and cordials from the cellar, and my cousin, then a child, thought pulling down meeting-houses a delightful event, which she wished might happen every day.

The Third church in Newbury from the first was progressive. In 1750 they voted, *nemine contradicente*, that "the scriptures be read in publick on the Lord's day." Reading from the Bible in the pulpit was not customary amongst the first congregations. I never remember hearing a chapter read until Parson Woods was ordained, and he only did so occasionally. In 1769 the church at Oldtown voted to introduce the Scriptures at public worship. When I first went to meeting, Watts' psalms and hymns were in use and they had been generally adopted by the churches.

In 1794 an organ was placed in the First church in Newburyport. It was, for those days, a large and handsome instrument. Round the top of the pipes were festoons of crimson silk; above them, in large gold letters, was the motto, "Praise Him with Organs." This remarkable innovation greatly shocked the more rigid, and the new instrument became the chief topic of conversation in town and country, in the commercial mart, and by the domestic hearth. It was denominated a "papistical device — a popish fiddle." Much was said about the "tooting tub," and "sarving the Divil on an orgin," while the Rev. Samuel Spring discoursed most disdainfully respecting "our neighbor's box of whistles." Notwithstanding the opposition, the organ retained its place, sending forth melody Sunday after Sunday, in the old meeting-house, and, with the bell and weathercock, was transferred to the new church. The interior of this building has received but little alterations. The front gallery pews were square, and when first erected the pulpit was higher than now, and surmounted by the sounding-board, then considered necessary for a speaker. This pulpit was reached by stairs leading from the back porch, and the platform beneath it was railed off like an altar; two gates opened into this compartment, to the right and left; within, in front, was the communion table, behind it stood three large arm chairs, with crimson seats. The pulpit cushion was of crimson velvet. From the centre of the ceiling depended a large glass chandelier for wax candles. It is a thousand pities this had not been preserved, as "a thing of beauty is a joy forever."

In those days evening services were rare events. When Dr. Parish was ordained, the parish in common with every other was so much divided on doctrinal points, that much vexation and delay occurred. It was not until the evening of the third day after the council had been convened that the ordination services took place. The parish ever after celebrated the anniversary of his ordination by an evening meeting. On one occasion I accompanied Mrs. Moses Colman. She took a pair of tall brass candlesticks and mould candles with her. The candlesticks were placed on the ledge on the front of the square pew, and the candles lighted that we might see the hymns. Nearly every pew was similarly lighted, there were candlebra on the pulpit, and candles on the communion table and in the singing seats; a few in tin sconces were hung along the walls, still the house was not very brilliantly illuminated. The Pleasant street meeting-house was dedicated in October. The sermon was preached by the Rev. John Andrews; the music was unusually fine; altogether it was a great occasion. A dense mass of human beings filled every available space of the large church; the ladies were resplendent with elegance, many strangers were present, and the dignitaries of the town and parish; the day was a festal one throughout the place.

Upon their removal to "Port," both Gen. Peabody and Col. Bartlett joined the first society, but in a few years, as their wives inclined to the more Calvinistic preaching at the Old South, pews were taken there. Both ladies soon after became communicants, and all the Peabody children, with the exception of the youngest, who was born in the District of Columbia, were baptized at this font.

Sophronia Peabody accompanied her uncle Leonard Smith to the dedication. Mr. Smith had purchased the upper corner wall pew on the side towards Green street, and to accommodate his large family two pews had been let into one. This pew was so crowded, Fronie and her cousin, Sophy Smith, were were perched on the window seat, where they vastly enjoyed the scene.

The new church gave great satisfaction, and for several years was crowded every Sunday. This society counted amongst its members many eminent persons. Patrick and Nathaniel C. Tracy, Judge Parsons, and his law students, amongst which was John Quincy Adams, the discarded lover of Miss Mary Fraiser, the daughter of Moses Fraiser, esq., whose pew was in close contiguity to that occupied by young Adams, whom the Fraiser family did not consider a sufficiently brilliant *parti* for the lovely Mary, then one of the celebrated beauties of the day. There were the Carters, Davenports, John Bromfield, the Cross families, Michael Hodge, Nicholas Brown, Col. Edward Wigglesworth, Joseph Marquand, Gen. Jonathan Jackson, David Moody, Jonathan Greeley, Judge Greenleaf and his son Col. Greenleaf, Major Joshua Greenleaf, the Balches, Stones, Johnsons, Noyeses, Toppans, Coffins, Jenkins, Mr. Prout, Mr. Israel Young, Dr. Micajah Sawyer, Captain Hudson, and many other distinguished persons and families.

The triangular piece of land on which the old meeting-house stood, was sold to the town for eight thousand dollars. The citizens subscribed thirty-five hundred of this sum. From this land Market square was formed, the well dug, and the town pump placed very nearly on the site of the pulpit of the old meeting-house.

CHAPTER XL.

In 1729 the inhabitants of the upper part of the second parish in Newbury petitioned the General Court to divide the west parish into two precincts. A map drawn that year shows that there were one hundred and eighty-four houses in the parish, and the families numbered one hundred and eighty-three.

March 20, 1781, the second parish voted "to desire the General Court to confirm the setting off of the fourth parish from the second," which was done by a committee, February 22, according to a vote passed by the second parish, January 6th, consenting to the division.

April 15th, 1729, the inhabitants of the upper part of the west parish, made an agreement "to build a meeting-house fifty feet by thirty-eight, and twenty foot stud." This was the old meeting-house on Meeting-house hill. The Rev. William Johnson was ordained over the new parish, September 15th, 1731.

The Johnsons are an old English

family. The first ancestor on record was Maurice Johnson, esq., M. P. for Stamford in 1523. He had two sons, Robert and Francis.

Robert Johnson, archdeacon of Leicester, married Maria ——; died in 1625, leaving one son, Abraham, born in 1577.

Abraham Johnson married Anna Meadows in 1597; they had one son, Isaac. Mrs. Johnson died young, and in 1602, Abraham Johnson married a second wife, Cicerly Chadderton, by whom he had eleven children: Laurence, Maurice, Robert, William, Edward, Ezekiel, Nicholas, Francis, Henry, Cicerly, and Elisabeth. Mr. Johnson removed with his family from Milton Bryan to Canterbury, county of Kent.

Isaac Johnson, the son of Abraham Johnson by his first wife, in 1623 was united in marriage with the Lady Arabella Piennes. This couple with two sons by the second wife, William and Edward, emigrated from Canterbury to America. The early death of Lady Arabella Johnson, which cast so deep a gloom over that infant colony in the wilderness, has become indelibly interwoven in the early history of the Massachusetts settlement.

William Johnson settled in Charlestown in 1630, and his brother Edward in Woburn. William Johnson in 1633, married Elisabeth Storey of Charlestown; they had five children: Rahanna, Elisabeth, Joseph, Jonathan and Nathaniel.

Nathaniel was married in 1668, to Joanna Long of Charlestown; they had three children: Nathaniel, William and John.

William Johnson, son of Nathaniel and Joanna Johnson, came from Charlestown to Newbury in 1698. Nov. 9th, 1702, he married Martha, third daughter of Captain Daniel Pierce of the "Pierce" farm, Newbury. They had six children: Isaac, William, born May 31, 1706; Eleazer, Elisabeth, Martha and Lydia. William Johnson died in 1741, aged 70 years.

William, son of William and Martha (Pierce) Johnson, graduated at Harvard in 1727. Soon after his ordination, he married Betty, daughter of Dr. Humphrey Bradstreet. They had nine children: Sarah, Martha, Mary, Dorothy, Anna, Hannah, William, Daniel and Bradstreet.

Sarah married Mr. David Chase, who resided on his farm near the present Rocks bridge.

Martha became the wife of Dr. William Hale of Old Rowley.

Mary married my grandfather, Joseph Little.

Dolly was twice married; first to William Folsom, of Newmarket, N. H., who died young; second to Squire Blanchard of Chester, N. H.

Anna married Dr. Tenney of Bradford; he died the second year of his marriage from the small pox, which he took in performing the duties of his profession. He was a most promising young man, and his death was sincerely mourned throughout the community. The widow Tenney married Mr. Joseph Moody of Amesbury.

Hannah married Master Simeon Chase.

William, Daniel and Bradstreet settled in business in Newburyport. William married Temperance Little; their two daughters, Temperance and Mary, died unmarried. The only son, William, went to Amesbury and engaged in the carriage business.

Daniel married Hannah Woodman of Newbury, June. 1764; they had two daughters. Hannah, who married Mr. Stephen Frothingham, and Betsey, who married Mr. Thomas Beck, and went to Portland, Me. Daniel Johnson's second wife was Mary Horton, to whom he was married Feb., 1787.

Bradstreet Johnson married Susanna Brown, and died childless.

Madam Betty Johnson died August 2d, 1756, in the 43d year of her age. Parson Johnson married a second wife, a widow Sargent, from Amesbury. He died February 22d, 1772, in the 40th year of his ministry, aged 66 years. The stone erected by the parish to his memory bears this inscription:

> "He was a gentleman of good understanding, of uniform piety and virtue, of a very amiable temper, tender and affectionate in his family connections, a benevolent and faithful friend."

Parson Johnson was reverenced and beloved in an unusual degree both in his family and the parish. My mother was his especial pet; she could recollect standing between her grandsire's knees, while he taught her the alphabet, and though only five years old at his decease, she could read the Bible quite fluently.

Eleazer, my great-grandfather's youngest brother, married Elisabeth Pearce. They had nine children, Eleazer, William Pearce, Nicholas, Joseph, Philip, Jane, Sarah, Elisabeth and Martha. Mrs. Johnson died soon after the birth of Martha, and Mr. Johnson in 1766, was married to Sarah Bailey. They had one son, John Bailey Johnson. My great uncle, Eleazer Johnson, died in 1792.

Eleazer Johnson jr., married Hannah Greenleaf in 1777. Their children were Eleazer, Joseph, Hannah, Abigail and Jacob Greenleaf.

William Pearce Johnson married Sarah Greenleaf Oct. 1770. Their children were Mary, Catharine, William Pearce, Sarah, Eleazer 4th, and Jonathan Greenleaf.

Nicholas, the third son, married Mary, daughter of Matthew and Anna Greenleaf Perkins, Dec. 1776. Their children were Nicholas, Anna Greenleaf, Mary Perkins, Elisabeth, Sarah, Philip, Abel Greenleaf, Benjamin Greenleaf, and Henry.

Joseph, the fourth son, married Elisabeth Dole. Their children were Joseph, born 1769, died 1785; Richard, born 1771, lost at sea with Capt. Whitcomb and crew in 1718; Eleazer, born May 9th, 1773, married Sarah Newman June 11th, 1797; Elisabeth, born July 1775, married Richard Dole. Philip, the youngest son, married Dolly Noyes in 1773. Their children were Dolly, Sally and Philip.

Jane, the oldest daughter, married Nathaniel Nowell; Sarah, Phineas Parker; and Martha, Capt. Desaunette. Elisabeth, my great-grandfather Johnson's oldest sister, married Isaac Hall. Their daughter, Hannah Hall, married Edmund Bartlet; their children were William, and Hannah who died young. Mr. William Bartlet married the widow Betty (Coombs) Lascom, the daughter of Philip and Lydia Johnson Coombs: Martha the second sister, married Ralph Cross; the youngest, Lydia, Philip Coombs, who came from the island of Guernsey, and was the first of the family in Newburyport; it was their daughter Betty who married William Bartlet.

Isaac Johnson, the first of the name in America, and one of the original settlers of Massachusetts, arrived at Salem June 12th, 1630, and died Sept. 30th, following. He ranked by virtue of his birth, learning and wealth, next to Gov. Winthrop, and was so placed in the colonial records. His wife, Arbella or Arabella, was the daughter of Thomas the 14th Earl of Lincoln. Gov. Winthrop named the ship in which they came to this country for her.

Edward and William, half brothers of Isaac, came to America, in 1630, probably with Gov. Winthrop. Edward was a merchant and historian, as he wrote the "Wonder Working Providence of Zion's Savior," which was a history of New England from 1628 to 1652. It was printed in London in 1654, and copies of the original edition are highly prized by bibliographers. He was also speaker of the colonial Legislature, and one of the members authorized to treat with the commissioners of Charles II. He resided at Charlestown, and was one of the founders of Woburn, as Isaac was of Boston. Edward, as may be seen from the foregoing, was a man of great note in the colony. He was the first of the family in this town, as it is recorded that he traded here about the year 1634. As this was a year prior to the arrival of the party with Messrs. Parker & Noyes, this trade must have been with the Indians, or some isolated pioneers. He kept the town records of Woburn from its foundation until his death.

Below I give some extracts from various works regarding Isaac Johnson.

Bancroft, in his "History of the United States," says:

"The zeal of White soon found other and powerful associates in and about London, men of religious fervour: Winthrop, Dudley, Johnson, Pynchon, Eaton, Saltonstall, Bellingham, etc., famous in colonial records."

In another place it says:

"The virtues of Arabella Johnson, a daughter of the house of Lincoln: could not break through the gloomy shadows which surrounded her, and as she was ill before her arrival, grief soon hurried her to the grave. Her husband, one of the first men in the colony, zealous for pure religion, in life the greatest furtherer of the plantation, and by his bequests a benefactor of the infant state, was subdued by the force of disease and affliction, but he died willingly and in sweet peace, making a most godly end."

Lossing's "History of the United States," says:

"Amongst these was Isaac Johnson, a principal leader of the enterprise, and the wealthiest of the founders of Boston, and his wife, the Lady Arabella, a daughter of the Earl of Lincoln. She died at Salem, and her husband did not long survive her."

Blake's Biographical Dictionary confirms what I have noted regarding Edward, stating also, that he went to Merrimack in 1632 with a license to trade. Concerning Isaac it says, "Boston was settled under his conduct. He had the largest estate of any of the colonists, and was the greatest furtherer of the plantation." His lot in Boston was the square between Tremont, Washington, Court, and School streets, and he was buried at the upper end of his lot, which gave occasion for the first burial place, to be laid out around his grave. This is the church yard of King's chapel. His house was on a hill near Tremont street.

Thomas Johnson, kinsman of William, was amongst the earliest shipbuilders on the Merrimack river. He owned the ship-yard near the bottom of Ship street, and was one of the first settlers in that locality. His home was on the corner of Ship and Water streets, and at the time it was built there was only the residence of Dr. Humphrey Bradstreet and one other house below on Water street.

William Johnson came from Charlestown and succeeded Thomas in the business, and soon became a wealthy man. In the town records, 1731, we find, "Town voted liberty to William Johnson and others to build a wharf at the foot of Chandler's lane (now Federal street."

The ship carpenters were then one of the most influential classes in town, and William Johnson was at their head. At his death in 1741 he bequeathed one half of his ship yard, and his homestead, corner of Water and Federal streets, to his son Isaac; his house corner of Water and Ship streets and the other half of his ship yard to his son Eleazer. He left legacies to his son William, the clergyman, and to his daughter. He was a wealthy man for those times, and possessed two or three farms, well stocked, a number of houses, barns, ware-houses, a long wharf, a ship yard with all the machinery, tools and implements of art used in the business, lumber, a negro girl, etc. The wharf originally cost twenty thousand dollars, and as much more was afterward spent upon it. When it came into the hands of a descendant, and the ship yard merged into Johnson's wharf, some thousands were spent in putting a substantial stone wall around it. Here Capt. William P. Johnson, who was first a ship carpenter, then a successful ship master, when the Johnson ship yard was no more, on the Johnson wharf, carried on a large and profitable business. He owned the first ship employed in freighting in Newburyport, the "Industry" which was employed in taking tobacco, from the James river to Europe. He can be truly called the father of the freighting business which was such a source of profit to the place. Capt. Nicholas Johnson, Capt. John N. Cushing, and Henry Johnson, esq., afterwards owners of the Johnson wharf, there successfully persued the same business until their removal to the "Cushing wharf," which is still owned in the family. The Johnson wharf was sold to Mr. William Bartlett in 1830 for eight thousand dollars, and was called the Bartlet wharf. Again in 1855 it was sold for forty-two hundred dollars, and has passed from the family.

William Johnson's vessels constantly arrived at Newburyport, from Honduras, the West Indies, the Straits, and the north of Europe. He was the first person in Newburyport who put blinds to the windows of his house.

Eleazer Johnson led the band that seized the tea and burned it in market square before the destruction of the tea in Boston harbor. The story is as follows: Eleazer Johnson standing one day, upon the timber of his yard, called his men about him, and after a few patriotic words gave the order, "all who are ready to join, knock your adzes from the handles, shoulder the handles and follow me." Every adze in the yard was knocked off, and the stout, athletic man, who would have marched through a regiment of "red coats," had they stood in his way, taking his broad axe as an emblem of leadership, and for use, marched at the head of the company to the powder-house. There that well tried axe opened a way through the door, and each man shouldering a chest of tea, again fell into line. They marched direct to where Market square is now located, defiling round the old meeting-house. Johnson's axe opened a chest, and box and tea were on the ground together, each man as he came up followed suit, then with his own hand Johnson lighted the pile and burned it to ashes.

Through the troublous times that followed, the Johnsons stood at the head of the "Sons of Liberty." Eleazer's sons were, like himself, intelligent, enterprising, and patriotic. His son Philip volunteered and participated in the battle of Bunker Hill. His son Eleazer, who commanded a "Letter of Marque" in the revolution, the brig "Dalton," was captured, and he and his crew were imprisoned at Plymouth for two or three years, in the famous "Old Mill Prison." His son Nicholas, who commanded the "Count de Grass," was the first to display the stars and stripes from his mast-head on the river Thames. His son William Pearce Johnson, master of brig "American Hero," in 1776, hearing, when in one of the French West Indian islands, that war had begun, loaded with arms and ammunition, which he safely landed in Boston. This was the first material aid furnished the patriots. Like his ancestors, William P. Johnson possessed great muscular power. In a test of strength with the late William Bartlett, his neighbor, he lifted eighteen fifty-six pound weights, and was declared the strongest man in town. Eleazer Johnson was above the ordinary size, with black hair and eyes.

The Johnson coat of arms are:

GULES, THREE SPEAR HEADS ARGENT, CHIEF ERMINE. CREST—RAVEN'S WINGS REVERSED.

The Greenleafs, with whom the Johnsons so frequently intermarried, have been a family of great consideration in Newburyport. Three brothers of the name emigrated here. Benjamin, a descendant of one of these, died in 1783, having been a representative in the legislature and otherwise honored with marks of public confidence. Jonathan and Benjamin were nephews of the first-named Benjamin. The Greenleafs sprang from the French Huguenots. They removed to England in the sixteenth century; thence to America. Stephen Greenleaf, son of Edmund, built one of the earliest wharves in the vicinity of the market, in 1680. On that spot next the town landing was the yard in which Jonathan Greenleaf, his kinsman, worked as a mechanic. Mr. Greenleaf became the owner of this yard, and furnished many vessels for the mother country before the revolution. He owed all that he was to his industry and natural talents; having few educational advantages, he became well informed, won the confidence of all, and was constantly in some public office.

He was on the first "committee of safety" in Revolutionary times, was a member of the Continental Congress, of the governor's council, the State senate, and a representative to General Court for many years. In 1782 the town of Newburyport voted thanks for his long and faithful service in General Court. He was considered one of the great men of his day: one of the ablest, most eloquent, and most influential men, a man of such persuasive powers that he was commonly known by the designation of "Silver Tongue."

CHAPTER XLI.

The Rev. David Toppan, the successor of the Rev. William Johnson, was ordained April 18, 1774. He married Mary, daughter of Dr. Enoch Sawyer of the west parish. He was appointed professor at Harvard University in 1792, and died August 27, 1803, aged 51 years.

Leonard Woods, D. D., was settled December 5, 1798, and installed at Andover Theological Seminary in 1808.

In 1789, intelligence of the success that had attended the labors of a young English missionary in New Brunswick, having been brought to the Rev. Mr. Murray, pastor of the Presbyterian church, as it was a period of much religious interest, not only in his society but throughout the town, the clergyman forwarded a most pressing invitation to the young divine to come hither. The invitation was accepted, and the summer of that year the stranger commenced his ministration in Newburyport.

Charles William Milton was born in London the 29th of Nov., 1767. A protege of Lady Huntingdon, he graduated at the Seminary established by her munificence for the education of young men in the gospel ministry.

Mr. Milton was ordained a missionary in Spa Fields Chapel, London, 17th of Feb., 1788, and commenced the labor of his vocation in the British Provinces. From his first advent, the young preacher created a great sensation in Newburyport and vicinity. He was invited to settle in Amesbury, but his admirers in Newburyport could not permit him to go, but formed a new society, the fourth, and settled him as their pastor. This measure, so little anticipated by Mr. Murray when he solicited Mr. Milton's presence, must have been galling to the pastor of the Presbyterian church, as the larger part of those forming the new Independent society were seceders from his flock.

As the town refused the society the use of the town house, the members for a while met for worship at the residence of Mr. Anthony Morse in Milk street. In 1793, the present Prospect street church was erected, and Mr. Milton was installed March 20, 1794. His popularity continued for years, the large church being filled, often crowded.

This building was at first built with two towers and belfrys, as now, but the interior was much more massive. There were galleries on three sides, the pews were square, the pulpit like all pulpits in those days, there was a sounding board and deacons' seat. Two beautiful glass chandeliers lighted the house; these, though the church has been modernized, the society has had the good taste to preserve.

I was about fourteen years of age

the first time I heard Parson Milton preach; he was in the pulpit when I entered the meeting-house. In those days the seats, which were on hinges, were raised during prayer, in order that the worshippers might stand more conveniently. As the congregation rose, up went the seats with a clap, and the "amen" was followed by a slam, bang, which rattled the windows and reverberated through the building in a most anti-reverential manner. Here and there a seat was cushioned for an invalid or elderly woman, but it was a rare thing for a pew to be thus furnished throughout, and a carpeted floor had never been thought of. Col. Greenleaf caused a deal of talk by cushioning his pew in the new Pleasant street meeting-house with cushions covered with red velvet edged by fringe.

I had scarcely become seated when up jumped Parson Milton from the pulpit, in his gown and bands, like a jumping jack out of a box, and, with up-raised hands, gleaming eyes, the thick curls falling to his shoulders, in quick, curt tones, he shouted, "Let's pray." Up jumped the congregation: slap! went up the seats. I was scarcely on my feet, or had regained the breath which had been fairly taken from me, when "amen" was pronounced; down, bang! went the seats, and a hymn was given out. I doubt not that the sermon was sound and pithy, but the preacher's manner so wrought upon my nerves that I could scarcely listen, and the final amen was hailed with great satisfaction. I was only too glad, as the pew doors were flung wide and the men and boys clattered down the aisle, to follow them into the winter sunshine of the quiet street.

By his good sense, urbanity, and originality, Parson Milton obtained a strong hold upon the affection of his people. His preaching was bold and energetic, often interluded by the most odd and startling illustrations: at times he soared into a perfect rhapsody of impassioned eloquence. The manner of the man pointed every word, a manner peculiarly his own; his tones and gestures must be heard and seen to be appreciated; they were the power by which he swayed the multitude. Wholly absorbed in his subject, he often cast aside rules and regulations, making a law unto himself.

The sexton of his society was a Mr. Currier. This name, in the then common parlance, was called Kiah. On one occasion, at an evening lecture, Parson Milton nearly upset the equanimity of his hearers, by shouting, in the midst of his sermon, without the slightest pause between the sentences, "The Lord said unto Moses, Kiah snuff the candles!" Describing one of his church members, who was a dealer in lumber, he said: "Brother —— is the crookedest stick that ever grew on Zion's hill." One Sunday, in his vehemence, he pushed the Bible from the the desk, and the sacred volume, much to the consternation of the congregation, went, slap! upon the floor in front of the pulpit.

On a warm Sunday afternoon, the Parson espied one of his parishioners asleep in his pew, near the pulpit. This man's christian name was Mark. Leaning forward, in a quick, loud tone he exclaimed, "Mark!" The sleeper started and opened his eyes, when in a lower tone was added, "the perfect man, and behold the upright." He was a true friend of sailors; every Sunday his invariable petition arose "that God would bless our seafaring brethren." Parson Milton died May 1, 1837, aged seventy years.

Several members of the Presbyterian church, being dissatisfied with the settlement of the Rev. Daniel Dana as their pastor, withdrew from the society and formed the second Presbyterian church. The society was incorporated November 24th, 1796. That year Harris, Pleasant, Broad and Essex streets were accepted by the town, and the meeting-house erected on Harris street by the new Presbyterian society was dedicated in December. The first pastor of this society was the Rev. John Boddily, who was born in Bristol, England, and educated at Lady Huntingdon's college. He was ordained at Westbury, England, in 1780, and installed in Newburyport, June 28, 1797. Mr. Boddily died in 1802, and was succeeded by the Rev. John Giles. This gentleman, also an Englishman, was born in Caerlon, Monmouthshire, in 1758; he was settled over the society in Harris street, July 20, 1803. Parson Giles was the great Democratic, or, as he was commonly styled, Jacobin preacher, rivalling Dr. Parish, of Byfield, his Federalist opponent. People would rush to town from all quarters to listen to the Democratic discourses of Parson Giles, and the meeting-house would be thronged, while *vice versa*, the town folk would go out to Byfield to enjoy the eloquence of the celebrated Dr. Parish's fiery Federalist harangues. The church in Harris street was the nucleus of the Democratic society of the place—Dr. Smith of Mount Rural, Capt. Benjamin Pierce, the Williams' family, the Hortons, Capt. Richards, Mr. Samuel Noyes of the "Farms," and other leading families,—for though Newburyport was emphatically a Federalist town, there was still a most respectable minority of Democrats.

From my earliest recollection, there were Baptist churches in Haverhill and New Rowley, but the society in Newburyport was not formed until 1804. This sect had obtained a few converts through several previous years. I have elsewhere mentioned an unsuccessful attempt to form a church. The first regular service was held in a school-house on Marlborough street, July 22, 1804; a young licentiate preacher, Joshua Chase, conducted the service. On Sunday, the 14th of the October following, Stephen Goodwin, David Burbank, Benjamin Goodwin, Bart Hurd, John Flood, Nathaniel Pettingell, and Mrs. Rebecca Dorman, were baptized. These were the first ever immersed in the town. The 2d of May, 1805, a church was regularly organized. Soon after, the young licentiate was ordained as an evangelist and went to another field of labor. In the autumn, an engagement was made with the Rev. John Peak, who preached alternately in the Marlborough street school-house and in a small building at the "Plains." This continued until Mr. Peak made it a condition of his permanent settlement that the society should worship in some central location in Newburyport. For a time they met in a building called the "Tabernacle," on Temple street. In 1807 the society began to build a brick meeting-house on Liberty street, which was completed the next year, and the next, 1809, the Rev. Mr. Peak was ordained pastor.

Capt. William Cutler, of Newburyport, married a French lady, a member of the Roman Catholic church. To baptize her infant, and perform other sacraments, Bishop Chevereaux, of Boston, occasionally visited Mrs. Cutler at her residence. There were some half dozen French exiles and other foreigners in the place, also Catholics, who would assemble on these visits, in a chamber which Mrs. Cutler had fitted up for an oratory. These were the first Catholic services ever held in Newburyport.

Sophronia Peabody when a child was intimate with Mrs. Cutler's little girl. One Saturday as the two were returning home from school, Frasiette said to Sophronia: "The bishop is coming to say mass to-morrow. Mamma expects him this afternoon in the four o'clock stage. We have fitted up the oratory real pretty, and if you will never, *never* tell, I will show it to you." Mrs. Cutler, a very quiet and discreet person, avoided all publicity that might cause remark or animadversion, consequently this caution in Frasiette. Fronie having given the required promise of secrecy, the two mounted to the second story of Mr. Cutler's house. Slowly opening a door, Frasiette, reverently crossing herself, admitted her visitor into a dimly lighted apartment, richly furnished, and hung with several pictures from scripture subjects; at the upper end was an altar covered with a handsome cloth, upon which was a crucifix, wax tapers, and other appurtenances for worship. Gliding across the room, the little Frasiette devoutly knelt and whispered an *ave*. The dim, religious air of the room, and the solemnity of her companion, made a vivid impression on my young cousin. Scarcely would she then have believed that her baby brother, Joseph Little, in after years would graduate at a Catholic college, marry a catholic lady, and live and die in the bosom of that church, which, as a New England boy, he was taught to shun and abhor.

CHAPTER XLII.

From its settlement, Newbury, for a new place, was remarkably well supplied with the means of education. For the first few years, Mr. Parker and Mr. Noyes taught the boys of their charge, but in a short time a regular schoolmaster was maintained. His election and the appropriation for his salary being one of the items in the warning for the annual town meeting. Provision was also made for the study of Latin.

The first schoolmaster of Newbury was Anthony Somerby. In the year 1639, "for his encouragement to keep schoole for one year, he was granted foure akers of upland, over the great river, on the neck; also sixe akers of salt marsh, next to Abraham Toppan's twenty akers." In 1675, Mr. Henry Short was hired at a salary of £5 for the first six months, and sixpence a week from each scholar.

As the population increased and extended, difficulties arose respecting the location and support of the school. There was the first settlement on the river Parker, the Riverside village on the Merrimac, and the West village near the Artichoke river. As these settlements were at a considerable distance from each other, each holding distinct interests, it was but natural that the town meetings became the arena of much zealous contention upon the school question. The Parker river settlement usually contrived to secure the largest appropriation, while the remote village at the "Plains" with difficulty secured a mere moiety. In 1680 the town voted to pay a salary of £60 a year, and hired Mr. Emerson as teacher. The minority rebelled, refused to employ Mr. Emerson, and hired a Mr. Burley for £20. The "Generall Courte" was called upon to settle the matter. It decided in favor of Mr. Emerson, but as the town was unwilling to pay the high salary of £60, Mr. Emerson was requested to teach at the old salary of £20; at his refusal he was dismissed with only one dissentient vote. The next year Mr. Burley was secured as master at the usual salary of £20. He taught nearly two years, and was succeeded by Mr. Edward Tomson who resided at the "Plains." Up to 1691, the school was located at Oldtown; that year it was voted that it should be kept a third of the year at each of the villages. Mr. Seth Shone was hired as master: he was to teach readers free. Latin scholars were to pay 6d, and cipherers 4d a week.

In 1693, Mr. John Clark was called to preach and keep a grammar school at the west village for one year. In 1694 Mr. Christopher Toppan was employed; he was to receive "£20 in money, and 30s in good country pay, so long as he shall carry on one-half of the ministry, and £30 in good country pay, so long as he shall keep the writing and grammar school." Nicholas Webster succeeded Mr. Toppan; he was to have £30 in country pay, 4d a week from "lattin" scholars, and "nothing a week" for readers, writers, and cipherers. From 1700 to 1711, Mr. Richard Brown, afterwards minister at Reading, was the teacher. In 1713, Mr. John Woodbridge was hired at a salary of £25; he taught the school for eighteen years, his salary being gradually raised to £40 per annum.

In 1725 the Third parish was formed. This parish, as I have previously stated, had the care of the educational interests of its children, obtaining what money was possible from the town and making up the remainder by a tax upon the parish. In 1728 the town voted £30 for each of the three parishes; the Third parish added £30 to its share. The Third parish school was then kept in the house of John Ordway, near the head of Queen, now Market street. In 1732 Master Woodbridge was succeeded by Master Stephen Sewell, who taught for nearly fifty years. In 1740 the Third parish raised £120 to have a grammar school, which was taught by Mr. Samuel Moody, and a writing school, which was taught by Mr. Leonard Cotton. At the incorporation of Newburyport, in 1764, a committee was appointed to provide, at the public expense, good and sufficient schoolhouses and the best masters that could be procured. The grammar school was located on Greenleaf's lane, now State street, in the town-house, which had been built by the Third parish two years previous. This was a two-story wooden building, surmounted by a belfry and spire, and stood near the upper corner of Essex street, on a part of the Clement estate. Mr. Joshua Moody was the first teacher. At the "March meeting," 1764, Mr. Moody resigned, and Mr. Eleazer Porter was hired for a time. In July the selectmen offered the school, at £70 a year, to Mr. James Lovell, an usher in a school in Boston. Mr. Lovell requested time to decide upon his answer. After waiting several weeks, Mr. Samuel Parker was placed over the school. He taught until 1767, and was succeeded by Mr. Moses Holt, who taught three years, when Mr. Jeremiah Fogg took the school, at £60 a year. Mr. Fogg taught three years, when Mr. Nicholas Pike was appointed at a salary of £80. Master Pike was a renowned teacher. He was also town clerk, a selectman, and a representative to the State legislature; after the Province became a State he was a justice of the peace. Mr. Pike was a great mathematician. His arithmetic was the first ever issued in this country; it was in universal use until Master Walsh's appeared. Mr. Pike taught the school until 1791, with the exception of one year, when his place was filled by Master Woodbridge. Mr. Samuel Moody succeeded Mr. Pike, taught two years, and was followed by Rev. Eliphalet Gillett, who, in 1794, gave place to another distinguished teacher, Master Michael Walsh. In 1796 the brick school-house at the lower end of the Mall, near the site of the ancient windmill, was built. Master Walsh taught until 1803, when he was succeeded by Joshua Lane. He was followed by Moody Noyes, and by John Loud, who kept until 1806. The school having greatly declined, the salary was raised from $420 to $600, and Mr. Eben Coffin hired to teach. He was a superior teacher, and taught until 1810, when Joseph Dana succeeded him. In a few months Mr. Dana became preceptor of the Newburyport Academy, and Mr. B. D. Emerson took the school. In 1811 he was succeeded by Asa W. Wildes. In 1816 Mr. Wildes resigned, and Mr. B. D. Emerson again took the school. In 1818 Mr. Frazier was teacher, but not giving satisfaction, Mr. Wildes was persuaded to again take the school, which he taught until 1823.

The two writing schools established by the town in 1764 were located: one on Bartlets lane, now Winter street, and the other on a lane which is now School street. The school in the North school-house was formally opened by Parson Lowell, with a prayer and an exhortation, in which the pupils were told "to obey and reverence the master in school, and at all times to conduct themselves in a proper and orderly manner."

The Rev. Mr. Parsons opened the South school with prayer and good advice to the boys. The master of the North school was John Vinal from Boston; he was succeeded by John Mycall, I. Hills, R. Long, T. Thompson, Enoch Titcomb, Henry Titcomb, Wm. Sawyer, Wm. Farnham, Archibald McPhail, Henry Titcomb and Jonathan Coolidge.

Master Stephen Sewell was the first teacher at the South school; he continued to teach until his powers having become impaired by age, Bishop Norton was appointed usher; he succeeded Master Sewell, retaining the school until 1790. He was followed by Joseph Moody, Joseph Newman, Robert Long, Samuel Goodhue, Ben. Cheever, Ben. Whitmore, George Titcomb and Newman Brown. This school in 1822 was in the new school-house standing on the site of the old one. In 1796 the writing schools were so full, a centre school was formed in the room vacated by the grammar school, in the old town house, where it remained until 1609, when the second story was added to the school-house at the lower end of the mall, and the school removed to it. The masters in the centre school were Samuel Toppan, Paul Noyes, Benjamin Clanin, James Burnham, Samuèl Colman, Benjamin Gould, Asa W. Wildes, George Titcomb, Benjamin Whitmore and S. Goodhue.

In 1805 the "north end" petitioned for a school-house. A school had been organized, which was for a while taught in the upper loft of a barn belonging to Capt. Morrison on Kent street. The brick school-house was built, which stood upon Kent, corner of Russia street. The masters of this school were William Pipkin, Robert Harvey, Daniel Haskell, George Rogers, Rev. H. Wheeler, Nathan Brown, Josiah Bartlett and George Titcomb.

Master Robert Harvey was also clerk at St. Paul's Episcopal church. He was an excellent teacher, and a most efficient church officer, much beloved and respected by the rector and the society. Previous to this date, tin foot-stoves, holding within an iron pan filled with hard wood coals, had been the only protection from cold in any house of worship, but about the time of Master Harvey's appointment to the office of clerk, a large, cast iron stove had been placed in the broad aisle of St. Paul's church. One cold morning, finding that the wood fire did not give the requisite heat, as uncle Nat Bailey, the sexton, was ringing the bell, Clerk Harvey proceeded to fix it. In so doing he smutted his hand, which inadvertently was passed over his face, smearing it most ludicrously. As was then the custom, at the appointed time the clerk rose in his desk, and with his usual grave dignity gave out the hymn, the first line of which most singularly read,—

"Behold the beauties of my face."

The effect was irresistible, and a suppressed smile spread over the congregation, while the unconscious clerk calmly finished the verse.

Master George Titcomb was an excellent penman. During the winter he usually taught a private evening writing school. He was also noted for making the quill pens then wholly used.

There was no public school for females until 1790; then four "dames'" schools were gathered for girls between five and nine years, in which were taught reading, spelling the catechism, sewing, knitting, "good manners and proper decency of behavior." These "dames" were Ann Bradish, Elisabeth Chandler, Anne Obin and Margery Rosseau. In 1792 the daughters of those paying a tax of over three hundred pounds, were permitted to attend the grammar school, an hour and a half after the usual session during the summer, when the number of male pupils was diminished, to receive instruction in reading and grammar from the masters. This arrangement not proving satisfactory, was discontinued at the end of the season.

In 1791 two schools for the instruction of small boys were organized. In 1804 four morning schools were established for girls, which were kept from six to eight o'clock, and Thursday afternoons, for six months in the year. Notwithstanding the early hour these schools were well attended. They were taught by the masters of the boys' schools in the four school-houses of the town.

In 1812 these morning schools were discontinued, and three grammar schools for girls were established. One was located in the Court House, the "north end" school was taught in the second story of the school-house on Kent street, and the third was on Beck street. The teachers were Miss Chadbourne, Miss S. I. Moulton and Miss Clarissa Call. Private schools were extensively patronized. Those for young children were usually taught by middle aged or elderly women, in cap and spectacles. There were Dame Moody, Marm Emerson, Marm Fowler at Belleville, and others. Distinguished private schools for both sexes were taught by gentlemen. Several of the teachers of the public schools, at times taught private schools. Master Long kept in a low, ropewalk-like building, a rude structure, with an immense fire place, and a wall from which large patches of plastering had been detached, while the remainder was in a cracked and shaky condition. Though at that time a teacher considered it necessary never to neglect the axiom "spare the rod and spoil the child," even then Master Long was noted for severity. "Oh my! how he did lick the boys!" was the exclamation of a former pupil, as she recalled her school days. Master Walsh had a flourishing private school, in a school-house back of the church on Harris street. Master Archibald McPhail, for a time, taught a very select and genteel school, in a long, low, wooden building on Green street, on the lot where the Catholic church now stands. Later Master Titcomb taught in this building a private school for boys. There was also a number of select schools for young ladies in the town. In my childhood Marm Dod and Miss Phillipa Call were famed instructresses. Mrs. Catharine Wigglesworth Brown, the widowed daughter of Col. Wigglesworth, had a large and genteel school for several years in Newburyport: afterwards she was the Principal of a flourishing seminary in Georgetown, D. C. Miss Akerman, Mrs. McCulloch, Miss Susan Tenney, Miss Elisabeth White and Miss Stanwood, had private schools for Misses. Dr. Samuel Colman, for a time, taught a private school for young ladies, in a room over the "Herald" office. After his decease this school was continued by his daughter Mary Ann, at her mother's residence on Water street. Miss Brice, an English woman, taught in the old "Tabernacle," Temple street. This lady and her negro maid servant were conspicuous characters at that period.

At each of the female schools, in addition to knitting and plain sewing, ornamental needlework was taught, and in some, instruction was given in drawing in India ink and painting in water colors; also, every girl was taught to embroider letters in marking stitch. One was considered very poorly educated who could not exhibit a sampler; some of these were large and elaborate specimens of handiwork; framed and glazed, they often formed the chief ornament of the sitting room or the best chamber. When they merely comprised the alphabet, in the variously designed letters of printing and writing, finished by a verse of poetry, or a text from Scripture, the whole enclosed by an ornamental border, they were quite pretty specimens of needle work; but sometimes, when more ambitious attempts were exhibited, they were sufficiently grotesque. I have seen wrought under the letters, a square, three-storied house flanked by a pot of flowers, the pot, and what was intended for a rose bush, as tall as the house, with a horse on the other side twice as large as either. Pocket-books and cushions worked in crewel, had given place to wrought muslin, and pictures worked on satin. Mourning pieces were in vogue, though some preferred scriptural or classical subjects. One could conscientiously pronounce these productions remarkable specimens of art. The needlework was usually very neatly executed, but the false perspective and queerly drawn figures, rendered most of them "simply ridiculous." Miss Dod had some handsome copies of the pictures of the Washington family executed in her school, and Mrs. Katy Brown's school was distinguished for the pictures executed by its pupils. Sophronia Peabody, of this school, embroidered a mourning piece, a memorial to her sister Fila, who died in her fifth year. In the foreground, on a green mound stood a white monument surmounted by an urn; the front of the pillar bore the name and age of the deceased; above drooped a luxuriant weeping willow: beside the tomb knelt a lady, clad in the height of French fashion, very properly drying her tears on a large handkerchief in the right hand; beyond stretched a bit of landscape, put in by Mrs Brown in colored chalks, which showed that the lady had a fine talent for landscape painting. The parting of Hector and Andromache was a favorite picture amongst the girls of Mrs. Brown's school. The couple were represented in a final embrace on the portico of a palace. Massive pillars supported the roof; the floor was of alternate squares of black and white, representing marble. A little apart stood the nurse bearing the infant heir in her arms, while the back ground showed a a plain dotted by tents. Coats of arms were also embroidered on white satin with colored silk. These pictures were tastefully framed by Mrs. Moses Cole. Miss Peabody's was framed in gilt, in an oval of enamel, with gold stars in the corner.

Miss Mary Ann Colman was a good teacher of water color painting; the fruit and flower pieces executed at her school were natural and well done. She also taught painting on wood; several work-boxes and work-stands, painted under her instruction, are still to be seen in the residences of some of our older citizens.

Besides these schools there were several noted academies in the vicinity. As a boarding-school "finish" was considered requisite to complete a genteel education, these became flourishing institutions. The academy at Atkinson, N. H., was one of the first established in New England; that at Bradford had been founded several years. The Lynn academy was at that time a noted school. When Miss Peabody was fifteen, it was decided that she should receive the benefit of an academic course. My aunt, who was piously inclined, would have preferred Bradford, but as Mr. Leonard Smith's youngest daughter, Sophia, and the daughters of several of Gen. Peabody's Boston friends were at Lynn academy, the general and his daughter inclined to that seminary; as the gentleman that year represented the town in the State legislature, and it was convenient for Fronie to accompany her father on his way to and from Boston, Mondays and Saturdays, Lynn received the preference.

In 1807 the Newburyport academy was incorporated. Gen. Peabody was active in this measure, and he was so much pleased with Mrs. Boardman, the preceptress of the Lynn academy, that through his endeavors she was secured for the new academy at Newburyport. Mr. Amos Clark was the first preceptor, assisted by Mr. Archibald McPhail. Mr. Chandler succeeded Mr. Clark, assisted by Mr. Adams. Mr. and Mrs. Alfred Pike were preceptor and preceptress of this institution for several years. Later, Mr. Eben Bailey, son of Mr. Paul Bailey of West Newbury, taught a large private school in Newburyport. Mrs. Lord was the principal of an excellent school at the academy. Her pupils executed many fine paintings in water colors; some of their paintings of fruit and flowers on white velvet were very beautiful. This lady's marriage with Dr. Richard S. Spofford, was regarded by her pupils and the public as a loss to which they could scarcely have been reconciled, had they not rejoiced in the prospect of her happiness and usefulness amongst them in a different sphere.

Master Cheever and Master Whitmore for many years were noted teachers in Newbury.

The first Sabbath school in Massachusetts was organized in Newburyport in 1814. These schools were held in the chapel of the North church, a small wooden building on Titcomb street, and that of the Old South church, a dingy brick edifice on the upper side of Beck street. The school at the North was formed by Miss Phebe Harrod, Miss Louiza Farnham, who married the Rev. Dr. Orville Dewey, and Miss Eliza Epps Carter, who became the wife of the Rev. David Kimball, of Rockford, Ill. That at the Old South, was under the direction of Miss Ann Wheelwright, who first married Mr. Samuel Adams of the Newburyport Academy, second her cousin John Wheelwright, Miss Dolly Greenleaf, afterward Mrs. Pearson of Portland, Maine, and Miss Eliza Gould, who became Mrs. Rappello of New York city. Four of these ladies, Miss Harrod, Mrs. Dewey, Mrs. Kimball and Mrs. Rapello, are still living in the enjoyment of a hale old age.

In 1817 a union school from each of the societies in the town was organized at the Court House.

Mr. John Pearson was the first superintendent, he was succeeded by Mr. Samuel Tenney and William B. Bannister, esq. This continued a year or two, then the different societies formed a school for themselves as at present, but for a time an annual union service was held in Parson Milton's meeting-house, the children with their teachers occupying the wide galleries of the spacious building. A union teachers' meeting was also continued for some time.

Miss Mary Hodge was one of the most active and efficient amongst the first Sabbath school teachers.

CHAPTER XLIII.

At an early date, the colonists of Newbury commenced the construction of water craft. The first vessels designed for fishing and the coasting trade were built on the river Parker. As the settlement increased, the waterside people became largely engaged in shipbuilding; many vessels, as I have previously stated, being built for English owners. The first ferry across the Merrimac was at Carr's Island, and one of the first building yards was established there by Mr. George Carr. I have stated that my great-grandfather Johnson's father had a shipyard as early as 1695, near the bottom of Chandler's lane, now Federal street, and the business was continued in the Johnson family for two or three generations. In 1759 Mr. Gideon Woodwell owned a yard near the foot of Muzzey's lane, now Marlborough street, and as early as 1730, Mr. Samuel Moggaridge had a dwelling house and building yard at the rocky point farther up the river, afterwards known as Moggaridge's point. At that time Mr. Ralph Cross was a prominent builder, and Mr. William Gerrish had an extensive yard reaching from South, now Bromfield street, to Somerby's court, and from the river back to Hancock street. Ship yards were scattered along the river bank from Pierce's farm to Moggaridge's point. In the summer of 1766 seventy-two vessels were upon the stocks, all in process of construction. During the Revolution many privateers were built in Newbury and Newburyport. At the close of the war, ship building again became active, but the ships of those days were small, none exceeding two to three hundred tons burthen. About 1790 Mr. Elias Jackman established a shipyard near the Chain bridge. This bridge, built under the supervision of Mr. Timothy Palmer, was opened to the public November 26, 1792. About this time Mr. Orlando B. Merrill established himself in ship building at Bellevilleport. Mr. Merrill was the inventor of the water-line model. Previous, only skeleton models had been used. There were several other prominent ship builders at the "Shipyards;" Mr. Elias Briggs sent forth a large number of vessels, and the yards of Messrs. Stephen and Benjamin Dalton, Joseph Coffin, and Messrs. Jonathan and Thomas Merrill, from year to year resounded with the cheery sounds of industry.

I have stated that Major Ephraim Emery married Miss Mary, daughter of Mr. Peter Russell of Bradford, who was a distinguished shipbuilder. Their oldest daughter, Mary Emery, married Capt. John Remick. This gentleman was engaged in ship building as a master carpenter during his life. In his latter years Maj. Emery resided with his daughter and son-in-law at their residence in Bellevilleport, and there the old revolutionary hero, who for several years had patiently borne the affliction of blindness, breathed his last in 1825, aged 67.

At the south end, Mr. Gideon Woodwell had been succeeded by his son, Capt. John Woodwell, who carried on an extensive business at this period. Immediately preceding the great fire of 1811, many small craft and boats were built at the south end.

CHAPTER XLIV.

Though the European troubles had impeded commerce, Newburyport was as prosperous as her sister seaports. Her foreign, West India and coasting trade, combined with the country traffic, caused the wharves and business streets to wear the aspect of a thriving mart.

The first wharf at the "water side" was built in 1656, near the site of the present Market house, by Mr. Paul White, along with a dock, warehouse and stillhouse. In 1678, Marchant (Richard) Dole procured the grant of land lying near "Watts his cellar," where he built a wharf and dock. "Watts his cellar" was also in what is now Market square. In 1680 the town granted liberty to Ensign Stephen Greenleaf and Mr. Daniel Davidson to build a wharf at the point of rocks above "Watts his cellar." The same year Nathaniel Clark obtained a portion of the flats, upon which to build a wharf. The town also voted to grant the petition of Benjamin Rolfe, Doctor John Dole, and Richard Dole, for four or five rods on the flats, from Watt's cellar spring to Ensign Greenleaf's, for a place to build a wharf. Robert Coker, in the behalf of his son, Benjamin Coker, proposed for a place to make a wharf. Year after year other wharves were added down the river until a continuous line stretched from the ship yards to Joppa.

In the year 1811 the first was Pillsbury's wharf at the foot of North, now Oakland street. The second was Sevier's, near the foot of Broad street. The distillery of William and Abraham Williams stood near the head of this wharf, just below the residence built by Capt. Sevier, afterwards purchased by Joseph Williams, jr., from which the wharf was known by the name of the Williams wharf. Richard's and Caldwell's wharves came next. Below was that of Major Samuel Coffin. This wharf ran out into deep water; upon it was another large distillery, and twenty sail of vessel could be seen there at a time, discharging cargoes of molasses from the West Indies. Horton's and Newman's wharves ranged below. Moses Brown's was at the foot of Green street. Here was a third distillery, and this was the focus of Mr. Brown's extensive business. Titcomb's wharf came next; then, Greenleaf's, Ferry, Boardman's, O'Brien's, Jackson's, Jewett's, Atwood's, Carter's, Marquand's, Hudson's, and Davenport's. Below was Lunt's mast yard; then came Haskell's, Bartlet's, Johnson's and Coombs' wharves. The lower wharf was owned by Maj. David Coffin, who was then one of the most thriving merchants.

At that time every vessel placed upon the stocks was wholly completed and equipped for sea before it sailed over the bar. This brought a multiplicity of business to the town. Along the wharves stretched lofty warehouses crowded with merchandise. Carts and drays rattled up and down, incoming and outgoing vessels came and went, the merry songs and "heave ho's" of the sailors, blended with the cheery tones and hearty jests of the stevedores, carts from the interior unloaded and loaded — at every turn was bustle, industry and activity. Here were the spacious sail and rigging lofts, pump and block makers' shops, and ship chandlers stores, every thing that pertained to maritime trade. Mr. Joshua Norton, Joseph Stanwood and the Messrs. Davis and Haynes, had large sail lofts; Thomas Prichard a rigging loft on Ferry wharf; Enoch Toppan a block maker's shop on Carter's wharf. Maj. Joshua Greenleaf did most of the ship iron work at his large smithy on Liberty street. Mr. Gordon had a similar establishment at Bellevilleport. This gentleman was somewhat economical in his household. At that period cheese was a customary appendage of the dinner table, being considered an accessory to digestion. Mr. Gordon employed several workmen. One day a large cheese was placed on the table; after the meat had been disposed of, Mr. Gordon took a knife to cut the cheese; turning it over, he exclaimed, "this is a good cheese, a pretty cheese, too good to spoil!" and laying down the knife, he rose and called his men to their work. That afternoon a large anchor was to be forged, the fire was kindled, the iron heated.

"That is a good heat!" exultantly exclaimed the master.

"A good heat," with one voice responded the men.

"A grand heat," reiterated the master.

"A grand heat," again responded the men.

"Then why don't you strike?" impatiently demanded the master.

"It is a good heat?" queried the foreman.

"Yes, yes, strike, strike I tell ye," hurriedly ordered the master in a quick authoritative tone. "Strike, strike."

"Don't you think it is too good a heat to spoil?" quietly returned the foreman, while not an arm was uplifted.

The hint was taken; the cheese brought with a loaf of brown bread. The luncheon eaten and well washed down with grog, the anchor was forged with a will. Mr. Kenniston had then just set up his forge at the shipyards. Sargent's gunsmith shop was on Water street, and Mr. Joseph George did an extensive blacksmith's business at his stand on Inn street. Mr. Robert Dodge had a smithy on High street for carriage work. Carriage building, which for many years had been a thriving business on the main road, had just been introduced at Belleville.

In 1785, before Washington street was laid out, Mr. John Tracy had a rope-walk running from the Quaker burying ground to the river. A Mr. Crocker at an early date built a rope-walk on State street, running from where the Whitefield church now stands towards Fair street. He afterwards built another near Frog pond, which subsequently became the property of a Mr. Cummings. When the Newburyport turnpike was built it was laid out directly through this walk, which consequently was removed. Mr. Cummings in company with a Mr. Akerman afterwards did business in a walk running from South, now Bromfield, to Marlborough streets. Abel Greenleaf had a walk which ran from State street, where stands the store of Capt. John Buntin, to Green street. E. Swett built a walk which extended from Fair to Federal, opposite Charter street; this afterwards was purchased by Nathaniel Tracy; and Mr. Swett built another running from Federal to Lime streets. Moses Kent built one from Federal to Fair street, where Orange street now is; this was moved to the south side of Federal street, where it became the property of Edward Wigglesworth; afterwards it was purchased by Robert Gardner and moved to South street, where, in company with a Mr. Laskey, a large business was done at the time of the great fire. Messrs. Eleazer Johnson, and Young and Pettingell had walks extending from South to Marlborough streets. Andrew Laskey had a walk on Milk street which ran to Water street. Mr. Green Pearson one from Washington to Water street; this was I think the walk built by Mr. John Tracy. Edward Wigglesworth built one which ran from Lime to South street above Newbury; this was sold to Eleazer Johnson, moved south of South street, and afterwards owned by Andrew Laskey, and finally by Mr. George Donnell, who is still living, 1880, the oldest man in the city. E. & I. Swett built a walk south of Marlborough street. The Gardner rope-walk was afterwards owned by David Evans, whose sons went into the cordage business in other towns. Near that Deacon Amos Pettingell built a walk which later was owned by Pettingell and Donnell. Eleazer Johnson built another near the last named which was afterwards owned by Mr. Wormstead and son.

Below, in Newbury, skirting the river and round "Flat-iron point," was an irregular collection of small low houses, forming the fishing hamlet of Joppa. Here in the season the river bank would often be lined with wherries which had just been brought in loaded with fish, which the sun-burned, bare-footed women, in brown homespun short gown and petticoat tucked to the knee, with the older children, aided the toil-worn fishermen to carry to the great fish-flakes on the uplands below the long rope-walks. Round the open doors toddled wee, white-haired urchins, while others sailed ships and mimic boats in the pools and eddies of the flats.

Beside the distilleries I have mentioned, Mr. Joseph Williams had a large establishment at the foot of Strong street, and Caldwell's on Merrimac street was even then noted, for its rum, anise and other cordials. Mr. John Berry Titcomb had a bakery and flour store back of the North church. and Mr. Gunnison carried on an extensive business on Titcomb street. Pulaski Woodman had a bake-house near the head of Market street, and Messrs. Theodore and John Pearson's bakeries were on Centre street. Mr. Samuel Wheeler had a bake-house and store on the same street, and Ebenezer Pearson one on Middle street.

On the site of the present Market house was a row of low, open butcher's shambles, occupied by Mr. David Tenney, Jeremiah Colman and David Emery, these two doing business as the firm of Colman & Emery. In addition a number of butcher's carts came in two or three times a week from adjacent towns. These after supplying their customers, occupied a stand in Market square. Previous to the demolition of the meeting-house, it was their custom to range back of that building with other country traders, a row of oat troughs having been nailed to the sacred edifice for the purpose of baiting horses. The chief of these out of town butchers at that time were Mr. John Follansbee and his son John, and Mr. Samuel Bailey from the upper parish in Newbury, and Mr. Williams from the lower parish; Mr. Clements, Mr. Kendrick, and Capt. Sawyer from Amesbury. Mr. John Dodge had a large soap and candle manufactory near Market square. At the north end were the wool pulling and leather dressing establishment of Messrs. Butler Abbott and Henry Merrill. Above were two large tanneries owned by Mr. John Balch and Mr. Eben Savory, each of whom carried on an extensive business.

CHAPTER XLV.

The town had been greatly improved in the past ten or fifteen years; new streets had been laid out and graded, and many fine stores and dwellings erected. State street as a whole presented a view of two-storied wooden buildings, mostly painted pale yellow, with green blinds or shutters. Interspersed were lofty brick blocks and edifices, and on the lower side adjoining Water street was a row of old, unpainted buildings, remnants of the more ancient town. On the upper side of the street, the first house from High was an old fashioned one with a long, sloping back roof. Here lived "Scrabble" Titcomb. How he obtained this sobriquet I am unable to say. Next were the new and palatial residences of Mr. Joshua Carter and Gen. John Peabody. On the opposite corner of Harris street lived Master Pike, in a large, substantial house; then came the Tracy mansion, at that time occupied by Jacob Coburn as a hotel. The next was an old wooden structure, occupied by the widow Wood; the next belonged to Mrs. Burt; Mrs. Searle also occupied it as a dwelling, and shop for dry goods and millinery. Below was the old Wyatt house then occupied by Mr. Ebenezer Stedman. On the upper corner of Pleasant street stood Dr. Micajah Sawyer's handsome residence; on the other corner the year previous a large three-story wooden block had been built. Here Cornhill commenced; before the street had been graded this was quite an eminence, high and warm land; for years it was planted with corn, and thus obtained its name. The corner store in the block was occupied by Arthur Gilman for dry goods; then came those of Paul Noyes, John Porter, Pierce & Gordon, Moses Kimball, jr., Francis Somerby, and William Hoyt. William Francis had a hair dressing shop at the lower end. The upper rooms were let to Joseph T. Pike and Paul Bishop, tailors; James Hodge, shoemaker; and the law offices of Edward St. Loe Livermore, Little & Bannister, and John Stuart. Next, on the lower corner of "Thread-needle alley," came the "Wolfe Tavern," a two-story, wooden building, somewhat dingy with age; before the principal entrance, which was reached by a flight of steps from the sidewalk, from a tall post swung the sign, a likeness of Gen. Wolfe; from this sign the house derived its name. This was also the "Eastern Stage Company's" house; to and from its doors rattled the gaudily painted stage coaches, and in the rear its numerous fine horses were stabled. This house for many years had been kept by Moses Davenport, but latterly it had passed into the hands of Mr. Prince Stetson. Below the "Wolfe Tavern" was the "Phœnix Building," an imposing four-storied brick structure, a fine specimen of architecture, with handsome copings, and between the upper windows, arched niches ornamented with statues. Here was the custom house, Ralph Cross, collector; the post office, Caleb Cross, post master; the office of the Phœnix Insurance Company; the remainder of the lower floor was improved by Philip Bagley and son, auctioneers, and Joseph Jackman, dry goods. Prince Stetson had hired the chambers as additional sleeping rooms to his hotel; the fourth story was "Madison hall." Below the Phœnix came Blunt's building, a second large four-storied brick block; the stores were occupied by Joseph Hooper, crockery, Joseph Coolidge and Moses Osgood, dry goods: Howard S. Robinson improved part of the chambers as a dwelling, the others were rented to Charles Norris & Co. for a printing office, and David Fairman, an engraver. Next came Peabody's corner, three stores; here Samuel Stevens had a hardware store, John Chickering one for dry goods, and Thomas C. Whipple a book store; above, in the chambers, were the Newburyport library, and Benjamin Lord, tailor.

The first building on the lower corner of State street, from High street, was the handsome brick house built by John Berry Titcomb. Next came the elegant Dalton establishment, then owned and occupied by Moses Brown. Dr. Andrews, pastor of the First church, resided in the third house; next came those of Mrs. Carr, and Jonathan Marsh, esq. The Balch place came to the corner of Temple street. Col. Stephen Bartlett's house was on the lower corner; then came the Moulton house, and that of David Wood. Below was the bank building, Newburyport Bank, William Bartlet, president, and Samuel Mulliken, cashier; the remainder of the building being occupied by Mrs. Bodily as a boarding house. The next lot, extending to Essex street. had been occupied by the Town hall. In 1809, Gen. John Peabody offered to erect a handsome three-story brick block on this site, the upper story of which he would furnish as a hall for the town, to be known as the "Town hall," with whatever rooms should be desired for public use in the other stories, if the town would convey to him the old town-house and the land upon which it stood. The town accepted this proposal, and the present block was erected. The "Town hall" was finished and furnished in the best style. The names of the States were painted above the windows, with other appropriate decorations. In the second story was a room for the selectmen, and the watch-house was in the L on Essex street. The first three stores were occupied by James Caldwell, Prescott Spalding, and David Peabody & Co., for dry goods; below was the book and chart store of Ebenezer Stedman, sign of the golden ball; the store on the corner of Essex street was rented by Solomon Davis, for dry goods, and the upper rooms were occupied by Sam'l L. Knapp and other lawyers and persons, as offices. On the lower corner of Essex street was Stephen Greeley's shoe store. Next came the old Clement house. Here, when I was a child, a man walked across State street on a tight rope, stretched from one of its chimneys to that of the "Wolfe Tavern," an event which made no little sensation in the staid town. Below were Osgood & Brackett, shoe makers; John Knowlton, cabinet maker; Jonathan Woodman, jr., silversmith; Morrill's boarding house; Barber Newman's shop; Ebenezer Dole's variety store, and Daniel N. Dole, silversmith. In the chamber above this store Obadiah Pearson worked at tailoring. The two last stores were those of Gilman White, crockery and glass, and Moses Cole. painter and gilder.

George Little, the first of that name in Newbury, had two sons, who married two daughters of Tristram Coffin. Capt. Joseph married Mary, and Moses Lydia. Each of these had a son named Tristram. One of these Tristram Littles owned the property from Market square to Fair street, between Liberty and Water streets. On his estate he built a princely mansion, which at this time stood a little back from State street. Though hoary with age, it still retained much of its ancient elegance, and was the home of two bachelor brothers, Michael and Hazen Little, descendants of Tristram Little. Tristram (son of Capt. Joseph Little) married Anna, daughter of Stephen Emery. Their oldest child, Mary Little, married Capt. Michael Dalton, whose son, Tristram Dalton, was born in Newburyport, May 28, 1738, and graduated at Harvard University at the early age of seventeen. He studied law as an accomplishment, the fortune which he inherited from his father not requiring him to practice it as a profession. His wife was Ruth, eldest daughter of Robert Hooper, of Marblehead. Mr. Dalton took a deep interest in agriculture and horticulture, which was shown in the extensive garden of his residence on State street, and his estate on Pipestave hill, West Newbury. His was a most hospitable mansion; his town and country houses were honored by the presence of the distinguished of our own and foreign lands as guests. As eminent for piety as he was for mental endowments, St. Paul's church, of which he was a warden, shared in his generous liberality. He was a representative, speaker of the House of Representatives, and a senator in the legislature of Massachusetts, and a senator of the United States in the first congress after the adoption of the federal constitution. When Washington City was founded, Mr. Dalton invested his entire fortune in lands there, and lost it by the mismanagement of a business agent. At the same time a vessel, which was freighted with his furniture and valuable library, was lost on the way from Newburyport to Washington, and he thus found himself, after living sixty years in affluence, penniless. Several offices of profit and honor were immediately tendered to him by the government, and he accepted the surveyorship of Boston. He died in Boston, May 30, 1817, and his remains were taken to Newburyport, where they were interred in the burial ground of St. Paul's church.

Round the corner of Middle street was James Kimball's grocery store, Whittingham and John Gilman's book store, and Nathan Ames, shoemaker. Above was the Herald office, Ephraim Allen, editor and printer; beyond was the dwelling and milliner's shop of Mrs. Jones. Thomas Dodge's house and joiner shop, Hannah Bradbury's house and milliner shop, and the dwelling house of Nancy and Eliza Batchelder, milliners. On this street were the cabinet and chair making shops of Clark Morss, Elijah Bliss, Southy Parker, Daniel Abbott, E. Dole, G. Parker, and S. Dole; and the groceries of E. Dole, P. Tenney and P. Thurlo. On Market square were Samuel Thompson, tobacconist, Joseph Lesley's cooper shop, Edward Rand's dwelling house and hardware store, Daniel Smith and Aaron Davis, apothecaries, Enoch Plummer, Ephraim Titcomb and Moses Moody, groceries; Anthony Smith kept hardware and groceries, and Perkins & Dean kept two stores for hardware. Here were John M. O'Brien's attorney's office, and Daniel Balch's shop for watch making; James Locke's, Edward Toppan, jr's., James Kimball's, Francis Todd's, and Samuel Foster's dry goods stores; Edward Little & Co's book store: over this store was Enoch Pike's tailoring establishment. The office of the Union Insurance Company, Stephen Holland, president, and the residence of Dr. Bradstreet, were on the square, with Thomas Hale's hatter's shop and two ship chandlery stores belonging to Abner Wood and Major Joshua Greenleaf. On Liberty street were the residences of Major Joshua Greenleaf, Ephraim Allen, and the old Emerson house. Below the market, on Water street, were John Wood's warehouse at the head of Ferry wharf, and the groceries of Daniel Burnham, William Bayley, Joseph Edwards, Benjamin G. Sweetser, Moses Sweet, Moses Clark, and Widow Greenleaf: William Boardman kept hardware, groceries, paints, etc. Next to Mr. Bayley's grocery was Billy Watkins' property: two houses and stores, with two back stores. This Billy Watkins, an eccentric old bachelor, was one of the notorieties of the town. Below was Humphrey Cook's hatter's shop, and that of Thomas Lord; David Moody and Thomas Moody had malt houses, Mrs. Richardson a milliner's shop, Joseph O'Brien's house and store, the Harrod house, and Joseph Brown, auctioneer. John Hart's tavern, Benjamin Appleton's hatter's shop, Marm Seward's boarding house, a boarding house kept by Hannah Prime, Joseph Toppan's house and dry goods store, Stephen Gerrish & Son's house and dry goods store, John Greenough, hatter, Clement Star, house and shop, T. & A. Wheeler, grocery and boarding house, Benjamin H. Toppan, coppersmith, Timothy T. Ford's house and dry goods store, and Capt. Dunlap's house and shop. At the head of Marquand's wharf was the residence of Joseph Marquand, a spacious and handsome mansion; several of the neighboring buildings were his property, and below on the wharf his six spacious warehouses.

Mr. Abraham Jackson's place of business was on the corner of Centre street, and he had two large warehouses on his wharf. Mr. Joseph Moulton and his son William, had a large jeweller's and silversmith's shop on Broadway. Mr. David Wood made clocks, in a shop which was one of the front rooms of his dwelling house on State street. It was common to convert the front room of a house into a shop. Most of the smaller groceries and variety stores were kept in this way. A door led from the shop into the living rooms of the family; thus the mistress of the domicile could tend the shop, while attending to her household duties. Mr. Wood's clocks were the tall, mahogany-cased time-keepers then fashionable. The dial, in addition to the usual face, was furnished with a second hand; some told the day of the month, the maker's name being inserted in the centre, below a bouquet of roses. These clocks were in great demand, scarcely a house was without them in all the region about. Mr. Samuel T. DeFord and Charles L. Emerson carried on a large business in hats and furs on Merrimac street. Mr. Porter Russell Messrs. Edward and Abner Toppan did a large business in the manufacture and sale of furniture. Mr. Abner Toppan had a two story shop contiguous to his house on High street. Mr. Stephen Toppan on Toppan's lane was a distinguished architect and builder. Mr. Timothy Palmer was celebrated, not only as an architect and carpenter, but as a bridge builder; several of the best bridges in the country were from his designs. Miss Mary Jenkins' millinery establishment was in her house on Water, corner of Market street. Green and Harris streets were now lined with handsome houses, most of which had been built since my recollection. The first house on the lower side of Green from High street was built by Mr. Potter, who carried on a thriving business at cabinet making. The next was Mr. Tom. Clarke's. The house on the corner of Green and Harris, and the next on the upper side of Harris street, Mr. Leonard Smith built for his two sons, John and William, and here they had recently installed their brides. John married Mary, daughter of Jonathan G. Parsons, and great-granddaughter of Rev. Jonathan Parsons, and William, Miss Mary, second daughter of Mr. Abraham Jackson. On the corner opposite stood the residence of Mr. Allen Dodge. Col. John Greenleaf's came next, then Mr. Israel Young's. That of Jonathan Gage, esq., was on the upper corner of Pleasant street, and Robert Laird's house and brewery were on the one opposite. Below the brewery came the Washington Hall building. A two-story wooden edifice, the hall in the second story, dwellings and a school room below. On the corner of Water street stood the General Titcomb house, one of the old and splendid colonial mansions now somewhat lapsed into decay and let as a tenement house. The first house on the upper side from Brown's square was built by Judge Bradbury. After he left the town it was purchased by Capt. Robert Jenkins. Mr. Joseph Cutler built the house above, but at this time it was owned and occupied by Mr. Abraham Jackson. This gentleman, a descendant from an English family of note, was for some years one of our first merchants. Mr. Jackson twice married. The first wife was Mary Mitchell, of Boston, the mother of one son, Nathaniel, and two daughters, Ann and Mary; the second, Hannah Parsons, granddaughter of Rev. Jonathan Parsons, also had one son and two daughters, Isaac Rand, Ellen and Charlotte. Miss Ann long ranked among the brilliant stars of society, possessing a vivid imagination and much theatrical talent. One who ever listened to her thrilling tales, would never forget her descriptive ability, or her tragic powers.

Mary, Mrs. William Smith, was one of the most attractive of women, possessing rare attainments. After her husband's death she established a flourishing seminary at Alexandria, D. C., where she drew around her the daughters of some of the most distinguished families in the country; her house became the centre for the best society in the "District;" the names of the greatest statesmen of the period, and many eminent foreigners were enrolled among her personal friends.

Ellen married Admiral George Frederick Pearson, U. S. Navy. A vivacious and cultivated lady, Mrs. Pearson adorned the elevated position to which she was called, winning the esteem of those with whom she became connected. Isaac Rand Jackson died young. At the time of his death he was Charge de Affairs from United States to Denmark. He married Louisa Carroll, granddaughter of Charles Carroll of Carrollton.

Previous to the purchase of the house

on Green street, Mr. Jackson's residence was on Water street, near that of Joseph Marquand. When the oldest son, Nathaniel, was eighteen, Mr. Marquand being a representative at the General Court in Boston, young Jackson passed the night at his neighbor's. Before retiring, Mrs. Marquand would order a large armful of wood and some half dozen mould candles, then bid the young man good night, with the remark: "Now, Nat, read just as long as you please."

In the Revolutionary war one of Mr. Marquand's prizes contained a library, the property of the Governor-General of Canada, which that dignitary had forwarded to England preparatory to following himself. Naturally a devourer of books, this large collection of the best authors was a rare treat, and night after night the visitor, forgetting time. pored over the pages, which often were of the old fashioned brownish paper, and fine type, until his eyesight entirely failed. This weakness of the eyes, changed his whole career. He left his father's counting room, and, as supercargo, entered upon a life on the "ocean wave." For years foreign lands and tongues were more familiar than his own. He became an apt business man, a distinguished linguist, a remarkably well informed and most accomplished gentleman. His knowledge of Spanish was such that in the war of 1812, while sailing under Spanish colors, he was kept three days on board of a British man-of-war without disclosing his nationality, though every artifice was used to catch him off his guard. On the third day he was permitted to return to his ship, which proceeded on its course. Some time after having been captured, Mr. Jackson, when on parole in London, met an officer of the vessel in which he had been detained. This Lieutenant had striven by every device to startle young Jackson into some unguarded exclamation, but without avail. Instantly recognizing the pseudo Spaniard, he gave his hand with a cordial greeting, exclaiming "I knew you was a Yankee all the time, who ever saw a blue-eyed Spaniard? But you was such a deuce of a clever fellow we could not detain you."

Mr. Jackson married, in Gottenburg, Miss Johanna Tod, a lady of Swedish birth, but of Scottish parentage. His eyes having regained their strength he ceased his wanderings. At his house in Newburyport he often entertained distinguished foreigners. Bishop Cheverеaux, on his visits to the place, never left without calling to enjoy a chat in his native tongue; later several young men from the Spanish West India islands availed themselves of his instruction in learning English. The tidings that Nat. Jackson had contracted a marriage abroad made no small stir amongst the belles of Newburyport, but time showed the wisdom of his choice. Lovely, devoted, well did Mrs. Jackson fulfil the vow to love and cherish for better for worse, for richer for poorer, in sickness and in health. The friend and companion, as well as the watchful and judicious mother of her children, a kind neighbor and faithful friend, none knew her but to love her. To the choice circle admitted to her intimacy, she became dear as a sister, and the youthful companions of her sons and daughters, will ever cherish the memory of one, who, by her grace and urbanity, her sympathetic interest in their joys and griefs, her many little devices for their entertainment and amusement, made so many sunny hours, which will ever gleam undimmed amidst the recollections of the past.

Capt. and Mrs. Jackson reared a gifted family of four sons and three daughters. The second daughter married Capt. Joseph C. Hoyt, one of the most successful ship masters of Newburyport, who died on the 5th of June, 1880. Andrew, the second son, died in boyhood. Thomas the eldest, and Cornelius Souchay, the youngest, settled in St. Louis, where both died, the former in middle life, the latter in early manhood. Highly beloved and respected, a large circle, both at the east and west, mourn their early death. To the versatility of talent, hereditary in the family, to Souchay was given a fine artistic genius, a Hogarthian power to portray, with lifelike vividness, as if by magic, the persons and scenes around him, slight pencil sketches, but these depict a power that needed only practice, to have placed him amongst the most eminent of world-renowned artists. Nathaniel, the third son, won a brilliant record in the war of the rebellion. Entering the army as Colonel of the first Maine regiment, three months men, he continued in the service, after the return of the regiment. Wounded at the battle of Gaines' Mills, he was promoted to the rank of Brigadier-General for his gallantry. He accompanied Sherman through his Southern campaign, leaving the army, at the end of the war, with the rank of Major-General by brevet.

The arms of Jackson (Southgate) co. Middlesex, are:

GULES, A GREYHOUND COURANT, IN A FESSE OR, BETWEEN THREE PHEONS OR. CREST—A GREYHOUND PASSE SA, COLLARED OR, RESTING THE DEXTER FOOT ON A PHEON OF THE LAST.

The next house, on the corner of Green and Union (now Washington) street, was built by Capt. Babson, from Gloucester, who came to Newburyport for business facilities. It was purchased by Col. Fowle, and after his decease it was occupied by Joseph Cutler, who married Col. Fowle's widow. Mr. Cutler, the cashier of the Merrimac Bank, died suddenly, early in the present century. The lower half of the house, at the time of Mr. Cutler's death, was occupied by Mrs. Cutler's nephew, Mr. Joseph Hooper. This gentleman, a grandson of Robert, commonly styled "King" Hooper, of Marblehead, and Benjamin Harris, the distinguished merchant of Newburyport, and son of Joseph Hooper, the royalist, was born after his father went to England. In several ways this young man was despoiled of a large fortune. His father's property was confiscated by government; his furniture had been previously burned by his indignant townsmen; through treachery and fraud he lost an estate in Boston, on Pemberton hill, which by right belonged to his mother. Pemberton square has been laid out on this property. Nothing daunted, Mr. Hooper gathered the remnants of his patrimony and opened a crockery store in Blunt's building, State street. Soon after he was united in marriage with Miss Mary Whitmore, the daughter of Col. Joseph Whitmore, a veteran of the Revolution, whose residence was on Fair street. Mr. and Mrs. Hooper reared a large and highly-talented family of sons and daughters. Afterwards Mr. Hooper occupied the three-story house on Washington, near Boardman street, for some years the residence of Enoch S. Williams, esq. In the rear of this house, Mr. Williams established the first comb factory in the place, and in this house Mr. and Mrs. Hooper's fourth daughter, Lucy, the able writer, was born. Though she passed from earth in early womanhood, her name had become enrolled among the sweet singers and celebrated authors of America.

The Hooper coat of arms are:

OR, ON A FESSE BETWEEN THREE BOARS, PASSE AZURE, AS MANY ANNULETTES OF THE FIRST. CREST—BOAR'S HEAD ERASED AT NECK, AZURE. BESSANTIE ARMED AND CRINED.

The Harris arms are:

AZURE, A CHEVRON ERMINE, BETWEEN THREE HEDGEHOGS, OR ON A CHIEF, THE PRUSSIAN EAGLE WITH IMPERIAL CROWNS. CREST—A HEDGEHOG OR. SUPPORTERS OF ARMS, ON THE DEXTER SIDE EAGLE, ON SINISTER A STAG.

Mrs. Joseph Cutler, as Miss Alice Hooper, had been a celebrated beauty. Her portrait, by Copley, has excited universal admiration. The lady is painted in a dress of blue satin, with antique bodice, full skirt, and demi-open sleeves, finished by double lace ruffles, with stomacher to match, necklace and ear-jewels of pearls, hair brushed from the forehead and turned over a roll at the back. One hand hangs gracefully at her side, the other, outstretched, catches the sparkling drops from an old-fashioned aqueduct. Beyond is a wood, lighted by a shimmer of sunset glow; through openings the eye catches glimpses of an open country, stretching far in the distance, with a gleaming horizon, barred by ruddy cloud streaks. Words are inadequate to describe the perfection of this painting. The shadow of the lace upon the arm is a wonderful specimen of art, and one listens to hear the tinkle of the fountain, or stoops to catch the pellucid drops from the maiden's fair hand.

Newburyport at that time was rich in Copley's paintings. Mr. Joseph Hooper had a likeness of his father, and Mrs. Nathaniel Tracy, whose maiden name was Mary Lee, niece of Mrs. Robert Hooper, had life-size portraits of her father and mother. The pair are painted in the dress fashionable at the time of their marriage. Mrs. Lee is depicted coming from a garden laden with roses. These are magnificent pictures. I have been told that the artist ranked them among his very best. The only picture by this distinguished artist at present remaining in the city of which I have any knowledge, is a pastel, half size portrait of the third daughter of Robert, or "King" Hooper of Marblehead, Rebecca, wife of Lewis Jenkins. Mr. Jenkins for years kept a dry goods store on State, corner of Essex street, at the sign of the golden ball. He died in 1799. The portrait is that of a young lady in the dress of the period, cut low, square in the bosom, and trimmed with rich lace, the hair turned over a roll, and ornamented by flowers. The face and figure present the delicate beauty, and high bred grace which characterized the ladies of the Hooper family. This picture has descended to a grandniece, Mrs. Caroline (Gallishan) Currier of Belleville. Robert, or King, Hooper was born in Marblehead. His father came from Wiltshire, England, amongst the earliest settlers of this country. Robert married Ruth, daughter of Mr. Joseph Barnard Swett, a prominent merchant. They had six sons and four daughters, Mrs. Dalton, Mrs. Cutler, Mrs. Jenkins, the fourth, Hannah, who married a White. His son Stephen owned the "Hooper farm," on Pipestave hill, afterwards purchased by my uncle John Coker. Mr. Robert Hooper was one of the principal founders of Marblehead prosperity. His fellow-townsmen held him in high esteem, and styled him "King Hooper," as a mark of honor. Mr. Hooper owned a fine country seat in Danvers, which is now the property of Mr. Francis Peabody. This was a magnificent estate, one of the handsomest of the grand old colonial mansions, with appointments and grounds to match; the place was famed for its beautiful trees. The walls of the best rooms were hung with tapestry, and the furnishings equalled it in splendor. At the commencement of the Revolutionary war the British for a time quartered troops upon the place, and so well was it stocked with all that was requisite for man and beast, that the soldiers were not obliged to go elsewhere for supplies.

Though his son Joseph chose to remain loyal to King George, Robert Hooper was a true patriot. At the beginning of the war he refused the offer to be made King's Commissioner, an extremely lucrative situation.

The Rev. John Pierpont, during his residence in Newburyport, occupied the Cutler house for a time.

On the upper corner of Green and Union streets, was the mansion built by Judge Parsons, then owned and occupied by Leonard Smith. Mrs. Smith was a sister of General Peabody. Mr. Smith at that time ranked amongst our wealthiest and most active merchants. Above came the long, low school-house I have mentioned. The corner bordering on High street was an open field. The first of the three-story houses on Harris street, from Green, was built and at that time occupied by Obadiah Parsons, the second by Samuel Dole, the last, next to State, by Capt. Samuel Chase.

The lower side of Tyng street and Toppan's lane formed the dividing line of Newburyport from Newbury. The house on the corner of High and Tyng streets was built by Thomas Coker, who also built the house on the upper corner, in Newbury; the one below, down Tyng street, was built by Humphrey Webster. The second on High was the residence of Abner Toppan; the three-story house on the corner of High and Broad streets was built by Moses Fraiser, esq.; at this time it was owned and occupied by Capt. Jacob Greenleaf. The next, on Broad street, was built by Capt. Moses Goodrich; the one below by Thomas Coker. this gentleman was the father of my uncle John Coker, of West Newbury. At this time the house was owned and occupied by a Mr. Brown. The handsome residence of Tom. Thomas came next; below that, Moses Coffin, the father of Mr. Emery and Col. Frederick Coffin, had built a three-story house; further down was the residence of Capt. Fletcher.

Mt. Rural, the estate of Dr. Josiah Smith, bordered the upper side of High street, from Toppan's lane nearly to Kent street; fields intervened to Common pasture lane, now Johnson street. The first house on the lower side below Broad was the residence of Dr. Bond; the next had recently been erected by William Swain; the brick house on the corner of Kent street was built and owned by Messrs. Enoch and Stephen Toppan: a field separated Kent from Buck street. Capt. Buck's handsome brick house was on the lower corner of Buck street; Mr. Woodman's below. Opposite, on the lower corner of Pasture lane, was the new three-story house of Capt. William Hoyt; below was the residence of Capt. Charles Goodrich; next came the elegant mansion of John Tracy; below was the Dexter house, then Caldwell's tavern. On the lower corner of Olive street stood the old Frothingham house, the birth place of the wife of Lord Timothy Dexter; below came the Bassett house and the residence of Mr. Porter Russell. A house owned by Mr. Williams was on the upper corner of Boardman street; and Capt. Lunt's on the lower. The elegant residence of Dr. James Morse, rector of St. Paul's church, came next: below were the handsome mansions of Capt. Tristram Coffin, Capt. William Faris, Mr. Abner Wood and Jonathan Pettingell. The old Pettingell house was below on the upper corner of Winter street. Next to the Dexter house garden, on the upper side, was the Titcomb house, and a two-story house, built, I believe, by a Mr. Somerby; next was the rectory of St. Paul's parish, at that period occupied by the widow of Bishop Bass. Below were the handsome three-story houses built and occupied by Capt. Wyatt and Samuel A. Otis, esq.; next came the Carey house, the former residence of the Rev. Thomas Carey of the first church; Mr. Philip Bagley's, Enoch Toppan's, and that of Deacon Parker followed, with the Cooper and Packard houses. Below Star alley was the Horton house and a row of old style domiciles; on the corner next the mall stood the mansion of Daniel Farnham, esq. Jacob W. Pierce occupied the house on the lower corner of Winter street; next came the Marsh house and the old Bailey place; below, St. Paul's church and church-yard. On the opposite corner of Market street was the Morse house, famous in the annals of witchcraft, a picturesque old fashioned building painted red: below came the Hodge house, and the residence of Dr. Adams on the upper corner of Court street. Below the mall, on the upper side, were the residences of William Moulton and William Greenleaf, the academy and the handsome mansions on the ridge, Judge Livermore's, Capt. Abraham Wheelwright's, Mr. Stocker's, Capt. Eben Wheelwright's, Deacon Solomon Haskell's, Richard Pike's, Capt. John O'Brien's, Capt. Philip Coombs', and Elias Hunt's. The old Prout house and that of Capt. Benjamin Pierce stood below. Dr. Charles Coffin's was the last house before crossing the Newbury line.

On the lower side the first house from Newbury was that of Samuel Milliken; then came Capt. Micajah Lunt's, the old Tom Cross house, Capt. Samuel Swett's, Anthony Davenport's, and Capt. Holland's, on the lower corner of

Federal street. Fields stretched from Federal to the lower side of State street; the old Buntin house stood on the upper corner. The four-story brick block on Brown's square had been recently built. On Market street were the handsome residences of the Hortons, Stephen Frothingham, Edmund Bartlett, and Capt. Isaac Stone. The Hoyt mansion was on Boardman street, with the Johnson's, Gallishan's, and Capt. Pulsifer's. Mr. Butler Abbott had a handsome establishment on Kent street; Capt. Samuel Bailey's residence was on Spring street. Captains Eleazer and William P. Johnson, William Coombs, and William Bartlett, esq., occupied handsome houses on Federal street. Capt. Nicholas Johnson had recently purchased the large brick house on the Boston turnpike, built by William Wooart, esq; Mr. Seth Sweetser built and occupied the one below. Capt. John Coombs resided on Water, corner of Lime street; Judge Greenleaf's residence was on the corner of Union and Titcomb streets. The Atwood house stood on Lime, corner of Atwood street. Besides the residences I have named, there were many others, both spacious and elegant, scattered throughout the town. A stable was attached to the better class of houses, and many of the more common had a barn for the accommodation of a cow if not a horse. Most families had one or more cows, which in summer were pastured in the upper or lower common; when returning home at nightfall they made quite a drove. The more prominent citizens usually had a horse, and some kept a coach and span.

There were three Masonic lodges: St. John's, St. Peter's and St Mark's. St. Peter's occupied Washington hall; I think St. John's assembled in Madison hall in the Phœnix building, and that St. Mark's joined with St. Peter's.

Samuel Bartlett, a younger brother of Col. Bartlett, occupied the lower half of his house. Mr. Samuel Bartlett was a Mason. When I was a child the brethren often assembled at his residence. They occupied the front chamber, where they would keep up a most tremendous racket until a late hour.

Mrs. Bartlett was a delicate woman with small children, and my aunt was subject to nervous headaches. I wondered that they bore the infliction with any patience. For myself I obtained a great dislike to the order, and firmly believed in the red hot gridiron and every other diabolical invention.

CHAPTER XLVII.

At this time the old English style had not wholly passed from society; there was more of precedent and caste than now.

The professional men and their families held the first rank, then came the merchants, town and national officers, shipmasters, the more prominent and wealthy mechanics, etc. Politics separated the elite; though sometimes meeting on common ground, usually there was but slight social fraternization. There were Federal and Jacobin clubs, military companies, balls and parties. One lady would not call upon another of the opposite party; gentlemen were scarcely civil to each other; much rancor, bitterness and scorn were shown upon both sides. The artillery company were Jacobins, the "Silver Greys" Federalists. The leading Jacobins were Capt. Benjamin Pierce, the O'Brians, Mr. Marquand, Capt. Russell, Dr. Smith, of Mt. Rural, the Williams family, Capt. Richards, and others.

Most of my town relatives were Federalists. Through my Johnson, Little and Smith ancestry, I was connected with the Johnsons, Crosses, Coombs', Wheelwrights, Noyes', Bartletts, and other of older families. At their residences, and those of my uncles Peabody and Bartlet, I met the most brilliant stars in the Federalist galaxy. My great-uncle Daniel Johnson was the black sheep amongst his Federalist brethren. At Gov. Gerry's election the opposition got up all sorts of slurs: one was a caricature called a "Gerrymander." Uncle Daniel took pains to procure a copy which he sent to me. The Democratic party also had the ascendency in the legislature. In 1812 the old senatorial districts were rearranged, and the Federalists, in derision, drew this figure, as representing Essex county:

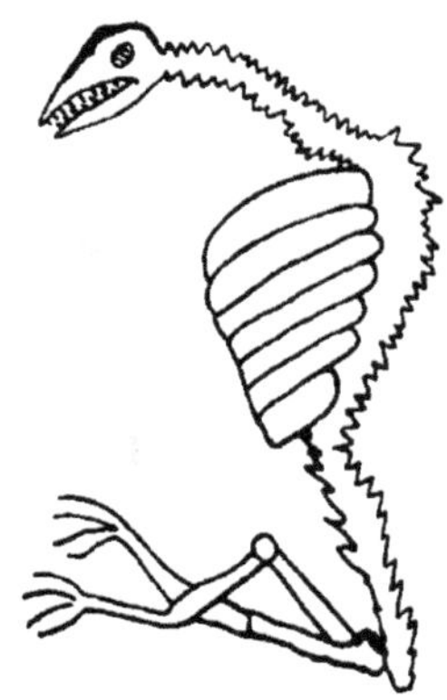

A Gerrymander.

The picture uncle Johnson sent to me was in the Newburyport Herald, and covered two-thirds of one page of that sheet.

The Embargo Act wholly disarranged the business of Newburyport; for a time it brought much suffering. It was but natural that opposition to the policy of the administration should be nearly universal. On the first anniversary of the passage of the act, the flags were hung at half mast, the bells were tolled, and minute guns were fired: while a procession of sailors bearing crape on their arms marched through the streets, headed by a dismantled vessel drawn by horses on a cart. This craft bore a flag inscribed: "Death to Commerce." On the quarter-deck stood a sailor with a glass in his hand, and a painted motto bore the words: "Which way shall I steer?" Occasionally the sailor threw the lead. Opposite the custom house he delivered an address appropriate for the day and the Federalist party.

In 1809 the Embargo gave place to the Non-Intercourse Act. Negotiations with Great Britain followed, which resulted in the release of our citizens impressed into her service. In 1810 France repealed her continental decrees. Business revived, and shipbuilding again became active.

The brilliant coterie of which Judge Parsons, and his law students, Robert Treat Paine, Rufus King, John Quincy Adams and other talented young men, the Jacksons, Daltons, Tracys, Greenleafs, Hoopers, and other distinguished families, the Misses Fraiser, Atkins, Searle, Bradbury, Farnham, Thomas, Jenkins, and other belles and beauties, who graced the assemblies at the old Tabernacle in Temple street, in my mothers girl-hood, had been succeeded by another generation. Of the clergymen's families, the three daughters of Parson Giles had just entered society. Dr. Andrew's oldest son was in college and Margaret was in her teens. Dr. Spring's oldest sons were also collegians. Dr. Dana's and Parson Milton's children were small. Dr. Morss had recently married Miss Martha Boardman. Dr. Micajah Sawyer was the senior physician, his two daughters, Mrs. Lee and Mrs. Schuyler, had been married several years. I vividly recall the grandeur of their nuptials. Dr. Francis Vergnies, a Frenchman, a physician of much skill, and extensive practice, lived and died a bachelor. His home for many years was on the lower corner of Union, (now Washington,) and Market streets. Dr. Nathan Noyes had married Miss Mary Niles, of Hanover, N. H., and established himself in Newburyport, where he was fast becoming a celebrity. Dr. Bricket, had moved into town from the lower parish in Newbury, where he still had a large practice. Dr. Prescott, who had recently established himself in the place, with his wife and lovely daughters, was fast acquiring a wide spread popularity. Dr. Johnson, a young man and unmarried, had just received his diploma.

Theophilus Bradbury, judge of the Supreme Court of Massachusetts, died in 1803. Judge Parsons, when a student, read law in the office of Theophilus Bradbury, who was a member of Congress from this district during Washington's administration.

Judge Livermore was then the oldest and the most distinguished of the legal fraternity of the town; he was also our representative to Congress. His daughter, Miss Harriet Livermore, from childhood had been noted for eccentricity; her singular conduct and conversation was a frequent topic for remark.

William B. Bannister esq., had recently formed a partnership with Edward Little.

Tom Carey, the son of the late Rev. Thomas Carey, a talented, highly educated, polished and entertaining young man, would probably have acquired a high reputation, had he not, like too many others of that generation, succumbed to the demon of dissipation. Possessed of wealth, a handsome person, pleasing address and rare accomplishments and culture, with a power of adapting himself to any society, great wit, humor and generosity, notwithstanding his convivial proclivities, as yet he held posts of trust and honor, gentlemen hailed him as the prince of good fellows, and ladies, with whom he was a general favorite, smiled their sweetest at his approach.

One evening, Tom Carey and a number of other young men had been holding an orgie, in a low tavern near Market square. About midnight they sallied forth, "half seas over." The northern sky was brilliant with an aurora, but in their muddled condition Tom's companions took it for a fire at the north end, and commenced to give an alarm. "Shtop, shtop," cried Tom, "don't scream, its only the Rora Bolis, keep to the west, keep to the west!" The next afternoon, sobered and shaved, curled, powdered and cued, in fine broadcloth, Wellington boots, bell crowned beaver, kid gloves and gold headed cane, Mr Carey accompanied by Dr. Spring, as school committee, was making the round of the schools. As they passed down State street, old Morrill, a rough, saucy blackguard, stood at the door of his boarding house, and espying the pair, he shouted, "Keep to the west Mr. Carey, keep to the west." Tom had the grace to color, while his companion looked the curiosity he was too polite to form into a question. Mr. Carey passed the matter by some remark, and for a time it was noticed he was remarkably circumspect in his conduct, but the story became current, and "keep to the west," remained a jest for a long time.

William H. Prince, Ebenezer Moseley, Sam L. Knapp. John Scott and Moody Noyes, were all young lawyers boarding at Coburn's Hotel in the Tracy House. Tom Carey also boarded with Coburn. This bevy of young attorneys were a special attraction to the belles of the period. The previous Fourth of July Squire Moseley delivered an oration in the Pleasant street meeting-house; there was a procession, fine music, and a grand gala through the day and evening. Young Moseley acquited himself with great eclat and some of the enthusiastic misses plaited a crown of laurels as a gift for the orator, but not having the courage to present it, he never knew the proposed honor, though ever after he was known amongst them as the "laurel crowned Demosthenes."

Sam L. Knapp was a splendid man, the prince of beaux, winning his way as by enchantment, particularly distinguished as a belles-lettres scholar, he wielded the pen of a ready writer, his imagination was vivid, his power of description graphic, his conversation both brilliant and instructive.

Moody Noyes, a promising young man, modest and retiring in society, died young. Jacob Gerrish was another young lawyer, and Stephen Hooper, a son of Mr. Stephen Hooper of the Pipe-stave hill farm.

Messrs. Clark, Chandler and Adams, Archibald McPhail, Asa W. Wildes, Benjamin A. Gould, George Titcomb and Joseph Gleason, the editor and publisher of the "Statesman," the Democratic newspaper, were favorites in society. Arthur Gilman, John Porter, David Peabody, George Peabody, Francis B. Somerby, Edward Toppan jr., Joseph Huse, George Cross, Oliver and Prescott Spalding, Abner, William, James, John and Alexander Caldwell, and their cousin William Caldwell, Moses Osgood, John Chickering, Jonathan Coolidge, Henry Frothingham, John R. Hudson, Edward S. and Isaac Rand, Isaac Rand Jackson, Joseph Marquand, Joshua Aubin, Sewell Toppan, Joseph Abraham, Robert and William Williams, Nathaniel, John, William, Thomas, Leonard and David Smith, Samuel T. DeFord, Simeon Wade, Eben and Charles Hale, Nathaniel Greeley, the Johnsons, Greenleafs, Stones, Noyes, Balches, of Newburyport, Joseph Balch of Belleville, Joseph T. Pike, David, Abner and Jerry, sons of Abner Wood, William and George, sons of the widow Wood, were prominent among the rising young men. George Wood afterwards became a well known author. Besides these a number of our young men were engaged in business in foreign ports, or as masters or supercargoes of ships; amongst these were Capt. Nathaniel Jackson, Captains John and Benjamin Harrod, Capt. Green Sanborn, and Capt. Richards.

Capt. Nathaniel Jackson had just brought home his lovely wife. This lady, her infant son, and his Swedish nurse, clad in the costume of her country, attracted much attention. Mr. and Mrs. John Dean and Jacob W. Pierce and wife were young, married people. Nicholas Johnson had recently led to the alter Miss Sarah, oldest daughter of Mr. Anthony Davenport. John and William Smith had just established their brides in their elegant homes. These ladies with Mrs. Tom Thomas, Mrs. Thomas Hooper, who was a daughter of Judge Bradbury, Miss Ann Jackson, Mr. Leonard Smith's niece, Hitty Smith, and his daughter Sarah, were the acknowledged queens of society.

The three daughters of Dr. Smith of Mount Rural, Miss Mary, Hannah, Judith, and Caroline Little, and the six daughters of Mr. John Balch of Belleville, Mr. Joseph Williams' only daughter Caroline, Mr. John Tracy's daughters Margaret, Mary, Elizabeth and Catharine, the daughters of the late Nathaniel Tracy, Louisa and Helen, Miss Sukey Fowle, and Miss Sally Cutler, Mr. Daniel Balch's daughters, the Misses Searle, Harrod, Frothingham, Johnson, White, Wheelwright, Marquand, Davenport, Stocker, Faris, Greenleaf, Wood and Pierce, Miss Sarah Hale, Maj. David Coffin's only daughter Mary, Mr. Moses Brown's only daughter Mary, Miss Margaret Andrews, the Misses Giles, Miss Mary Ann Oxnard, Hannah Bartlett, Betsey Lawrence, Martha, Sally and Katie Caldwell, and their cousin Sally Caldwell, Sophronia Peabody and her cousin Sophia, the youngest daughter of Leonard Smith were the most prominent belles. Miss Lydia Osgood, the youngest daughter of Deacon Osgood of the upper parish Newbury, was a general favorite in this circle; no festivity was complete without her.

Miss Ann Thaxter, a step daughter of Joshua Carter, had been married a short time previous to Nathaniel Parsons of Boston. In his visits to his fiancee Mr. Parsons created a sensation in the neighborhood, as he dashed to the door, in his coach and four, with a darkey in livery holding the ribbons, and the splendor of the wedding was long remembered. After the bride had become settled in her city home, her two intimate friends, Mary Brown and Sophronia Peabody, paid her a visit. The house, which was near Bowdoin square, was a large brick structure; a gateway led through a paved court to a spacious stable. Over this gateway from an arched iron railing was suspended a square glass lantern. This was customary at that period, at the better class mansions. The interior of the house was magnificent both in proportion and finish. Mirrors were inserted in the drawing room doors to enhance the effect. The furniture had been imported expressly for the house, it was both rich and stylish; glittering chandeliers, and other ornaments embellished the rooms; the silken canopy to the bed in the guest chamber, was gathered around an oval mirror set in the centre of the arched top. The whole mansion was resplendent with French luxury and novel elegance.

The first class dwellings of Newburyport, were mostly square structures, three stories in height, or of two stories with dormer windows in the roof; some were gambrel roofed houses. There were generally four rooms on the lower floor, a spacious hall from which a flight of broad, low stairs, with elaborately carved balusters led to the story above. Usually an L was attached for an outer kitchen, and a court yard, frequently flagged, led to a stable beyond. Gardens were attached to most residences, those on the upper side of High street usually had extensive grounds. The heavy claw-footed furniture of a previous date had been followed by lighter, in the French style. Stiff looking, slender legged chairs and sofas were primly ranged round the room, with card table to match in the piers; these sometimes had marble tops. Above them hung large Dutch mirrors. Often the walls were adorned with one or more family portraits; these though not Coply's were usually good pictures. The French Revolution had sent many refugees to our shores who had been compelled to turn their talents and accomplishments to account. Mr. Moses Cole painted fine portraits, and he was well patronized by his townsmen. An engraving of the Washington family was a favorite picture that could have been seen in many houses. Carpets had come much more generally into use. The Turkey carpets bordered and fringed had given place to those from English looms, though Turkey rugs were still highly esteemed. Very pretty carpets in striped patterns of home construction had become fashionable, and those from rags for common use were often seen.

The dining or sitting room almost invariably held a large mahogony sideboard. Beneath generally stood an ornamental liquor case, and upon the top were some half dozen cut-glass decanters filled with wine, brandy and other liquors; these were flanked by trays of wine glasses and tumblers. The old fashioned silver tankard had become obsolete, but a display of silver tumblers was considered desirable. The chambers were still furnished with hangings to the bedsteads, but bureaus had supplanted the case of drawers. In many mansions stairs led from the china closet to a private cellar, which usually was well stocked with choice wines and liquors. Our foreign trade gave facility for obtaining the best brands; few families were without a larger or smaller supply. Cider was put in the common cellar and used as freely as water. On one occasion Mr. Nathaniel Tracy caught his negro serving man carousing with a brother darkey in the wine cellar, drinking "to better times" from a silver goblet brimming with choice old Bordeaux. Chaises were now in general use; there were a few barouches; four-wheeled wagons were superseding the two-wheeled spring cart. Coaches drawn by two horses, sometimes four, were the fashionable equipage; several were kept by families in the town.

The attire fashionable for a gentleman at that period was similar to that I have described as worn by Tom Carey. Small clothes were still stylish for evening parties and balls. The French mode prevailed in the costume of the ladies. Short, scant ruffled skirts, short waists; for young ladies short sleeves, and low necks, especially so in the bosom; an under handkerchief fitted so neatly it was scarcely discernable, and tuckers finished the neck. Long gloves, sashes, and a great variety of ornaments were worn in full dress. The hair was worn high, often the back hair having been divided, half fell in curls on the neck while the remainder was wound round the comb; at other times it was wholly braided and twisted into a crown upon the head, the front hair clustered in short curls over the forehead or on the temples. The elder ladies wore variously fashioned caps and turbans. Ear jewels were universally worn. The strings of gold beads so general in my mother's girlhood were then deemed old-fashioned; necklaces and chains had taken their place; often a miniature painted on ivory set in gold was worn on the chain. Both my Aunt Peabody and Bartlett had good likenesses of their husbands, which were fine paintings. Brooches, bracelets and rings were of various patterns, some exceedingly elegant in design. Rich thread laces were much in demand, and linen cambric. The gentlemen's shirt bosoms were ruffled with this fabric. Silk bonnets were worn, but straw was the style. A black satin cloak with cape and sleeves was the usual outdoors garment for older ladies, for the younger, silk pelisses in fancy colors were fashionable; both reached below the knee and were finished by a trimming of black lace. Long cloth wrappers were made for common wear. White dresses were worn entirely by young ladies when in full dress, and usually on Sundays. However cold the weather or wet the walking a white cambric, with a green, blue, or lilac silk pelisse, a straw bonnet trimmed to match, white silk stockings and kid slippers of the same hue of the pelisse, or cork soled morocco walking shoes, with a sable muff and tippet, was the street dress of a young lady of ton. Muslins and gauzes over under dresses of satin, with rich trimmings of lace, ribbon, spangles, bugles etc., were the mode for evening attire. Silks were seldom worn excepting by older ladies, and woolen fabrics were only admissible for home wear. A deal of fun was made of Mr. John Balch's daughters, because their mother very sensibly compelled them to wear crimson bombazette dresses to a party one snapping winter night, with the thermometer below zero. On pleasant days fashionable ladies devoted the morning to calling or receiving visitors. Cake and wine were invariably handed to the guest.

One o'clock was the dinner hour for all classes. At the first stroke of the bells of the Pleasant and Federal street churches the streets were filled with a hungry throng rushing homeward. There was little ceremonious visiting of an afternoon, unless invitations had been issued for a tea party. At these the ladies assembled from four to five o'clock, Tea was served at six.

In most families there was a boy or girl bound to service until the age of eighteen. When the hour arrived this young servant passed round napkins upon a salver; next a man or maid servant bore round the tray of cups, the younger waiter following with the cream and sugar. Bread and butter and cake succeeded, these were passed round two or three times, and the younger servant stood, salver in hand, ready to take the cups to be replenished. If the gentlemen came to tea, and this was the only refreshment, sliced ham or tongue were usually added, but often there would be a hot meat supper at nine or ten o'clock. This was a customary meal in many families. In Mr. Leonard Smith's family it was as regular as either of those during the day. As both my aunts considered the practice unhealthy it was never introduced into their households. Dinner parties were common, when the table would be loaded with luxuries. After the dessert the ladies retired to the parlor for an hour's gossip, while the gentlemen sipped wine, smoked long Dutch pipes and discussed the affairs of the nation The ladies having been rejoined in the drawing room coffee was passed. These parties were often the scene of much conviviality, but "being a little after dinnerish" it was considered a slight matter, and any escapade in consequence was wholly overlooked. In 1780 the Marquis de Chastellux, the Vicomte de Vaudreuil, M. de Taleyrand and M. de Montesquieu visited Newburyport; they came from Portsmouth over the Merrimac Ferry and stopped at the "Wolfe Tavern." These foreigners had a letter of introduction to Mr. John Tracy, but before it was delivered Mr. Tracy and Col. Wigglesworth called to invite them to pass the evening with Mr. Tracy. I copy the account of this visit from a description written by the Marquis de Chastellux, as it is a perfect picture of the tone of society at that time and for a long period after. M. de Chastellux writes, "This Colonel remained with me till Mr. Tracy finished his business, when he came with two handsome carriages, well equipped, and conducted me and my aide-de-Camps to his country house." (This was the mansion on High street above the former Dexter house.) "This is in a very beautiful situation, but of this I could myself form no judgment, as it was already night. I went, however, by moonlight to see the garden, which is composed of different terraces. There is likewise a hothouse and a number of young trees. The house is handsome and well finished, and everything breathes that air of magnificence accompanied with simplicity, which is only to be found among merchants. The evening passed rapidly by the aid of agreeable conversation and a few glasses of punch. The ladies we found assembled were Mrs. Tracy, her two sisters, and their cousin Miss Lee. Mrs. Tracy has an agreeable and sensible countenance, and her manners correspond with her appearance. At ten o'clock an excellent supper was served. We drank good wine, Miss Lee sung, and prevailed upon Messrs. de Vaudreuil and Taleyrand to sing also. Towards midnight the ladies withdrew, but we continued drinking Madeira and Xery. Mr. Tracy, according to the custom of the country, offered us pipes, which were accepted by M. de Taleyrand and M. de Montesquieu, the consequence of which was that they became intoxicated and were led home, where they were happy to get to bed. As to myself, I remained perfectly cool, and continued to converse on trade and politics with Mr. Tracy."

In addition to the entertainments I have described were evening parties and balls. These parties were often large, and music was usually provided for dancing, with a choice and elegant treat. Sillabub at an earlier day had been a fashionable evening beverage. There were sillabub tables, small, square, four-legged ones, with a narrow ledge running round the sides, on which were placed the glass sillabub bowl and ladle, the mixture, which consisted of milk, wine or cider, sugar and spice, being dipped into tall, slender stemmed glasses. The introduction of tea brought sillabub into disuse. Ices had not then become general. Cream whipped to a froth, sweetened and flavored, was much favored. Served in glasses it looked very pretty, and "whips" were the one genteel thing for an evening soiree. Jellies, various cakes, fruit, wines and hot punch were the usual additional refreshments.

The old Tabernacle upon whose floor the stately minuet of a preceding generation had been danced had given place to the new Washington Hall on Green street, which had a spring floor, considered especially excellent for dancing. It was reached by two flights of stairs leading from the lower entry to the one above; two ante rooms opened into this, from which doors led to the hall, which was lofty and spacious. Large windows draped with red faced on either side; at the upper end was a gallery for musicians; opposite were two fireplaces where huge logs crackled and sparkled. Round the sides was a platform, slightly raised above the spring floor, upon which stood rows of yellow wooden settees. Two glittering chandeliers were suspended from the ceiling. Upon the mantels and orchestra stood glass candelabra and candlesticks.

Here during the winter a series of monthly assemblies were held, at which the young people danced contra dances, four-handed and eight-handed reels, while their elders amused themselves at the card tables spread in the ante rooms. A black waiting maid, and two or three sable male waiters were in attendance. The refreshments were similar to those at the parties.

It was expected the morning after a party or ball that the gentlemen should call upon their fair partners to inquire respecting their health. It was common for them to drop in of an evening socially. Sam L. Knapp rendered himself especially welcome, and Tom Carey's varied information and fine voice fitted him for a most entertaining companion. Singing was a universal accomplishment. In a few houses a spinet or harpsichord could be found, but as yet there were but four pianos in the town. These belonged to the daughters of Parson Giles, Miss Mary Coffin, Miss Catharine Davenport and Miss Sophronia Peabody. A French refugee, formerly a nobleman, whose name I cannot recall, came from Boston once in two weeks to give these young ladies lessons.

The organs in St. Paul's and the Pleasant street church were played by Mr. Daniel Bayley and William Wood, the brother of the author, George Wood.

The pianos were small, slender-legged, tinkling instruments, imported from Paris. The music was love songs, dancing tunes, etc., "Hail Columbia," "Yankee Doodle," the old revolutionary song, "Why should vain mortals tremble at the sight of death and destruction on the field of battle," "Moll Brooks," "What can the matter be," "The Campbells are coming," and the duet "Shepherds have you seen my Flora pass this way?" were favorites. I copy an ode entitled "Freedom's Anniversary," from a music book published in 1808:

"This day fires our minds,
This day fires our minds,
This day fires our minds
With a flame as arose,
When our sires drew the steel,
Which laid prostrate our foes,
With mirth inspiring lay,
We'll celebrate the day,
Till the orbs cease to roll or the earth melts away.

Brave heroes who fought,
Brave heroes who fought,
Brave heroes who fought,
And have labored to crown
Columbia's rich fields in the pride of renown,
From your station on high one moment look down
On myriads of wretches that grovel around;
To Afric's broad zone turn the wings of the mind,
Traverse regions unknown and nations unnamed,
Or fly to famed Asia and there you will hear,
Oppression's loud clangor, hoarse grating the ear;
Or haste to proud Europe, her regions explore;
Mark the myriads that starve, yet kings they adore;
Disgusted with tyrants, disgusted with slaves,
Extend fancy's pinions and mount o'er the waves,
To your own native clime, for there you may find
The wisest and happiest of all human kind.
Thus highly exalted, ne'er cease to adore
The God of the skies, and his mercies implore.
This day fires our minds,
This day fires our minds,
This day fires our minds
With a flame as arose
When our sires drew the steel
Which laid prostrate our foes,
With mirth inspiring lay,
We'll celebrate the day,
Till the orbs cease to roll or the earth melts away."

There is a Thanksgiving anthem:

"Sing aloud to God our strength,
Sing aloud to God our strength,
Sing aloud to God our strength, to God our strength,
Make a joyful noise to him with psalms, to him with psalms, to him with psalms, to him with psalms,
Praise the Lord all ye nations, praise him, praise him, praise him all ye people,
For his mercies are great, his mercies are great.
We will rejoice and give thanks, will rejoice and give thanks, will rejoice and give thanks, will rejoice and give thanks.
Let us come before his presence, before his presence, before his presence, with thanksgiving, with thanksgiving, with thanksgiving, with thanksgiving, and enter his courts with praise.
Thou, O Lord, hast crowned the year with goodness, with goodness, with goodness.
The pastures are covered o'er with flocks,
The vallies are also covered o'er with corn,
The vallies are also covered o'er with corn.
Hallelujah, hallelujah, hallelujar, hallelujah, hallelujah, amen.
Hallelujah, amen, amen, hallelujah, hallelujah, amen, amen."

CHAPTER XLVIII.

For some years an orphan asylum had been established where some half dozen girls were reared and instructed, until of an age to become bound to service in some family, there to remain until eighteen. This institution was located on Federal street, and at that time was under the supervision of Mrs. Joanna Akerman. The orphans were dressed in uniform. On Sunday, headed by the matron, they demurely walked two and two, in procession, to the Old South meetinghouse, where a pew in the gallery was appropriated to their use.

That spring, to the horror of the more rigid, two dancing schools were opened, one by Mr. Ingalls, at Union Hall, the other by Mr. Nichols, who "gave lessons as taught by the celebrated Italian master, Mr. Dochoun. Gentlemen desirous of practising the small sword, cut and thrust, broad sword, and a powerful defence with the cane," were desired to leave their names at the bookstore of Thomas & Whipple. A convenient bathing house was also established on Water street, above Market square.

At this time two newspapers were supported in Newburyport, "The Herald," which was the Federalist organ, and the "Statesman," Democratic. A large circulating library was well patronized, and there were several good private libraries in the town. These were anxious times, and the news from Europe was impatiently awaited. Buonaparte was in the midst of his career, his progress was eagerly watched, and the accounts of his success were read with wonder and avidity. Byron and Scott had begun to enchant the world. "Elizabeth, or the Exile of Siberia," was the new novel which every one was perusing.

In speaking of the business of the town I omitted the truckmen, comprising a tall, stalwart band of men, who in their long white frocks, made a goodly show in Fourth of July and other civic processions. Sometimes of an afternoon, when the business for the day was over, they would drive in a line through the streets, their fine horses, and long, tilting, clattering trucks noisily breaking the quiet monotony. In the winter, on their sleds, in this way, they frequently volunteered to aid in breaking the paths. In addition to these drays a large business was done by ox teams, one or more pair of oxen yoked to a two-wheeled cart. Mr. Nathaniel Bricket, Mr. Samuel Wheeler and Mr. Charles Chase were noted teamsters.

Back of the Pond stood a collection of low, unpainted huts. This village was styled "Guinea." Here were the homes of the colored population, of which there was quite a number. These were mostly descendants of servants formerly held as slaves in our first households. Many considering themselves as still connected with the old master's family, in any emergency always looked to it for advice, care and consideration.

In those days of huge wood fires, it was no uncommon thing for the burning of a chimney to endanger a whole neighborhood. A law was enacted that every chimney should be swept once a year. Lilly White, a tall, lithe negro, was the principal sweep, followed by his little apprentice boy bearing a bag of clothes. Lilly perambulated the streets, brandishing his brooms and crying:

"Lilly White has come to town,
To sweep the chimney up and down,
If he does not sweep them clean
He shall not have his pistareen."

Clement Paul, a genteel waiter, was a favorite in the upper circles. Joe Fatal, Col. Greenleaf's darky, Old Cambridge, who could remember being kidnapped when a child and brought to this country in a slave vessel, Jimmy Paul, Sip Burnham and others were useful members of society, and respected citizens. Many colored women did washing, and black Luce was a famous nurse. Old Luce Pero, a beggar tramp, generally accompanied by one or more children, was the horror of the more infantile population; the threat "old Luce Pero will catch you," was sufficient to quell the most turbulent urchin. Coburn had a remarkably aristocratic darkey employed in his hotel. Much admiring a pair of boots which Ebenezer Mosely, esq., had purchased, the negro waiter strutted into the store of Osgood & Brackett, and with a pompous air ordered a similar pair; adding, much to the amusement of Messrs. Osgood

& Brackett, "Let 'em be jes like Squire Moseley's, only a *quarter dollar better.*"

No fish market had been established, fresh fish was vended about the streets in wheelbarrows. Clams in the shell were sold; none were then shucked. Sometimes the "Algerines" from Seabrook peddled about boiled clams taken from the shell, but clams were regarded as a plebeian dish, from which many persons turned in disgust. The chief fishmongers were Flood, and Jim Ball.

The famous witch of the town was a woman known as Madame Hooper. Her early history has remained a mystery. She came to Newbury about 1760, and for a time was the dame of a school at the south end; afterward she became a famous fortune teller, rivalling in celebrity Moll Pitcher of Lynn; her home on Cottle's Lane being visited by persons of all ages and classes from near and afar. In person Madam Hooper was short and stout, with a strongly marked countenance, glittering gray eyes, and a full set of double teeth; her appearance was that of one born and bred in good society, though from the first a peculiarity had been evinced in her demeanor which increased with years. She was well educated and accomplished, and brought with her on coming to town, a very extensive and handsome wardrobe, rich brocades and the like, which were worn without remodelling to the end of her long life. These antique garments, with a unique bonnet of her own fashion, combined with an oracular, sibyllic manner, were calculated to inspire credulous people with the awe and wonder which she coveted. Children ran at her approach, and their elders from fear of the "evil eye" were lavish in courtesy. Thus the witch carried matters with a high hand, visiting where she chose, generally acting her own pleasure without much regard to the wishes or convenience of others, few venturing to cross one whom so many considered as possessing supernatural powers. This reputation was artfully sustained. Often her visitors were received in impurturbable silence, but when an answer was vouchsafed it usually was verified. This foresight and sagacity succeeded in securing dupes for many years. She kept a pet fowl, black in plumage, with a clipped bill and claws, which was regarded as her "familiar." Madame Hooper lived to an advanced age, but at length died in poverty and degradation, unmourned but not unremembered. Her name had become a household word, which has been handed down through the generations as one of the marvels of the past. Perhaps if the secrets of her life could be unmasked we should pity rather than condemn.

Billy Watkins was a somewhat eccentric individual, who owned a large estate on Water street. Foony Gerrish, a wig maker, often became the jest of the populace. Though illiterate, he evinced a desire to rank amongst the educated. On one occasion a person in the bar room of the "Wolfe Tavern" perceiving him seemingly intent upon perusing a newspaper which was held bottom upward, inquired, "What is the news, Mr. Gerrish?" "Terrible gales," hurriedly returned the old man, "terrible gales, ships all bottom upwards." Wishing to be thought a man of business Foony bought a ledger. That morning he sold a wig, for which, much to the purchaser's astonishment, he declined to take payment, "he would charge it." At night he detained one of the young clerks in the neighborhood to note it down. Having written the date the young man inquired the name of the debtor. Foony looked puzzled, scratched his head, he "never thought to inquire the name," but after a moment's deliberation he added, "Never mind, put it down, one wig to a man that looked like an Amesbury man." Whether Foony received the price of the wig from this dubiously described individual I am unable to state.

Another notoriety was "Bumble Bee Titcomb," a carpenter by trade. While at work at his bench a bumblebee lighted near his hand. Mr. Titcomb raised his hatchet, ejaculating, "Now, old fellow, your end has come! Say your prayers, for death is nigh. One, two, three—strike!" Down went the hatchet, cutting off the end of Mr. Titcomb's thumb, while the bumblebee, having flown up and stung the end of his nose, buzzed exultantly away through the open door. Ever after the carpenter was known th.oughout the town as "Bumble Bee Titcomb."

Another of the celebrities of the town was Mr. Enoch Toppan, commonly called "Rhymer Toppan," as he was never at a loss for a rhyme. One day, at the market house, Mr. James Carey and Mr. Richard Adams laid a wager respecting Mr. Toppan's instantly returning an answer in rhyme. Mr. Toppan was across the square. From the steps of the market house Mr. Carey sang out, "Mr. Toppan, so they say, buys his meat and never'll pay." To which was responded, "Jimmy Carey, if that be true, I'll always have my meat of you." Mr. Carey was obliged to "stand treat."

For years the chief wonder of the place was Lord Timothy Dexter, his hairless dog and his images. This man was born in Malden in 1743. He came to Newburyport in early manhood and married a Miss Frothingham, from the old Frothingham mansion on the corner of High and Olive street. In a short time he obtained a large fortune by taking advantage of the markets and by lucky adventures. His first successful speculation was buying up continental notes when depreciated, and selling them when a prospect of redemption had raised their value. His speculations in mittens, warming-pans, whalebone and the like, are widely known. Though ignorant and illiterate, and doubtless somewhat indebted to luck for his good fortune, still it is evident the man was both shrewd and sagacious. His vanity was inordinate. Under any circumstances it is probable he would have proved an eccentricity, still, such were the convivial habits of the period, and constantly surrounded as he was, by a band of sycophantic boon companions, who spurred him on to all sorts of ridiculous sayings and doings, one can scarcely judge what the character of the man would have been under the teetotal regime of Neal Dow. Having bought the fine Jackson mansion on High street, nearly opposite his wife's maiden home, he began to beautify it after his own design. Mr. James Wilson was a carver of figure heads of ships. Dexter conceived the idea of employing Mr. Wilson to embellish his house and grounds with wooden statues. These figures were remarkable specimens in wood carving. In this work Mr. Wilson displayed the power of a sculptor; it is a pity he never aspired to works of greater durability. The figures of Washington, Adams and Jefferson, over the front door, were excellent, and the other figures, the eagle upon the cupola, and the animals, were life-like and in good proportion. Dexter built a tomb in the garden; on its completion he got up a mock funeral, had his wife and family arrayed in mourning, acted his part as corpse, and was borne to the sepulchre with due funeral rites. After his resurrection and return to the house he beat his wife because she did not weep while following him to the grave. He kept a person in his house named Jonathan Plummer, who styled himself "physician, preacher, and poet laureate, to his excellency Timothy Dexter, Earl of Chester, and Knight of the two open-mouthed lions." In those days it was the practice to send notes to be read at public worship before the long prayer, requesting suitable petitions in time of affliction, or on occasions of joy. Below is a note sent by the poet laureate, and read in his pulpit by the Rev. Charles Milton:

"Jonathan Plummer jr., desires to return thanks to the transcendently potent controler of the universe, for his marvellous kindness to him in raising him from a desperately low and perilous indisposition, to such a measure of strength and health that he is again able with gladness of heart and transporting rapture of mind, to wait at the celestial portals of wisdom. The said Plummer also desires to give thanks to Alpha and Omega, the first and the last, the beginning and the end, for his astonishing favor, his captivating mercy, and his personal regard to him in snatching him from endless grief and everlasting woe, in a miraculous manner; by light in dreams; for causing the day to dawn in his heart, and the dayspring from on high to illuminate his dark and benighted understanding; for chasing far from him the gloomy fog of infidelity, and enabling him triumphantly to rejoice in the glorious light and liberty of the Gospel, wherein his blessed Redeemer has crowned his happy life."

The Rev. Parson Milton's response to these requests was, "O Lord, have mercy on this over-pompous brother, whose wordy rhetoric has just startled our ears; save us from cant, bombast, and all the wiles of the devil. Amen."

I copy a document of Plummer's, headed "The Author's Last Will and Testament." "Preparatory Address to the Readers. Ladies and Gentlemen: At the request of a number of worthy friends, I now furnish you with my last will and testament. You will doubtless think it a very singular production, and you will think right; for, excepting a few lines in the beginning, which are partly borrowed from the last will of a celebrated writer, and the last paragraph, which is taken from Fisher, I believe nothing like it has ever been published or written.

But the will is not more singular than the usage which occasioned it. What this usage was I shall not now undertake to disclose, for to do justice to the subject would I believe require a considerable number of volumes; and besides, my abilities are inadequate, vastly inadequate to the ponderous task. Was the celebrated Cicero again permitted to live in our world I fancy he might talk day and night on the subject, might entirely exhaust his unequaled eloquence, might move earth and perhaps Heaven, to pity, to commiseration, and to tears, and perhaps not half disclose the affecting scene, not half display the inexpressible anguish with which the barbarous treatment of a certain man has oppressed my tender soul.

The resentment which I now display is not the effect of any sudden and unreasonable gust of passion. I have long dispassionately considered the subject, and the influence of religion, of justice, of duty to parents, of good breeding, and of every other incentive to moderation, folly only excepted, has been in this case eagerly sought after, listened to, and properly regarded by me.

I, Jonathan Plummer jr., of Newbury, in the Commonwealth of Massachusetts, seriously considering the uncertainty of human life, do, while in a sound state of mind, and in tolerable bodily health, make this my last will and testament; being determined to dispose of all my earthly property, not as custom may prompt, but as justice and equity seem to direct. I most humbly recommend my soul to the extensive mercy of that supreme, eternal, intelligent Being, who gave it me: at the same time most earnestly deprecating his justice. If I die in Newbury or in any place within twenty miles of it, I desire to be buried in the burying ground which is near the meeting house, of the first parish in this town, and that I may be carried to the grave from my own apartment. Should my father, or any, or either of my brothers have the hypocrisy to follow me in mourning, or to walk between my coffin and the other people who happen to attend my funeral, I desire my executor to endeavor to prevent their so doing. Should my mammy and my oldest sister outlive me, I desire them to walk next to my coffin dressed in decent customar mourning, and as many of the ladies whose names I shall mention in this will, as happen to attend my funeral, to follow them, but not in mourning. As the usage I have received from my father and brothers has given me tortures which no tongue can express, I do not mean that they shall be much the better for my property which I may happen to leave in this world. But, nevertheless, as my father happened somehow or other, when he first made a will, so far to forget his enmity as to bequeath me about a thirtieth part of what he was then worth, as a grateful return for this almost miraculous favor, I give and bequeath to him the sum of seventeen shillings; which is not far from a thirtieth part of what I was possessed of when I for the first time committed a will to writing. As something influenced my father to order the sum which he bequeathed me to be handed to me in ten annual payments, his conduct influences me to treat him in the same manner. I desire my executor to pay him the above seventeen shillings in ten different yearly payments. One shilling, eight pence, one farthing and a half yearly, the first nine years after my death, and the tenth year one shilling, eight pence, two farthings and a half. But should my father die before he has received all which I bequeath him in this manner, it is my will that my executor keep what remains in his hands of the seventeen shillings at the time of my father's death, for his own proper use and benefit. This is all the money which I can conscientiously give my father, but at the same time I wish him riches more durable, more inestimably valuable than gold. I wish him that precious light of Christ which once partly illumined his now (in my opinion) benighted understanding. I wish him, and was it in my power, I would bequeath him such a portion of the blood of the meek and lowly Redeemer, as would wash him from all sin, enable him to face me at the bar of the righteous judge at the great day, and rescue him from those torments which the abuse which I have received from him so amply and so eternally deserves. My mamma having used me as a son, I should be glad to leave all the rest of my property to her, if it was not nearly the same thing as leaving it to my father and brothers; but her interest is so nearly connected with theirs, and the good which I have received from her has been so many hundred times counterbalanced by the evil treatment which I have received from them, that I cannot conscientiously reward her kindness any farther than by giving her a share in common with the rest of the ladies mentioned in this will.

It is my will that my executor, soon after my decease, convert all my real and personal estate into ready money. That he shall collect what happens to be due me, and sell all my property, of whatever kind it happens to be, by public auction or private sale, one or both, as he shall think proper; and that after deducting the aforesaid legacy of seventeen shillings, paying all my just debts, and taking pay for his own time, trouble and expense, and what time, trouble and expense he shall then expect to be incumbered with as executor to this my last will and testament. After doing this I say, it is my will that he soon after equally divide all the remaining part of my money among the following amiable ladies, as many of them I mean as happen at that time to be alive, viz: My mamma, Miss Anna Bayley, the two oldest daughters that are not now married, of Capt. Jonathan Poor, Misses Judea Plummer and Hannah Plummer, daughters of Mr. Jeremiah Plummer; Misses Else Adams, Rhoda Plummer, Rebekah Noyes, Margaret Robinson, Mary Hook, Charlotte Ilsley, Jemima Knight, Hannah Adams, daughter of the late Mr. Richard Adams deceased, Ruth Short, daughter of Mr. James Short jr., Eunice Pearson, Mary Noyes, and the very amiable Sarah Little, daughter of Mr. Richard Little, the transcendently amiable Misses Else Tucker, Mary Tucker, Elizabeth Tucker, Charlotte Tucker, Clarissa Tucker, Catharine Tucker and Hannah Tracy; the handsome Mrs. Mary Noyes, widow of the late Capt. John Noyes deceased, and the blooming widow Huldah Noyes the consort of Mr. William Stickney; the consort of Mr. John Holland, and the consort of Mr. George Adams of Newbury in the Commonwealth aforesaid; Mrs. Judea Kent and Mrs. Elizabeth Pike, spotless widows; the transcendently lovely Mrs. Lydia St. Barb, Abigail Cutler, Hannah Boardman, Sarah Wigglesworth and Katherine Wigglesworth: the eminently amiable Misses Mary Barber, Elizabeth Greenleaf, daughter of Mr. Abner Greenleaf; Lucy Lunt, Sarah Smith, Catharine Murray, Elizabeth Ingalls, Maria Ingalls, Mary Moulton, Mary Sweat, Eunice Sawyer, Abigail Boardman, Sarah Couch, Anna Couch, Anna Dodge, Isabella Thompson, Lydia Thompson, Hannah Noyes, Jane Noyes, Sarah Alexander, Mary Alexander, Mary Moody, Sarah Moody, daughters of Mr. Benjamin Moody of Newburyport, in the Commonwealth aforesaid; Mrs. Eleanor Weeks of Candia in Chester, and Miss Elizabeth

Plumer of Exeter, in the state of New Hampshire.

I meant to write the aforesaid list of names for certain reasons, without any epithets denoting the qualities of the ladies, but it is very difficult for me to speak about such heavenly lassies without these epithets, and I doubt whether even the pope or his nuncio, if he knew them as well as I do, could go through the task which I meant to perform. Had I allowed free scope to my inclination I should have added a shining epithet to each of the respected names, nor should I then have done more than each of the lovely ladies deserve from my pen. I am sensible that the total sum of my fortune is but trifling, but I hope to make a considerable addition to it, and should I die without being married, I mean that the aforesaid ladies shall have all that I leave after seventeen shillings are deducted from it, be it more or less. They saw me afflicted and tormented by a man from whom I might naturally expect better usage; and while I believe this man was laboring to destroy my character and retard my fortune, with enmity more abusive than death, more cruel than the grave; when I was warmly contending with poverty, rags and wretchedness, I received from these ladies such friendly treatment as rendered my low estate not only tolerable but in some measure happy, while some less virtuous ladies seemed to rejoice at my misfortune, and denied me the common civilities of life, even the favor of walking the ground with them. The above named ladies not only failed to imitate them in these respects, but gave me reason to think that they wished to see me in better circumstances. The value of the civilities which I have received from them is greatly enhanced when I consider the immense wisdom and angelic beauty of a great part, and the captivating amiableness of the whole number. Considering these things, I know no bounds that I ought to set to my gratitude, love and esteem. Had I ten millions of dollars to dispose of more than I have, I would freely will it all to them. I wish them the most consummate earthly felicity, and was it in my power to insure them seats in paradise, I should not eat nor drink with half the pleasure that I should take in conveying to them the most delightful mansions in those realms of bliss. I think it apparent from Scripture that departed souls retain a remembrance of the friendly deeds of their benefactors in this world, and I confess that I am not without hopes of being serviceable to those lovely nymphs in the regions which we shall inhabit beyond the grave; even after ten million times ten million years have rolled away, I hope to give them fresh marks of my present unfeigned and boundless regard.

I make, constitute, ordain and appoint Mr. Edmund Knight of this town, sole executor to this my last will and testament, hereby renouncing, disallowing and disannulling all former wills, testaments, executors, legacies or bequests by me in whatever manner named, willed bequeathed, hereby ratifying and confirming this and this only to be my last will and testament. In testimony whereof I have hereunto set my hand and seal."

Dexter owned a farm in Chester, and consequently styled himself Earl of Chester. He erected handsome building on this estate, and these were decorated with several images, which were a wonder in that region for a long time. The poet laureate's description of his lordship and the Dexter mansion ran in this wise:

"Lord Dexter was a man of fame,
And celebrated was his name.
His house was white,
And trimmed with green,
And on the top an eagle seen.

Lord Dexter, like King Solomon,
Hath gold and silver by the ton;
And bells to churches he has given
To worship the great King of Heaven,

Two lions stand to guard the door,
With mouths wide open to devour
All enemies who dare oppose
Lord Dexter or his shady groves.

The images around him stand,
For they were made at his command;
Looking to see Lord Dexter come,
With *fixed* eyes they see him home."

Dexter gave the Harris street church $333.33 to purchase a bell, and a similar sum was presented to St. Paul's society. He evinced a praiseworthy liberality in aiding any enterprise that would benefit the town, taking over a hundred shares in the Essex Merrimac bridge. On the Fourth of July following its completion he delivered an oration there, which, says the Essex Journal, "For elegance of style, propriety of speech, and force of argument was truly Cicceronian!!"

Lord Timothy also greatly improved the roads around his mansion. His offer to pave High street, and to build a brick market house, if they might bear his name the town rejected; but the two thousand dollars he bequeathed in his will, "the interest of which he directed the overseers of the poor annually to distribute to such of the poor of the town as are the most necessitous, who are not in the workhouse," was accepted and acknowledged with gratitude and thankfulness." Determined to rank amongst those whose names never die, Dexter wrote a book entitled "A Pickle for the Knowing Ones." A sufficiently original production to obtain its author's aim. Punctuation was omitted till the last page, which was closely covered with the various marks, the readers being directed "to pepper and salt it as they pleased."

Dexter died in 1806 and his house was rented for a tavern. The widow of his only son, Samuel, and his only daughter, Mrs. Bishop, boarding with the landlord's family. As the images decayed they were removed, but the three presidents remained over the front door for many years. As the tomb in the garden was near the house, it did not become Lord Timothy's mausoleum, he was interred with his wife and son on Burying Hill, the garden tomb continuing an object of interest to visitors at the hotel until a comparatively recent date.

The streets of Newburyport, though greatly improved, were often unprovided with gravelled sidewalks. There were but few pavements, and those principally before some of the larger mansions. The bricks were usually laid side up, some presenting a zig-zag or herring bone pattern.

Prior to 1800 the town commenced to plant shade trees. Lombardy poplars were a favorite avenue tree. The Boston turnpike had a row on either side as far out as "Old Maid's Hall," and it was common to see three of these stiff trees before a house, towering sentinel like on the edge of the sidewalk.

On Merrimac street nearly opposite Broad, is an ancient house which was formerly a noted inn, known as "Spaulding's Tavern." The Stone house, on a farm near the Upper Green, Oldtown, is another very ancient mansion. This farm was first owned by Mr. John Spencer, who sold it to Capt. Daniel Pierce. Capt. Pierce erected a dwelling of stone, after the style of an old English manor house. This was the girlhood home of Martha Pierce, the mother of my great grandfather Johnson. Afterwards the place was owned by Mr. Nathaniel Tracy, whose family resided there some years; it next became the property of Capt. Offin Boardman, who built the wooden wing at the upper end of the house, and the L in the rear. Capt. Boardman sold the estate to Mr. John Pettingel, and at the time of which I am writing, it was known by the name of the Pettingel Farm. At one time this house, on account of its safety, was the depot for the town's powder. One of Mr. Pierce's negro slaves, having placed a lighted candle in a keg of powder, blew out one side of the house, and much to her consternation lodged herself amongst the limbs of a large apple tree. There are many legends connected with this antique dwelling, which, if its walls could speak, would many a tale unfold. There is a tradition that in the early days, the males being absent, an Indian who came with evil intent, was forced by the females of the family into a chest in the cellar, where his earthly career soon closed, and that thereafter his shade haunted the spot.

Another ancient family residence is situated in the "Farms District," Newbury. The place originally belonged to John Hull, who died in 1670. At his decease it was purchased by John, oldest son of Mr. Nicholas Noyes, who built the house soon after. The homestead has descended from father to son to the sixth generation. John's son and grandson were both named Daniel. Maj. Samuel Noyes and his son Samuel to Luther, his fourth son. The seventh generation are in his family, and two of the eighth have been born there. The house, a substantial edifice, was built in a style unusual for a farmhouse in those early days. The front hall is wainscotted, and a handsome staircase, with the elaborately carved balusters then fashionable for the first-class mansions, leads to the second story. The kitchen fireplace has been reconstructed, but when built it was huge even for the period; an ox could easily have been roasted whole in its capacious recess. This house has been the birthplace of several clergymen, physicians, and other distinguished persons. Dr. Daniel Poore's mother was one of the daughters of the family; her son was named for his grandfather, Daniel Noyes. On this Noyes farm is located one of the most promising of the newly discovered Newbury mines.

CHAPTER XLIX.

In the autumn of 1810 Mrs. Moses Colman was taken ill of a slow fever. As she would have no one but Sallie to nurse her, I remained in Byfield several weeks. During this time the household were troubled by a series of mysterious and untoward events. Mr. Colman missed a ten dollar bill from his desk drawer in a remarkable manner, the hens quitted laying, a cask of choice cider that had never been tapped was found empty, and Jerry's fine parade horse which was at pasture on the farm, presented a low and jaded condition. Jeremiah Colman and David Emery had been for some time officers in the troop. At that time Jerry was captain and David first lieutenant of one of the companies forming the regiment of cavalry. "What could have happened to Jerry's horse!" His father said "he looked sorry." At this juncture, Charles Field, the colored boy brought up in the family, now a youth of twenty, evinced great religious concern. His state was such that Dr. Parish was requested to visit him. The keen witted clergyman, after conversing with Charles, avowed lack of faith in his professions. "He had seen his mother in such states. It was his opinion that this show of piety was to cover some rascality. He had said as much to the fellow, and bade him ease his soul by confession, and by making every restitution possible." The next day to my surprise, I discovered the missing bank note in Mrs. Colman's cap box. It was immediately ascertained that Charles had for weeks been riding the parade horse to Newburyport, a series of dances having been held in Guinea which he had attended. Having hidden his Sunday suit in the hay mow, after the family had retired he stole out, dressing himself in the barn, saddled and bridled the horse, which had been stealthily brought up from pasture in the evening, using the military equipments, then dashed down to Guinea in grand style, exciting the envy of his brother beaux, and the great admiration of the sable belles. The ten dollar bill was taken to exhibit his grandeur and that of the family. On moving the cider cask, preparatory to its being refilled the straws with which its contents had been sucked from the bung were found with a heap of egg shells, which explained the former scarcity of eggs. Charles was brought to confess his misdeeds, with many professions of sorrow and promises of amendment. Such was the affection felt for one reared in the family from infancy, that he found a ready forgiveness.

A short time after my return from Byfield I was summoned to town. Col. Bartlett had at length succumbed to the disease that had threatened for many years; he was in a confirmed consumption, confined to his chamber, and most of the time to his bed.

Four years before, my aunt, who was childless, had adopted a little girl, and as she was wholly devoted to her husband, the care of this child and the superintendence of the house devolved upon me. These were sad but busy days. Mr. Benjamin Hale was acting stage agent for Col. Bartlett; he came every morning for orders, and through the day there were more or less callers concerned for one who was a general favorite. During the past year alarms of fire had been frequent; it was evident some person of evil intent was plotting mischief. The citizens had become watchful and solicitous. The stable, where the next spring the fire commenced, had been set on fire two or three times, but the flames had been extinguished without an alarm. David Emery prevented one conflagration with a bushel measure of water; he had led his horse to Mr. George's shop, and was waiting for the men to come from dinner to shoe him. The street was quiet. David tied his horse and sat down to wait; at that instant he descried smoke issuing from the window of the stable opposite. Springing up, he caught a bushel measure that stood by the pump, and filling it ran to the loft. The chamber was empty with the exception of one corner, where a heap of the hay chaff had been scraped together which was burning briskly. Mr. Emery dashed on the water in the measure, which sufficed to quench the flames.

In February the incendiary was more successful. One evening in that month, Mr. Gilman White's crockery store on State street was burned. About nine o'clock the bells gave the alarm. I ran to the front door to ascertain the location of the fire. As the latch was lifted I was confronted by David Emery; he bore one child in his arms and held another by the hand. "Here, Sally," he hurriedly exclaimed, giving me the infant, "these are Ann and Charles Stetson. Gilman White's store is ablaze, and Mrs. Stetson has gone to Topsfield. Prince has sent the children to you." I took them into the sitting-room, while Mr. Emery hurried away. Little Charles did not wake; the girl brought Eliza Bartlett's cradle, at which that young miss, wakened by the hubbub, made a great ado; but I managed to lay the infant down still sleeping. Having silenced Eliza, I placed Ann Stetson, a quiet, pleasant child, in my bed. The fire was confined to Mr. White's store. Soon after midnight Mr. Stetson came and took Charles home, but Ann remained till her mother's return.

The third of May, the first circus that ever visited Newburyport came into town; an Italian troop, Messrs. Cayetano & Co. A board pavilion was erected in an unoccupied lot between Pleasant and Harris streets; this was furnished with seats in the pit, which surrounded the ring; above was a gallery, with boxes comprising the dress circle. There was a stand for musicians. The exhibitions were on Monday, Wednesday and Friday afternoons; the doors opened at half-past three; the performance commenced at half-past four. Tickets to the boxes were one dollar; to the pit fifty cents; children under ten years of age half price. This was a most respectable and fine looking company, their horses were splendid animals, all the appurtenances in the best style. The performance commenced by the "Grand Military Manœuvres by Eight Riders." As the company furnished but six, upon their arrival at the Wolfe Tavern they applied to Mr. Stetson to fill the cortege. He referred Cayetano to Samuel Shaw and David Emery, as two of the best military riders in the place. These gentlemen hesitated respecting joining such a show, but by the solicitation of friends their scruples were overruled. The matter was kept secret; only a select few knew of their intention, and the uniform would prove a perfect disguise. Col. Bartlett was so feeble, I hesitated with regard to accepting Mr. Emery's invitation to the circus, but my uncle insisted upon my going, "he was curious to hear about it, wished he could see Sam and David ride, he knew they could sit their horses with the best of them." My plans came near being reversed, through the conversation of a band of callers on the morning prior to the Wednesday afternoon performance, which I had engaged to attend. Little suspecting that I had any special interest in the play, these pious women invoked the wrath of Heaven, and its most awful judgments upon the company and all who should patronize them. "A mean, low set of foreigners, their presence was a disgrace to the town; they wondered the selectmen should grant them a permit. No one of the least respectability would think of showing themselves in such a place as this circus." Abashed, I reported to Uncle Bartlett. He declared the talk all nonsense, and bade me go. Finding that my Uncle Peabody and Sophronia were going and that most of the elite had purchased tickets, I ventured to dress for the occasion. Mr. Emery escorted me to a private entrance on Harris street, where we joined Mr. and Mrs. Shaw. The gentlemen having conducted us to a box, went to don their uniform. We were soon joined by General Peabody and his daughter, and Dr. Prescott and his daughters. Col. Greenleaf occupied the next box. I soon espied Mr Moses Colman and his son Jerry in the pit, and as seat after seat and box after box filled with the wisdom, wit, beauty and fashion of the town and vicinity, I leaned back in my seat, satisfied with my company, and glad that to please my uncle and David I had not been over scrupulous.

This was prior to the formation of brass bands. The music consisted of some half dozen performers on the bugle, clarionet, bass-viol and violin. Various airs had been played while the audience were gathering. As the moment arrived for the performance to commence, at a bugle call, in dashed the eight horsemen, in a showy uniform in single file: they rushed around the ring, then followed a series of splendid feats of horsemanship and military tactics. I do not think I should have known either Mr. Shaw or Mr. Emery had they not given a little private signal. They did themselves great credit, rode better even than the trained equestrians. Cayetano was highly delighted, and was most profuse in his encomiums and compliments. The military exercise over, Master Tatnal performed several gymnastic feats. He was followed by Master Duffee, a negro lad, who drew down the house by feats of agility, leaping over a whip and hoop. Mr. Codet signalized himself in feats of horsemanship. Mr. Menial, the clown, amused the audience by buffoonery and horsemanship. Mr. Cayetano executed on two horses the laughable farce of the "Fish woman, or the Metamorphosis." With a foot on each horse he rode forward, habited as an immensely fat fishwoman, in a huge bonnet and uncouth garments. Riding rapidly round the ring he divested himself of this and several other suits, ending in making his final bow as an elegant cavalier. The young African next performed feats of horsemanship and vaulting, danced a hornpipe, and other figures, ending by dashing round the ring, standing on the tips of his toes. The horse, Ocelet, posted himself in various attitudes, danced and took a collation with the clown. Mr. Cayetano performed the Candian Peasant, and feats of horsemanship with hoops, hat and glove, terminating by the leap of the four ribbons separated and together. Mr. Cayetano performed the pyramid, young Duffee on his shoulders as "Flying Mercury." Then came the Trampoleon exercise by Messrs. Menial, Codet, and the young African: somersets over men's heads and a leap over six horses. The next scene was the Pedestal: the horse of knowledge posted in different attitudes. The performances concluded with the Taylor riding to Waterford upon the unequalled horse Zebra.

by Mr. Menial, the clown. This was a most laughable farce, Zebra being a Jack trained to the part. This elicited a storm of applause, and the play ended with cheer after cheer. The circus gave universal satisfaction, and from Newburyport they went to Exeter, intending to make an Eastern tour.

CHAPTER L.

"There is a destiny that shapes our ends,
Rough hew them as we will."

The memorable Friday evening, the thirty-first of May, 1811, the sun set in unclouded splendor, gilding the church spires, and gleaming upon tree tops, window panes, and the masts of the little fleet anchored at the wharves up and down the river. For the last time its rays illumined the ancient town; when it sank behind the western heights it bade a final adieu to many an antique landmark and to many a goodly heritage. The last lingering gleam died away from the old "port," which henceforth would only be known in tradition and song. For the last time busy feet trod those long lines of lofty warehouses; carts and drays rattled up and down the wharves; the evening stage coaches dashed up to the Old Wolfe tavern; merchant and artisan turned the key, and wended their way homeward; the tea urn steamed on the luxurious board in stately mansions, and the more frugal supper was served in the dwellings of the mechanic and laborer. Little did they reck that ere another day should dawn, each would be reduced to a perfect equality, alike homeless and penniless. That the old town of the primeval settlers and of Revolutionary fame would have passed into oblivion, that one period had ended, that henceforth a new town was to arise, a new order of things to be instituted, new customs and business to be established, new men and measures to be represented; but the old town of Newburyport, with its commerce, its prestige and aristocratic splendor had gone forevermore.

As home duties claimed my presence I returned to "Crane Neck" the last week in May. The night of the thirty-first, the family, with the exception of my mother and myself, retired at nine o'clock. We were sitting by the smouldering fire, sadly talking over my winter's experience, when a knock came upon the back door. Surprised, I rose, and drawing aside the fastening, opened it upon William Thurrell, who hastily exclaimed, "Sallie, Newburyport is on fire." Repeating his words to mother, I ran to the eastern end of the house, and throwing open the door, I stood transfixed. It was then only half-past nine, and it was so light that at that distance I could have read fine print.

The family and neighborhood were aroused; the young men saddled their horses or harnessed teams, and hurried to town. The others watched and moaned in a helpless anguish nearly bordering on despair. The house soon became thronged. People came from miles back, to the hill. We had a good glass, and from the range of the Pleasant street church steeple, which we momentarily expected to see enveloped in flames, saw that the fire was still below the residences of Gen. Peabody and Col. Bartlett, but we knew that much of their property must be burned, with that of other relatives and friends. Recalling David Emery's activity, courage, and self-forgetfulness, I knew that he would rush into the thickest of the fight waged against the devouring element, and I could not but feel anxious for his safety. It was a fearful, a terrible night. If I could have been on the spot, could have but a helping hand! —but to be thus compelled to gaze in inactivity was horrible. All night long the flames swelled and surged, with a roar like that of the distant sea. Towards morning came the sound of explosions, when great pillars of smoke, flame and sparks, would spring up towards the sky. By sunrise the fire had become subdued; but a dense smoke veiled all the intervening space, and the sun came up the heavens red and lowery, its rays obscured by the dense atmosphere.

Some of the neighbors came home in the morning, but my uncle, Ben Little, and my brother James remained through the day. It was evening ere we learned the full extent of the great fire. This conflagration commenced soon after the ringing of the nine o'clock bell, in the unoccupied stable in Mechanics' Row, Inn street, in which the former incendiary attempts had been made.

It was a pleasant moonlight evening, and probably over a hundred persons were walking the streets in the vicinity. Suddenly a tall spire of flame shot up into the sky, and in an instant the whole neighborhood was aglow. No rain had fallen for several weeks; a brisk westerly wind was blowing, which threw the flames directly upon some of the principal stores. The alarms of fire had of late been so frequent that the fire department were unusually efficient. There were three or four as good hand engines as could be purchased, worked by willing and sturdy hands, and several fire companies in perfect organization, each member of which was supplied with two leathern buckets, and a knapsack containing two canvas bags, of the capacity of four bushels each, for the removal of clothing and bedding. The buckets were painted green, with the owner's name inscribed within a gilt scroll on the side; the name was also stamped upon the knapsack and bags. The rules of these societies required the apparatus to be hung in the front entry of the owner's residence, and once a month members were detailed to examine into their efficiency.

In addition wardens were appointed, who, armed with long poles, ordered and directed at a fire. There were also ladders placed at frequent intervals about the town, hung upon a fence or building, protected from the weather by a board nailed slant-wise above it. The bells rang the alarm, but before a stream of water could be brought the stable was enveloped in flames, which in an incredibly short time consumed the two unimproved stables, the tavern and grocery of Joseph Jackman, Mr. Nathan Follansbee's grocery store, and a dwelling house belonging to Mr. Matthew Perkins on Inn street. Notwithstanding the fire department in full ranks worked with the energy of twice their force, aided by every exertion of the citizens, the flames could not be subdued, but soon swept down to the market, thence to State street. Every one rushed to the rescue; long lines were formed to pass water; the high bred lady stood side by side with her servants, and humbler neighbors; all distinction of cast, age or sex, was lost in this vortex of misery and terror. Assistance came from Newbury, Amesbury, Salisbury, Rowley, Ipswich, Danvers, Beverly, Haverhill, Topsfield, Bradford, and towns across the river in New Hampshire. Engines were brought from Salem and some other towns, but the flames spread in such various directions as to baffle all exertions to subdue it. In a few hours it prostrated every building on the north side of State street, from Pleasant street to Market square, and on the opposite side from Essex street. It proceeded into Essex street on the northeast side to the house of Capt. James Kettell, where it was checked; into Middle street as far as Fair street, on the northeast side, and a few rods there on the southwest side into Liberty, within one house of Independent, and down Water street as far as Hudson's wharf, sweeping off every building within the circle. The whole of Centre street was laid in ashes, and the whole row of buildings in Merchants' Row on Ferry wharf: all the stores on the wharves between the market and Marquand's wharf, including the latter. This cleared about sixteen and a half acres, in the most compact and wealthiest part of the town. Nearly two hundred and fifty buildings were burnt, most of which were stores and dwelling houses. Upwards of ninety families were rendered homeless; nearly every dry goods store was burned, four printing offices—the whole number, including the Herald office, the custom house, the surveyor's office, the post office, two insurance offices—the Union and Phenix, the Baptist meeting-house, four attorneys' offices, four book stores, the loss in one of which was $30,000, and also the town library.

Blunt's Building and Phenix Building for a time presented a barrier to the destructive element, and hopes were entertained that they would be saved, but by a sudden change in the wind the flames were carried directly upon these immense piles. State street at this time presented a spectacle most terribly sublime, the flames meeting in an arch across it. The wind increased in strength, and it was seen that the new brick Baptist meeting-house on Liberty street was doomed. This was full of goods and furniture, deposited there as a place of undoubted safety at the commencement of the fire.

At two o'clock the fire raged in every direction. The authorities commenced to blow up and tear down the buildings in its path. About four o'clock the danger diminished, and at six the fire had in a great degree spent its fury.

The scene during the night was most terrible. The moon gradually became obscured and at length disappeared in the thick cloud of smoke which shrouded the atmosphere. The glare of light was intense, and the heat that of a sultry summer noon. The streets were thronged with those whose dwellings were consumed, conveying the remains of their property to places of safety. Every kind of a vehicle was pressed into this service, from a hand barrow to a stage coach.

"The incessant crash of falling buildings, the roaring of chimneys like distant thunder, the flames ascending in curling volumes from a vast extent of ruins, the air filled with a shower of fire, and the feathered throng fluttering over their wonted retreats, and dropping into the flames, the lowing of the cows, and the confused noise of exertion and distress, united to impress the mind with the most awful sensations."

I copy the description of Elder John Peak, the pastor of the Baptist society, whose church and dwelling with part of his furniture and clothing were bruned. He writes, "I saw the roof of our meeting-house tumbling in, leaving the brick walls principally standing. But what an awful sight! Bright flames ascending to a great height; explosions of powder, spirits, etc.; vast columns of cinders and flames ascending in quick succession to the clouds; a dense smoke ascending from the burning of tar, rosin, pitch, etc., formed thick clouds which spread over all in awful majesty. The roaring of the flames, accompanied with wind, the sound of the trumpets and voices of the firemen, the crash of buildings, the cry of the sufferers for help to secure their goods, and the increasing progress of the conflagration, altogether, was the most appalling scene I ever witnessed."

Much household furniture and clothing was burned that might have been saved at the commencement of the fire, had this not have been at such a distance that many whose houses were destroyed never suspected danger till too late; so swift was the destruction, and so meagre the means of transportation, that loss was unavoidable.

On Market square, Mr. Edward Rand's store was burned, but his house was saved. Perkins & Dean had two stores, one a fire-proof building, which was principally preserved; the remainder of the upper side of the square was swept clean. Mr. Abner Wood and Maj. Joshua Greenleaf lost two large ship chandlery stores, and three brick stores on Water street. Maj. Greenleaf's dwelling house, barn, smithy, etc., on Liberty street, were also consumed. On Ferry wharf was a block of lofty buildings called Merchants' Row; these were occupied by John Wood and others, warehouses; Samuel Brown, ship chandlery; A. & E. Wheelright, three stores, groceries, iron, etc; Jacob Stone, groceries; Zebedee Cook, groceries; Robert Dodge, flour; Joseph Stanwood, jr., sail loft; Thomas Pritchard, rigging loft.

On Boardman's wharf, Offin Boardman lost six stores and warehouses; these were occupied by Amos Toppan, Benjamin G. Boardman and John Ordione. At this wharf a schooner was burned to the water's edge.

On Atwood's wharf, Margaret Atwood owned three warehouses; these were occupied by John Wood and B. G. Sweetser.

On Carter's wharf, W. Boardman lost one warehouse, Enoch C. Toppan a shop, block maker, Nathaniel Carter a house and barn.

On Marquand's wharf, Joseph Marquand had six warehouses, a rigging loft, counting-room, etc. On Water street, at the head of the wharf, two dwelling houses and three stores; all of these were burned, including his elegant residence, one of the splendid mansions of the town. At this wharf the brig Washington lost its mainmast, rigging, etc.

On O'Brien's wharf, Capt. Joseph O'Brien lost one store, and his dwelling house at the head of the wharf, with another store on Water street.

On Jackson's wharf, Mr. Abraham Jackson lost two warehouses, three stores, and a house on Water street.

On Jewett's wharf, Mr. Jonathan Gage lost one warehouse. The south side of Cornhill, from Charter to Essex street, comprising the Newburyport bank and the Peabody building, with the dry goods stores of James Caldwell, S. Davis, David Peabody & Co., and Prescott Spaulding, were not burned;

these were the only dry goods stores on State street that were saved. George Peabody at that time was a clerk inthe store of James Kimball, on Market square, which was burned.

CHAPTER LI.

On the evening preceding the fire, Frank Somerby, Ben. Tappan and David Emery had been walking in the mall. When the nine o'clock bell rung they turned homeward; they had reached the head of State street when that tall spire of flame darted skyward. Shouting "Fire," the trio ran down the street. "Head for my store," said Mr. Somerby, as Mr. Emery turned into Charter street to get his bags and buckets. David still boarded with his brother, and both belonged to the "Washington Fire Association." Tossing his watch and pocketbook into the hands of Margaret Lakeman, who resided in the family, he seized his fire apparatus and ran to Mr. Somerby's store, from whence he proceeded to Wolfe Tavern; after that had been cleared, he assisted in the removal of the bedding in the rooms occupied by Mr. Stetson, in the Phenix building. From that time he worked through the night, going from house to house as they became endangered, assisting the ladies to pack their valuables—a task in which he was peculiarly efficient. Within doors most of the time, too busy to look or think, at dawn he found himself on the farther confines of the fire; with amazement he gazed around—could it be daybreak? he thought it not later than twelve o'clock; could it be possible? For the first time he realized the extent of the terrible conflagration; for the first time thought of his own property, which characteristically had never entered his mind in his anxiety for others. Mr. Colman was equally oblivious, in aiding the members of his fire company and packing his household goods, which, as the fire surged up State street, were put in readiness for removal.

Being so near the river, the shambles, through the exertion of Capt. Israel Young, were saved; but a stable on Market square, owned by Dr. Smith of Mt. Rural, which Mr. Emery occupied, was burned; his loss however, was small, as his wagon was at the slaughter house on the turnpike, and his horse at pasture there.

A year previous, through commercial disaster and the dullness in trade engendered by the embargo, Gen. Peabody had been obliged to suspend business; his affairs were soon satisfactorily adjusted, and he commenced the erection of a new brick store on Market square; this building was just completed, and a fine stock of new goods had been put in that last week in May, in the expectation of opening to the public on the first of June.

On the afternoon of the 31st of May, Sophronia Peabody and her cousin David had taken tea at Deacon Osgood's, in West Newbury; they were on the summit of Pipestave Hill, on their way home, when that spire of fire shot into the sky. Mr. Peabody put his horse to a run; in breathless suspense they dashed to town, in dismay and terror watching the swift progress of the flames. As the couple drove into the yard of the State street mansion, David threw the reins to a boy who came to stable the horse, while he and Sophronia hastened to the store. Miss Peabody secured some rich lace, and a few other light but valuable articles, which she took home; these were the only goods in the whole of that large, new stock which escaped the flames; the rest unfortunately were taken to the Baptist meeting house, which later in the night was consumed with its contents. In addition, the General lost three other stores on Market square, and three on State street, the whole of "Peabody's Corner," and two on the opposite side of State street, which were owned in company with Mr. David Wood; one of these was occupied by Jonathan Woodman, jr., silversmith; the other was Newman's barber's shop.

By the change in the wind that took the Phenix and Blunt buildings, the upper part of State street became endangered; for a time fears were entertained respecting my uncle's elegant residence. Water was carried to the roof, the plate and much of the clothing was packed: but another shift of the wind averted all danger.

The day after the fire Col. Bartlett was borne on a bed to the residence of his brother-in-law, Gen. Peabody, and Mr. Stetson took Col. Bartlett's house for a hotel. The brick addition was built, and this continued to be the location of the "Eastern Stage House" for about two years. The Tuesday succeeding the fire I went to town; I found Col. Bartlett much more comfortable and cheerful than I had dared to hope; his good judgment and business tact were never more conspicuous than in a short consultation held with Gen. Peabody while I was in his room. The General, with reason, appeared nearly crushed. Seeing that her father had become somewhat inspirited by his relatives' firmness, Sophronia proposed that we should go out to view the ruins. Entering Market square from State street, we paused a moment on the site of that new store which had been the goal of so much promise, then proceeded down Water street, taking a circuit of the whole area. In many places heaps of rubbish were smouldering in the cellars. It was indescribably sad to see the large space covered with charred debris and half-fallen chimneys; those belonging to dwelling houses were mostly standing to above the ovens. The sight of these domestic appurtenances brought such a vivid picture of household desolation that I turned hastily away and left the scene.

As many strangers were in town, drawn thither by the double motive of viewing the ruins and doing spring shopping, the dry goods stores in the Peabody building presented quite a lively aspect. At David Peabody's store we met his fiancee, Miss Sally Caldwell, the daughter of Mr. William Caldwell. On passing Dr. Andrews' residence Miss Margaret came to the door; she was followed by her little sister Hannah, carefully holding a basket and box, in which were packed her dolls, playthings and picture books. Mrs. Andrews had kept her younger children asleep during the whole of the night of the fire; this gave Miss Hannah great offence; "her things might have been all burned up;" thenceforward, through the summer, they were kept in readiness for a removal at a moment's notice. There is but one step from the sublime to the ridiculous, many ludicrous incidents occurred at the fire. Little Eliza Bartlett, awakened by the noise and glare, clamorously demanded her best wrought muslin dress, thinking that it was some grand gala illumination; and a lady carefully conveyed what she supposed to be choice plate, a long distance, finding to her dismay upon arriving at her destination, that her burthen consisted of two flatirons.

Tea was announced upon our return; I had not intended to stop, but my aunts insisted upon this. Their equanimity and heroism excited both admiration and wonder; their nobleness of character was fully displayed in this time of trial; without neglect or confusion every duty was performed in the sick room and throughout the household. A stranger would never have imagined that such a change in the domestic arrangements had occurred in such a brief space of time.

From the purchase of his house Col. Bartlett had rented the lower half; at the time of the fire it was occupied by Mrs. Prout and Miss Nabby, the maiden sister of the late Mr. Prout. As Mr. Stetson needed the whole house, these ladies, with their young serving-maid, Ann Mason, had also become boarders in Gen. Peabody's family. On my account the meal had been served early; the gentlemen were not present, but the circle of ladies did their best to sustain a cheerful conversation, which was aided by the prattle of the children. I could scarcely swallow; and it was with a sigh of relief that I turned my horse's head homeward. Wishing to relieve my Aunt Bartlett of all unnecessary care I took her little adopted girl with me. General Peabody's second daughter, Adeline, a most lovely child, had been a sufferer from hip disease for some months; she came to Crane Neck soon after. I had one or both of the little girls with me most of the summer.

On Monday morning, June 3d, at 9 o'clock the inhabitants of Newburyport assembled to take into consideration the state of the sufferers by the fire, and to devise means for their relief. At this meeting the following persons were chosen a committee on behalf of the town to solicit that aid of a benevolent public which the distress of a great portion of other citizens so forcibly claimed, and to adopt the necessary measures for affording immediate relief to the destitute, and to distribute among the sufferers at their discretion all moneys or other property which might be received:

Jeremiah Nelson, Isaac Adams, Eleazer Johnson, Jacob Stone, Nicholas Johnson, jr., selectmen; Joseph Dana, William Woart, Isaac Stone, Nicholas Johnson, Aaron Pardee, William Bartlet, Moses Brown, William Coombs, John Pettingell, Samuel Coffin, Joshua Carter, James Prince, Michael Hodge, jr., Benjamin Pierce, William Russell, Stephen Howard, Robert Foster, Samuel Tenney, John Stuart, Samuel L. Knapp, Daniel A. White, Nicholas Pike, Thomas M. Clark, Joseph Williams, William Cross.

The selectmen of the town were authorized and appointed to receive all moneys and other donations for the use of the sufferers; and Wm. Bartlett, Woart, Moses Brown, Benj. Pierce, T. M. Clark, Nicholas Johnson, Joseph Williams, John Pettingell and Isaac Adams were appointed to solicit subscriptions, and receive donations from the inhabitants of Newburyport. The sufferers in need of immediate relief were requested to apply at the store of Capt. William Russell, Market square, where also contributions of provisions were gratefully received.

In a town meeting held on Friday,

June 7th, it was voted, "that in future no buildings should be erected within the limits of the town more than ten feet high, unless the same be built of brick or stone." From this vote sprang the large number of low wooden shops called "ten footers," which for a number of years disfigured the streets.

The 13th of June was set apart as a day of fasting and prayer, in consequence of the heavy calamity with which the town had been visited. In the forenoon a sermon was delivered in Rev. Mr. Dana's meeting-house by Rev. Mr. Miltimore of Belleville; in the afternoon the Rev. Dr. Buckminister of Portsmouth preached at the Rev. Dr. Spring's meeting-house; in both instances there were crowded audiences.

By the invitation of Rev. John Giles and his society, Elder John Peak preached in the Harris street church the Sunday succeeding the fire. In the morning the Baptist clergyman took his text from Isaiah 5th, 24th, "Therefore as the fire devoureth the stubble, and the flame consumeth the chaff, so their root shall be as rottenness, and their blossom shall go up as dust: because they have cast away the law of the Lord of Hosts, and despised the word of the Holy One of Israel." The afternoon sermon had for its object "Comfort to the afflicted who put their trust in the Lord."

The following Sabbath the Baptist society occupied the court house, in which they worshipped until the erection of the new church. This society was peculiarly bereaved by the fire. In addition to the loss of their meeting house, eleven of their principal members were amongst the greatest sufferers. Capt. Joseph O'Brien, who had been one of their most prominent benefactors, lost $30,000. At a society meeting June 11th, it was voted to appoint the Rev. John Peak an agent, to solicit aid towards the erection of a new house of worship. The clergyman made a tour as far south as Philadelphia and Baltimore, visiting most of the Baptist societies on his route. After his return he went as far east as Hallowell. This mission was eminently successful, and steps were immediately taken to procure the land for a new meeting-house; a committee of three was appointed to circulate subscription papers at the north, south and central parts of the town. That for the centre received no subscribers; at the south end one individual subscribed fifteen dollars; at the north end five hundred dollars were subscribed. Consequently it was decided to place the new meeting-house on Congress street. A plan for a building fifty feet by forty-two, with gallery, was approved, and the work commenced in April, 1812. The site of the old meeting-house, with the basement, bricks etc., were sold for the benefit of the original proprietors. After the new house had been begun, Dr. Bolles' society, of Salem, presented a subscription amounting to $440.17. This church was completed the last of July, and with the land cost less than than $4000. "The house was dedicated without parade, with fervent supplications for the divine blessing on the church, congregation, the word which should be dispensed there, and on their kind benefactors."

The Rev. Dr. Spring also made a tour for the purpose of soliciting funds, traveling as far south as Virginia. This call was met most generously; Philadelphia, with the aid given to Mr. Peak, contributed $3000, and a Moravian society in Pennsylvania added $60 to the funds forwarded from that state; besides many donations from distant parts of the country, the neighboring cities and towns were most prompt and liberal in their contributions; Boston gave $24,315.25; Charlestown sent $1,744.-55. Of this $150 was presented by the firemen to their brethren in Newburyport: Salem presented $1000 and contributions of clothing; Portsmouth and all the smaller towns gave as largely in proportion to their means. Those of our citizens who were able showed great liberality towards their unfortunate fellow citizens; provisions, furniture and clothing were given in large quantities from Newburyport, Newbury, and the other adjoining towns; Mr. William Bartlett presented $3000, Mr. Moses Brown $1500, and other gentlemen contributed as their means permitted; the Shaker families at Canterbury and Enfield sent five wagon loads of furniture, bedding, clothing and food, which were received with the warmest thanks.

The 1st of June the circus of Messrs. Cayetano & Meniel was in Portsmouth; these gentlemen wrote to Samuel Shaw and David Emery that if they would come over and ride in the military exercise, they would advertise a benefit for the Newburyport sufferers. This proposal was accepted with alacrity, and the proceeds of the exhibition, which amounted to sixty dollars, were handed to the Newburyport Relief Association. Such a noble charity from foreigners and strangers was duly appreciated by our townsmen, and it was with genuine grief that some two or three years after, they received the tidings of the loss of the whole troop on their passage from New Orleans to Havana.

Of the money received, as just a distribution as possible was made. No one whose remaining property amounted to the value of five thousand dollars received any appropriation. From the first few days after the fire the burnt area in the vicinity of Market square and State street presented a most busy aspect; the debris was quickly cleared, and the foundations of most of the present buildings were laid; before winter many dry goods and grocery stores were opened, and by the second year the town bore a much handsomer appearance than before the fire; but the war with England and other causes combined to curtail business, and it was years before the traces of the great fire were wholly obliterated.

Col. Bartlett lingered till November. For many weeks he laid helpless as an infant, and the end came gently; without any painful struggle, his transition to another world was in perfect keeping with his calm, genial character. Earthly cares and duties finished, he departed, in the hope of a new and blissful life in that world "where there is no more death." His widow bowed in submission, casting her burden upon that Savior who alone could give comfort. His relatives, friends, and the whole community mourned the loss of one, who at the early age of thirty-eight had been called from their midst.

Col. Bartlett was buried under arms, and the funeral, which was from Gen. Peabody's residence, was largely attended. Dr. Dana conducted the service, then the military formed in the order of escort; behind the hearse a negro attendant led the Colonel's famous charger—a splendid white horse;

from his bridle floated bands of crape; the housing was of black; across the saddle depended the uniform boots, with spurs attached, and upon it were laid his sword and cap, with its long white plume; next came a long procession of gentlemen on foot, and a long line of mourners in carriages concluded the cortege, which to the solemn beat of the muffled drum slowly moved to the Old Burying Hill, where dust was rendered to dust. A volley having been fired over the grave, the musicians struck up a lively air, and the remains were left in the full hope of a glorious immortality.

The famous white horse became the property of Mr. Benjamin Hale, who succeeded Col. Bartlett in the stage agency. Though obliged to part with her favorite, Mrs. Bartlett, through the kindness of Mr. Hale, never felt his loss, as she had only to name the time when a ride was desired, and the horse was immediately put at her disposal.

My preparations for marriage were nearly complete, but nothing definite had been decided upon, when to my utter astonishment, one evening in March David Emery came with the announcement that he had hired the Pillsbury place in Belleville, and had come to take me down with him in the morning to inspect the premises, and assist in making farther arrangements. I was completely dumbfounded. The Pillsbury domain consisted of a farm of sixty acres, on which was a large, old-fashioned house, which for many years had been a noted tavern for drovers and country traders. With the most perfect *sang froid* Mr. Emery stated his intention of immediately putting up a large slaughtering house, and that he had already hired Mr. James Carey to assist in the butchering business. Mr. Carey, his wife and two children were to occupy a part of the house. "I was expected to become the mistress of a public house on a large farm, with an extensive butchering establishment attached!" "Yes, and I could do it." Efficient help had been secured—a girl from Lock's Hotel, who knew every "rope in the ship." Lock had succeeded Coburn, who had been appointed deputy sheriff.

Somewhat encouraged, I began to gather my scattered ideas and to take a more coherent view of things; but it was after a restless night that I set forth with Mr. Emery in the morning. The place of our destination had formerly been the homestead of Mr. Edward Rawson, to whom at the first settlement of the township five hundred and eighty-one acres of land had been granted, which was termed Rawson's Newbury plantation. Mr. Rawson was the first town clerk of Newbury, and one of the wealthiest and most influential citizens. Afterwards he became Secretary of the colony of Massachusetts and moved to Dorchester. The unfortunate marriage of his youngest daughter, Miss Rebecca Rawson, to an Englishman named Thomas Ramsey, under the assumed name and character of Sir Thomas Hale jr., nephew of Lord Chief Justice Hale, Whittier has woven into his charming tale entitled "Margaret Smith's Journal," and this first home of my married life was the scene of that romance.

In 1651 (O. S) Mr. William Pillsbury purchased of Mr. Edward Rawson forty acres of land for the sum of one hundred pounds. The deed of this purchase is still held by the Pillsbury family. The present house was built

in 1700, by Mr. Daniel Pillsbury. Originally it consisted of the main building; the several additions, which so materially enhance its picturesque appearance, have been made as the needs of the occupant required. At this time the estate had passed through three generations to the heirs of Mr. Joshua Pillsbury, who a few years previous had purchased a farm in Boscawen, where he had recently died. Pilesburgh or Pilesborough, now Pillsbury, Essex, England, Arms. Per fesse sable and azure, on an eagle displayed argent; three griffins' heads, erased of the second. Crest, an Esquire's helmet· Motto, *Labar ammia vincent.*

A piercing March wind swept with great force across "the plains;" I was completely chilled before we reached our destination. The old tavern looked dreary and uninviting. With a sinking heart I stepped from the sleigh and accompanied Mr. Emery to the door. The premises were occupied by a family named Poor. Mr. Emery having introduced me to Mrs. Poor, went with Mr. Poor to the barn. My hostess led the way to the large kitchen next the street; the breakfast dishes had not been cleared, and the room bore a most untidy aspect. A chair having been dusted, I was requested to take a seat at the fire. Gathering my handsome, light, drab cloth pelisse about me, I ventured to do so. While warming my benumbed feet the landlady never ceased making apologies; she had not expected me so early, she had small children, etc. I stopped the talk as speedily as possible by rising to go over the house; the spacious rooms were dingy, dirty, and meagerly furnished; everything looked sombre and cheerless; I felt as though they were peopled with all the defunct Rawsons and Pillsburys: in fancy, gliding before me, I saw Miss Rebecca Rawson, whom the scamp Thomas Rsmsey so shamefully married, then robbed and deserted in a foreign land, and who soon after met with a tragical death, being swallowed up by an earthquake in Port Royal. Mr. Emery's brisk step and quick, business tone dispelled these illusions. Alterations and repairs were discussed; whitewash, paint and paper would work wonders. Quite inspired, I rode down to my Uncle Peabody's.

Considerable trade had sprung up between Newburyport and Alexandria and Georgetown, and several of our citizens had become residents of the District. Gen. Peabody had decided to join them: preparations were in progress for the families' removal to Georgetown early in the summer.

Mr. Bartlett still boarded at her sister's; her future was undetermined. I had long coveted the two card tables and some other articles of furniture that had stood in her parlor. Much to my delight I found that they could be purchased; Aunt Peabody was glad to let me take some of her surplus things. I returned home that night well satisfied; order was beginning to be evolved from the chaos of my brain, and courage was upspringing for the new career marked out for the coming years.

The wedding was on the 22nd of April. No one was present but the family. Dr. Parish performed the ceremony. I wore a white India muslin, the skirt edged by an ornamental border wrought in colored worsted; bands of similar embroidery finished the neck and short sleeves, with a girdle to match. My walking dress was a short pelisse of light drab silk, trimmed with black lace; the bonnet matched the pelisse, trimmed with bias folds of the silk bound with white satin, and white satin strings. The hair in full curls upon the temples, formed a sufficient face trimming. Mr. Emery had a blue coat with brass buttons; drab pants, white vest, a drab overcoat, and a very stylish black beaver; we both wore white kids.

Mr. and Mrs. Carey with their two eldest children, Sophronia and Hannah, were already settled in their rooms at the upper end of the house. On my arrival I found myself not only the landlady of a public house, but the mistress of a family numbering seven persons; besides Betsey Downing, the maid servant, there were three hired men, Daniel Smith, Aaron Palmer, John Webster, and a boy of fourteen named Guy Carlton Mackie. This lad had been cast a waif upon the world; his experience had been both varied and romantic; his last feat had been to escape from a British man-of-war, where he had been brutally treated, as his scarred back bore witness. Mr. Justin Smith picked him up in Boston and brought him to Newburyport to tend in his restaurant; he might as well have employed a monkey. As the lad, in common with most boys had taken a huge liking to Mr. Emery, Mr. Smith implored him to take him; "he could manage him if it was in the power of mortal to do it." Accordingly I was received by this hopeful, cap in hand, with the most graceful of bows. For two years he continued the most faithful and devoted of servants; my word was law, and he was equally obedient to Mr. Emery. Ever alert, quick-witted, possessing a knowledge of the world far beyond his years, he proved a valuable addition to the *menage.*

The March previous Capt. Jeremiah Colman and First Lieutenant David Emery had both received promotion; Captain Colman became Major of the regiment of cavalry, and Lieut. Emery took the command of the company. On the Monday following our marriage there was another choice of officers, when Jeremiah Colman was chosen Colonel and my husband Major. Thus, in the period of one month, David Emery received both a captain's and major's commission in the troop, besides assuming the responsibility of marriage and the management of an extensive business.

Belleville presented at that time the same neat and pleasant appearance as now. At the junction of the main ferry and bridge roads, facing High street, stood the old-fashioned hay scales. The first house round "Newton Corner" was that of Mr. William Wade; next came the fine residence of Mr. Robert Dodge; below stood Varnum Howe's house and hatter's shop, the Gordon house and blacksmith's shop, the residences of Mr. Amos Atkinson, Col. Eben Hale, Mr. Folsom, Mr. Russel, Mr. Oliver Hale and Messrs. Moses L. and Theodore Atkinson. Below came the Quaker meeting-house and the mansion of the late Dr. Edmund Sawyer, then occupied by his widow and family, and that of the Rev. James Miltimore, the Pillsbury place, the Atkins estate and the residence of Capt. Reuben Jones. The house on the corner of Toppan's Lane was owned by Mr. Jonathan Harris, whose wife was Anna Toppan, a daughter of the late Edward Toppan. Down the lane came Mr. Stephen Toppan's house and the old Toppan homestead, then the property of Mr. Enoch Toppan.

The first house on the lower side of High street, from the bridge road, was that of Miss Eunice Atkinson, afterwards Mrs. Moses Currier; the next belonged to Mr. William Merrill; next came the residences of Mr. Moses Atkinson, Orlando Merrill, Jacob Little, Stephen Little, the homestead of Josiah Little esq., Mr. Thomas Hale's house and hatter's shop; William Wigglesworth's house and that of Mr. Moses Merrill; the next house belonged to "Marm Fowler," one of the ancient school dames; below was a small one-story house, and another of two stories, the latter belonging to Dr. Edmund Sawyer's estate. On this side of the street was Russell's chaise manufactory. The schoolhouse and meetinghouse stood together, above Moody's Lane; below was Samuel Moody's house and that of Mr. Thomas Emery; on the upper corner of Tyng street stood the house built by Mr. Thomas Coker.

The morning after the arrival at our new home our next neighbor Parson Miltimore called, and in his genial manner bade us welcome. This was the commencement of a friendship that continued to the end of the worthy clergyman's life. Mrs. Miltimore, an invalid, visited but seldom, but the young people became most pleasant companions. The three sons, Andrew, James and John Murray, and the three daughters, Dorothy, Eliza and Mary, had none of them yet left the paternal roof.

The next Sunday we attended service at the Belleville meetinghouse. This was the first building, the one burned by lightning—a good-sized edifice, with galleries, and a tall and graceful spire. A broad and two-side aisle led to the pulpit, which was in the style of the period; a sounding-board was suspended above the desk, upon which rested a green velvet cushion; the arched window in the rear was draped with a curtain of the same color; the pulpit cushion, and the seats of the three yellow, oval-backed, wooden chairs which stood beneath it were covered to match. A mahogany communion table occupied the platform in front, and two handsome glass candelabra were placed either side of the sacred desk; there was no chandelier, but the sconces for candles were hung around the walls.

The society was large and of the highest respectability. The Pillsbury pew, which we had hired with the place, was on the left side of the broad aisle from the entrance, and about half way to the pulpit; one seat, which was cushioned, was reserved for Grandma'am Pillsbury; the rest of the pew, like those throughout the house, were unpainted boards hung upon hinges. Some faces were strange, but many of the congregation were relatives or acquaintances. There were the Little families from Turkey Hill and Belleville. Mr. Nathaniel Emery, from the lower parish of Newbury. The Toppans, Atkinsons, Mr. Thomas Hale's, and all the families on High street above the meetinghouse, and many below, Mr. John Balch's and Capt. John Remick's, and most of the other families from Bellevilleport. The choir, as was then the custom, was composed of volunteers, all good singers, and accompanied by a bass viol.

Gen. Peabody had established a store for dry goods in Georgetown, D. C.; in June his wife and family left to join him. They sailed in the brig Citizen, Capt. Dole, of Ring's Island. This was a regular packet plying between Newburyport and the District of Columbia, owned by Messrs. Robert, Allen and Frank Dodge. This firm was largely engaged in the flour trade, and for its greater facility Mr. Frank Dodge had recently become a resident of Georgetown. This separation from my aunt and cousins was painful to the whole family, but especially so to me; I took my farewell the day prior to their departure. The spacious house was empty and closed: the furniture, trunks etc., were loading for the vessel. My aunt and cousin Sophronia maintained a calm, even smiling exterior, though I well knew that great heart sobs scarcely permitted utterance. John, the oldest son, a handsome, noble youth, courageously assumed the burthen of manhood, and the younger children clustered about me, giving their little messages and last kisses. It was inexpressibly sorrowful to leave my pet, my sweet, darling Adeline; the beautiful girl so lovely in her suffering, clung to me in an embrace that spoke volumes; and I could not but feel that this was a final adieu. Polly Smart, the faithful handmaiden of years, who adhered to my aunt like Ruth to Naomi, also came to say good-bye. Sad, sad was the parting, and it was through an irrepressible mist of tears, that from the upper window of the old Pillsbury house I watched the Citizen glide down the river and over the bar; watched until she became a white speck on the sky, then wholly disappeared in the distance.

Aunt Bartlett took the house and shop formerly occupied by Mrs. Searle, and with the assistance of two young lady acquaintances she set up a fancy goods and milliner's store.

The intelligence of the declaration of the war with Great Britain was received in Newburyport on the fourth of July. There had been a celebration, oration, etc., Major Emery had been on duty, and Col. Moses Newell, of the upper parish, who dined with us. I was apprised of the news at the table. There was much conversation, but my husband said little, and I knew by his grave taciturnity that he was troubled. At night, after the house was still he came into my private parlor, and sinking into the large rocking-chair exclaimed, "Wife, I fear I am ruined." Whether it was my father's democratic rearing, or a clearer insight, I cannot tell, but someway I did not share in this despondency, and soon succeeded in chasing the gloom from his brow.

CHAPTER LII.

The declaration of war caused much anxiety for the safety of the Citizen. Two days' sail from Georgetown, and she was boarded by a British frigate. At her appearance Capt. Dole strove to outsail her, but the third shot over his bows compelled him to heave to and answer the demands of "where from" and "where to?" At the third question "with what laden?" a clerk of Gen. Peabody's named William Brown, who accompanied the family, caught the speaking trumpet from the captain's hand, and shouted, "A few Yankee notions, such as women, children and spinning wheels." A boat was immediately lowered, but as the boarding officer found that Mr. Brown had given a correct invoice, and though the declaration of war had passed the senate, its ratification by the House had not been received, after a short delay the Citizen was permitted to proceed to her destination, which was reached in safety, and my uncle's family were soon domesticated in their Southern home.

In Federal New England the war was exceedingly unpopular, and the Governor of Massachusetts appointed a public Fast. In every seaport there was much distress. Labor was impeded; the most industrious were enforced to idleness; poverty took the place of plenty; this was too often followed by despondency, drunkenness and misery. Many a noble man became a mere wreck of humanity, and many a delicately bred lady descended into an unthrifty, slatternly household drudge, while their offspring, half clad and half fed, mixed unrestrained amongst the very dregs of the population. "It is an ill wind that blows no one good." The war which ruined hundreds, brought, notwithstanding my husband's forebodings, great prosperlty to the tavern; we could not have engaged in a more lucrative business. British manufacturers having quantities of goods upon their hands, ran cargo after cargo into their eastern provinces, thence they were passed across the border and taken South by ox teams; as our accommodations were excellent, the teamsters made "Emery's tavern" their headquarters. The first teams arrived in September—five carts loaded with a variety of goods. consigned to Boston merchants. From that time until the winter of 1815 more or less came every week. usually to stop over night; at sunset I have often counted a dozen or fifteen drawn up by the sidewalk, opposite the long barn, their motley coverings of patchwork quilts, coverlets etc., presenting a gypsy-like, semi-barbarous appearance. Gunpowder and other ammunition was also transported. One night we slept with a large wagon loaded with powder standing directly opposite the house, but as the fact was not known until after its departure in the morning. no fears alarmed the household or neighborhood, but Mr. Emery was careful that there should not be any repetition of the risk.

Commerce being entirely stopped, and the coasting trade greatly impeded, all imported goods commanded an exorbitant price. Flour rose to fifteen and eighteen dollars per barrel, brown sugar was twenty-five cents a pound, molasses a dollar fifty cents per gallon. Dry goods, crockery, glass etc., were equally dear. I paid a dollar a yard for calico, a common-sized looking-glass cost sixteen dollars, common tea-sets were from nine shillings to two dollars. My china set was sixteen dollars; blue-edged dining plate were a dollar per dozen, knives and forks were from two and and a half to three dollars per dozen. With the exception of corn and wool, all kinds of country produce was cheap. Good butter brought from ninepence to a shilling, and cheese from eight to nine cents per pound; potatoes were twenty-five cents per bushel. All kinds of butcher's meat was low. Owing to the high price of wool the pelts alone paid the cost of the live animal, and a good carcass of mutton could be bought for fifty cents. Cheap as this was, owing to the lack of work, many had not the money to buy even a small piece of meat. Mr. Emery was in the habit of giving away livers, heads, and the cheaper pieces. Young lads out of our most respectable families, on half-holidays and after school, were glad to give a helping hand at the slaughter house. receiving in pay a liver, sweetbread, or bones for a soup. I have often watched them as they passed the house with their baskets, their faces radiant in the expectation of a good dinner on the morrow. Some of our best mechanics were glad to dig potatoes on shares, thus securing a supply for winter. Mr. Emery having raised three or four hundred bushels, this was a mutual benefit. As the supply brought by the eastern coasters was diminished, wood rose to ten dollars per cord. Most of this was rafted down the river, but during the winter quantities came from New Hampshire; in good sledding I have seen a dozen loads in a line proceeding down High street.

Federalist ideas were so prominent the fitting of privateers was strongly opposed; but as this was the only hope for our marine, and as the administration had some strong supporters, during the summer a number of vessels cleared from Newburyport, "bound on a cruise." One of the most active in this business was Capt. Benjamin Pierce, a wealthy and influential citizen, largely interested in shipping. During the war he fitted out several armed vessels at his own expense and tendered them to the government. Capt. Pierce married Elizabeth Gerrish, who was connected with one of the most prominent and influential families of the town, and through a long life she was eminent for piety, benevolence and patriotism. Capt. and Mrs. Pierce had five daughters and three sons—Sarah Coffin, who married Thomas H. Battell and afterwards Mr. James Oakes of Boston; Elizabeth Maria, who married Mr. D. C. Moseley, afterwards, Hon. Joel W. White of Norwich, Conn., who was consul at Lions, France, for several years; Rebecca married Mr. George Reed, a prominent merchant of Boston; Mary became the wife of our respected citizen, J. J. Knapp, esq. After the fire of 1811 Capt. Pierce built the mansion on High street, which after his decease came into the possession of Mrs. Knapp, where she resided until her death. This lady inherited the noble traits of her parents, and to an advanced age, she was ever ready to listen to any tale of suffering, while her hand and purse were always open to extend relief. Caroline, the youngest daughter, is unmarried, and has long been a resident of New York city. The three sons, Benjamin, Charles and George, all died single.

One of Capt. Pierce's vessels, the brig "Decatur," was commanded by Capt. William Nichols. In July the sound of heavy guns called the population to the wharves and other outlooks commanding the water. Coming up the river was the "Decatur," gay with flags and streamers, followed by two English prizes, the brig "Elisabeth," taken on the 25th of July, and the "Duke of Savoy," whose captain was shot dead at the wheel; there was also a French schooner, captured from the French by the English and recaptured by the "Decatur." A great crowd awaited the landing.

CHAPTER LIII.

Upon hiring the Pillsbury place Mr. Emery had put up a bowling alley. This attracted the townspeople, and as it was a pleasant walk to Belleville, I had many callers. Several of the elderly gentlemen became habitually accustomed to saunter up to the tavern on pleasant afternoons, when they often dropped into my private parlor for a chat. Mr. John Tracy, paralyzed and feeble, was a frequent visitor; he was usually accompanied by his friend, Mr. Samuel A. Otis. Mr. Tracy was fond of recalling the events of his earlier days; his tales of the Revolutionary period were very interesting. During the winter that Boston was occupied by the British, Mr. Tracy went to the city to visit his ladylove; he had scarcely arrived, when he learned that Gen. Gage had gained intelligence of a vessel of his loaded with gunpowder which was nearly due, and had placed one of the fleet on the watch for her. Bidding his betrothed a hasty adieu, he again mounted his horse and retraced his steps with all speed, finding to his great joy upon his entrance into Newburyport, his vessel safe at the wharf.

As I have previously stated, Mr. Tracy and his brother Patrick were largely engaged in privateering. A succession of ill luck had proved almost ruinous. At the end of 1777 the brothers had lost forty-one ships. Mr. Tracy's only hope was centered in a letter of marque of eight guns, of which he had received no tidings. Walking one day with his brother, discussing the ways and means of obtaining subsistence for their families, a strange sail was espied making for the harbor. Mr. John Tracy jocosely exclaimed, "Perhaps it is a prize for me." Mr. Patrick laughed a doubtful laugh, but Mr. John immediately took a boat and went down the river. To his great amazement, on reaching the ship he found that it was really a prize belonging to him, worth five and twenty thousand pounds sterling.

As the summer advanced dry goods of every description became excessively scarce, consequently exceedingly high in price. Though in most families there was more or less spinning and weaving, and the click of knitting needles was a familiar sound, it was difficult to procure proper apparel; plainness in dress was enforced by necessity. This state of things engendered an illicit traffic which our people as good Federalists were slow to condemn. I was awakened one night by a tap upon the window of my bedroom. Somewhat startled, I still forebore to awaken my husband, who had retired much fatigued. Slipping on a wrapper, I raised the curtain and asked "Who is there?" "A friend;" was the reply, "make no disturbance, but call the Major; I must see him a few moments." I recognized the voice as that of Capt. Josiah Bartlett; at that time an active shipmaster. Mr. Emery hastily dressed, when it was found that Capt. Bartlett had a stagecoach at the door, filled with merchandise, gloves, muslins, laces, vestings, ribbons, and other articles of a like description. These were hastily placed in my best bedroom, from whence they were gradually taken to the stores in town. Capt. Bartlett continued to bring goods for some time. We often had bales of valuable cloth hidden in the hay mow; some were taken to Crane Neck and stored away in the large back chamber.

The collector of the customs, Mr. Ralph Cross, and Master Whitmore, another custom house official, were in the habit of walking up to the tavern of a pleasant afternoon; on one occasion I entertained the two old gentlemen in my parlor while Mr. Emery loaded a team at the barn with smuggled goods and drove away to West Newbury without exciting the slightest suspicion in the government officers, though the whole household were on the broad grin, and I was obliged to control my risibles and give a variety of private signals to the others to prevent an unseemly outburst of merriment.

Late in the autumn Mr. Luther Waterman and Mr. Joshua Aubin received notice that a lot of linen awaited their order at "Kennebunk wharves." How were they to get it to Newburyport! "The Major" was everybody's resource in a dilemma, and no excuse would be received; "he must get that linen." Mr. Emery hesitated; it was a job he did not relish. Besides having inherited his father's consumptive temperament, his health was such he could ill bear over fatigue and exposure, but overcome by his friends' importunity, he at length reluctantly made his preparations for the journey. Wishing to remain unrecognized, he donned his worst suit of clothes, to which was added a gray spencer belonging to my brother James, too short in the waist and sleeves; over this was drawn an old overcoat, which as it was minus several buttons, was secured by a red surcingle; an old slouched hat and a pair of striped woollen mittens completed the disguise.

In the summer of 1811, Mr. Emery had driven to market the first covered butcher's cart. This wagon had been made to order, and was A 1 in every respect. To this wagon, for the Kennebunk expedition, were harnessed "tandem," the Major's splendid parade horse, "Peacock" and our family horse, "Kate," a beautiful sorrel mare. I expressed to my husband the fear that the contrast between his dress and his team might excite suspicion. My disquietude became increased at finding after Mr. Emery's departure that our house dog "Turk," a handsome and noted animal, was missing. According to my husband's direction, he had been shut into my room, but "snuffing the battle afar," in some unknown way he obtained egress, and started ahead, keeping shrewdly out of sight until his master had advanced too far on the road to turn back.

Mr. Emery set out early on Monday morning. Wednesday night the welcome rumble of wheels, and his glad tones, brought the whole family to the door. A large hogshead marked "Rum," filled the wagon, which was driven to the barn and unloaded. Turk, quite tired out, sought his nook beside my parlor fire, whither he was soon followed by his master, who having refreshed himself by a change of raiment and a good supper, entertained me with an account of his adventures.

The journey to the "Wharves" was made in good time. The goods were stored in the warehouse of a retired sea captain. This gentleman had been largely engaged in the West India trade, and there were plenty of rum casks at hand. After some consultation it was decided to pack the linen in one of these, which was done. A certificate must be at hand, but as the one belonging to this cask could not be found, another was adroitly altered. It was late ere all the arrangements were completed, and the captain invited Mr. Emery to pass the night at his residence, where he was entertained most hospitably. The following morning the cask was hoisted into the wagon; there were plenty to assist, several very gentlemanly looking young men lending a hand with alacrity. It was nearly noon before everything had been completed. By mistake the lower road was taken. Wishing to avoid the ferry at Portsmouth, Mr. Emery inquired of a young fellow he met how it could be done. The gift of a cigar won his good offices, and he volunteered to lead the way through a cross-road that turned on to the upper route. Night closed in; the path led through dense woods; an early snow that elsewhere had vanished, covered the ground; here and there were small clearings, where a log hut loomed up amid the charred stumps, its one or two small windows, radiant from the pine knot within, and crowded with faces that the crunch of the wagon through the snow had drawn thither.

The main route having been gained, his conductor left him. Having driven till past midnight, he came to a large tavern; after repeated knocks a boy's head was thrust from a window, who shouted, "'taint the teamsters, Mr. Smith, it's a man." After further parley the door was opened, and the landlord, bearing a lantern, came out, excusing the delay; he was troubled with teamsters from the back settlements, who only came in to warm themselves and get a drink, and the lad had been directed not to disturb the house by their admittance. The horses were stabled and a good supper provided, of which Mr. Emery partook, with Turk, who with true canine sagacity, fully shared his master's responsibility. The meal over, the landlord lighted his guest up-stairs. "There are three other gentlemen in the chamber, but you will find an empty bed," he said, as he opened the door. True; there was an "empty bed," but the occupants of the two others had stripped it of every article of covering excepting the sheets. Making virtue of necessity, Mr. Emery quietly slipped in alongside of the solitary sleeper in the second couch. It was scarcely dawn when his light slumber was broken by the rising of the occupants of the first bed. After they had gone down Mr. Emery rose and dressed without disturbing his bedfellow. As preparations for breakfast were in progress, he sat down by the bar room fire to wait for a cup of coffee. As he did so, one of his room mates said to the other, "That fellow up-stairs has been to Portmouth and got a custom-house commission." Mr. Emery could not repress a start; there he had been snoozing beside an officer of the customs, having taken his bed by storm. After a moment's consideration he concluded it best to order his horses and drive a few miles before breakfasting. Just as the wagon was brought to the door, the government appointee came below. Eyeing the team with a scrutinizing air, he bade Mr. Emery "Good morning," adding "Fine horses, sir; a handsome dog. From the eastward, I presume?"

The captain at the "Wharves" had given Mr. Emery several bunches of choice cigars. Handing his interrogator an Havana, Mr. Emery took the reins. The custom house officer politely thanking him, inquired, "if he had cigars to sell?" "Oh! no; only a few for his own use, and to present to a friend," Mr. Emery returned, giving him a half-dozen, Bowing his thanks, the officer asked, "Where that liquor was going?" expressing a doubt of the reliability of the cask. Mr. Emery was on the box, and away; too hurried to answer these pertinent queries. Nothing noteworthy occurred until he reached Hampton, when the weight of the linen was so great the transom bolt broke just in front of the tavern. Mr. Emery went down between the wheels. but received no serious injury. The whole village rushed to his assistance, and a blacksmith soon repaired damages. Mr. Emery was a personal acquaintance to every one of his assistants, but he could not repress a slight trepidation during his detention; this was increased by the good-natured hostler's appearance with hammer and wedge, to drive the hoops of the cask, fearing it might leak.

"We won't lose any of the good stuff, Major." he said, as he mounted into the wagon. "Darn the old thing!" he continued, "it's a trump, anyhow. If ever I see sich a ricketty thing hold out like that! Why, thunder and tow! it's calked here with oakum! Fireation! why don't it weep out? Well, I must say it beats the Dutch!"

The bolt was in its place. Mr. Emery gladly drove forward and reached home without any farther adventure. The following day the linen was taken from the cask, packed in boxes and carried into town.

That winter, Mr. Enoch Gerrish of Boscawen, came with a large pung loaded with calicoes and cotton shawls, which he had smuggled out of Canada. The shawls were quite pretty, having white or buff centres and high-colored borders: they sold for four dollars apiece. I took calico for a dress and a shawl; two other shawls were sold in the house; the remainder of the goods were slyly conveyed in the evening to the store of Miss Dolly Carnes. This new stock brought a rush of custom to that spinster's establishment, which at that time was in the Dr. Coffin house on High street. Shawls were in great demand. The previous autumn many ladies had knit or net them from woollen yarn of their own spinning and coloring. My husband's grandmother. Ruth Little, net several, and his cousin, Sally Little, knit one on large wooden needles for me, which I had colored at Pearson's Fulling Mill. This shawl was very pretty, and most comfortable. being both soft and warm.

Wood was so scarce and high, peat came into general use. Mr. Emery owned a peat meadow, and we burned peat mixed with wood in all the fireplaces, but the bar room was heated entirely from peat. Mr. Emery contrived for it a grate, which rested upon large iron fire-dogs. The room was low but very large, and this peat when in full glow, radiated so much heat that a seat was comfortable at the farthest corner from the fire in the coldest weather.

With the sleighing came country teams, loaded with butter, cheese, poultry etc. Sometimes the house was crowded. Many of our Boscawen friends were accompanied by the ladies of the family; these were my private guests, with whom I went shopping and visiting. I lived in such a whirl, self was unheeded. We were doing well, making money; everything was bright and lively; only now and then I realized how fatigued I daily became. One cold night a large party drove to the door; Mr. Emery was absent: I told Guy to have a good fire in the bar room. The lad threw on a bushel or so of peat: this had only commenced smoking when the men entered. "What in the world is this? what has the Major here?" exclaimed one, poking the turf with his whip stock. "Well, I guess we shall get warm round this pile of dirt!" said a second indignantly. "Confound the stuff! this don't look like David," complained a third. The summons to supper was given; by the time it was over the peat was thoroughly aglow. Ranging their chairs in a circle about the fire, the party made themselves comfortable with their tobacco pipes. It was not long before one chair was moved back, then another, still a third and fourth, when a general eulogium was pronounced upon the "Major's durned stuff."

Mr. Emery kept a quiet, orderly house; a ban had been placed upon political discussion, parties were at such variance, so much animosity was often expressed that this was the only safe course; but upon this evening, having the room to themselves, the gentlemen commenced the all-absorbing topic. They were pretty equally divided in sentiment, and being friends and neighbors, for a time the discussion was carried on pleasantly, in temperate terms; but the peat fire, temper, etc., bid fair to bring on a tempest. My parlor opened into the bar room; I had been a listener to the whole conversation, and was just debating the propriety of going to the disputants, when Mr. James Corser of Boscawen, who had been reclining on the bunk which Guy occupied nights, slyly lifted the whip, and applying the handle to his lips, sent forth an exact representation of a bugle blast. The company sprang to their feet as one man; a general laugh ensued, politics were forgotten, while Corser entertained them with a unique mimicry of various musical instruments, and other drolleries, which in these days would have given him a fortune as a public exhibitor. Our peat fire greatly surprised and pleased a young Irish peddler, who had brought a piece of his native bog in his pocket all the way from the old country, to show as a curiosity, and to look at when homesick, never dreaming that there were peat bogs in America.

CHAPTER LIV.

Mr. Carey had been hired for a year; when this had expired he went in to business for himself and moved on to the Boston turnpike. Mr. Charles Bancroft took his place, and a second wagon was put into the business which was driven by Mr. John Pillion. Phineas Whittier from Boscawen and Richard Garland from Gilmanton were the farm hands.

Everything went on as usual through the summer. Little did we foresee the trouble in store. On the 25th of August both Mr. Emery and Mr. Bancroft were taken ill of fever. Mr. Bancroft went to his home in Amesbury, where after lingering eight weeks he died. Mr. Emery had a slow, intermittent fever, which ran forty days; he was very sick; two attacks of pleurisy for a time gave small hopes of his recovery, but after the fever turned he began to slowly rally, and though confined to the house through the winter, in the spring, though feeble, he again resumed business. During this long illness hosts of friends rallied to our assistance; I have ever cherished deep feelings of gratitude for the affection and sympathy then shown.

Mr. Whittier attended Mr. Bancroft's funeral, at which he took a cold, which brought on a severe typhoid fever. Meantime the house was overflowing with company; my brother James had come to take charge, but I was often compelled to settle accounts and attend to other business. I had plenty of good help, and Mrs. Whittier came to her son, still, for months I was not free from anxiety respecting the invalids, neither eating nor sleeping with any regularity. "As thy day is, so shall thy strength be." Owing to a kind Providence, I was sustained through all these arduous duties.

In 1812 Dr. Dean Robinson became a resident of the lower parish in Newbury. In a short time he acquired great popularity and an extensive practice, not only in Newbury and Newburyport, but in the adjacent towns. Handsome, possessing a winning address, everywhere his reception was most cordial; no physician ever commanded more universal love and respect. Previous to his coming to Newburyport he had married the widow Farnham, of Andover. Dr. Poore had become aged and very deaf, all communication with him being held by the aid of an ear trumpet; but still he continued his daily rounds, the saddle-bags strapped to the saddle, plodding along on his staid old horse, the companion of years.

One afternoon the eccentric old gentleman rode up to Dr. Robinson's door and beckoned to Mrs. Robinson to come out. The lady answered the summons, when stooping down and peering into her face, her visitor exclaimed, "They tell me your husband is so much handsomer and younger that he will get all my practice; but you tell him that if he does I can beat him in one thing, *I've the handsomest wife.*" Having delivered this pronunciamento with his usual nasal accent, in a tone of unquestionable positiveness, the Doctor jerked up his reins and rode abruptly away, leaving the astonished Mrs. Robinson standing by the roadside in a state of bewildered amazement, from which it took some moments to recover. With a hearty laugh the lady returned to the house, and her graphic description and apt mimicry of the scene became a source of great merriment to her husband and friends.

Dr. Robinson had been chosen surgeon to the regiment; in this way Mr. Emery had made his acquaintance. Though Dr. Noyes and Dr. Vergenies were called, he was the attending physician through the illness of both Mr. Emery and Mr. Whittier. His solicitude and care were unwearied; to my husband and myself he grew dear as a brother; a friendship was formed which never varied in the future, but continued to the end of the Doctor's long and useful life.

In September the news of Perry's victory on Lake Champlain brought great rejoicing. Guns were fired, bells rung, crackers snapped, horns sounded, every demonstration of joy that noise could express was made. Mr. Emery was scarcely convalescent, and the din proved too much for his weak nerves.

After worship had been discontinued at Queen Ann's Chapel, the building fell into decay; the bell hung in the belfry for ten years, when one stormy night the steeple blew over and the bell was thrown into the road. Mr. David Whitmore wheeled it into his barn, where it remained for some time. At Mr. Whitmore's request the bell was removed to the residence of Mr. Josiah Little, till the building of the schoolhouse on High street, when it was hung in the belfry, where it was used to summon the scholars to school, and on Sundays the congregation to meeting, as the tower of the meetinghouse had never been furnished with a bell. The boys, with their usual delight, in noise, kept this bell in such a constant jingle through the day that at length I was obliged to have the clangor stopped.

In October, Mr. Solomon Babb took the place of Mr. Whittier. Mr. Babb came into the family at a time of peculiar trial, but he was found equal to every emergency, and for thirteen years he continued our factotum, both out of doors and within.

In December Daniel Thurston Colman, the oldest son of Uncle William Colman, of Byfield, supplied the place of the deceased Mr. Bancroft. Mr. Colman continued in the butchering business for many years, until failing health compelled him to yield his place to his son. He has recently deceased, having for some time been the only surviving member of those then attending the market, and for many subsequent years.

In March, a recruiting band being in town drumming up recruits for the regular army, Guy Carlton Mackie, following his native-born instincts, ran away from school, and without giving us the least warning, enlisted and marched away without one word of farewell. We were heartily sorry for the lad, but as he was off before we learned that he had left school, nothing could be done, and Mr. James Carey's younger brother David supplied his place, and took the new suit of clothes Guy left, they proving a perfect fit. Several years after Guy ran in to see us a moment, being on his way with a detachment of soldiers from one of the eastern to a southern port, and that is the last we ever heard of him, though an interest was always cherished in his future career.

In the summer of 1814 the news of Napoleon's abdication brought a second gala to the town. The success of the allies was celebrated by a display of flags upon the shipping, the ringing of all the bells, excepting that of the Second Presbyterian meeting-house—Rev. Mr. Giles, and the firing of a grand royal French salute of twenty-one guns, and at sunset a New England salute of five guns. In the evening the town hall, observatory, and other public buildings were brilliantly illuminated, and transparencies with appropriate mottoes were exhibited. Parson Giles was too consistent in his political opinions to permit his bell to add its tones to this jubilee. This course was supported by the Democratic citizens, and there were members in the Federalist ranks who disapproved of the manifestations, especially the New England salute of five guns.

The week after my marriage, the three-story house nearly opposite the Pillsbury place, was raised by Mr. Humphrey Webster, who then resided in a similar house which he had built on Tyng street. The hard times preventing the completion of this building, it stood for some time unfinished.

In April, 1813, on the night before Fast, Miss Margaret Lakeman was married to Mr. Joseph Magowen, at the residence of Col. Colman. My husband and I attended the wedding; it was between ten and eleven when we returned. Nothing unusual was then seen or heard. About midnight I was awakened by the dogs; Turk and another large dog at the barn were barking furiously, and a small dog that shared Guy's bunk added his voice to the concert. Rising, I opened the door into the bar room, inquiring, "What is the matter?" Guy, in a sleepy tone replied, "that he had looked out, but saw nothing." I returned to bed; the dogs became quiet, and I heard no more until morning, when Bets Downing's outcry roused the whole family. Burglars had removed the putty from a pane of glass, passed in a hand and taken out the nail which fastened the window, thus obtaining entrance into the kitchen next the shed. Having made a good meal of hashed meat and bread, they took a large silver spoon, a couple of overcoats, two or three pairs of boots, some stockings and underclothing, Betsy's reticule, containing her needle-book, thimble and scissors, a Bible and a History of Joseph. The barking of the dogs evidently hastened their departure, as two or three pieces of nankeen and some other articles that had been taken from the drawer of a desk in the room were left scattered over the floor. A large wagon loaded with chocolate stood by the barn, but the dogs proved an effectual guard, not a cake being taken.

From our house the thieves proceeded to that of Mr. Russel, where they stripped a large clothes-horse of the week's ironing. Mr. Russel, a carriage builder, had a large family, small children, and apprentices. Most of the lads were minus clean clothes for Fast; even the infant's clothing was all taken.

Robbery was not common in those days, and this caused a great stir. Notwithstanding a general search, no trace of the miscreants was found, with the exception of Guy's boots, which were nearly worthless, and the leaf from the Bible upon which was written David Emery; these were picked up in a thicket by the roadside a short distance beyond the Essex Merrimac bridge. As two men had been seen prowling around the unfinished house, the neighborhood became alarmed, and Mr. Emery advanced Mr. Webster five hundred dollars for its completion, taking a mortgage on the property. The house was soon finished and rented to Mr. Aaron Stevens.

At the commencement of the city of Lowell Mr. Webster was amongst the first mechanics to go thither. The first money there earned paid that mortgage. No stage had then been put on the road, and Mr. Webster walked the whole distance from Lowell to bring the money.

The spring of 1813 George Peabody came to say farewell, having concluded to join his uncle at the South. This was the first step in the ascent to his future prominence and wealth. One person's misadventure sometimes makes another's fortune. Had it not been for the great fire, and Gen. Peabody's removal to the District of Columbia, though doubtless George would have become wealthy and powerful, it is not probable he would have occupied the place he subsequently filled. After a business connection with his uncle of about two years, young Peabody entered the wholesale drapery business with Mr. Elisha Riggs. In 1815 the house was transferred from Georgetown to Baltimore, and in 1822 branch houses were established in New York and Philadelphia. In 1830 Mr. Elisha Riggs having retired, Mr. Samuel Riggs entered the firm, which under the style of Peabody, Riggs & Co., became one of the leading houses of the country. After several trips to Europe, in 1837 Mr. Peabody took up his residence in London, and commenced his successful career as banker and broker.

Monday, the 13th of February, 1815, news arrived that a treaty of peace had been made at Ghent. It was good sleighing. Col. Colman and my husband started that morning for Boscawen. Glancing from the window I espied Edmund Baker, a lad formerly employed at Gen. Peabody's, running a horse up the street. As he neared the house he sprang up in the stirrups, and swinging his hat above his head, vociferously shouted, "peace, peace." Dashing to the door, he screeched "Where's the Major? Peace, peace." Throwing up his hat and catching it, he began to hurrah, again calling loudly for the Major. I had scarcely made the excited lad comprehend that the Major was away, before I espied Zachariah Davidson coming in a sleigh; his horse was at the top of its speed, and he was shrieking "peace, peace," at the top of his voice. Drawing up before the door, he too commenced shouting for the Major.

Having ascertained that the good news was really true, and informed Mr. Davidson of the Major's absence, "Zach" drove on to spread the glad tidings, and Edmund returned to town, "awfully sorry that he could not have told the Major first."

In a few moments others arrived; the house became thronged, and the whole populace went half crazy with delight. Tuesday evening Col. Colman and my husband arrived. Having learned the welcome news in Concord, they at once retraced the road home.

Belleville was counted Democratic—or Republican, as the party was then termed—Belleville port had been especially noted for Jacobinism. Belleville decided to celebrate the ratification of peace, which was done by the President on the seventeenth. The next Monday afternoon an address was delivered in Belleville meeting-house by young John Merrill, son of Mr. Orlando Merrill. The house was crowded. John Merrill was then engaged to his future wife, a daughter of Mr. Robert Dodge. The Dodge family occupied a pew next to ours, and when the young man entered, habited in Parson Miltimore's black silk surplice, which had been loaned for the occasion, a gown being at that time a fashionable garb for a public speaker, and with grave decorum accompanied the dignified clergyman up the aisle and pulpit stairs, the three Dodge girls were convulsed with laughter; their sly glances to me so excited my risibles, that I had much ado to recover equanimity, and I could see that Miss Elizabeth was excessively nervous through the exercises. There was a prayer by Parson Miltimore, an appropriate ode was sung, then the young orator rose to perform his task. I could but sympathize with the Dodge family in their anxiety for his success, but the young man acquitted himself admirably. His oration won great applause, and from that epoch the gentleman took his place amongst our most gifted and prominent citizens.

In the evening there was a grand illumination throughout the parish. The old Pillsbury house was as brilliant as tallow candles could render it, and the ancient mansion looked prettily picturesque with its lights twinkling in its and many various sized and shaped casements.

CHAPTER LV.

Soon after the declaration of peace we had the pleasure of a visit from cousin Sophronia Peabody; she came and returned with Capt. Dole in the "Citizen." Miss Peabody had borne the transplanting to Southern soil most kindly; she had secured many warm friends in the District and Maryland. She had much to tell of a life of which we knew little, and scenes and events which have become historical. Her ideas had changed and expanded, and her natural elegance of manner was rendered still more conspicuous by a dash of Southern polish. We laughed heartily over an account of the first party she attended in Washington. Full of the New England Federalist notions, she promptly refused to dance with a most unexceptionable partner, simply because he was a most prominent Republican, being obliged in consequence to play wallflower through the evening. Some compensation was given by a presentation to Madame Patterson Bonaparte.

At the time of this lady's marriage General and Mrs. Peabody were on the road to Philadelphia, and the General had the honor during a shower to escort the bride a short distance under his umbrella. His praise of her beauty and elegance had rendered the lady an object of especial interest to us, and Miss Peabody greatly enjoyed sitting beside her for a half hour, while she carried on a lively conversation in French with the Spanish minister.

Though receiving every kindness that could be rendered to strangers in a strange land, slight things often showed even then the latent fire which in after years was destined to break forth in devouring flames—the cavalier disdain for the less refined but equally proud puritan. Edward, Gen. Peabody's third son, a bright lad of seven summers, having unintentionally given offence to one of his schoolmates, that young urchin persisted in following him round, shouting "Yankee tank, Yankee tank!" Edward bore this until he considered forbearance no longer a virtue, when he gave the young Southron such a thrashing that his puritan descent was ever afterward fully respected.

The negroes were a constant source of novelty and amusement. My cousin related many tales of their faithfulness, and many funny anecdotes evincing the peculiarities of the race. An extremely tidy, economical New England woman, my aunt was somewhat horrified at the general thriftlessness of both whites and blacks, while she astonished the neighborhood by her activity and energy. Having employed a negress to scour the white, hard-finished wall of the parlor, she greatly excited that individual's ire by compelling her to clean the wall to the ceiling overhead, instead of stopping half way as intended. The woman in her wrath declared that "anybody might see Missus Peabody was nuffing but a Yankum *woman;* a Southern *lady* would never have known whether the plaster was cleaned or not."

During the war, Mrs. Madison found it as difficult to procure articles of luxury as those of less exalted station. Being in a dilemma respecting curtains for the "Blue room" at the White House, she rode over to Georgetown to inspect Gen. Peabody's stock. He had a piece of blue silk damask, but it was only half the requisite quantity. What could be done? An idea suggested itself to the General. The furnishing of the best parlor and chamber of his State street house had been purchased in Italy by Capt. Caleb Lufkin, it having been ordered by a nobleman of that country for his palace, but for some cause was never used, but sold. The upholstery and curtains were of a thick, heavy, watered silk, with broad satin stripes, and of a most beautiful tint of yellow. Part of the curtains were then not in use, as in that warm climate white muslin was preferable. These curtains were brought for Mrs. Madison's inspection; she was delighted, and took Gen. Peabody in her carriage to Washington, to assist in planning the drapery. It was found that in size the golden curtains fitted the windows admirably, and mixed with the blue, they gave the room a charming effect. Thus the Newburyport hanging received the distinction of gracing the Presidential mansion. The silk woven for a European aristocrat, thus decorated the residence of the Democratic chief magistrate of these free and independent United States.

Miss Peabody's description of the burning of the Capitol was exceedingly interesting. The approach of the British had been anxiously watched by the people of the District, but not a doubt of the supremacy of the American arms was entertained, until the morning of the twenty-third of August. Early on that day a rumor arose that the United States troops had been defeated at Bladensburg. This report was soon confirmed by the appearance of the retreating militia. Squad after squad of soldiers passed in rapid flight during the morning. The panic became general; most of the citizens packed their valuables and started for the country. Washington became nearly depopulated; everything in the form of an animal or vehicle being pressed into service. Through the day this miscellaneous and incongruous procession had passed Gen. Peabody's residence; it was nearly four o'clock in the afternoon; the stream of passers had greatly diminished when the cry arose, "The President! the President!" and a coach dashed past, on the back seat of which sat Mr. Madison. The weather was excessively hot and the President had taken off his hat; there was no mistake, he was recognized at a glance.

Could this be possible! The family gazed in speechless amazement; then the brave, noble-spirited John burst forth in a torrent of indignation. "Catch Yankees to have allowed the President to run in this fashion! they would have died first, every mother's son of them, if they were all Federalists." Gen. Peabody shared his son's excitement. His military ardor was completely roused. "Never was a building better located for defence than the Capitol, if the soldiers, instead of running away, had spent the day in intrenching, something might have been done." The General paced around with the impatience of a caged lion. He was urged to remove his family to the plantation of a friend a few miles back, but riding was painful to Adeline's lame hip, and the others preferred to remain and abide events. Towards night it was reported that the iron works, where cannon and ammunition had been cast, were on fire; but this was a false rumor. The British troops without any halt pressed forward directly into Washington; about eight in the evening the advanced guard entered the city, and in about an hour the kindling fires showed that the work of destruction had commenced. It was a still, sultry, moonlight night; not a breath swayed the flames which rose up; straight, mighty pillars of fire, forming a unique and magnificent spectacle. Gradually they widened and brightened, till the Capitol, the buildings of the several departments, and the bridge over the Potomac, were wrapt in one sheet of fire. From the portico of their house the Peabody family watched the panorama, this disgraceful vandalism, with feelinge that can better be imagined than dsscribed. At a late hour the two younger boys, Joseph and Edward, were fairly driven to bed; at breakfast they were not to be found. Much startled, the family were about to institute a search, when in marched the two young heroes, clad in their last winter's scarlet suits, which they had donned for the occasion, thinking that these clothes would "pass muster" amongst the British, their hands and pockets full of half-burnt charts, rulers, paper, knives etc., that they had picked up amongst the ruins. With a grand air they reported the notice they had received. One officer had patted Edward's curly head, and inquired "if he would not like to be a soldier?" To which the pert youth replied, "that he intended to be one, when he would whip the British soundly for thus dastardly burning our Capitol." This speech was received with roars of laughter; and one officer in a splendid uniform, said, "he would give a round sum to own that Yankee boy, that he was made of the right stuff."

Fears were entertained of marauders; but none of the soldiers crossed into Georgetown. During the afternoon an accident spread great dismay through the army. A quantity of powder had been hidden in a dry well, which was covered with plank. A party were lounging over the platform smoking, when a spark fell through a crevice and a terrible explosion followed. Some of the group were killed and others wounded. This accidental occurrence was regarded as a Yankee trick, and it spread both consternation and horror through the British ranks. The Yankees were full of tricks. Who knew but that the whole area was undermined! Terror multiplied terror, till a panic took possession of the troops and they scarcely dared to move; every order was performed with fear and caution. In the evening this terror was heightened by a most terrific thunder storm; the oldest inhabitant could not recall its equal. Glare succeeded glare—a perfect sheet of lightning, while the thunder roared, rattled, crashed and pealed; rain mingled with hail poured down like a second flood, and the wind blew a perfect tornado. The negroes declared "the Lor Gor Ormity was taking up our side for sure." Perhaps the British entertained the same opinion. The fleet was driven from their moorings in the river and dashed against each other, experiencing considerable damage: tents were overturned, horses broke loose, altogether it was a fearful night. The morning showed the enemy in full retreat. Before sunset the rear guard had marched forth, and in a few hours the last straggler had disappeared.

CHAPTER LVI.

The 9th of September, 1815, my first child was born, a girl, who lived but twenty-four hours. I remained feeble for a long time, and it was difficult to say "Thy will be done." Parson Miltimore proved a precious friend at this season, and Dr. Parish often called with words of comfort and cheer.

When Mr. Emery hired the Pillsbury farm, Daniel Colman came to Newburyport to take the situation he relinquished in the business with Col. Jeremiah Colman. That gentleman had recently purchased a residence in Newbury, on the Boston turnpike, whither he had removed. The last of October Mr. Daniel Colman was married to Miss Nancy Pike, the second daughter of Mr. Henry Pike, of Ring's Island. The young couple commenced housekeeping in half of Col. Jeremiah Colman's house, and there the wedding took place, a very pleasant family gathering. Dr. Parish performed the ceremony. The good Doctor often boasted of having married the three brothers to three of the handsomest and best women to be found. A large L was soon added to the house, giving accommodation to the two families; but for some months the two sisters-in-law shared the kitchen, one having a fire in one corner of the capacious fireplace and the other in the opposite, the brick oven being used alternately. Mrs. Jeremiah Colman was fond of adverting to this period, always ending her recital with "and we never had one word of difference."

The next year, 1816, was memorable as "the cold summer." The 1st of June Mr. Daniel Colman and wife, and Mr. Emery and myself, started on a journey to Boscawen. We set out early Monday morning, a raw, pitiless day, and this weather continued through the trip. We wore winter clothing, and fires were as acceptable as in January. Thursday was election day. We went into Concord in the morning to be present at the inauguration of the Governor. As it seemed fitting to dress for the august occasion, Mrs. Colman donned a blue crape, and one of those smuggled shawls that I have previously described. I wore a black crape, and a black, worsted summer shawl. Mr. Colman and Mr. Emery escorted us to the meeting-house. The wind blew a gale, with an occasional shower of snowflakes; it was so powerful that it was difficult to reach the church even with the gentlemen's assistance. Having become seated we strove to enjoy the scene; but in vain. Our teeth fairly chattered in our heads, and our feet and hands were benumbed. Mrs. Colman had a troublesome tooth, and that began to ache unbearably. We were truly thankful when the services closed. But our dinner at the hotel, in a large cold hall, was fully as uncomfortable. We were only too glad to order our horses; but the wind was so powerful that in passing over Concord bridge I thought the chaise must be overturned; even Mr. Emery, who never feared anything, was a little discomposed. The night was passed at a hotel on the Chester turnpike, where in company with other travelers, we shivered round a rousing fire, complaining of the cold room.

There was frost every month during the year; but little corn ripened that season. As the Pillsbury place was high, warm land, we had a good crop. It was the same at Crane Neck; my father raised the usual quantity; but on many farms not a kernel ripened. This produced great distress. In the following spring seed corn shelled brought three dollars per bushel.

On the 1st day of April in this year,

during the only heavy thunder shower of the season, the Belleville meeting-house was struck by lightning and speedily consumed. It was the afternoon for the annual spring town meeting, which was held in the lower parish meeting-house, and only two or three men in the whole vicinity were at home. About half-past two I sat down before the fire in my room to warm my feet. Turk laid down beside me. It had been thundering some moments, but the shower came up apace. Suddenly a terrible clap burst overhead; the lightning coming down the chimney crinkled upon the hearth about my feet. Turk jumped half way to the ceiling, then sank on the floor, trembling with fright. For a moment I could not stir. Thinking that the premises must have been struck, with a mighty effort I gained my feet, and by aid of the furniture reached the end window. Smoke was curling round the corner of the barn. Supposing it to be on fire, I was endeavoring to get to the door to call Mr. Babb, when he, shouting, "The meeting-house is struck, the meeting-house is on fire," seized a couple of pails of water, and with the boy ran up the street. The Portsmouth stage, Zachariah Davidson driver, was exactly in front of the meeting-house when the bolt struck, and the two leading horses were brought to their knees. Mr. Davidson ran his team down High street, giving the alarm. The few men about the neighborhood and a small army of women were soon at the scene of the conflagration. No water was at hand, and the fire spread with such rapidity little could be done; only a few hymn-books, Bibles and pew doors were saved. The engines and fire companies came up from town, and the men ran their horses from town-meeting, but it was only to witness the fall of the sturdy frame of the sacred edifice. This was a severe loss to the society, but it was a dispensation of Providence, and no complaint could be made. Arrangements were immediately entered upon for the building of another house, which was completed and occupied before cold weather. During its erection the society worshipped in the court-house.

I did not fully recover from the shock I had received for some hours: and ever after, at the approach of a shower, Turk always, if possible, hid himself under a bed, showing great fear.

After much dissension, the society in the upper parish of Newbury voted to refer the site for a new meeting-house to a committee of disinterested persons. Judge Timothy Pickering of Salem, and Governors John Taylor Gilman and Jeremiah Smith of New Hampshire were selected. These gentlemen very properly decided that it should stand on the plain, a little below meeting-house hill. A neat edifice, of which the new church at Belleville was almost an exact counterpart, had been completed, and on the 12th of June, 1816, the Rev. John Kirby of Middletown, Conn., was ordained.

Two years previous, the 1st of June, 1814, the Rev. Gilbert Williams, of Fog's Manor, N. J., had been ordained pastor over the second parish in Newbury. On the 31st of October, 1816, the Rev. Leonard Withington, of Dorchester, was settled over the Oldtown Society. Dr. Withington had even then, though a young man and a stranger, made his mark, and his ordination was a season of rejoicing and festivity.

Of the pleasant family circle I had entered at my marriage, no one was more respected and beloved than the widow of Col. Dudley Colman. Her father, John Jones, esq., a gentleman of wealth and position, was great grandson of Michael Wigglesworth, author of "Day of Doom," and grandson of Rev. Samuel Wigglesworth of Ipswich Hamlet, now Hamilton. Her mother was Mary Whipple of Grafton. Mary Jones Colman was his only daughter: her only brother, Nathaniel Jones, died in early manhood, leaving three sons, Nathaniel, John and Samuel, and one daughter, Mrs. Katharine (Jones) Brown, the distinguished teacher in Newburyport, and Georgetown, D. C. After her husband's decease, Mrs. Colman resided amongst her children. Previous to his settlement in Salem the Rev. Henry Colman was ordained over a society in Hingham. As was customary for clergymen in country parishes, usually there were a few lads boarding in the family, fitting for college under Mr. Colman's instruction. Peculiarly adapted for the office of teacher, a mutual regard was formed between master and pupils, which continued through life.

John Jones, the youngest son, married Eliza, daughter of Josiah and Olive Neal, and settled in Brookfield; he died young, and his widow married his brother Charles, of Brookfield. Mr. Charles Colman was an active, courageous, enterprising man, and unusually well informed; he could speak both French and Spanish fluently. In the war of 1812 he was taken prisoner, held as a hostage, and confined in the jail at Quebec. With two others he esacaped. Hving stolen a calf, which they managed to dress and roast, they made the best of their way through the woods for several days, but were so blinded by mosquito bites they were unable to proceed, and were recaptured. Afterwards Mr. Colman was taken to Halifax. At the disbanding of the army he returned home, where he learned that at the time he was taken prisoner a Colonel's commission was on the way to him, which he failed to get. But later he received the deed of one hundred and sixty acres of land, as other soldiers. Bridget Colman, the only daughter remarkable for her beauty, married a French gentleman named Chappetin, and went to Providence, R. I.

Aunt Colman was accustomed to make an annual visit to her Newbury relatives, which caused much family festivity. Early in March we received intelligence that Mrs. Colman might be expected on the next Wednesday in the two o'clock stage from Portsmouth. Punctually at the time appointed our visitor came. Dinner over, she called for the swift and began to wind the yarn to knit a petticoat, those garments at that time being universally worn. The stitches having been cast on two long wooden needles, her fingers flew with a rapidity seldom equalled, while an entertaining conversation was sustained in which a thorough knowledge of the world was shown, a keen insight of men and modes, coupled with extensive reading, expressed with a keen wit, and sparkling versatility of language which was most engaging.

Invitations had been sent for a family gathering the next afternoon. The ladies came at three o'clock, the gentlemen joining them at tea. A merry evening was enjoyed. Father, and Uncle Ben Colman and Uncle Searle were brimming over with jokes and anecdotes, in which they were fully sustained by their sons and nephews. Aunt Dudley was unusually entertaining. Aunt Doctor, (as the widow of Dr. Samuel Colman was usually termed,) a stout, dignified lady, became remarkably genial; her daughter Mary Ann, the distinguished teacher, in a quiet way added much to the conversation; her second daughter, Hannah, afterwards Mrs. Wait of Baltimore, a great beauty, looked unusually lovely. Aunt Searle's black eyes danced with glee, and Mrs. Jeremiah and Daniel Colman, with their little girls, completed the circle. At nine o'clock the company separated with expressions of satisfaction and the hope of many future reunions. Friday it stormed. One ought to have seen Aunt Dudley's fingers fly! That evening the petticoat was completed—a feat scarcely equalled in the annals of knitting.

CHAPTER LVII.

The summer of 1817 President Monroe made a tour to New England. On June 16th a meeting of the citizens of Newburyport was called in the Town Hall to prepare for the distinguished visitor's reception, and the following gentlemen were chosen as a committee of arrangements:

Ebenezer Moseley, Abraham Williams, Robert Clark, Richard Bartlett, Stephen Howard, selectmen; with William Bartlett, Joseph Marquand, Moses Brown, William B. Bannister, Joshua Carter, Thomas M. Clark, William Cross, Daniel Swett, Joseph Williams and Josiah Smith esq. The committee invited the Hon. Jeremiah Nelson to join them.

The following named gentlemen were appointed marshals for Newburyport:

Maj. Joshua Greenleaf, Maj. Abraham Perkins, Capt. William Davis, Col. Enoch Plummer, Capt. Thomas Burrill, Capt. Joseph T. Pike, Maj. Ebenezer Stone, Doct. John Brickett, Butler Abbot, Maj. Gilman White. Newbury, joined in the reception, and Col. Ebenezer Hale, Maj. David Emery, Maj. Daniel Smith, Capt. John Emery Bartlett, Adj. George Waterman, acted as marshals from that town.

On July 7th, the following military order was issued:

"Pursuant to Division orders, a military escort has been ordered to receive the President and his suit at Ipswich. The field and staff officers of the several regiments in the Brigade, together with such captains and subalterns as may be so disposed, will assemble in Ipswich in uniform, and mounted, on Thursday, 10th inst., at 9 o'clock, to join in the escort.

Regiment of Cavalry under the command of Col. Jeremiah Coiman.

Brigadier General of the 2nd Brigade and Staff.

Maj. General of 2nd Division and suite.

Part of the Committee of Arrangements.

Officers of the several Regiments in the 2nd Brigade, 2nd Division, M. M.

Cavalcade of Citizens.

The escort will receive the President at Ipswich and attend him through the Brigade.

Maj. John Scott and Maj. David Wood, jr., are appointed Marshals, and will arrange the escort.

BENJAMIN STICKNEY,
Brig.-Gen. 2d Brigade, 2d Division, M. M.

The cavalcade to form at the Lower Green; carriages to proceed in the rear of the procession."

Owing to unavoidable delay the President did not reach Newburyport until

Saturday, the 12th of July, which was an extremely hot day. During his severe and long sickness, thinking that his health would never again permit military duty, Maj. Emery resigned his position in the cavalry, consequently he had no connexion with the troops on this occasion, but he acted as marshal. He still retained his parade horse Peacock, and Col. Eben Hale rode our handsome mare Kate. The marshals wore chapeaus ornamented with a black cockade, a gilt eagle in the centre, and swords with scarlet sashes. As Col. Hale and my husband cantered down High street you would rarely see two finer or better mounted horsemen.

"The cavalry under Col. Colman, the field and staff officers under the direction of Majors John Scott and David Wood jr., took up the escort and proceeded to Parker river bridge, where the President was met by the Hon. Bailey Bartlett, sheriff of Essex, with his suite, together with the committee of arrangements, when Colonel Moseley, as their chairman, addressed him as follows:

Sir,—A number of the citizens of Newburyport and vicinity, desirous of paying you their respects, have taken this liberty to meet you on your journey, and with your permission will accompany you to Newburyport, where the citizens of that town will be happy in a more formal manner to pay you their salutations."

The President left his carriage and mounted his horse. On reaching the Newburyport line, the peal of bells and the roar of cannon, from Capt. Coffin's well disciplined company of Artillery, announced the approach of the distinguished visitor. The President was greeted by loud hurrahs from the throng lining both sides of High street. At the Mall he was received by the Washington Light Infantry, Capt. Balch, and passing under a civic arch which was tastefully decorated with wreaths of flowers, he passed through an avenue of youth of both sexes, arranged on each side. The school children wore a uniform of white and blue, which was most becoming. In front of the Court House waved a revolutionary flag. The procession, after proceeding the length of the Mall, marched down Market street, through Union, down Green, through Merrimac and Market square, up State street to Gilman's Hotel. This was the Eastern Stage House, kept by John Gilman, which had been removed some two or three years previous from Col. Bartlett's late residence on the corner of Temple street, to the mansion built by Gen. John Peabody, on State, corner of Harris street, lower half of the present Merrimac House.

At the hotel the President was greeted by a larger assembly than had ever before collected in the town; and as he entered, accompanied by Gen. Swift, Mr. Mason, other officials, and the committee of arrangements, the gratulatory shouts of his fellow citizens rent the air. The chairman, Col. Moseley, spoke as follows:

"Sir,—The citizens of Newburyport, by their committee, beg leave to present their sincere respects to the Chief Magistrate of the United States.

Having been called by a free and intelligent people to preside over their most important concerns, it must be peculiarly grateful to your feelings at the commencement of your arduous duties to be made more particularly acquainted with their local interests, and to receive their affectionate and respectful salutations. It is no less pleasing to us than happy for the nation, that we derive the honor of this interview, from the practical operation of that maxim of your illustrious predecessor, the Father of his country, in his last affectionate address to his fellow citizens, that timely disbursements to prepare for danger frequently prevent much greater disbursements to repel it. A numerous and wealthy population, stretching along an extensive seacoast, present to a foreign enemy many alluring objects of attack, and the present period of peace and public tranquility appears peculiarly favorable for your patriotic efforts for our defence and security. Enjoying as we do the blessings of a free government, our attachment cannot be the less ardent when administered by one who took an honorable and active part in those measures by which it was obtained. We trust that under your administration, by the smiles of a kind Providence, a spirit of peace will be generally diffused, the venerable and pious institutions of our fathers preserved, and the citizens meet their appropriate reward in the labors of agriculture, manufactures and commerce, and in extending the sciences and arts.

Accept, sir, our best wishes, that you may prosper in the important objects of your journey, and at the close of your labors receive a consolation, the most dear to a patriot, in the happiness and prosperity of his country."

The President replied, "That he received with great sensibility the attentions of the citizens of Newburyport—that his principal object in making this tour was to see the situation of the people in different parts of the country, and the entrance and harbors of the principal towns, and to acquire such information as would enable him better to discharge the duties of his office; that in his journey he had been highly gratified with the prosperous condition of the people, and that their situation was far more happy than that of any other in any part of the world, and that we could not be sufficiently thankful to that bountiful Providence which had conferred upon us such distinguished blessings." The President concluded with desiring "that his grateful sentiments for the kind and respectful manner in which he had been received by the citizens might be communicated to them."

After mutually exchanging civilities with his fellow citizens the President and suite sat down to a sumptuous dinner, served up by Mr. Gilman with much elegance and taste. Gen. Swift presided at the table. Among the guests were Major Gen. Dearborn, Com. Bainbridge, Brig. Gen. Miller, Dr. Waterhouse and Gen. Brickett, with the reverend clergy from this and many of the adjacent towns. Gen. Swift announced the following as the toast of the President: "Happiness and prosperity to the inhabitants of Newburyport." The President having signified his pleasure to dispense with the escort of cavalry, retired into another apartment, and after taking an affectionate leave of the committee of arrangements he ascended his carriage amid loud and reiterated cheering and resumed his journey. At Amesbury he tarried about an hour, viewed the factories, expressing his admiration at their situation and his gratification at their flourishing condition. He arrived in Portsmouth between six and seven o'clock.

The President was highly gratified with the local situation of the town.

Liberal feelings ruled the day; it embraced all as Federalists, all as Republicans. The regiment of cavalry commanded by Col. Colman, conducted in a manner gratifying to spectators and highly honorable to themselves. Collected as they were, from the remote parts of the brigade, great credit is due these troops for the alacrity with which they obeyed, and the promptitude with which they executed the command of the Brigadier General. They at once presented a pleasing specimen of good order, correct discipline, and soldier-like deportment.

The following card was inserted in the Newburyport Herald of July 15th:

"The committee of arrangements in behalf of the citizens, present their thanks to the teachers of the respective schools, and the marshals of the day, for the very handsome and interesting manner in which the children were presented to the view of the President on the day of his arrival, and which called from him expressions of high approbation."

CHAPTER LVIII.

The September following I was taken with a slow typhoid fever, which ran forty days, by which I was left extremely feeble, and confined me to the house during the winter. My sister Susan was with me most of the time, and the tedium of a slow convalescence was enlivened by a bevy of youthful neighbors.

Mr. Enoch Toppan's two sons, Moses and Edward, and their sisters, Hannah and Margaret, were still at the homestead. Mr. Stephen Toppan's oldest daughter, Mrs. Green, had returned to her father's house a widow, with three daughters and one son. Esther had married Mr. William Boardman, but Harry, Charlotte, Nancy and Stephen were at home. Mr. Abner Toppan's oldest daughter, Sophia, had married Mr. Oliver Crocker and gone to New Bedford, Betsey and Ariana were unmarried, Abner and Stanford lads in their teens, Harriet and George mere children. With Mrs. Reuben Jones' nieces, Mary and Maria Stanwood, the young people from these families formed a gay group, with whom my sister immediately became a favorite, and the quiet of my room was often broken by a ripple of girlish glee, and as I became stronger the young gentlemen greatly enjoyed dropping in of an evening.

In October was received the sad intelligence of the death of our dearly beloved cousin, Adeline Peabody. Her departure was not unexpected, but it brought an irrepressible grief, though we well knew that our loss was to her an inestimable gain. The following truthful and touching lines were written by a friend, a gentleman of Georgetown, D. C.:

"LINES

Occasioned by the death of Miss Adeline Peabody, a young lady who died after a long and distressing illness at Georgetown, D. C., Oct. 9th, 1817, aged 19 years.

"Knowing this, that the trial of your faith worketh patience; but let patience have her perfect work, that ye may be perfect and entire, wanting nothing."—St. James.

Patience! at length thy 'perfect work' is done,
And Adeline has rest among the dead;
Her ravished soul awakes, the eternal sun
Burst through the clouds that gathered round her head.
On eager wings the immortal spirit soars;
Her sister angels hail her to the skies—
Oh! glorious flight from earth's encumbering clay,
From scenes where woe their constant vigils keep,
Where cares perplex the anxious heart by day,
And sorrow drives from night the balm of sleep!

Yet can affection bid such worth farewell,
As thine, sweet Adeline, without a tear,
Or cause, in pensive tenderness, to dwell
On virtues that thy memory endear?
Thy love that shed its genial warmth around,
Thy manners, gentle, affable and kind,
Thy generous friendship—candor without bound,
Thy spotless purity of heart and mind!
O bright ensample of unsullied youth,
O holy faith and piety sincere,
'Twas thine, appointed by the word of truth,
To view the early grave without a fear;
To see with joy the sure approach of death;
The blessed privilege to thee was given,
And some bright seraph, as he caught thy breath.
Gave thy departing soul a glimpse of heaven."

Grief and joy go hand in hand. In the December following cousin Adeline's death my brother James was married to Miss Sarah B. Little, the second daughter of my husband's uncle. Edmund Little. The bride and groom were second cousins. Intermarriage is a family trait amongst the Littles, which is likely to continue to the latest generation. My brother and his bride set up housekeeping at the old homestead, as James was needed to assist his father on the farm.

In February Mr. Thurston Colman was married to Miss Nancy Harris. This young couple went to housekeeping in the house on the lower corner of Tyng street; but they soon moved into Mr. Harris's house, on the corner of Toppan's lane, where he resided through his long life.

As vigor did not return with spring, Dr. Robinson recommended a journey to Saratoga. I was so feeble that many of the family strongly objected to so long a jaunt; but Mr. Emery was desirous for the trip.

In 1815 the sign was taken down, and from that time we entertained only the drovers, who could not dispense with the yards. Three of the butchers had left, John Pillion for Providence, R. I.; Mr. Joseph Mead had married and settled on his father's farm, in Meredith, N. H. Mr. Colman's marriage left only Mr. Babb and the boy in the family. Betsey Downing had gone as cook to a boarding-house in Boston, and her place had been supplied by Betsey Durgin, a young girl mother Colman had brought up at Byfield. Thus an opportunity was afforded for a short absence from home; consequently preparations for the tour were commenced, though my strength was scarcely sufficient for the effort. Mr. Joe T. Pike cut and made in his best style a blue cloth riding-habit for the journey; it was trimmed with buttons and velvet in the tip-top of fashion. Aunt Bartlett's establishment furnished a drawn green silk bonnet, with a short sarsenet veil. This was then the genteel mode for traveling. We owned a handsome chaise; Kate and Peacock were harnessed to it tandem; a traveling trunk, which had been made expressly to strap to the vehicle, was put in place, the box stowed with luggage, and on the morning of the second of June we turned our horses' heads Saratogaward.

Our first stop was at my Aunt Coker's. Mr. Coker had recently sold the Crane Neck farm and purchased the Hooper place, on Pipestave Hill, whither they had removed. The Dalton place adjoining was then owned by Captain Joseph Stanwood. In the palmy days of Newburyport commerce, the old gentleman would sit at his chamber window, spyglass in hand, watching for one or another of his vessels to appear at the bar, at sight of which his horse was ordered, and he was in town to meet her at the wharf. After dining at my father's we rode over to the West parish in Haverhill to pass the night with my Aunt Chase. Mr. Amos Chase had some years previous purchased a large farm there, and the house was merry with a fine family of stalwart boys and handsome girls. After a most pleasant visit we proceeded to Pembroke, and the following morning rode into Concord to breakfast. It chanced to be election day. Stickney's Tavern was thronged with the members of the General Court and their wives. After breakfast, as I was chilly, Mrs. Stickney ushered me into a back sitting-room, where there was a fire. My sanctum was soon invaded by some half-dozen of the *elite* of the New Hampshire ladies, to whom, after the early morning ride from their homes, the warmth was exceedingly grateful. Some of these thus accidentally thrown together were acquaintances; the others were introduced. There were Mrs. General this and Mrs. Colonel that, Mrs. Judge and 'Squire so-and-so; titles fairly rained. After the recognitions and introductions were over, all eyes centered on me, and there came a dead pause; then two or three of the chief dignitaries whispered together, after which, one who instituted herself spokeswoman approached and politely inquired, "to which member I belonged?" I explained that I was a stranger on a journey. "You are from below?" questioned my interlocutor. "Yes," I returned, naming my place of residence. As I ceased speaking the group thronged about me. "Would I please excuse, but was this the newest style for riding dress?" Having examined my habit and bonnet minutely, and farther inquired respecting Boston fashion, the conversation was abruptly ended by the entrance of Mr. Emery, accompanied by the respective Generals, Colonels, Judges and Esquires belonging to the fair dames, most of whom were his friends. Wine was brought, and after a merry chat we separated, the New Hampshire party to assist in the election ceremonies and festivities; we to proceed to our friends in Boscawen, where we remained until the next week Wednesday. While there Mrs. Deacon Enoch Little of Little's Hill, gave a Little party, at which twelve were present, the number having been gathered together at a half-hour's notice. Wednesday morning we bade our Boscawen friends adieu, and proceeded on our route. The day's ride brought us to Newport, where we passed the night; the next we slept at a country tavern high up amongst the mountains. Friday morning Connecticut river was crossed. The ferryman resided on the Vermont shore. Mr. Emery having blown a summons from the tin horn suspended from a post for that purpose, after a tedious delay a rickety ferry boat was pushed off and rowed toward us. I was mortally afraid the old thing would sink in mid stream, but greatly to my relief we gained terra firma in safety. That night was passed at Castleton, at a tavern on a large farm. Fifteen handsome cows attracted my attention as they came to the yard to be milked. My hostess, seeing that I was interested in her dairy, took me to look at her cheese, very large and fine ones. As we came back, the landlady's daughter drew me to the open door to hear a whippoorwill. The child was much astonished to learn that I had heard "her bird," as she termed it, before.

The next morning this little girl came with the request that the lady from Newburyport would go to her grandmother's room a few moments. Following my small guide, I entered a light, cheerful apartment leading from the kitchen, where I found a pleasant-faced old lady seated in an arm-chair beside a linen wheel. Her knitting-work, Bible, hymn book and spectacles lay on a stand near; a woolen wheel stood on the other side of the fireplace, and in the corner opposite the bed was placed a small loom. To the remark "that this looked like a hive of industry," the old lady replied that she needed something to wile away the time, and her son had fitted up this room for her accommodation, so that when tired of one occupation she could take another. "They tell me you are from Newburyport, my dear, and I wished to see you, for that is the place where the blessed Whitefield died and lies buried. Of course you have visited his tomb?" I was compelled to reply in the negative, which greatly surprised the good woman. "Lived so nigh all your life, and never visited Whitefield's tomb! Why, I allers thought if I went within forty miles of the place I would make a pilgrimage expressly to visit the sacred shrine. Go to see it on your return, I beg, for my sake. Visit the dear saint's last resting place." Having listened to the recital of her conversion through Whitefield's preaching, with several anecdotes of the great revivalist, I bade the old lady good morning, to resume my journey. In a few hours the state line into New York was crossed, and the Dutch origin of the inhabitants soon became apparent. The road, much used for drawing lumber, was deeply rutted, and owing to recent rains exceedingly muddy. During the morning, espying a red flag floating from a pole in the distance, Mr. Emery drove cautiously forward, supposing it to be a signal of danger. Approaching a small stream, we found that the bridge had been swept away and a party of men were then replacing it. Here was a dilemma! The master builder said "he could get the chaise and horses across, but how could he manage for the lady?" The string pieces, timbers a foot and a half wide, were already laid. I told him if he would take my hand I would walk across, which I did, much to the admiration of my escort and his fellow laborers, who pronounced me a brave little woman. The chaise was taken over plank put down for the purpose, and the horses having swam across, were again harnessed and we resumed our journey. Fort Ann was passed early in the afternoon. Here the log causeway that had been built for the passage of Burgoyne's army, was being taken up, though one side was left while the other was rebuilt. For two miles the horses walked through mud reaching to their fetlocks.

Sunday morning we strayed from the direct road into a cart path through the woods, which after devious picturesque windings, brought us into the midst of a cluster of white, one-story cottages, surrounding a neat church. Drawing up before the first house, a woman came to the door in a short, loose gown and petticoat, patched with various colors, a white cloth cap, and bare feet. To Mr. Emery's inquiry respecting the route she stammered, "I will call mine goot mon." "Mine goot mon" instantly appeared, smoking a short pipe. He expressed surprise at seeing such a turnout, complimented Mr. Emery upon his skill as a driver over the primitive path we had crossed, and directed us to follow a new rail fence across a pasture, which would return us to the main road without difficulty. After a drive of a mile it was regained, and the delay was not regretted, as by it we obtained a glimpse of what seemed a foreign country. Dinner was taken at a Dutch tavern, owned by the landlady, whose husband was a New Englander. The house, a large. one-story building, with the other appurtenances, were the acme of neatness; the interior of the inn was as clean as scrubbing and whitewash could render it, but there was not a bit of paint or paper, nor a carpet in the whole premises. We had an excellent dinner, served in good style. The landlady waited upon the table, and greatly amused us by the declaration, "that she had married a Yankee in preference to a Dutchman, they were so much smarter, and treated their wives with so much more respect."

That afternoon we passed the Hudson at Glen's Falls, one of the most picturesque of cataracts. The bridge was just above the falls, and our horses trotted across it pretty briskly, while we were enveloped in the spray.

Ohio was then the El Dorado of promise to emigrants. Quite an exodus was transpiring in western Vermont, and many were on the road. A short distance beyond the Hudson we overtook a cart drawn by a yoke of oxen, loaded with household goods. Upon a feather bed sat a middle-aged woman, while her lord drove the patient team, and a barefooted girl trudged behind, driving a cow. Near sunset the famed watering place was reached, then a mere village. There were but two hotels—wooden buildings with stoops—though every family was in readiness to receive boarders. According to advice, we drove to the smaller of the two hotels, which was kept by a Mr. Donney, who with his wife were natives of Connecticut. This was an excellent house, and Mrs. Donney was untiring in her exertions for my comfort. Being early in the season the place was comparatively empty. There were about a dozen boarders in the house, amongst whom was a Mr. Clark, and his stepdaughter, Sophia Parker, formerly belonging in Boston, then residing at Salem, Vt. They were very pleasant people; Miss Parker became an inseparable companion. A Mr. Amory from Boston, an aged gentleman and a confirmed invalid, was boarding at the other hotel. He sent to have Mr. Emery call upon him, as they were originally from one stock; it was the same name.

The morning after our arrival Mr. Emery escorted me to the springs before breakfast. Congress Spring was enclosed by a railed platform, but its surroundings were still as nature left them. "Round Rock" and "Flat Rock" were in the midst of a pasture. The whole village presented a barren, straggling appearance. I never could swallow more than three tumblers of the water at a time, but some would imbibe double or treble that quantity. One lad often boasted of regularly taking his eight glasses. Many amusing scenes were enacted at the springs. Such wry faces, spittings and sputterings are seldom witnessed. The wife of an army officer gave the company a deal of merriment by her grimaces and ejaculations. Mr. Emery could not drink the water, but it proved beneficial to me.

An old lady, who with her daughter and son-in-law, came in a wagon from her home on a farm some twenty miles back, amused us greatly. She was suffering from weak eyes, and concluded to try the efficacy of Saratoga water as a remedy. Declaring herself too tired to go to the spring, she entered the parlor and despatched her daughter's husband with a two-quart pitcher, which was filled and placed on the table beside her, when she vigorously commenced the task of imbibing it. Every mouthful elicited the most ludicrous grimaces, accompanied by a variety of odd ejaculations, "But she didn't ride twenty miles for nothing, you must live and larn; she was determined to give that water a good try if it did taste like pisen." In a couple of hours the pitcher was emptied. The water having been topped off by a hearty dinner, the dame remounted her wagon, which was stowed with an array of kegs, jugs and bottles, which had been filled to take home. assuring us as she said good-bye, "that she raly believed there was something in that water, she felt better aready."

I was interested in a party of Quakers on their bridal tour, who came to the village in a large Dutch wagon, which had been cleaned and furnished with chairs for the accommodation of the bride and her sister. The chief object of the visit was the purchase of a bridal bonnet, which was brought, tried on, and exhibited with pride and pleasure. I praised the head gear, as I saw it was expected, though the new bonnet of white satin, Quaker shaped, was so identical with the old one, that I could not have told one from the other. Upon hinting this to the young wife, she hurriedly exclaimed, "Oh, the old one is not fresh; see this spot!" pointing to the tiniest of specks, and I came to the conclusion that womanly vanity and fondness for dress were not wholly smothered under the Quaker garb.

Emigrants to Ohio were daily passing through the village, presenting more or less thrift in their outfit. One wealthy yeoman moved his family in a frame building drawn by his numerous draft animals, while a large drove of cattle and sheep brought up the rear. The caravan presented a singular spectacle as it moved slowly past, the smoke curling from the stovepipe, and the women busy at their household tasks within the house.

A party of Dutch laborers stopping over night, ordered milk for their supper. Finding that it was sweet, they turned it to curd with cider. At my expressions of surprise at their taste, Mr. Donney informed me that it was the boast of an orderly Dutch housekeeper, that the bottom of her sour krout and bonny-clabber firkins were never visible

The following Sunday morning we bade adieu to Saratoga, and commenced the homeward route. Not a specimen of the male gender was visible during the day. The Erie canal had then been just commenced, and every man and boy throughout the region, "had gone to see the canawl."

Wednesday we returned to Boscawen. Friday morning the journey was resumed, home being reached Saturday evening, after an absence of a month. I came back a new person, with health and strength completely restored.

CHAPTER LIX.

On the evening of the 19th of December, 1816, occurred the great Goodridge sham robbery. Major Elijah P. Goodridge of Bangor, Maine, passed Pearson's tavern and the Essex Merrimac Bridge shortly before nine o'clock. A little over an hour had elapsed when he rushed into the toll-house hatless, his clothes soiled, one hand bloody, and in an excited, incoherent manner declared, "that he had been waylaid by three men just over the brow of the hill beyond, who had beaten him over the head, fired at him from a pistol, wounding his hand, and having dragged him into the field adjoining, had there robbed him of a large sum of money, leaving him senseless; that upon consciousness returning, he had made the best of his way back to the island." Mr. Pearson took the Major into the house and a physician was summoned. The wounded man continued to talk in a distracted manner of being amongst thieves and in a den of robbers, but at length recognized Mr. William Potter, the driver of the Eastern mail stage to Portsmouth, and requested him to go to the scene of the outrage and search for his horse and effects.

Mr. Potter went, accompanied by several others with lanterns. Just over the brow of the hill a pistol was found in the road; a rail was down in the fence, and in the gap a few drops of blood were seen. Major Goodridge's pocketbook lay open under the fence, with his watch, knife and papers; a rod beyond his portmanteau, valise and whip were found, and thirty-six dollars in bank notes; the handle of the whip was also spotted with blood. The search for the horse proved fruitless, but Major Samuel Shaw, coming from Hampton with a baggage wagon belonging to the Stage Company, soon after passing the bridge, found that a stray horse was following his team, which he kept behind down High and State streets to the stable at Gilman's hotel. This stray horse was the missing animal.

Dr. Carter of Amesbury dressed the wounded hand. The patient talked wildly, and appeared in a deranged state, complaining of excruciating pain in his side and in the back of his head. Doctor Israel Balch was present with Dr. Carter. The Major was put in bed and Dr. Carter remained with him till morning; he was then apparently so delirious that Mr. Pearson called Dr. Richard S. Spofford. That afternoon he was taken to the residence of Mr. John Pearson, in Newburyport. He fainted on the way, and continued delirious for two or three days, when he gradually grew better, and after a while was able to go to Danvers, where his friends resided.

This affair caused a furor of excitement. People feared to travel alone after nightfall. There was a great demand for sword canes, and a strict watch was instituted for three suspicious individuals. Upon his recovery Major Goodridge stated, "that at the time of the robbery he had upon his person and in his portmanteau $1086 in bank notes and $669 in gold belonging to himself; in addition, he had money sent by him to pay over from three to five hundred dollars. One hundred and twenty was paid at Freeport, thirty dollars he left in the post-office at Dover to go to Rochester, the remainder was to be paid in Newburyport."

As the gentleman's character was unimpeachable, and he ranked amongst the first in business circles, it was difficult to question his veracity, still, doubts respecting his story were whispered. At the intelligence, Mr. Emery went directly to the bridge. He said little on his return, only declared it a most singular robbery. As some wrappers to the gold bearing Major Goodridge's mark were picked up near Pearson's tavern, the Major caused Mr. Ebenezer Pearson, the inn-keeper, to be arrested, but as no proof of guilt was found he was immediately acquitted. About a week after, Major Goodridge having obtained the presence of Deputy Sheriff Jacob Coburn, and accompanied by one Swinnerton, of Danvers, with a divining rod, commenced a search of the premises on Deer Island. After a time a bundle of soiled and torn papers belonging to Major Goodridge were taken from the vault of the privy, and six pieces of gold wrapped in a cloth were thrown from the snow back of the house.

Mr. Pearson was a second time arrested, only to be acquitted with the heartiest acclamation. The old gentleman, then seventy years of age, had ever been one of our most respected and esteemed citizens, and the indignation of the populace had been aroused at what was deemed an outrage upon one of Mr. Pearson's age and social standing. At his acquittal this second time the enthusiasm of the crowd assembled at the court house could scarcely be expressed. Amid hilarious shouts the old gentleman was placed in a coach, which as it was good sleighing was upon runners; the horses were unharnessed in a twinkling, and a band of young men drew Mr. Pearson the whole distance to his residence, the procession being augmented by a long line of friends in sleighs.

Hearing the huzzas, I ran to a window commanding a view down High street. What was coming I could not divine; but on a nearer approach I descried Mr. Pearson. The old gentleman was affected to tears; and he earnestly strove to prevent this ovation; but it would have been as easy to have stayed a whirlwind. Altogether it was a most unique scene, a demonstration to worth which was long remembered.

A person named Taber, and two brothers, Levi and Laban Kenniston, were next arrested. Taber had been to Berwick, and was known to have been on the road about the time of the robbery. Some one hinted a suspicion against him, which Major Goodridge eagerly grasped.

The landlord of the Dexter House and his son gave the clue to the Kenistons' arrest. The afternoon prior to the supposed robbery the brothers stabled their horse at the tavern. They next inquired of the landlord's son, Mr. Samuel R. Caldwell, if they could have lodging, and at what hour the house was closed, then went out, saying they would take a walk. About seven o'clock that evening Mr. Sam Caldwell saw them near the house in earnest conversation with a man he did not know. They did not return that night, but the next morning came into the stable and inquired if their horse had been watered; they then unhasped a door and went down under the stable. Mr. Caldwell watched them from a hole in the floor. About an hour after the oldest brother went into the house. At breakfast there was much talk about the robbery. Levi said, "Well, I am glad I wa'nt there." This farther aroused Mr. Caldwell's suspicion, and he asked the pair where they had passed the night. They replied, "at Mr. Ephraim Titcomb's cellar." Upon this information, after the guests' departure, Mr. Sam Caldwell went to inquire of Mr. Titcomb respecting the strangers. Mr. Titcomb knew the Kenistons, they were at his cellar the afternoon before the robbery. Laban had just come from jail, and had no money; he owed Mr. Titcomb for board, and left his bundle for security till he should pay. Levi had a turkey; he said he had no money and could not pay his brother's bill. The evening of the robbery they were in and out; after supper, not far from seven o'clock, they went out together with one M'Intire, and were gone till past ten o'clock. The following morning Mr. Titcomb told Levi that his brother could not go away until his bill was paid. Levi told Mr. Titcomb to take the turkey; he then took out a new bill of the Newburyport Bank, a two or three dollar bill, and Mr. Titcomb took out what Laban owed.

Mr. Caldwell, never suspecting but that there had been a bona-fide robbery, considered it his duty to inform Mr. John Pearson, at whose house Major Goodridge was then stopping, respecting these to him suspicious individuals.

On the 4th of February, Maj. Goodridge with a party of friends, having obtained the services of Samuel T. Leavitt, a deputy sheriff in New Hampshire, proceeded to arrest Levi and Laban Kenniston, and to search their residence, which was at the dwelling of their father. Money in small sums was found in various places in the house. This was claimed by different members of the family. After a strict search two doubloons were unearthed in the cellar, under a pork barrel. One of these was enclosed in a wrapper which bore a mark which Major Goodridge claimed to have put upon it in Bangor, and a ten dollar bill of the Boston Bank, found in a drawer, which Major Leavitt thought was counterfeit. Major Goodridge also claimed it, showing his own handwriting on the back, which looked as though an attempt had been made to erase it.

The circumstantial evidence was so strong against the brothers Kenniston that they were held for trial, as was also the man named Taber.

Mr. Joseph Jackman of Newburyport, left town for New York on business, about a week after the robbery. Major Goodridge expressed his suspicions of him, and engaged Mr. John Pearson and his son to write to their friends in New York to have Mr. Jackman watched. He next proceeded to New York, and obtained the assistance of a marshal of the city, a Mr. Hoyt, to search Jackman's room, when some wrappers of gold which Major Goodridge claimed as bearing his mark, were found loose upon the floor, with some old rubbish and papers.

On Tuesday, April 4th, 1817, Taber and the brothers Kenniston were brought to trial at the Supreme court holden at Ipswich, before Hon. Samuel Putnam. Samuel L. Knapp, esq., was counsel for Tabor. Daniel Webster then recently admitted to the bar, and the Hon. Joseph Bartlett were counsel for the Kennistons. A motion was made by Mr. Knapp that Tabor might be tried severally, which was granted. On Thursday morning the trial of the Kennistons commenced.

Major Goodridge testified to what he had previously stated. "While at Alfred, while his baggage was being taken in to the inn, a person entered who said he was going into the country; this man he has since had reason to suppose was Taber."

"After he went to Danvers he was endeavoring to pick up every circumstance that might be a clue to the robbery. There he had the first notice about Taber from John Page, who referred him to one M'Kinstry for a more particular description; met M'Kinstry at Breed's in Lynn, who particularly described Taber, and told him he might be found in Boston, and advised witness to arrest him by all means, as he had made up his mind that he was guilty. After being in Boston two or three days, witness went out to find Taber; met with him there near Boyden's, a little west of the market, offering some hair combs to a person; judged it was he from description; he had a mark a scar under his eye; inquired if his name was Taber; he said yes; asked him to step into the house; he declined and proposed going back into the yard. Witness inquired of Tabor whether he was acquainted with the people about the bridge; Tabor said he could point out the robbers, that he had formed his opinion who they were. Pressed him hard to disclose; he said if he should tell what he knew about it, it would be more than his life was worth, those persons would kill him. Before parting he said he would for three hundred dollars tell all he knew, but did not say how much that was. Witness then went to Mr. French, who was to furnish the money and consulted with him; had agreed to meet Taber at a place appointed on the Monday following; Taber did not keep his engagement, and avoided meeting the witness; was there advised by his friends to disguise himself, which he did in the dress of a sailor, and went in the evening with Capt. Silsbee and Mr. Jones to find Taber; after finding him and conversing with him alone, he consented to give the names of those who had committed the robbery for four hundred dollars, and trusted to the honor of the witness to pay if the information should prove true; witness then went to consult Silsbee and Jones; afterwards went to Tabor, and he gave the names of a number of persons who had been concerned in the robbery; he said the prisoners were two of them, and now had part of the money if they had not spent it; told where they resided. Witness thought it best to begin the investigation with the prisoners, as they were the least artful; went on to Danvers with Mr. French; informed Mr. Page, who consented to go and assist in searching the Kennistons; French and witness then went on to Hampton, and remained concealed at Langmaid's; sent for Mr. John Pike and employed him to go to Newmarket and ascertain whether the Kennistons were at home; after he returned, got a warrant, sent for Major Leavitt, a good officer, and early in the morning went with him and Mr. Towle and arrested the Kennistons at their house. After securing the prisoners, proceeded to make a thorough search through the whole house; found some gold; heard Major Leavitt say he had found a counterfeit bill in a drawer in a room at the north part of the house; witness had not been in that room before Major Leavitt went in. After finishing the search they went with the prisoners to Major Coffin's house, about three miles. There Major Leavitt took out of his pocket-book a ten-dollar Boston bill which the Major had thought counterfeit. On examining it witness saw the writing on the back of it, "James Poor, Bangor," and knew the bill; it was a good one; there appeared to have been an attempt to erase the writing."

Major Goodridge said "he had the bill with him when he was robbed; knew it by the words on the back of it in his own handwriting; received it about a week before he left Bangor; never saw it after he enclosed it with his other bills in a piece of cambric handkerchief till he saw it at Major Coffin's."

The search at the Kennistons continued a long time before anything except the counterfeit bill and some parcels of silver money were found; witness happening to open a door, saw a boy and girl climbing on a bed; they started when they saw him; he called the officer, and told him he had better search the bed; Majors Coffin, Upton and Goodridge went in, saw a pair of pantaloons hanging up over the bed, which the boy and girl seemed to be aiming at; took the pantaloons down and found in them some silver and a doubloon without any paper on it; this gave new spirits, and the search was continued more closely; some were searching in the cellar; took down the loose stones of the wall, dug in the sand at the bottom, turned over the potatoes and moved the barrels. Upton suddenly called and said, 'Here, I have found the whole hoard!' and showed a doubloon which he had scratched up where a pork barrel had stood. Maj. Leavitt picked up another; one of the doubloons had a wrapper with witness' figures on it, which he made at Bangor. By this time the neighbors had collected, and helped search the house critically; searched it throughout; nothing else material was found except a quantity of silver dollars in a tin dish, in a case of drawers; thinks from twenty to forty, but did not count them—the prisoners said the money was not theirs. The prisoners were carried before a magistrate. Some time after, some of the wrappers of the gold with the witness' figures were found at Mr. Pearson's, at the bridge, in a vault of the privy, some of them very much defaced; some also were found at New York with Joseph Jackman, and a receipt torn up small; could identify one with his own name and the name of the receipter, Thomas Curtis, of Boston, which he had about him when robbed; before he left Bangor put up his papers and took many receipts for the purpose of settling with people in Boston; had left the pieces of papers at New York with the police officer; Jackman was one named by Taber, and in consequence of that information he had arrested Jackman."

It was proved that Taber returned from his journey to Berwick, and had been incarcerated in the jail in Boston for debt on the 12th of December, and though he obtained bail for liberty of the jail yard, he was confined within the jail limits at the time of the alleged robbery. Accordingly the Solicitor General entered a *nolle pros* on indictment against Taber, and he was sworn as a witness.

Taber testified "that this was the first time he ever saw Major Goodridge except at the examination in Newburyport. No person ever came to him in disguise in Boston, and he never had seen the Kennistons till that day."

William Jones of Boston testified that "he was present when Major Goodridge conversed with a man who was understood to be Taber; he was dressed in a light surtout." It was proved that Taber did not own and had never worn such a garment.

The silver and paper money were accounted for by Aaron Kenniston, the father of the prisoners; he had no gold in the house. He gave Levi the two-dollar bill, out of which he settled with

Mr. Titcomb when his son went to Newburyport.

It was proved that Major Goodridge was in the cellar at the Kenniston's taking down the wall, when the gold was found under the barrel, and Sheriff Upton thought that Major Goodridge first called attention to the pantaloons where the first doubloon was found; but Major Leavitt thought Major Goodridge had not entered the room where he found the marked bill.

Doctor Israel Balch was present with Dr. Carter. "He observed when he looked at the patient the patient looked away; he saw no wounds on his head or side; the pupils of his eyes were dilated a little, thought it might be owing to the darkness of the room; thought he was not deranged but playing the crazy man. He said he could not move himself in bed, but when he thought he was alone, the Doctor saw him rise up, place his earlocks and forelock in order, throw out his right arm, expectorate and spit in the fire. Hearing a noise, he laid down, covered himself up, and began to talk incoherently."

David Lawrence testified that he was at Mrs. Martin's, in company with Joseph Jackman, from 7 to 9 o'clock, on the evening of the 19th of December. Mrs. Ann Martin and Miss Fanny Griffin corroborated this statement.

The examination closed at 10 o'clock on Friday morning. Mr. Webster's argument for the prisoners, and that of the Solicitor General for the commonwealth, with the charge of the judge, was closed about 5 o'clock in the afternoon. On Saturday morning, at the opening of the court, a verdict of not guilty was returned, and the prisoners were discharged.

Though Mr. Joseph Jackman proved his presence at the house of his neighbor Mrs. Martin, on the night of the 19th of December, as the wrappers and torn receipt were taken from his room in New York, he was brought to trial at Salem November, 1817. Andrew Dunlap esq., of Salem, and Ebenezer Mosely esq., of Newburyport, were his counsel. At this trial the jury could not agree, and the case was a second time brought up at the April term. The indictment read as follows:

"At the Supreme Judicial Court of the Commonwaelth of Massachusetts, begun and holden at Ipswich, within and for the said county of Essex, on the 1th Tuesday of April, in the year of our Lord one thousand eight hundred and eighteen, the jurors for the said Commonwealth, upon their oath, present, that Joseph Jackman, resident in Newburyport, in said county of Essex, trader, on the nineteenth day of December, 1816, at Newbury, in the said county of Essex, neither was with force of arms, nor with force and violence, but Elijah P. Goodridge, with force and violence, shot his own hand with his own pocket pistol without the least doubt, then passed the village, for the place is now called Shamhill, and Essex Merrimac Bridge. Then E. P. Goodridge threw the same pistol into the river; that must be his object in going over to Mr. Pearson's, he could not have any other object. Elijah P. Goodridge, in the said peace of the said Commonwealth, then and there being, feloniously did put sundry bank bills to the amount of $36 in the field; and laid some small change, and one or more pieces of gold, and a very new gold watch carefully placed under the fence —all was supposed to have been done by the hand of said Elijah. There Elijah P. Goodridge did rob himself against the said peace of the said Commonwealth, and contrary to the form of the statute in such case made and provided."

Thursday morning at ten o'clock the jury were empaneled for the trial. The jurors were Stephen Barker, Andover, foreman; David Emery, Newbury; Gibbins Adams, Newbury; James Darling, Beverly; Nathaniel Hawkes, Saugus; Joseph Tufts, Danvers; James Abbot, Andover; Benjamin Hawes, Salem; Amos Burnham, Ipswich; Benjamin Foster, Manchester; Jacob Greenleaf, Newburyport; the judge, Hon. Charles Jackson, counsel for the Commonwealth; Hon. Daniel Davis, solicitor general; counsel for the prisoner, Hon. Daniel Webster, Boston; Ebenezer Moseley esq., Newburyport; Andrew Dunlap esq., Salem.

The excitement, which from its commencement this remarkable incident had aroused, had at this time become intense. Mr. Jackman had hosts of friends, and the sympathy of the community, but Major Goodridge also possessed many friends, who would not for a moment entertain the idea that he could have perpetrated such a tremendous fraud as a sham robbery.

Major Goodridge reiterated his former statement of the robbery, and of his finding the wrappers and receipt in Jackman's room. The papers were produced and exemplified. Jackman claimed the papers as his. Major Goodridge had stated that he drew the charge from his pistols every day on his journey. Webster called for the pistols and inquired for the old ramrods that were in them at the time of the Kennistons' trial. The Major replied that they were worn out and broken. Webster then inquired what had become of the worms or screws that were on the old rods. The reply was, "There was none." At which Webster exclaimed, "Do you undertake to say that you drew the charges every day on your journey without a worm or screw!" Goodridge was at a loss what to say, but at length replied, "he believed there was a screw on one of the rods. He bought the pistols eight or nine years ago; for the last three years no one had seen them, as he feared persons would borrow them to fight duels." This was disproved by Mr. Eleazer Wyer of Portland, who testified to selling Major Goodridge the pistols while he was stopping at Burnham's Hotel on his journey from Bangor. The remainder of the witness' testimony was similar to that at the Kennistons' trial. The examination of witnesses over, Mr. Webster commenced his address to the jury. This was one of his most masterly efforts, one which those who were present always referred to with pride and admiration. He proved that it was impossible for either of the accused parties to have been on the spot at the time of the alleged robbery. The two wagons driven by Shaw and Keyser, and the mail stage, must have passed within three rods of Goodridge at the time he describes the robbery was taking place. The bullet went through the sleeve of his coat. He might intend it should have gone through nothing else. It was quite certain he could not have received the wound in his hand in the way he described. There was not the least mark of beating and wounding. The blow on the head which brought him senseless to the ground neither broke the skin nor left any mark whatever. He fell from his horse on frozen ground, without any appearance of injury. He was drawn through or over a rail fence with such force as to break the rail, but not at all to leave any wound or scratch on him. A second time he was knocked down, kicked, stamped upon, choked, and in every way abused and beaten till sense had departed and the breath of life hardly remained, and yet no wound, bruise, or discoloration, or mark of injury, was found to result from all this. Look to the appearance of the field. The portmanteau was there, the straps which fastened it to the saddle were carefully unbuckled. This was very considerate for robbers. It had been opened and its contents were scattered about the field. The pocketbook, too, had been opened, and many papers it contained scattered on the ground. Nothing valuable was lost but money, and the money belonging to other persons was not taken; the robbers found out that it was not the prosecutor's and left it. His watch was safe under the fence, the seal laid carefully on the grass; the timekeeper had not even ceased ticking. Had Major Goodridge the money with him that he mentions? If so, his clerks or persons connected with him in business must have known it, yet no witness was produced. Nothing could be more important than to prove that he had the money, yet he did not prove it. Fixing his eyes upon the prisoner with a glance that caused him to quail with conscious guilt, Mr. Webster ended this memorable harangue by a burst of eloquence scarcely equalled in the annals of jurisprudence.

The case was closed, and the jury retired the latter part of the afternoon. Eleven were unanimous for the verdict of no robbery; Mr. Hawkes of Saugus alone dissented. The evidence was conned and discussed until a late hour, but without avail. Provoked and weary, the eleven at length desisted from farther argument, and several lighted cigars. Tobacco smoke was annoying to Mr. Hawkes—seeing its effect, the majority caught the cue; every one took a cigar; a fresh box of Havanas were ordered, and soon the room was suffocating. The obstinate juror begged hard for air, but not a breath was admitted. "Would he unite on the verdict?" "No." Puff, puff, went the cigars, I believe one of the gentlemen managed to smoke two at once. The air grew chokingly dense; tears rose to the smokers' eyes. Mr. Emery said he could not have borne it much longer himself, when the obstinate dissenter succumbed, fairly smoked into acquiescence. Windows were thrown open, and the jaded men refreshed themselves by a bath and breakfast. The court opened at the usual hour when the verdict was rendered.

Thus ended the great Goodridge case, one that had caused more distress and expense than scarcely any other upon record. For a time it destroyed the happiness of several households; innocent men were held in durance, and at the Jackman trial in Salem one of the jurors lost his life. A tumbler was broken on a tray of refreshments brought from the hotel to the courthouse, and the unfortunate man swallowed a piece of the glass, which severed the jugular vein, causing death in a short time.

The only plea in extenuation for Major Goodridge is that in those days a failure in business was much more of a disgrace than at present. "Being broke," was something difficult to surmount. Finding himself in a financial dilemma, the Major concocted this plan to settle his affairs; but he overshot the mark. I believe he went South; but wherever his sojourn, he must have been the victim of remorse, for the fatal mistake that ruined his worldly career.

Immediately after the verdict of a sham robbery had been rendered, a gibbet was erected on the hill where it had been represented to have occurred, and Major Goodridge was hung in effigy. This gibbet remained many years, but at length fell to pieces from the decay of age.

CHAPTER LX.

On March 31st, 1818, the Essex Agricultural Society was formed; it was incorporated on June 12th. Mr. Emery was among those who formed this society, his certificate of membership reads:

"Received payment by the hand of Robert Dodge, the assessment of three dollars, for the Essex Agricultural Society for David Emery.

ICHABOD TUCKER, Treasurer.

May 6th, 1818."

Both Col. Colman and Major Emery were enthusiastic and untiring in forwarding the concerns of this society, and both were active on duty at its annual cattle shows, until failing health and the infirmities of age prevented; but to the latest hour of their long lives their interest in the advancement of the society was maintained; that society which in company with kindred spirits they had formed, when the improvement of stock, and science as applied to agriculture. had scarcely attracted a thought throughout our rural community; a band of men whose memory Essex county may recall with pride, all of whom have now passed to the green pastures and still waters of the celestial land.

The following winter our family circle was enlivened by the presence of Uncle Samuel Smith, who with his wife came to pay a farewell visit prior to their emigration to Ohio.

My grandmother had died suddenly the September previous. Though Mr. Smith had become a distinguished preacher of the Methodist circuit, his mother never tolerated his change of faith. I could not but rejoice that she had gone to rest without being disquieted by this Western scheme.

Uncle Sam was enthusiastic in the prospect of sowing the seed of truth in the new country now being fast reclaimed from the wilderness, and his wife was as hopeful and ambitious for her husband and family as she had been on their removal to Vermont. After a sojourn of several weeks, they bade their New England relatives and friends a final adieu, for though both lived to an advanced age, neither ever revisited their birthplace. That spring the family became located on a farm upon the Little Sciota river, not far from Chilicothe.

In the April of 1818 Mr. Joshua Pillsbury came from Boscawen and assumed the care of his ancestral acres, being the seventh in descent from William Pillsbury, who came to Newbury in 1651. We moved to the house on the lower side of High street, second above Kent, which had been built by Mr. William Swain, but was then owned by Mr. Abner Wood. Mr. Emery hired the field opposite, to which his slaughter-house and piggeries were drawn. In a few weeks he purchased this lot of Mr. Allen Dodge and Mr. Joseph Toppan for $500.

The next year he erected a large barn upon the hill. In addition to the usual appliances of a stable, a chimney was built at the lower end, and a room lighted by three windows was finished. This apartment had a fireplace, a large set kettle, and a good sized closet; a trap door opened upon stairs leading to the cellar beneath, in which was a wooden cistern, a pump above furnishing the premises with water. This room was for the convenience of packing beef and trying lard, two branches of business in which Mr. Emery was largely engaged. Mr. Babb was still our factotum. John Faris and Mr. Michael Creasey were the regular butchers, but Mr. Paul Lunt of Belleville, Mr. Stephen Emery and his son Moody, and Mr. Jonas Bartlett from the lower parish in West Newbury, were often employed. Not unfrequently from fifteen to twenty hands were at work, and as many as twenty beeves' carcases would be weighed off at once. The field below the buildings was fenced for a sheep pasture; a hundred head were often collected there. Three wagons were run to supply town customers, the barreled beef and pork supplied the fishing fleet and outward-bound vessels, and the surplus was sold in Boston.

In 1822 Mr. Creasey having established himself in business, his place was filled by Mr. Henry Mowatt. That spring, my youngest brother, Joseph Little Smith, came to Newburyport, and in company with Mr. Emery established a wholesale and retail grocery store on Market square, at the upper corner of Inn street. This was the depot for Mr. Emery's beef and pork trade. My brother boarded in our family.

There were a number of fruit trees on the lot Mr. Emery had bought; he planted others, and the elm back of the house, and commenced other improvements preparatory to the erection of a house. The elm near the barn was set out several years after by Robert Peabody while an inmate of the family. The next year he purchased the field between his lot and Mount Rural. This had formed part of the estate of the late Daniel Farnham esq., by whom it had been bequeathed to his daughters, Mrs. Sybil Sawyer and Mrs. Catharine Flag, who sold it to Mr. Emery for $650.

"Squire Farnham had formerly owned the whole of that end of the ridge. The first wife of Dr. Smith of Mt. Rural was another of his daughters. In 1820, by the death of his father, my husband's namesake, David Emery Colman, a boy of six years, was left an orphan. Mr. Emery took him into the family; he was a handsome, bright little lad, and he remained with us till his twelfth year, when he was put on the farm of Mr. Thomas Chase in West Newbury.

In May, 1819, my Aunt Bartlett was married to Capt. Joseph O'Brian. Captains Joseph and John O'Brian were of Irish descent, their father emigrated to America and settled in Machias, district of Maine. Both of the sons were successful shipmasters and merchants. Capt. John O'Brian, as I have previously stated, distinguished himself in the privateer Hibernia during the war of 1812. Capt. John O'Brian married Hannah Toppan; their children were Jeremiah, John, Hannah and Marcia Scott. Hannah became the third wife of her cousin Joseph O'Brian. Marcia married Rev. Dr. Jeremiah Chaplin, president of Waterville College, Maine. Both of these ladies were authors of some celebrity.

John O'Brian Chaplin was professor of Greek. Latin and English literature at Columbian College, Washing.ton, D C. Hannah Chaplin married Rev. Thomas Jefferson Conant of Brandon, Vt., employed by the American Bible Union of New York, in translating the Bible; professor in Rochester University until 1857; formerly professor at Waterville and at Madison University.

Captain Joseph O'Brian's first wife was Rebecca, daughter of David and Mary (Johnson) Moody. Their children were David, William, and others deceased before 1812—Dennis, Joseph, Thomas and Valeria.

The O'Brians were of a highly distinguished race, a great Milesian family of the name who descended from the Kings of Thomond. Arms, Gules, three lions proper, or. Crest, a naked arm embowered, the hand grasping a sword all ppr. Motto—"*Vigueur der dessus.*" "Strength from above."

Capt. Joseph O'Brian having lost his residence on Water street at the great fire, had purchased the house on High street, built by Capt. Samuel Swett, who had moved to Georgetown, D. C. As the Baptist meeting-house was located so far to the north end, Capt. O'Brian, being a zealous Jacobin, had taken a pew in the house of worship on Harris street. For many years Mrs. Bartlett had been connected with the First Presbyterian church, and she highly respected and esteemed its pastor, the Rev. Dr. Dana; but for some reason Capt. O'Brian objected to his performing the marriage ceremony. Mrs. Bartlett was equally averse to Parson Giles. After much discussion the pair agreed to disagree, and the Rev. Dr. Morse was called to tie the nuptial knot according to the ritual of the Episcopal church. Mrs. O'Brian, however, like a dutiful wife, ever after attended on Parson Giles' ministrations with her husband and family.

In the spring of this year the west part of Newbury was set off into a separate township, and incorporated by the name of Parsons, which was soon changed to that of West Newbury.

In the same year Col. Jeremiah Colman succeeded Mr. Benjamin Hale as agent for the Eastern Stage Company, an office which he filled until the opening of the Eastern railroad. Soon after accepting the agency Col. Colman purchased the house built by Mr. Obadiah Pearson, on Harris street, and moved thither. The business at the market was continued by Mr. Daniel Colman, who bought the residence on the turnpike, where he became a prominent citizen of Newbury, and an influential member of Oldtown parish. For many years he was a selectman of the town, one of the overseers of the poor, and the superintendent of the Sabbath school connected with the society, under the pastorate of the Rev. Dr. Withington. In addition he was often called to fill posts of trust and honor outside of his town and parish. The latter part of his life was passed on the ancestral farm in Byfield. Col. Jeremiah Colman was also an active member of the Oldtown society, filling the office of deacon for several years.

The next year, 1820, the navigation law was passed, which restricted vessels from taking cargoes to the British colonies, and from bringing cargoes to our ports. As Newburyport had a large eastern trade, this proved extremely injurious to our shipping interest. In addition, the exorbitant duties imposed by France and other continental nations on American goods and tonnage greatly depressed the maritime enterprise of the place.

Capt. John Murray Miltimore, the youngest son of the Rev. James Miltimore, at this time commanded the ship Jane. On arriving at Bordeaux from Norfolk, to his consternation he learned that a duty of $18 per ton had been imposed, an amount which the full value of both vessel and cargo would scarcely cover. In this dilemma Capt. Miltimore proceeded immediately to Paris to lay the case before the American consul, and Mr. Albert Gallatin, our minister to the Court of St. Cloud. The matter was carried before the government, and the duty on Capt. Miltimore's ship was removed and the law greatly modified. That same year a piratical fleet appeared in the West Indian waters, which for several years continued the terror of the sea.

The winter of 1820 and 1821 was remarkably cold. The river was passable for the heaviest teams on the ice from Haverhill to Black Rocks. China cups cracked on the tea table from the frost, before a rousing fire, the instant the hot tea touched them; and plates set to drain in the process of dish-washing froze together in front of the huge logs, ablaze in the wide kitchen fireplace.

That spring has been rendered memorable from its incendiary fires. Two alarms having been given, a strict watch, and other precautions, were instituted. A third fire was set in the barn belonging to my Uncle Bradstreet Johnson on Temple street, which was consumed, with Mr. Johnson's dwelling-house and the residences of Mr. Tommy Balch and Mr. Andrew Frothingham, opposite. The alarm was given about ten o'clock, and the fire raged till morning. Mr. Johnson was aged and feeble, and with difficulty he was moved from the burning house, in which he lost nearly the whole of his clothing and household effects. He was taken to the residence of his nieces, Tempy and Mary Johnson, which stood next below on the street, where his relatives and friends supplied his immediate need. He continued with these nieces until his death, some two years after. The Eastern Stage Company purchased his estate and erected the large brick stable still standing, for their use.

In the September following, the Rev. Gilbert T. Williams, from ill health, was dismissed from the pastorate of the First church in West Newbury. He died on the 24th of September, 1824, aged 63 years. He was succeeded in 1826 by Henry C. Wright. The Rev. John Kirby, of the second parish, in 1818 went South for his health, and on December 5th was drowned at Okrakok bar, North Carolina. He was succeeded by the Rev. Elijah Demond, who was settled on the 7th of March, 1821.

In March of that year, Newburyport voted to erect the present almshouse.

In 1822 the shambles gave place to the present brick market house.

In that same year, the Lancasterian or monitorial system of teaching was introduced into our public schools, which continued for several years.

As Mr. Abner Wood was desirous to occupy his house, on the 22nd of April, 1821, we moved to the house on High, lower corner of Tyng street. The establishment was owned by Mr. Luther Waterman, and the large house, stable and garden, was rented for forty-five dollars a year.

On the 22nd of January, 1821, my

sister, Susan Little Smith, was united in marriage with Mr. Edward Toppan. The name Toppan was originally Topham, taken from the name of a place in Yorkshire, meaning upper hamlet or village. The pedigree as far back as traced, commences with Robert Topham, who resided at Linton, near Pately bridge, supposed to be in the west riding of Yorkshire. He made his will in January, 1550. His second son, Thomas Topham, was of Arncliffe, near Linton. He died in 1589, and was buried in the church at Arncliffe. Edward Topham, alias Toppan, eldest son of Thomas Toppan, was of Aiglethorpe, near Linton, and has his pedigree recorded in the college of arms, with armorial bearings. One of his sons was a lieutenant-colonel in the service of Charles I., and was killed at Marston Moor in 1644. William Toppan, fourth son of Edward Toppan of Aiglethorpe, lived for some time at Calbridge, where his son Abraham was baptized April 10th, 1606. The family still exists in England, and are now of Middleham, in the northwest part of Yorkshire on the river Ouse. As early as 1637, Abraham Toppan resided at Yarmouth; his wife was a Susanna Taylor, a daughter of a Mr. Taylor and his wife Elizabeth. After the death of Mr. Taylor, the widow Elizabeth married a Mr. Goodale; after the death of Mr. Goodale she came to Newbury, where she died April 8th, 1647. Her four daughters were Susanna, the wife of Abraham Toppan; Joanna, the wife of Mr. John Oliver, and of Capt. William Gerrish; Elizabeth, the wife of Mr. John Lowle; and Ann, the wife of Capt. Thomas Milward, all of Newbury. In the first volume of the fourth series of the publications of the Massachusetts Historical Society, pp. 98 and 99, is the following: "A Register of the names of such persons who are 21 years and upward, and have license to passe into forraigne parts from March 1637 to the 29th of September, by virtu of a Commission of Mr. Thomas Mayhew, Gentleman." Among these persons are the following: Abraham Toppan Cooper, aged 31; Susanna, his wife, aged 31, with their children Peter and Elizabeth, and one mayd servant Anne Goodin, aged 13 years, sailed from Yarmouth 10 May, 1637, in the ship Rose of Yarmouth, Wm. Andrews Master."

In October, 1637, Abraham Toppan was in Newbury, as appears by the following extract from the town records:

"Abraham Toppan being licensed by John Endicott Esq., to live in this jurisdiction, was received into the town of Newberry as an inhabitant thereof and have promised under his hand to be subject to any lawful order that shall be made by the towne.

ABRAHAM TOPPAN.

Oct. 1637."

Abraham and Susanna Toppan had seven children, Dr. Peter, Elizabeth, Abraham, Jacob, Susanna, John and Isaac.

Jacob, born in 1645, married Hannah Sewell Aug. 24th, 1670; their children were Jacob, Samuel, James, John, Hannah, Elizabeth, Abraham, Anne and Sewell.

Mrs. Toppan's maiden name was Wigglesworth; she was the widow of John Sewell.

Abraham Toppan, born June 29th, 1684, married Esther Sewell Oct. 24th, 1713; the children were Edward, Elizabeth, Patience, Samuel, Jacob and Michael.

Edward Toppan, born Sept. 7th, 1715, married Sarah Bailey Sept. 7th,

40

1743; children, Abraham. Anna, born 1746, died 1757, Sarah, Mary, Patience, Joshua, Stephen, Edward, Enoch, Anna, Abner and Judith.

Enoch Toppan, born May 7th, 1759, married Mary Coffin Feb. 2nd, 1794, and Mary Merrill, Aug. 19th, 1797; children, Moses, Edward, Margaret, Hannah and Mary.

The arms of Topham or Toppan are:

ARGENT, A CHEVRON GULES, BETWEEN THREE SHANES' HEADS ERASED SABLE. CREST, TWO CERPENTS ENTWINED AROUND A CROSS PATEE FILCHEE.

Jacob Toppan owned a large tract of land through which Toppan street, then Toppan's lane, was laid out, where, in 1694, he built the present large and commodious dwelling known as the Toppan house. He was succeeded in the homestead by his son Abraham, his grandson Edward, and his great-grandson Enoch.

Edward Toppan, born April 7th, 1796, was the husband of my sister. Mr. Toppan had erected a house below his father's, on the opposite side of the lane, whither he took his bride. His brother Moses married Cornelia Brown, Feb. 2nd, 1828, and continued on the homestead.

My sister's marriage was satisfactory to the whole family, but especially so to me, as it brought her into my immediate vicinage. The new house, with its neat furniture was most inviting. Mrs. Toppan, a thorough housekeeper, possessing much energy, skill and taste, made an excellent wife and mother. Though a farmer's wife, and the mistress of a large family, hers was an unusually orderly household, and though no duty was neglected, time was found for social intercourse, hospitable entertainment, charitable deeds, the cultivation of a flower garden, and a variety of house plants, while her ingenuity and skill were often exhibited in little adornments in dress, or for the dwelling, and as gifts to relatives and friends.. Mr. Toppan, a most excellent husband, father, neighbor and citizen, held important positions in the town, and in the parish of the First Religious Society. A consistent Democrat, he twice represented his native place in the State legislature.

In the spring of 1821 Capt. Joseph O'Brian moved to Reading, Pennsylvania, and with his two sons, Dennis and Joseph, went into the dry goods business under the firm of "Joseph O'Brian & Sons, sign of the 'Golden Ball.'" Thomas O'Brian, in company with Thomas Foster, set up in the shoe business, as the firm of "O'Brian & Foster."

I had been so intimately associated with this aunt from infancy that I scarcely knew how to live without her; her departure caused a loneliness which was not at once dispelled; and her adopted daughter, Eliza Bartlett, was also greatly missed.

The next spring the family received with great pleasure a visit from my Aunt Peabody; she was accompanied by her third daughter Sophila. Learning that the "Citizen" had arrived with the expected guests, Mr. Emery and my brother Joseph hastened to the wharf. They found Mrs. Peabody and her daughter in Mr. Dodge's counting-room, awaiting a carriage to convey them to the residence of Mrs. Peabody's sister, Mrs. Samuel Noyes, at the "Farms," Newbury. Mr. Emery received the greeting of an old friend; but he was obliged to introduce his companion. Mrs. Peabody could scarcely realize that the tall, handsome young man could be "sister Prudy's little Joseph," and the little Sophila had changed as much to the gentlemen.

At dinner I was entertained with an account of the meeting, and naturally inquired respecting my cousin Sophila's personal appearance. Mr. Emery replied, "that she was not as handsome as Sophronia, that she was a complete Southern girl." My brother's handsome black eyes sparkled as he added, "that he thought her full as handsome as her elder sister, and that she was the most graceful and polished young lady he had ever met;" altogether he pronounced her "perfectly charming." I was somewhat amused, and was not as much surprised as Aunt Peabody, at her nephew's extremely considerate attention in driving her and her daughter about the vicinity to visit their numerous relatives. The visitors returned home in October, when the cousins' engagement was openly declared. No one thought of objecting on account of consanguinity, and the lady had rendered herself a general favorite. Marrying cousins was a family trait; my husband and my brother James and his wife were second cousins; Mrs. Toppan and her husband were also relatives, as Mr. Toppan's grandmother was a Little, from Turkey Hill; my brother and his affianced had but followed the family predilection of Little cleaving to Little in preference to the rest of creation.

The wedding took place the next October, at Gen. Peabody's residence in Georgetown. The bridal pair came directly to Newburyport, and remained with us until a house was procured.

Miss Dorothy Miltimore had some years previous married Capt. James Rousseau; he was recently deceased, and the widow, with her two children, had returned to the paternal roof. My brother rented her house at the head of Strong street, and in six weeks the young couple went to housekeeping. Polly Smart, who for years had been a faithful servitor in Gen. Peabody's family, had come North. At the time of Miss Sophila's marriage she was on a visit to Plymouth, N. H. Upon receiving the intelligence she hastened to Newburyport to meet the wedded pair, and remained with us until the house was secured, when she at once assumed the management of affairs. "What did that young thing know of New England housekeeping? She could embroider muslin and paint picters, but she knew no more how to take care of Joe Smith and his house than a baby!" So Mrs. Smith was installed in state in the parlor to receive callers and entertain her husband and his friends, while Polly, in her short gown and petticoat, and tow apron, her hair uniquely drawn under a net, her round honest face radiant with responsibility, clattered about with her strong bare arms amongst the pots and pans, a perfect autocrat of the kitchen.

On April 4th, 1823, my grandfather, Joseph Little, died at the ripe age of 83. He had suffered most patiently for some time from a cancerous stomach, and his departure had been long expected. My grandmother had a few years before been stricken with paralysis. Grandsir had been assiduous in his attention, and his departure was keenly felt by his widow: we all sadly missed the kind, genial old gentleman, and the old homestead ever after seemed lone and desolate.

CHAPTER LXI.

On August 31st, 1824, LaFayette visited Newburyport. On the 23d a town-meeting was called to arrange the reception. It was decided that the committee of arrangements should receive the General at Ipswich, thence he would proceed under the escort of a battalion of Cavalry, through Rowley to Newbury, Oldtown. At the head of South street this escort was to be joined by the Newburyport Artillery and the Washington Light Infantry, when the distinguished guest would be conducted through High and down State street to the Tracy mansion, then to the residence of James Prince, esq., where he would be entertained. Upon his arrival at the Prince house an address of welcome would be given by the Hon. Ebenezer Moseley. The houses along the line of the procession were to be illuminated; the signal for lighting would be a gun fired from Oldtown Hill. On the following morning an hour would be appropriated to the introduction of ladies and gentlemen, the time to be announced by ringing of the bells. A procession would then be formed of the commissioned officers of the brigade in uniform; State and municipal magistrates and citizens to accompany the General through the principal streets, escorted by the Byfield Rifle Corps, the Newburyport Artillery, and the Washington Light Infantry. This rifle company was the first organized in the State, and they were distinguished for accuracy of aim and other soldierly qualities. The school children were to assemble in the mall, the procession to pass through the lines. Citizens were requested to display flags on the vessels and other conspicuous places. The committee of arrangements were Ebenezer Wheelright, esq., Hon. Ebenezer Moseley, Anthony Smith, William Davis, Philip Coombs, Joshua Greenleaf, William Bartlett, esq., Hon, Samuel S Wilde, William Cross, Josiah Smith, Thomas M. Clark, Joshua Greenleaf, John Coffin, Abraham Williams, John Merrill and Caleb Cushing, esq.

The marshals of the day were Capt. Edmund Bartlett, Maj. Thomas Perkins, Maj. David Emery, Messrs. George Cross, Nathaniel Foster, John Scott, esq., and Nathan Brown.

Mr. Prince's elegant mansion was put in readiness to receive the distinguished guest. Mr. Emery took me to see the chamber he was to occupy. It was the apartment in which Washington had slept on his visit to the town, and the furniture had never been removed. The bedstead which had the honor to support both Washington and LaFayette on the night of their sojourn in Newburyport, was of mahogany, about the height of our modern bedsteads, with four handsomely carved posts reaching nearly to the ceiling. The hangings were of crimson silk damask, long curtains on rods, drawing around the bed, with valances draping the tester; the coverlet was like the curtains, and the whole were bordered by an ornamental gimp and fringe.

The seats to the mahogany chairs were covered to match; the rest of the furniture was rich and massive.

The dining-room was resplendent, with its handsomely appurtenanced sideboard, and the table was spread with great elegance. The spacious parlors were luxurious with their polished furniture, silken curtains and superb mirrors. Everything was fitting for the reception of the noble and honored visitor.

An arch was thrown across the head of State street which bore the inscription "The Hero of Two Continents." Many of the windows of the houses on the route of the procession were decorated with mottoes expressive of the most enthusiastic joy.

At an early hour on Tuesday evening, August 31st, the General arrived at Ipswich, amid the greetings of a large assembly of citizens. He was addressed by Nathaniel Lord, esq., and after partaking of a collation provided at Treadwell's Hotel, he proceeded towards Newburyport at 9 o'clock, attended by his suite, Maj. General Stickney and his Aid, and the committee of arrangements. The houses along the road in Oldtown, as well as in Newburyport, were illuminated. At the Lower Green the residence of Mr. Samuel Newman was conspicuous for the beauty and good taste regarding the lights. The hero's approach was announced by the ringing of bells, the roaring of cannons, and the display of rockets.

Unfortunately a drenching southerly rain set in the first of the evening, which marred everything. Notwithstanding the water poured down like a second flood, an immense crowd received the General. Upon arriving at the Prince house he was addressed by Hon. Ebenezer Moseley as follows:

"Gen. LaFayette,—The citizens of Newburyport are happy in this opportunity of greeting with the warmest welcome, a distinguished benefactor of their country.

The important services you rendered this people in the day of their distress, the devotedness which you manifested in their perilous cause, and the dangers which y u *sought* for their relief, are incorporated in our history and firmly engraven on our hearts.

We would lead you to our institutions of learning, charity and religion; we would point you to our hills and valleys, covered with flocks and smiling in abundance, that you may behold the happy effects of those principles of liberty which you were so instrumental in establishing. Our children cluster about you to receive a patriot's blessing. Our citizens press forward to show their gratitude. Our nation pays you a tribute which must remove the reproach that republics are ungrateful.

As the zealous advocate of civil liberty we give you welcome; as the brave defender of an oppressed people, we make you welcome—as the friend and companion of our immortal Washington, we bid you welcome."

To this a brief and appropriate reply was made, in which the General modestly hinted, that "the great attention paid him was far beyond his expectations or deserts—that his feelings of attachment towards this country could not be expressed, but only felt by a heart glowing with the most ardent affection."

A window was thrown up, and the General presented himself to the crowd. Every one strove to first grasp his hand; the shouts were hushed in the excess of affectionate feeling, while in kind rebukes he expressed his sorrow that any should be exposed for his sake to the inclement weather. Supper, which had been provided by Mr. Stetson, was then served. At the table, with the General and his suite, were the military officers, the committee of arrangements, the clergymen of the town and the marshals of the day.

I passed an anxious evening. My husband's health did not admit of exposure, and I knew he must be completely drenched. The bells and the guns announced the arrival of the cortege. About 11 o'clock I was startled by the entrance of a stranger, a cavalry officer from Andover, who brought an introduction from my husband. He was in delicate health and feared the worst from such a wetting. I supplied dry clothes and a cup of hot tea, while Babb, having stabled the officer's steed, built a rousing fire in the kitchen fireplace to dry his uniform. Mr. Emery arrived about 12; his military cloak had been some defence, still his clothing was saturated. The crowd had been great, and owing to the pelting rain there had been much confusion. A gang of pickpockets was following the General on his route, and several of our citizens were most adroitly despoiled of their pocket-books and watches. The marshals had been obliged to remain on horseback until the company sat down to supper. As the suits must be ready for service in the morning, the faithful Babb and John B. Porter, then a lad in the family, took them in charge while the tired owners sought repose.

On Wednesday morning the weather being unpromising, the procession was abandoned. After gracefully receiving all who chose an introduction, LaFayette entered his carriage for Portsmouth. An escort composed of cavalry, light infantry and artillery, accompanied him a short distance; the gentlemen of the committee of arrangements, and the marshals attended him to Leavitt's tavern in Hampton. In the afternoon the disappointed children were paraded on the mall; they had been furnished with LaFayette badges. The girls wore white dresses and blue sashes, upon which was stamped a portrait of the General; a similar likeness had been put on white satin ribbons about a quarter of a yard in length, which were attached to the buttonholes of the boys' jackets.

LaFayette returned to town between 12 and 1 o'clock Thursday morning. The houses on High street through Belleville and Newburyport were brilliantly illuminated, and every one was up to receive the beloved visitor.

The General remained here about two hours, and then set out for Boston, where he was under an engagement to review a body of troops at Lexington.

There were many interesting meetings during LaFayette's visit with old friends, his former comrades in arms, Capt. Gould and Mr. Edward Toppan, had served under him in Rhode Island; Mr. Lemuel Coffin had been under Col. Bayler of Washington's Life Guards, and witnessed LaFayette's brave conduct at Monmouth; Mr. Amos Pearson had been with him at the capture of Burgoyne; but of the many veterans of the continental army who were presented to the General, none produced a stronger title to notice than Mr. Daniel Foster; he was a non-commissioned officer in LaFayette's select corps of Light Infantry, and constantly about the General. This had been the pet corps of LaFayette, and he uniformed and armed it at his own expense. Mr. Foster advanced before the General, and holding his sword, welcomed his

EMERY PLACE.

former commander to our shores. He told him "he was proud to see him once more on American soil, and that his son's sons participated in his happiness on this joyful occasion." When La-Fayette saw one of his own infantry standing before him, one who had often commanded his quarter guard, and his own mark on the blade of the sword half drawn from the scabbard, he greeted the old soldier most cordially, embracing him enthusiastically, telling him "that he looked upon him as one of his own family."

Had it not been for the unpropitious weather, this reception would have been most auspicious; but the rain causing a change in the programme, some disappointment and mistakes ensued.

The Byfield Rifle Corps was to have joined in the Wednesday morning's procession; they came into town the evening previous to witness the arrival of the General and be in readiness for the next morning's celebration. Owing to the procession's being abandoned they were entirely overlooked. Mr. Emery found them a rueful set of men, without a breakfast. He immediately ordered the requisite refreshment, which, though it took nearly forty dollars from his pocket, secured him the kind remembrance of his own comrades, friends and neighbors.

CHAPTER LXII.

In August the county bought the estate above the jail. This property belonged to Mr. Thomas Somerby. On it was a good two-story house, which was sold to be removed, for the erection of the stone house occupied by the jail keeper. The Somerby house was put up at auction, and was knocked off to Mr. Emery for $190. By the terms of sale he was obliged to move it in one week; it was sold on Tuesday, and the next week Monday at half-past 5 in the afternoon, it was on his hill fronting his stable and slaughter-house. This was an astonishing expedition for those days, as none of the present appliances for moving buildings were at hand. Mr. Emery was obliged to go to Danvers to procure the wheels upon which the building was moved. The teamsters and farmers in the town and vicinity furnished the teams; a string of forty-two yoke of oxen drew the building to its place.

High street was lined with people to witness the novel sight; there had not been such a stir in the town for months, as in those days there was little to break the monotony excepting the daily arrivals of the various stages, and "court week," which was hailed with especial delight by the young ladies, as a season for evening parties, at which the lawyers and other distinguished strangers which the court drew into town, were entertained.

The evening of LaFayette's arrival the house stood upon posts, the cellar not having been completed, and I greatly feared that it would be blown over in the southeastern storm. No accident happened, and an L was immediately added. There was so little building at that time that the remodelling of the house attracted much attention, and visitors often went to view the building and the fine prospect which its site afforded. Mr. Moses Coffin and his sons did the joiner's work, and Mr. Marshall the masonry. The house was completed by November, and we took possession on the 22nd.

The next February my Aunt Thurrel died; her husband went before some two or three years. In March, her brother, and Mr. Emery's grandfather, John Little, died; he took cold at his sister's funeral and never went out again. In the same week we were called to mourn the loss of Jane Noyes, the only daughter of Mr. and Mrs. Samuel Noyes. Jane was a very beautiful and lovely girl of nineteen, and her death caused a sad void in the home and throughout the family. Her illness was lingering and distressing, but it was borne with a patience and even cheerfulness, which evinced the most lovely traits of a truly christian character. Leaning upon the Savior, she calmly met the approach of death, and with childlike trust at last fell asleep in Jesus. Jane Noyes was buried on one day, and Grandfather Little on the next.

The next October my brother Joseph moved to Boston, and went into the wholesale grocery business in a store on North Market street, in company with the Hon. Marshall P. Wilder.

The next spring Mr. Solomon Babb took possession of a farm which he had purchased in Meredith, N. H., bordering on Lake Winnipiseogee. This estate was bought with the savings of his period of service in our family. He not only secured a fine large farm, but had also sufficient funds to stock it and set up housekeeping.

In the August of 1824 Capt. John Emery Remick, then a lad of fourteen, the second son of Capt. John Remick, and grandson of Mr. Emery's uncle, Maj. Ephraim Emery, came to reside with us; he continued in our household until after his majority, and was ever regarded as a son in the family.

CHAPTER LXIII.

Methodism acquired but few adherents in this vicinity until 1819, when the Rev. John Adams, commonly known as "Reformation John," commenced his labors. The first meetings were held in private houses; then, an old schoolhouse on Marlborough street became the place of worship, while the prayer-meetings were still held at the dwellings of the converts.

A church had been built at Salisbury, and until 1825 the two societies were connected, Mr. Adams preaching alternately at the two places. On the Sabbaths when the service was held in Salisbury, many of the Newbury people crossed the river in boats to attend divine worship. At that period there were many itinerant preachers consecrated to missionary work; these travelled on foot, their clothing slung in a knapsack on their shoulders or on horseback, the saddle-bags depending from the saddle containing the sum of their worldly possessions.

Mr. Cutting Pettingell was one of the first converts, and his house was ever open to his brethren. Often at sunset one or more of these tired, dusty, wayworn travellers would arrive, explaining that they had been directed to the "Pilgrim's Home," as Mr. Pettingell's house had become designated.

In 1825, a small, one-story chapel, with an unpretending portico over the entrance, was erected in the midst of a field between South and Marlborough streets. Gates opening upon paths through the potato patch gave ingress to the building; the principal walk led from a gate at the head of Chase's court directly to the front door. This inconvenient location had been chosen on account of the cheapness of the site.

Among the first pew-holders were the Pettingells, Plummers, Hunts, Goodwins, Lunts, Thurlows, Capt. Joseph L. Colby, Mr. Benjamin Brown, Mr. David Watts. Mr. Moses Chase, Mr. Charles Shoof, Mr. Amos Currier, Josiah Plummer Noyes, Mr. Isaac Noyes, Mr. William Ilsley, Mr. Michael Wormstead, Mr. Samuel Smith, Mr. Benjamin Atkinson, Mr. Joseph Janvrin and Mr. Peabody Greenleaf.

In a few years Adelphi street was laid out; this brought the chapel into a pleasant and convenient situation, accessible from the sidewalk. The band, who in the face of much opposition had founded this new society, reckoned among its members some of the deepest thinkers and most respectable citizens of that part of the town; still they were subjected to much animadversion and derision. Many of the more zealous female members, discarding outward adornment, wore short hair and extremely plain attire; this, and their assisting to conduct the meetings, brought upon them the scorn and ridicule of the more worldly minded.

Greatly in need of a domestic, I was informed that a young girl named Ann Page desired a place. My invitation that she should call was immediately answered by a pretty, black-eyed girl of eighteen, lively and enthusiastic. To the chagrin and displeasure of her parents, Miss Page had embraced Methodism, and her mother declared "that if she would persist in disgracing herself, she must leave the paternal roof." Ann gave a graphic description of her conversion. One evening, from curiosity, she attended a meeting, declaring in her gay manner, "that she must hear the preacher, who shouted so loud that one could see the pudding he ate for dinner." The careless, thoughtless girl entered that old Marlborough street school-house to emerge a changed being. "Old things had passed away, all had become new." Her fine clothes were laid aside, her luxuriant locks were shorn, and in a plain calico, and a straw bonnet tied by a ribbon, drawn smoothly over the crown, she sought a place at service, that she might enjoy her religion without censure. The only boon she craved was to attend the Saturday evening class meetings and the Sabbath services. Though a total ignorance of the duties of a serving-maid was admitted, I was so much pleased with the girl that I hired her directly, and a most pleasant and efficient member of the household she became; willing, quick, lively and affectionate, she grew to be the light of the house. At the end of a year, her parents having become reconciled to her change of faith, she returned home to prepare for marriage. In that relation and throughout life she has exemplified the sincerity of her conversion. In her sportive manner she often testifies to the benefit that Methodism conferred in a temporal as well as spiritual sense. By being sent to service she gained the knowledge which is invaluable to a woman, a thorough training in domestic life.

The Boynton family date from the invasion of Ireland by the Norsemen, in the seventh century. A chieftain of the race obtained a victory on the river Boyne, and from that historic stream took the name of Boynton. The commencement of the family pedigree in England is as follows:

"Bartholomew Boynton, of Boynton, Lord of the Manor, in 1014, had Walter de Boynton, living in 1092, who had Sir Ingram Boynton Kent, 1113, who had Thomas Boynton, 1142, who had William de Boynton, 1166.

Sir William de Bovington, living in 1214, to whom Ingelram Monceau gave 2 messuages, 3 cottages and 7 bovats of land in Bovington, married Alecia, daughter of Ingelram Monceau, living a widow in 1221, when she gave two oxgangs of land in Bovington to Nun Appleton Priory.

Sir Ingelram de Bovington, seated at Acklam, 1229, married a daughter of Roger der Acklam.

William Boynton of Acklam, living in 1277, married Jaon, daughter of Sir John Wadsley.

Ingram de Boyton, held the 3d part of one knight's fee, in Acklam, Levinthorpe, Thornton, Martin, Cottesby and Rouceby 1313, married Margaret, daughter of Sir Walter Grindal—Isabel, daughter of Robert Nevile of Hornby 2nd wife.

Sir Walter de Boynton succeeded his father 1320, and heir to his brother John. He was knighted in 1356, being in the service of the Black Prince in Brittany; married daughter of William Aton of Ayton.

John de Bovington, gave 1 messuage, 1 taft, and 4 bovats of land in Bovington, for the maintenance of a chaplain, to pray at the altar of the Blessed Mary in Bovington, 'for his own soul, the souls of his father and mother, and the souls of all his ancestors, and the faithful dead.'

Sir Thomas Boynton of Acklam 1377, jointly with Thomas de Ingleby, had a grant from King Edward for free warren in Acklam, Cleveland, Aresome, Rousby, Newton, Smeaton and Boynton, co. York, and in 1392 Richard 2nd confirmed a gift of the fishery on the river Teyse at Catterick; married Catharine, daughter and co-heiress of Sir Geoffery Rossels of Newton, under Dunesburgh, Cleveland.

Sir Thomas Boynton, lieutenant and constable at Carlisle, under Henry Percye, son of the Earl of Northumberland in 1383, died before his father, married Margaret, daughter of Sir John Specton of Sawkill.

Sir Robert Boynton was governor of Berwick Castle in 1377, married Isabel, daughter of Sir William Normanville.

Sir Henry de Boynton, succeeded his grandfather, Sir Thomas, in 1402. He was suspected of being in the interest of Henry Percy, Earl of Northumberland, and his son, who had taken arms against Henry 4th in 1403; when the battle of Shrewsbury was fought, his oath was taken to be true to the king, yet three years after he was concerned with the said Earl, Thos. Mowbray, Earl Marshall, Richard Scrope, archbishop of York, and others who had taken arms, and flying to Berwick, was apprehended, and on the surrender thereof to the king, with seven others, executed July 20th, 1405; he married Elisabeth, daughter of Sir John Congers, of Sackburne.

Thomas de Boynton, aged 12 at his father's death, married Margaret, daughter of Peter Mirfield.

Sir William Boynton, brother and heir to Thomas de Boynton, married Jane, daughter of Simon Harding.

Sir Thomas Boynton of Akclam, married Isabel, daughter of Sir William

Normanville of Kilnwick. The will of Dame Joan Boynton of Yarm, was proved Feb. 7th, 1488. She had a license for an oratory at Sudbury Dec. 2nd, 1455, and also April 30th, 1463, to have service in an oratory wherever she chose, and in March 1473 Archbishop Nevile granted her the privilege for three years.

Sir Henry Boynton, lord of Barmston, married before 1473, Margaret, daughter and co-heiress of Sir Martin del See, Lord of Barmston, ob. before 1497. Dame Margery was a votary and patroness to the priory of Nun Cotham.

Thomas Boynton of Barmston and Akclam, in 1519 petitioned the Cardinal of York to have the chapel of Rousby consecrated and sacraments administered there. He died March 17th, 1523, and was buried in Rousby chapel; married Cecelia, daughter of Sir James Strangeways at Smeaton.

Matthew Boynton Esq., steward of the lordships belonging to St. Mary's Abbey, in York, died at York July 31st, 1541, aged 40. He had a grant of land for life from Henry 8th, of the high stewardship of all lands in the counties of York and Lincoln, forfeited by the attainder of William Wood, prior of Bridlington. In his will desired to be buried at Barmston, and leaves 20£ to the high altar in that church; married Ann, daughter of Sir John Bulmer of Wilton.

Sir Thomas Boynton, son and heir, aged 18 at his father's decease, and whose custody was given to Sir Ralph Evans, M. P. for Boroughbridge, 13th Elisabeth, high sheriff of Yorkshire, 18th Elisabeth, and knighted by her Majesty at Hampton Court January 1577, in the 20th year of her reign, was buried amongst his ancestors at Barmston. In his will he earnestly requests Henry, Earl of Huntingdon, (styling him 'that man of God,') to take upon him the guardianship of his only son; married 1st Ellen, daughter of Sir, Nicholas Fairfax, of Walton, was a minor in the king's wardship, with whom he had never company, but she was divorced from him, and married Vavavour of Hazlewood (1174); Margaret, 2nd wife, daughter of Sir William Henton, of Harpsham; 3d wife, Frances, daughter of Sir Francis Frobisher, of Altufts; 4th wife, Alice, daughter of Nicholas Tempest, of Helmsden. Cecely Boynton, second daughter of Sir Thomas, was maid of honor to Queen Elisabeth.

Sir Francis Boynton, high sheriff of Yorkshire, 1536, knighted at York April 17th, 1603, by King James, when he passed through that city on his way from Scotland, and had a deputation dated at York March 11th, 1615, for preserving game in the North and East Ridings. He died April 9th, 1617, and was buried at Barmston. At his death he was seized of the Manors of Barmston-cum-Winkton, Rousby, Acklam, Rudstone, a moiety of the manor of Middleton, Tyas, and lands in Barmston, and the rectories of Barmston and Bridlington; married Dorothy, daughter and heiress of Sir Christopher Place of Holnaby.

Sir Matthew Boynton, baptized at Barmston Jan. 26th, 1591, knighted by King James at Whitehall, May 9th, 1618, and by letters patent, dated the 25th of that month, advanced to the dignity of a baronet of Great Britain, M. P. for Heyden 1620. He was one of those rebels (?) chiefly entrusted in Yorkshire, for whom Sir John Hotham, and his son, Capt. Hotham, were contriving the surrender of Hull to the King. This Sir Matthew Boynton, had orders from parliament to have an eye on them, and endeavor to preserve the town if he perceived it in danger, pursuant to which he contrived the seizing him, and Col. Matthew Boynton, his son, actually took Sir John prisoner, and received pardon under the great seal Feb. 10th, 1625, high sheriff co., York 1628, 1644 and 1645. He had a deputation dated at Westminster April 5th, 1631, for preserving the game in the North and East Ridings, M. P. for Scarborough Oct. 25th, 1643, colonel of a troop of Horse, and governor of Scarborough Castle temp of Charles 1st and took an active part in the civil wars of the period. He died at Highgate, co. Middlesex, and was buried in the chancel of St. Albans, Holborn, March 12th, 1646. 1st wife, Frances, daughter of Sir Henry Griffeth Kent, and Bart. of Wicknow, co. Stafford and Burton Agnes, co. York (and sole heiress to her brother Sir Henry) by his lady Elisabeth, daughter of Thomas Throckmorton Esq. of Loughton, co. Warwick, lineally descended from the Kings of England, the Dukes of Normandy, the Princes of Wales, and the Earls of Northumberland, before and after the Conquest, of the Earls of March and Dunbar in Scotland, marriage settlement dated Sept. 27th, 1614, and died in July 1634, aged 36, and buried at Rousby, where a tomb is erected to her memory. 2nd wife, Katharine 2nd, daughter of Thomas, Viscount Fairfax of Emley.

Mathew Boynton, Lieutenant Colonel, was slain at Wigan, co. Lancaster, Aug. 26th, 1631, in the advance of King Charles' army towards Worcester; married Isabel, daughter of Robert Stapleton, of Wighill. Peregrine Boynton died Aug. 28th, 1645, and was buried at Barmston, whereon an epitaph is inscribed, 'This child God gave unto them when strangers in a foreign land.' Mary and other children."

This is all the record in England of the Boyntons coming to America.

Rev. Ezekiel Rogers arrived in this country with many respectable Yorkshire families, "godly men" and "most of them of good estate," in the autumn of 1638. The settlement of Rowley was commenced April, 1639. On the 3d of Dec. 1639 Mr. Rogers was installed pastor over the church.

The town was laid out in streets and lots. The record reads: "On Bradford Streete, To John Boynton, one lotte containinge an acree and a halfe, bounded on the south side by Michael Hopkinson's house lott, part of it lyinge on the west side, and part of it on the east side of the street.

To William Boynton, one lott, containinge an acree and a halfe, bounded on the south side by John Boynton's house lott, part of it lyinge on the west side, and part on the east side of the street."

John Boynton died in 1670.

William Boynton was made Freeman in 1640, died in 1665. William, the son of William and Elisabeth Boynton, was the first teacher in Rowley; he taught about twenty-four years.

William Boynton was one of fifty-eight, to whom, in 1667, Hog Island marshes were divided and laid out. In 1680 Rowley appointed nine tithing men for the inspection of families. Ivory Kilbarn was to inspect John and Caleb Boynton's families, and John Pearson the family of Joseph Boynton.

In 1691 the town paid Caleb Boynton £4. 15s. 3d. for his son William Boynton for military service in Canada.

In 1754 Stephen Boynton was out under Capt. John Lane at the eastern frontier, and in 1755 he was a private in a company under Capt. Thomas Gage, raised in Rowley to do duty at Lake George and vicinity.

John Boynton was out six and a half months under Capt. Jonathan Pearson of Newbury.

May 31st, 1757, James Boynton's name is amongst those forming Capt. John Pearson's Troop of Horse.

June 15th, 1759, John Boynton was one of Capt. Thurston's Alarm List.

In 1759 James Boynton was a private under Capt. Thomas Poor, of Andover.

In 1760 James Boynton was in a company raised under Capt. James Herrick, of Boxford, for the total reduction of Canada.

In 1779 Enoch Boynton was one of Capt. Thomas Mighill's company, who served in Col. Nathaniel Wade's regiment at West Point the term of three months.

Ephraim Boynton was fourth sergeant in the train band belonging to Capt. John Northend's company in Rowley. Ephraim Boynton married Abigaile, daughter of David Emery, of Newbury.

Joshua Boynton, son of John, born in 1640, held two hundred acres of the water front on the river Parker in Byfield.

His son Joshua, born in 1677, was deacon of the church in that parish for forty years; he died in 1770.

Joshua, born 1677, died in 1770.

Enoch B., born in 1759, died in 1798.

Enoch, born in 1730, died in 1805.

Enoch, born in 1799, died in 1859. His son, Methusela, was the father of Alfred Boynton, who married Abigail Moody; children, Alfred, Eben Moody, Charles and William.

Enoch Boynton, born in 1773, died in 1859; his wife, Alice Adams, died in 1811.

Enoch T. Boynton, born in 1804, died in 1826.

Adding Boynton born May 27, 1806. The Boynton Place on the old Newbury Turnpike was for years a noted tavern; many can remember the sign of the golden ball. Afterwards Enoch Boynton rendered it famous by his attempt at raising silk worms. He has now departed this life, and the inheritance of so many generations has passed from the family.

The descendants of John and William Boynton are numerous and widely scattered, but wherever located they show the characteristics of the race from which they sprang, energy, courage, and self-reliance.

The Boynton Arms are:

OR, BAR WAYS, GULES THREE CRESCENTS PROPER.
CREST, A LION RAMPANT.

CHAPTER LXIV.

The fiftieth anniversary of American Independence was celebrated in Newburyport with unprecedented honors. The day, which proved unusually fine, was ushered in by the ringing of bells, and a salute of twenty-four guns by the Newburyport Artillery. This was repeated at sunset. At 9 o'clock the military companies formed under command of Major Ebenezer Bradbury, officer of the day. At ten o'clock a procession was formed on the mall under the direction of the following marshals:

For the military procession, Maj. Caleb Cushing, Capt. Henry Merrill, Adj. Charles Kimball.

For the civil procession, Maj. David Emery, Messrs. William Hervey, Jacob W. Pierce, Moses Kent, John Greely, Samuel W. Thompson, Thomas Foster.

The escort consisted of the Ipswich and Bradford Light Corps, the Amesbury Artillery, the Newbury Cavalry, and the Newburyport Artillery and Light Infantry. These two companies, handsomely uniformed, the Artillery caps decorated by long waving black plumes, and the Light Infantry by white, produced a brilliant and imposing effect.

Music.

Major General Benjamin Stickney, Brigadier General Solomon Low and numerous officers of the Second Brigade in full uniform.

The officiating clergyman, the Rev. Dr. Andrews.

The orator, Hon. John Merrill.

The reader, George Cross, esq.

The president of the day, Maj. Joshua Greenleaf.

The vice presidents, Samuel March, esq., Col. Daniel Adams, Capt. Greene Sanborn, Stephen W. Marston, esq., and Dr. Richard S. Spofford.

The Committee of Arrangements.

Officers and members of the Franklin Debating Society, Municipal Authorities, Clergy of the town and vicinity. Next marched sixty revolutionary officers and soldiers, marshalled by Daniel Foster, esq., one of LaFayette's Life Guard, displaying the cap, plume and sword which he had worn while in service. Many wore the continental equipments; all a badge of blue ribbon imprinted with the magic figures '76. In the midst, borne by one of their number, was a tattered flag of the Revolution, which was unfurled at Bunker Hill, and there received the shots that rent it. This detachment was followed by four of the more infirm of their number in an open barouche, drawn by a span of superb white horses, among whom was that noble veteran, the aged Col. Edward Wigglesworth. Next came the National and State officers; the Newburyport Encampment of Knights Templars; King Cyrus' Chapter; St. John's, St. Peter's, St. Mark's Lodges in full regalia, bearing banners and badges; the Newburyport Marine Society; Merrimac Humane Society; the several Fire Societies; Engine and Fire Companies, each bearing appropriate banners. The truckmen in white frocks made a fine show; these were succeeded by a long line of citizens, the procession being closed by the children of the several schools in uniform, wearing badges with appropriate mottoes, under the care of their instructors.

The procession moved through High, Federal, Middle, the Market square, Green and Pleasant streets, to the Pleasant street church, which had been handsomely decorated by the ladies, the front gallery and side wall pews being reserved for them.

The orchestra, led by Mr. Thomas B. White, was composed of members of the different choirs of the town.

The exercises in the church commenced by a Voluntary on the organ by Edward L. White. The following anthem from the Oratorio of Joshua, was performed in fine style:

RECITATIVE.

"Thou, whose shining throne eternal stands
Above the heavens, who holdest in Thy hand
The fate of worlds; and in Thy royal robes
Adorned with suns and stars, dost fold the globe;
Thou art our Sovereign, and alone to Thee,
God over all! Columbia bends the knee!
For this to-day, receive, O King of kings,
The grateful tribute which a nation brings."

Chorus,

"From every heart let holy incense rise!
With Hallelujahs, fill the vaulted skies!
Ye herald angels, sound our song again,
While we, on earth, repeat a long Amen!"

The prayer which followed, by Rev. Dr. Andrews, is spoken of in the Newburyport Herald's report as "peculiarly beautiful and appropriate, commanding attention and admiration for its clearness of method, felicity of allusion, and clearness of diction. That his impassioned eulogy upon our sainted forefathers, and his nervous delineation of the trials and sufferings of the heroic men who toiled and bled for our sakes, were not lost upon his auditors, was evinced by their fixed attention, and we could perceive more than one tear swell up from the heart of the veteran and steal down his careworn cheek."

After the prayer, the following hymn, by Hannah F. Gould, set to music by T. B. White, was executed with great effect:

"Who when darkness gathered o'er us,
Foes and death on every side,
Clothed in glory, walked before us,
Leading on, like Israel's guide?
'Twas Jehovah! He appearing
Show'd his banner far and wide.

When the trump of war was sounding,
'Twas the Lord who took the field!
He, His people then surrounding,
Made the strong in battle yield;
To our fathers, few in numbers,
He was armor, strength and shield.

In the God of armies trusting,
'Mid their weakness, void of fear,
Soon they felt their bands were bursting,
Saw the dawning light appear;
Clouds dissolving in the sunbeams,
Showed the band of freedom near.

Hark! we hear to Heaven ascending
From the voices of the free,
Hallelujahs sweetly blending
With the song of liberty.
Power Almighty! we the vict'ry
Ever will ascribe to Thee.

Lo the dove the olive bearing,
Plants it on Columbia's shore!
Every breast its branch is wearing,
Where the buckler shone before!
Praise the Eternal! he is reigning!
Praise Him, praise Him evermore!"

The Declaration of Independence was read by Robert Cross, esq., the Herald report says, "with much taste, skill, and judgment, and we considered it judicious in him at that peculiar juncture, to add the names of the signers of the Declaration."

The following Original Ode was sung to the air of "Scots wha hae."

"SPIRIT OF '76.

See the war cloud wildly driven,
By the pealing thunder riven,
Shrouding earth and rending heaven,
Arm for liberty!

Let no haughty tyrants vaunt,
Hearts of steel! your courage daunt,
Be his portion woe and want,
Who would faint or flee;

Think your fathers spurned the chain,
Dared the rough and stormy main,
Not for glory, not for gain,
But for rights you have;

Think your fathers came not here,
Rais'd the prayer and dropped the tear,
Perils met, unblanched by fear
For a coward slave;

Look around you, see their graves!
See above, your banner waves!
Hark! the voice of battle raves,
Up, and you are free!

By the name drawn from your sires,
By your homes and altar's fires,
By your hopes and fears, desires,
Strike for liberty!"

The oration by the Hon. John Merrill, the Herald continues, "was spirited and patriotic, imbued with genuine republican feeling, evincing correct sentiment, and adorned with laudable precepts."

This was succeeded by an Ode, written by a lady. Air—"The Pillar of Glory."

"Bring brightest laurels and let them be braided,
Weave oak and olive!—and ne'er be it told,
A leaf in the crown of our nation was faded,
Or lost, when we saw her full fifty years old!
Still round thy forehead seen,
Fresh be the evergreen!
Pride of the waters and Queen of the earth!
Loud all thy tribes shall sing,
Rock, hill and forest ring,
Echoing, Hail! to the day of thy birth!

Our colors adorn all the waves of the ocean,
Our eagle explores every region of air!
Long as the pinions of Time keep in motion,
May they ride in freedom, and valiantly there!
Penned on the brightest page,
Down to the latest age,
The deeds of our sires shall as sunlight descend,
May every bosom feel
Fired by a noble zeal,
The prize they obtained to enjoy and defend.

Ye who remaining with locks thin and hoary,
Your toils in the field to your sons still recount,
Proudly ye stand 'mid the heroes of story,
As towers o'er the hills our own snow-crested mount;
Loud when the cannon roar'd
Warm when the blood was pour'd,
With flocks bounding, thick as the foes falling then;
See the green valley teem,
Far where the silver stream
Shines like your swords, spread at rest thro' the glen.

Spirit of him who at Vernon is sleeping,
Bend in thy glory, and smile at our mirth!
See the glad millions, the jubilee keeping.
Which thou dids't procure by thy valor on earth;
Still hallowed be the day,
When we have passed away,
And years over years, shall like floods, roll along!
Then may posterity
Still be inspired by thee—
'Freedom and Washington' ever the song!"

The services were closed by the benediction by Rev. Dr. Andrews.

The dinner, furnished by Messrs. Tyler & Cook, was served in Market Hall, which was finely decorated. "In the interstices between the windows, evergreens had been interwoven so as to give the hall the appearance of a complete shrubbery, in which were birds confined in cages, who saluted the guests with their enlivening notes; and overhead was spread tent cloths, to impart a military air to the festival. At the farthest extremity of the hall, over the President's table, was extended an arch with this inscription: "July 4th, 1776," supported by pillars inscribed with the names of Washington, Warren, Ward, Stark, Varnum, and on the other Putnam, Prescott, Brooks, Green, LaFayette.

The president of the day, Maj. Joshua Greenleaf, presided, assisted by the vice presidents at the citizens' tables; at the military, Major-General Stickney and Brigadier-General Low did the honors, assisted by Major Ebenezer Bradbury, Capt. Daniel E. Stickney, Capt. Enoch Pierce and Capt. Dunnels.

The tables were handsomely laid, and the dinner was excellent. Due justice having been done the viands, the "feast of reason and the flow of soul" commenced. Thirteen regular toasts having been drank, the president rose and volunteered this sentiment—"This national jubilee—A grateful country will embalm the memory of the patriots and heroes, whose blood and treasure secured to us the blessings we now enjoy."

By Col. Daniel Adams, vice president, "Union, liberty, and independence. May they be sacred in the breast, and defended by the best blood of every American."

By Dr. R. S. Spofford, vice president, "The sublime principles of Free Masonry. An object of terror to the tyrants of Europe, but in America, a strong pillar in the temple of liberty."

By Capt. Green Sanborn, vice president, "Our free country.—May slavery, the foul blot, be soon erased from its escutcheon."

By S. W. Marston, esq., "Rufus King, Theophilus Parsons, John Quincy Adams, Charles Jackson and Jacob Perkins, our fellow citizens, at all times the glory and honor of their country."

By Gen. Stickney, "State of Massachusetts, abounding in natural and political advantages—possessing a sound head and vigorous constitution."

By Hon. John Merrill, orator of the day, "The United States—their citizens are distinguished for enterprise and intelligence. Although like Themistocles they may not be players on the lute, yet, like him, they know how to make a great city of a small one."

By Samuel March, esq., "The reverend clergy—may they be to the people of their charge—going before them, —a pillar of cloud by day, and a pillar of fire by night, teaching them the way in which they should go."

By Gen. S. Low, "The fiftieth anniversary of American Independence—we hail it as a pledge of a national feeling which still breathes the spirit of '76 into the vitals of the true sons of America."

By Maj. David Emery, "The Fathers and children of 1776—may the rich blessings they enjoy be multiplied to the Fathers and children of 1876."

By Hon. C. Cushing, "The present generation—my best wish for them is, that they may but prove wise and brave as their fathers, pure and lovely as their mothers, and the proud inheritors of the free soil, and the free souls, which are the boast of America."

Daniel Foster, esq., rose and spoke as follows: "Fellow Soldiers of the Revolution,—Allow me for a moment to express to you my feelings on this joyful occasion. We remain among the few survivors of the revolutionary army—that army which achieved the independence we are now assembled to celebrate. We enlisted in the good cause in a day of darkness, when our beloved country was assailed by most powerful foes, when her prospects were gloomy and discouraging. By the favor of Divine Providence, we were safely conducted through that long agony of suffering and blood. By His goodness we have been continued through half a century to see this glorious day. We then only dared to hope for the *common* blessings of peace and national independence. But our most sanguine expectations have been more than realized; our thirteen colonies have become a powerful empire, enjoying civil liberty and social order, and advancing at an astonishing rate in the career of improvement and national greatness. Let us hope that we leave these invaluable privileges in good hands, and that our children and children's children, by adhering to the principles of our immortal Washington, will transmit them unimpaired to the latest generations." Mr. Foster concluded with the following: "Our Sons—may they ever stand fast to the integrity of our national Union, and relying on Heaven, be always ready to defend with their blood the high privileges bequeathed to them."

By Robert Cross, esq., "Those societies and benevolent individuals in all countries, who are endeavoring to disseminate the principles of peace—their object may be impracticable; it is at least a noble one, and worthy of a fair experiment. Success to their cause; and at the next jubilee, may posterity have occasion to commemorate the universal abolition of war." "The above toast was received with great enthusiasm by the whole company, and what is worthy of remark, more particularly by our military brethren."

By Maj. Ebenezer Bradbury, "The march of mind—no retrograding, no countermarching or obliquity. Direct to the front!"

By William S. Allen, "Our yeomanry; stout hearts and strong hands—

'A country's pride,
When once it's lost can never be supplied.'"

By Tristram Coffin 3d, "The brave Greeks, who are struggling for liberty. May they convince the Turks, by the most convincing of all arguments—their swords—that they will be free."

By John Adams, esq., of Andover, "May custom and prejudice yield to the voice of improvement, and may wise innovations meet the approbation of sage experience."

By Capt. Richard Lovering, "The officers and soldiers of the Revolution. We carry the badges of '76, we hope we have the principles in our breasts."

Mr. Short. "The tree of liberty, watered by the blood of the Revolution—may our children suffer no canker worms to injure its sacred leaves."

By Mr. Nathaniel Ladd, "May the surviving officers and soldiers of the revolutionary army ever hold in grateful remembrance the hospitality of the citizens of Newburyport, towards us who fought and bled to gain the independence which we are assembled this day to celebrate."

By Mr. Nathan Follansbee, "The revolutionary heroes of '76—while we honor them as the fathers of our country, let us not forget the noble spirit of our mothers and grandmothers, who urged them on to victory."

This last toast elicited rounds of applause.

The following revolutionary officers and soldiers were at the dinner: Elias Pike, Gideon Woodwell, Daniel Flanders, Stephen Toppan, William Huntington, Amos Carlton, Amos Norton, Joseph Pike, Richard Short, Samuel Follansbee, Jonathan Lambert, Benjamin Poor, Timothy Curtis, Oliver Goodrich, Timothy Gordon, Nathaniel Pearson, David Pearson, Timothy Poor, Caleb Kimball, Samuel Balch, Benjamin Davis, Aaron Rogers, Joseph Floyd, Nathaniel Howard, Moses Short, Joseph Stanwood, Elias Cook, John Pafferd, John Bootman, David Dole, Moses Somerby, Joshua Pettengel, Farnum Howe, Jacob Fowler, Samuel Eaton, Moses Pike, Jacob Currier, Nathaniel Ladd, Ezekiel Merrill, Daniel Adams, Nathaniel Beck, Jacob Brown, Joseph Mootrey, Jacob Hodgkins, Thomas Stanwood.

It will be recollected that both John Adams and Thomas Jefferson died within a few hours of each other on this fiftieth anniversary. This singular occurrence created a great sensation throughout the country, and suitable funeral ceremonies were held in most of the cities and towns of the Union to express the national bereavement. On the 14th of July a funeral oration was delivered in the Pleasant street church by Hon. Caleb Cushing. The church bells were tolled from four to five o'clock in the afternoon, the public buildings were draped in mourning, the flags were at half mast. At four o'clock a procession of citizens formed on the mall, which marched through Green and Pleasant streets to the church. At five o'clock the services commenced by a Voluntary on the organ. A hymn was sung by the choir, and a prayer offered by Rev. Dr. Andrews, after which the following Ode, by Caleb Cushing, was sung:

"Forget not the valiant
  Who have honored our story,
The high and the gallant,
  Whose deeds are our glory;
They are gone, but they leave us
  The meed of their merit,
Nor can ages bereave us
  Of the fame we inherit.
Then forget not the valiant
  Who have honored our story
The high and the gallant,
  Whose deeds are our glory.

The soil that descended
  To our fathers in honor,
They nobly defended
  From shame and dishonor:
And when to the slaughter
  Our heroes were given,
The blood of each martyr
  Rose like incense to heaven.
Then forget not the valiant
  Who have honored our story,
The high and the gallant,
  Whose deeds are our glory.'

The eulogy having been pronounced, the exercises closed with the "Dirge of Adams and Jefferson." Tune "Judgment Hymn."

"The portals of the grave unfold—
  In dust Columbia's weeping!
Shrouded in death's dark pall, behold
  The patriot Fathers sleeping!
While to their God their souls have risen,
Still round each cold, deserted prison,
  Sorrow her watch is keeping.

Those names, whose beams effulgent met,
  Our freedom's charter lighting,
Within the Book of Life are set,
  In glory there uniting!
While thousands here the patriarchs blest,
Their title to immortal rest,
  The Lamb above was writing.

'Twas on a great, a hallow'd day,
  The mortal conflict ending,
The sister spirits dropped their clay—
  To Heaven, their home, ascending;
They rose, from care and suffering free,
Above the grave, with victory,
  And angel hosts attending!

When twoscore years and ten were gone,
  Since glad our nation started
From Slav'ry's night, to hail the dawn,
  Whence Freedom's rays first darted,
They saw the rising sun appear;
But, ere the evening clouds drew near,
  The hoary saints departed.

Sages, your name, your virtues still,
  Though from your dust we sever,
With sacred joy each heart shall fill,
  Your mem'ry perish never!
The earth one mantle still retains!
Tho' gone the Sire, the Son remains!
  Farewell, great Shades, forever."

CHAPTER LXV.

In 1825 a factory for weaving hose was established in a building on Brown's square.

In 1827 a school for instruction in working lace was opened, and for a time, of an afternoon, scarcely a young girl could be seen without a lace hoop or frame in her hand. Very elegant veils wrought in frames supported by a stand, were worked. For a period this lace business continued quite remunerative.

This year the Newburyport bridge was built; an elegant structure suspended from arches by chains, similar to the open part of the Essex Merrimac bridge. This gave place to the less graceful railroad bridge in 1840.

In January, 1824, my Aunt O'Brian's adopted daughter, Eliza Bartlett, was married in Reading, Penn., with Mr. John Heiner Weitzel. The next summer the young couple visited New England. Mr. Weitzel kept a general furnishing store in Reading, and he purchased six pairs of brogans for his store of Uncle Joe Little; these gave such satisfaction to the Dutchmen, his customers, that an order was forwarded for twenty-five pairs; this was succeeded by another for fifty, then a hundred, and so on. Thus commenced the Southern shoe trade of Georgetown.

On October 20th, 1826, my Aunt Peabody died in Washington, D. C., and the following 25th of February, 1827, Gen. John Peabody followed her to the spiritual world. They had been lovely in their lives, and not long divided by death.

Capt. O'Brian having died in 1825, his widow returned to New England. As her mother was a confirmed invalid she remained with her. In the autumn of 1826 Mrs. O'Brian was seized with paralysis of the brain, from which she died in January, 1827. Grandmother Little lingered about two years longer, when the spirit was released from the decrepit body, by which it had so long been enthralled.

In the summer of 1829 I paid my first visit to Boston. My brother Joseph resided on Eaton street. Opposite was one of the old colonial mansions, surrounded by a spacious garden. I was entertained by the attractions of the city. Amongst the most prominent were the New England Museum, and the Athenæum on Pearl street. On a visit some two years later, I first saw the model of a railroad, with miniature locomotive and cars, which was exhibited in the hall over the Quincy market.

In the spring of 1831, the Rev. James Miltimore having become too infirm to officiate in the pastoral office, we took a pew in the Pleasant street church. Dr. Andrews resigned soon after, and the Rev. Thomas B. Fox was ordained the 3d of August.

The advent of this young man brought a new era to the Pleasant street society, and to the town. The spacious house of worship became crowded. For better accommodation two lines of slips took the place of the ancient square pews in the front galleries. The beautiful glass chandelier was taken down to give room for one of bronze and gilt, with five burners for sperm oil. Similar single lamps were suspended throughout the edifice, and the pulpit was lighted by a drop lamp over the desk, with Argand burners on either side. The old-fashioned organ was replaced by the present fine instrument. A flourishing Sunday school was established numbering over a hundred pupils, under the instruction of a band of young men and maidens which the youthful pastor had gathered around him, and into whom he had infused his own eager enthusiasm for truth, progress and reform.

In October the clergyman was united in marriage with Miss Fereline Pierce, a daughter of the venerable Dr. Pierce of Brookline. This gave a season of gaiety to the parish, the Sunday school children being invited on the Saturday afternoon after the lady's arrival in Newburyport, to visit their pastor's residence, to kiss the bride, and receive a piece of bride-cake, an event which I am certain they have never forgotten. On the afternoon of the Communion Sabbath a service especially for children was instituted; they occupied the singing gallery forming the choir, and the front tiers of pews next the pulpit; their pastor standing upon the raised platform beneath it, using the communion table for a desk. There he preached from month to month a series of discourses familiarly termed "Little Sermons," which attracted many children outside of his parish, and which all who had the privilege of hearing must remember—words which have oft recurred in memory to warn and cheer through life's checkered scenes. Small hymn books were provided especially for the Sunday school; afterwards a liturgy for its use was introduced. The library received a large addition of instructive and valuable books. A society library was also formed, containing much choice reading. A course of "Expository Lectures" was held on the Wednesday evenings of each week, with an evening lecture on the first Sunday in the month—Communion Sunday. A great interest was aroused; many children were presented for baptism, and many persons united with the church. Mr. and Mrs. Edward Toppan and myself were included in the number, and Mr. Toppan was chosen to the office of deacon.

The following summer, lectures on Botany were given to the Sunday school children after the afternoon service; and in the autumn Mr. Fox got up a picnic in the woods around the "Devil's Den and Basin." The Sunday school was conveyed in hacks and stage-coaches; the society went in their own teams. This was the first picnic ever held in these parts. That winter, Mr. Fox, to the great delight of the participants, introduced tableaux. The next summer flowers were placed upon the table at the children's meetings; after a time a small vase adorned the table amidst the massive, antique, silver tankards, at the observance of the Lord's Supper. After a while this vase of flowers became a regular adjunct of the Sabbath worship.

Mr. Fox having been placed upon the school committee, a new era commenced in our public schools; and in after years he was principally instrumental in the formation of the High school for girls in Newburyport, which was the first in the state. To the youth of the town he was a most faithful friend and champion, and his memory will ever be gratefully cherished. As might be inferred, these innovations on old-time usages, "these new-fangled doings," caused no small stir throughout our quiet, staid, strict community. It was a period of much religious excitement. "Protracted," or four days' meetings were the vogue. Great revivals were in progress, and there was much controversy and sectarian bitterness; Mr. Fox and his society received a full share of contumely; his "little sermons" and lectures were derided, his picnics were termed "Fox's Caravans;" the tableaux were theatrical enormities, which could not be too severely condemned, and the flowers in the church were something too terrible to contemplate without a shudder—"Such Popish folly! Posies in the meeten'us! they might as well turn Papists at once."

Annually in the spring, a service had been held at the Orphan Asylum, when those unbaptized children who had been admitted during the year were consecrated by the rite. If a new clergyman had been ordained since the last service, it had been customary to invite him to officiate. According to custom, it was proposed to extend this courtesy to Mr. Fox; but such a fierce opposition was raised, that the members of the Asylum Society belonging to the Pleasant street congregation, withdrew from the association, leaving the opposition to conduct matters to their satisfaction. Funds in consequence became low, and the Asylum was eventually discontinued. Soon after, the Society for Aged Females was instituted.

Dr. Spring died in March. 1819, and the Rev. Luther F. Dimmick was ordained over the society of the North church the next December. The Rev. John Charles March was ordained over the Belleville society in March, 1832. The Rev. James Miltimore died in March, 1836, at the venerable age of 81 years. Parson Miltimore was an affable and courteous gentleman, a fine writer, and a most devoted pastor and friend.

Dr. Elijah Parish died Oct. 15th, 1825, in his 64th year. Thus was lost to the New England church one of its most distinguished members; but the fervent eloquence and fiery zeal of the great Federalist divine is still a cherished memory, and his quick wit and fine social qualities will remain as pleasant reminiscences to be transmitted to posterity.

At this time, Dr. Lyman Beecher was at the zenith of his fame. Upon his removal to Boston, my brother, Joseph L. Smith, became his parishioner; but not being fully satisfied with the preaching of the celebrated clergyman, through Dr. Shurtleff, his family physician, he became a reader of the works of Emanuel Swedenborg. Though not inclined to literary pursuits, in an incredibly short time he became thoroughly acquainted with the voluminous writings of the Swedish seer, and an enthusiastic receiver of his doctrine.

The New Jerusalem church in Boston was then in its infancy, comprising scarcely more than a dozen communicants. Mr. Smith became one of the most zealous and energetic of the society, devoting both his purse and his apt business talents to its service. This interest never flagged until his decease, which took place at the early age of forty-three.

Father, mother, sister and husband have also gone;—of the former household band, my brother James alone remains.

The only persons still living on High street, who resided there during my early married life, are Capt. and Mrs. Joshua Pillsbury, Mr. and Mrs. Richard Ordway, and Capt. David Wood.

That Centennial of our Independence which loomed so dimly in the far future when my husband gave his sentiment at the Fiftieth Anniversary, I have passed. I have lived to ride upon railroads, and receive messages by the electric wires; to have friends cross the ocean in steamships; to send messages back by the sub-marine cable; the telephone is in operation in several lines through our streets, and the phonograph is on exhibition in our public halls.

The first anthracite coal fire I ever saw was in an open grate in my brother's house, in Boston, about 1830. It was regarded with curiosity; and the idea of using such material for fuel elicited considerable derision in the community. Now, a wood fire is the curiosity. Kerosene and gas illuminate our dwellings in lieu of candles and fish or whale oil. The horse cars run through our streets, and steamboats navigate our river. Though our dwellings on the whole may not be as spacious and imposing as formerly, they are much more convenient and comfortable; the same may be said of the churches, public edifices, and stores.

Every department of life has been improved by science, art, and ingenuity. Though our schools may not exhibit the superiority commensurate with the increased expense, no one would wish to renew the ancient regime, or return to the former incommodious school-houses, with their huge fireplaces and sizzling green logs. Though there is more laxity on the Sabbath, and fine organs and choirs are requisite concomitants of religious service, still, considering the increase and change in our population, I see no decrease in true christianity; on the contrary, we are before our fathers in the truest interpretation of neighborly love and charity. Look at our institutions for the amelioration of the race; at the various societies for spiritual and moral advancement; if there is not as much of the letter there is more of the spirit of the Divine law. Much is said of the deterioration of society; perhaps it would be well to teach our children a little of the old-time courtesy, and as well to practise it somewhat more ourselves; but in that kindly social interest which constitutes true politeness, we are not deficient, and many of the every-day customs of our fathers would not be tolerated for a moment. Our young ladies would not so smilingly receive a band of young men reeling from the dining to the drawing-room, with the slightly deprecating remark that, "they were only a little over-dinnerish, and not to be minded." And the boys' battle-cry of "up-alongers and down-alongers, rush 'em. rush 'em!" has long since ceased. Another feature in the former social system would not now be permitted; I refer to the treatment often received by the little bound girls in families. I have often seen such children going to the pump in mid-winter, clad only in a homespun short gown and petticoat, with slipshod shoes, disclosing huge holes in the heels of their stockings, and an old hood tied over their tangled hair. Domestic servitude and labor of all kinds commands much more respect and regard for its rights and comfort than it did a hundred years ago. We hear much complaint of hard times and low wages. But what would our laborers think of working for fifty cents a day, or our domestics at receiving only two shillings and sixpence a week, with cotton cloth at fifty cents, and calico a dollar per yard! The best of mechanics received not more than a dollar a day; many, for a time, could not obtain work even at a lower price.

In physical knowledge and culture there is also a marked change. The laws of health are better understood and applied. As a rule our houses are kept neater, all are warm in winter, and in every way better prepared for health and comfort through the year. One would now be considered insane to dress through the cold season, as was the mode in my girlhood. Generally there are truer views of life amongst the youth in our community, less false pride, and more industry amongst the higher classes. Our young men form Christian Associations and similar societies; our young ladies employ their leisure in teaching in Sunday schools and week day sewing schools for poor children, taxing their skill and ingenuity on articles for charity fairs, while they visit the poor, sick and infirm, carrying not only solid aid, but the light of their bright, sympathetic faces. We see little of the "Lydia Languish," the sickly, sentimental, mincing style, which held fashionable ascendency for a period.

Art has taken a much higher rank

than of yore; though the public taste has not quite risen to a perfect standard, it has greatly improved. Instead of only three or four pianos in the town, scarcely a dwelling of any pretension is without an instrument of some kind; even in the humblest abode the strains of a cabinet organ are often heard, accompanied by the cultivated voice of a sweet singer.

Our public library and reading room furnish the best of books; these, with magazines and periodicals, and the libraries attached to the Sabbath schools, preclude that literary hunger which I often experienced in my youthful days.

Though there is yet room for improvement, on the whole, the world is steadily advancing in material and spiritual interests. Let every one "press towards the mark for the prize of the high calling of God in Christ Jesus."

"I have been young, and now am old, yet have I not seen the righteous forsaken, nor his seed begging bread."